GW00372505

35

October
2002

ECONOMIC POLICY

A European Forum

SENIOR EDITORS
GEORGES DE MÉNIL
RICHARD PORTES
HANS-WERNER SINN

MANAGING EDITORS
RICHARD BALDWIN
GIUSEPPE BERTOLA
PAUL SEABRIGHT

BOARD OF GOVERNORS
GEORGES DE MÉNIL Co-Chairman
RICHARD PORTES Co-Chairman
HANS-WERNER SINN Co-Chairman
MAURICE AYMARD
GUILLERMO DE LA DEHESA
RAY REES
ALFRED STEINHERR
XAVIER VIVES

Published in association with the European Economic Association

Blackwell Publishers Ltd for Centre for Economic Policy Research,
Center for Economic Studies of the University of Munich, and
Département et Laboratoire d'Economie Théorique et Appliquée (DELTA),
in collaboration with the Maison des Sciences de l'Homme.

STATEMENT OF PURPOSE

Economic Policy provides timely and authoritative analyses of the choices which confront policy-makers. The subject matter ranges from the study of how individual markets can and should work to the broadest interactions in the world economy.

Economic Policy is a joint activity of the Centre for Economic Policy Research (CEPR), the Munich-based Center for Economic Studies (CES) and the Paris-based Maison des Sciences de l'Homme (DELTA). It offers an independent, non-partisan, European perspective on issues of worldwide concern. It emphasizes problems of international significance, either because they affect the world economy directly or because the experience of one country contains important lessons for policy-makers elsewhere.

All the articles are specifically commissioned from leading professional economists. Their brief is to demonstrate how live policy issues can be illuminated by the insights of modern economics and by the most recent evidence. The presentation is incisive and written in plain language accessible to the wide audience which participates in the policy debate.

Prior to publication, the contents of each volume are discussed by a Panel of distinguished economists from Europe and elsewhere. The Panel rotates annually. Inclusion in each volume of a summary of the highlights of the Economic Policy Panel discussion provides the reader with alternative interpretations of the evidence and a sense of the liveliness of the current debate.

Economic Policy is owned by the Maison des Sciences de l'Homme, CEPR and CES. The thirty-fifth Panel meeting was held in Madrid with support from the Banco de España. We gratefully acknowedge this support, without implicating any of these organizations in the views expressed here, which are the sole responsibility of the authors.

ECONOMIC POLICY
A European Forum

PANEL

35
October 2002

CONTENTS

Editors' introduction

The three short papers of a mini-symposium on the international role of the European single currency and five of the other papers we are publishing were presented at the 35th Panel meeting held in Madrid on 12–13 April 2002. Another paper was presented at the previous Panel meeting in Brussels on 19–20 October 2001. In this introduction we group papers around broad policy issues and we place their contribution in the context of wider debates.

EUROPEAN PARLIAMENT

The European Union is engaged in a profound reassessment of its organization and goals. European leaders as diverse as Joschka Fischer, Jacque Chirac and Tony Blair have proposed major changes in the EU's organization, and the 'European Convention' led by Valéry Giscard d'Estaing is formulating concrete reform proposals. One great challenge is to reduce the EU's democratic deficit and here the European Parliament (EP) could be crucial. How would a more powerful European Parliament (EP) affect decision-making in an enlarged EU? It is surely impossible to answer this question conclusively, but one thing is clear. Any sensible answer must be based on a clear understanding of how the EP has functioned in the past.

Following this logic, Abdul Noury and Gérard Roland put together a massive new data set covering all recorded votes by Members of the European Parliament (MEPs) between 1989 and 1999. Their paper addresses two sets of questions. First, they investigate how voting coalitions within the EP have formed: do EP coalitions form along ideological lines as in national parliaments, or along nationalist lines as in so many other EU institutions? Second, the data covers a period in which the EP's powers were increased and EU membership expanded, so the authors investigate the impact of more power and a larger membership: does greater power enhance the cohesiveness of MEPs, and do MEPs from new members act differently? The answers are surprising and provocative. MEPs seem to have more party loyalty than country loyalty. Party cohesion and participation are stronger when the MEPs have more power. And MEPs from the new entrants are just as party oriented as MEPs from incumbent nations. From these results, the authors conclude that the question in their title should be answered in the affirmative, and that the EP should be given equal standing with the Council in all legislative matters.

The Noury–Roland findings are striking and sure to play a role in the debate on Europe's future. If nothing else, they show that the EP acts much more like a 'normal' parliament than most observers seem to believe. The *Financial Times*, for example, wrote that the EP was 'rarely decisive, barely coherent and often overruled' (10/4/2002). Noury and Roland prove this wrong. In their data, votes are very frequently near-unanimous, and many such votes reflect the position of the Parliament relative to Commission proposals, or Council decisions, or even Parliament initiatives. There is thus a concerted effort in the EP, whenever possible, to appear united in front of the Council and the Commission, especially in cases of institutional conflict. As Thierry Verdier's discussion makes clear and as acknowledged by the authors, of course, past evidence need not bear on the EP's future behaviour. The party-line voting behaviour of the EP may, for example, reflect the fact that national concerns are currently dealt with in the Council of Ministers, and one cannot yet be sure that major reforms granting the EP more power over issues with strong country-specific dimensions would not dramatically alter MEPs' voting behaviour.

EU AID

How is European integration changing the location of industry? And what part are national and EU aids to industry playing in this process? A paper published in issue 32 by Michele Boldrin and Fabio Canova cast doubt on the efficacy of EU aids in reducing regional income disparities. In this issue Karen Helene Midelfart-Knarvik and Henry Overman go further by looking at the evolution not of income but of industrial structure in the EU. They report analysis of a dataset linking regional industrial structure with influences including comparative advantage, agglomeration forces and both national and EU aids. They show that states and regions are becoming more specialized within the EU, but this process is very slow. While there is no evidence of polarization occurring at the national level, some regions are losing out. National state aids to industry appear to have little effect for either good or ill, since their effectiveness at attracting economic activity and employment is limited. The authors also find that European structural funds expenditure has a significant effect on the location of industry, notably by attracting industries intensive in research and development. However, and controversially, they find that this effect has mostly been acting *against* states' comparative advantage – R&D-intensive industries have been encouraged by these aids to locate in countries and regions that have low endowments of skilled labour. Only in Ireland, where structural funds reinforced rather than offset comparative advantage, have poor regions been enabled systematically to catch up with the EU average. The implications are striking, and reinforce the conclusions of Boldrin and Canova about the wastefulness of EU aid: it may have been effective at changing industrial structure, but only by changing it in ways that are unlikely to raise income in a sustainable fashion. There was vigorous discussion at the panel, and a number of panelists cautioned that the findings use data over a relatively short period to illuminate potentially long-run changes. We share this caution, but think that the paper's findings pose a challenge to EU regional policy that warrants serious further research.

UNION DENSITY

Many papers show that labour markets where unions are more important tend to feature low employment and high unemployment. Since lower employment (and less work) may well be exactly what workers bargain for when collectively asking for higher wages, accusing unions of reducing employment may be a little moot. Still, if unemployment is a problem, then it may be solved by reducing the influence of unions. That this is possible was proved by Mrs Thatcher many years ago, and economists can readily see the point of union-bashing policies: the combination of higher wages and low employment may benefit at least some workers but, like any monopolistic practice, damages other economic agents more. But exactly what policies and economic conditions determine the strength of unions? And is the role of unions really so simple and so negative as the simple reasoning above contend it to be?

Daniele Checchi and Claudio Lucifora's paper provides intriguing empirical answers to the former question, and a sophisticated answer to the latter. The authors, and an extensive literature, point out that collective wage bargaining services may provide insufficient motivation for workers to join unions. If wages are the same for union members and other workers, then each individual worker would rather let others pay union dues and support union activities. Individual interest and competitive pressure tend to break collusive behaviour, unless union membership offers private, excludable benefits. Checchi and Lucifora note that unions can and do offer such benefits in the form, for example, of protection from job loss and other labour market risks. Government policies meant to offset such risks should then reduce incentives for workers to join unions. The social costs and benefits of union activity and government policies depend on whether unions simply decrease competition and reduce efficiency or usefully protect workers from unfair markets, and on whether union activity offers protection more efficiently than policies or markets. Empirically, employment protection legislation, wage indexation, and other policies meant to protect workers from income and employment risk are indeed associated with lower union presence. There is also some evidence that higher rents are associated with stronger union presence, as would be implied by the monopolistic view of unions, and the results offer interesting accounts of policy and structural causes for unionization rate trends in European countries.

The paper treats unions as an endogenous institution, and argues on theoretical grounds that higher unemployment should, under some conditions, increase workers' incentives to join unions. This perspective intriguingly reverses the usual economic reasoning, where historically given unionization rates cause high unemployment among other things. As the Panel discussion makes clear, the two perspectives should be treated as complementary, and further work should aim at explaining both unionization and labour market outcomes on the basis of deeper politico-economic structural features of countries and historical periods. While available data make it difficult to do so convincingly, Checchi and Lucifora's paper casts reasonable doubt on the simple view of unions as anti-competitive entities bent on inefficient rent extraction, and will remain a standard reference for further theoretical and empirical efforts.

ACTIVE POLICY EVALUATION

Whether or not unions are ultimately responsible for the high, persistent, long-term unemployment observed in many European labour markets, in the same markets one also sees governments engaged in extensive and expensive policies meant to increase employment. In the previous issue of *Economic Policy*, the paper by Yann Algan, Pierre Cahuc and André Zylberberg showed clearly that the most direct among such policies, namely public job creation, can very easily backfire. If unemployment is an equilibrium phenomenon, brought about by high wage demands and other structural features, more public employment can easily add to wage pressures, reduce private employment and increase unemployment.

In this issue, Jochen Kluve and Christoph Schmidt focus more precisely on whether, at least, targeted 'active' labour market policies (ALPM) can improve the employment prospects of specific disadvantaged worker groups. Their paper offers a clear and informative discussion of methodological problems encountered when trying to assess whether a given policy intervention has the desired effects in practice. Not only does one need to define clearly the effects to be assessed, and be aware of possible equilibrium side effects (of the type studied by Algan *et al.*). But even just measuring the impact effect of a policy intervention or 'treatment' requires methodological sophistication. In fact, the 'other things equal' assumption called for by such measurement need not even hold true within the sample of individuals considered, whose assignment to treatment may well be systematically correlated with their other relevant characteristics, rather than random as it would have to be in a controlled experiment. (Readers may remember that in *Economic Policy* 33 we published papers by Torsten Persson and Andrew Rose debating similar methodological issues in a different context.) Kluve and Schmidt offer novel empirical as well as methodological insight. Like Checchi and Lucifora, they run regressions that intriguingly reverse common causality views, 'explaining' high ALPM expenditures with other labour market policies and institutions that tend to be associated with high, long-term unemployment. And they carefully review a large set of empirical papers on the effectiveness of specific ALMP programmes.

While it would not be surprising (at least to economists convinced that lower labour costs increase employment) to find that subsidizing employment can create jobs, this is a surprisingly rare outcome in the programme evaluation literature reviewed by Kluve and Schmidt. The authors discuss clearly, but cannot resolve, the difficult issue of whether ALMP may pass cost–benefit evaluation. But they do very usefully emphasize that it is often not even possible to detect an employment creation effect from such policy interventions, and that the EU Employment Strategy's recent emphasis on ALMP may very easily lead to misguided and wasteful policies unless accompanied by competent evaluation efforts. This is an important message, and the paper should be an important reference for further work aimed at explaining, for example, the different extent and character of ALMP across European countries.

CORPORATE TAXES

Falls in statutory tax rates on corporate income in many industrialized countries in the last two decades have been attributed by many observers to fiscal competition, triggered by increased mobility of capital. But statutory tax rates are often a poor guide to the effective tax rates that really matter for investment decisions. Michael Devereux, Rachel Griffith and Alexander Klemm document what has really happened to effective rates of corporate tax over this period. Their paper points out that countries that have been cutting tax rates have often simultaneously been reducing tax allowances, thereby broadening the tax base. Calculating the net effect of these two trends is complex; nevertheless it appears that on average across EU and G7 countries, effective tax rates on *marginal* investments – those that earn just the cost of capital – have remained fairly stable. It is tax rates on more profitable investments that have fallen. The authors discuss two possible explanations. One is that governments may be responding to a fall in the cost of income shifting, which puts downward pressure on the statutory tax rate; the consequent reduction in revenues leads to base broadening to reduce broadening the budgetary costs of this. A second explanation is in terms of conscious competition for more profitable intra-marginal projects, in particular those earned by multinational firms. Discussion at the Panel meeting indicated that it is much harder to be sure about the causes than about the phenomenon itself. In particular, there are divergences in trends across countries, suggesting that more partial explanations such as shifts in political ideology may be more persuasive than ones that purport to apply uniformly to the industrialized countries. Nevertheless, the paper discredits the myth of a simple 'race to the bottom' in corporate taxation, and is sure to spark a lively academic and policy debate.

FINANCIAL SERVICES VAT

The EU financial sector accounts for an important and growing share of Europe's GDP but the vast majority of this is exempted from value added tax (VAT). This exemption distorts prices, reduces government revenues, puts EU credit institutions at a disadvantage to their non-EU rivals, and opens the door to subtle tax-competition among national tax authorities. The only real justification for this odd exemption is technical. As it turns out, it is devilishly difficult to determine the value-added created by financial services that involve financial capital, so almost all countries exempt financial services. The few attempts to introduce VAT on financial services have been short-lived.

Harry Huizinga argues that the changed nature of bank–client relationships and advances in information technology have opened the door to a practical way of redressing this exemption. His solution is to 'zero rate' financial services provided to EU businesses but to charge normal VAT on services provide to households. This would certainly create an incentive for tax arbitrage, with, for example, households posing as businesses to avoid VAT. To avoid this, banks would have to verify their customers' VAT status. While this may be burdensome, the OECD-wide fight against tax evasion and the international fight against terrorism have forced financial institutions to know much more about their clients. Verifying a client's VAT status should thus be fairly simple.

In addition to arguing that his reform is feasible, Huizinga calculates the economic impact of reform. He finds that reform would significantly increase VAT revenues, while having little impact on the overall economic well being of Europeans. Households would see an increase in the price of financial services but given the relatively high incomes of mortgage takers, the burden of the tax would be approximately proportional across income classes.

Huizinga's discussants and other Panellists were significantly more pessimistic about the do-ability of Huizinga's proposal. Stijn Claessens argued that the very nature of financial services makes them amenable to accounting tricks and redefinitions that EU tax authorities would be hard pressed to keep up with. Fiona Scott Morton cited the example of mortgages that satisfied religious prescriptions against borrowing by redefining interest and amortization payments as rent. Charles Goodhart suggested that to avoid a 15–25% VAT, mortgages might be securitized and floated on credit markets with only minimal intervention by traditional financial institutions. While addressing such concerns fully will require further research, it is clear that the paper by Huizinga is an excellent and provocative first step.

FOREX MARKETS AND THE EURO

Readers may remember that in *Economic Policy* 34 a paper by Harald Hau, William Killeen and Michael Moore attracted much and very critical attention. At the following Panel meeting we organized a mini-symposium on the issue of whether the euro may or may not be in a better positition than its predecessors (chiefly the deustchemark) in international currency markets. All three papers made interesting theoretical and empirical contributions to this debate, and all are published in this issue.

Charles Goodhart, Ryan Love, Richard Payne and Dagfinn Rime offer an empirical analysis of transaction costs against the US dollar before and after the launch of the single European currency. They find that tradable spreads indeed appear larger for the euro than they were for the deutschemark, and propose a very simple explanation: when the euro replaced the mark, the smallest significant digit of price quotes happened to be defined as a larger fraction of typical exchange rates. As was already noted in the previous Panel's discussion, this 'granularity' intuitively tends to imply larger differences between dealers' bid and ask spreads. The authors foster confidence in that explanation by showing that the distribution and behaviour of spreads is quite similar before and after introduction of the euro when expressed in terms of minimum quote changes ('pips'). They also discuss whether reducing the granularity of price quotes would improve the market's liquidity and, in light of similar policy experiments in US stock markets, conclude that it may but need not do so.

Carsten Detken and Philipp Hartmann's paper analyses a broader set of foreign exchange data, confirming Goodhart *et al.*'s findings as regards increasing dollar-euro spreads transactions costs. Their data also indicate that such increases are not observed in other bilateral markets, and the spreads' persistence and correlation with the nominal euro/dollar exchange rate all confirm that the 'granularity' explanation has a real chance of being correct. Detken and Hartmann also examine recent evidence regarding other international uses of the euro, finding that domestic consolidation has the implications envisioned before introduction of the single European currency and that other possible trends are not easily detectable yet.

In the third contribution to the mini-symposium, Richard Lyons offers a clear discussion of evidence and explanations within a unified framework, provides additional evidence on customer (rather than dealers') behaviour before and after introduction of the euro, and explains why such seemingly small phenomena as a increase of transaction costs by a tiny fraction of a percentage point may indeed have major implications for the functioning of exchange rate markets.

We are pleased to see that the initially controversial empirical findings of Hau, Killeen and Moore emerge largely unscathed by analysis of more and better data. And, even though 'granularity' of price quotations offers a more immediate explanation of the empirical evidence, we remain very impressed by the subtle theoretical explanation put forward by those authors. Rich Lyons' clear and sophisticated account of currency spreads' practical relevance (even when almost mechanically driven by 'granularity') more than suffices to motivate publication of these papers, and the very substantial effort entailed by all authors' empirical analysis.

Readers will find at http://www.economic-policy.org Hau, Killeen and Moore's rejoinder, as well as a Web essay by Lyons arguing that while macro theory offers little guidance to the dynamics of exchange rates (as explained by Ken Rogoff in an earlier Web essay), microstructural theory has been able to offer powerful empirical insight into high-frequency exchange rate dynamics.

Like the mini-symposium discussant Ken Rogoff and many Panel members, however, we are less than completely convinced that success or failure of the single European currency project may be significantly affected by international phenomena. Introduction of the euro was not motivated by international-use considerations. Joining the euro area (for better or for worse) was motivated by countries' hope that markets would become more efficient and macroeconomic policies more effective and better guided. We are commissioning a set of very interesting papers for the April 2003 Panel meeting and plan to publish a special issue focused on early evidence of such phenomena. We hope our readers will enjoy this and future issues, and close this introduction thanking all authors, panelists, and anonymous referees (who play an increasingly important role in the journal's editorial process) for their invaluable contribution to ensuring that *Economic Policy* continues to offer competent, thorough and accessible analysis of topical issues.

European parliament
Should it have more power?

Many observers have expressed scepticism about granting more power to the European Parliament. The sceptics believe that Members of the European Parliament (MEPs) do not vote in a disciplined way and that they vote more often with their country group than with their European Party. Using a unique database consisting of all roll call votes by each individual MEP between 1989 and 1999 (over 6000 votes by over 1000 different MEPs), we show that the sceptics are wrong. Our data shows clearly that MEPs vote more along party lines than along country lines. Party cohesion is comparable to that of the US Congress and is increasing over time whereas country cohesion is low and declining. In short, politics in the European Parliament generally follows the traditional left–right divide that one finds in all European nations. These findings are valid across issues, even on issues like the structural and cohesion funds where one would expect country rather than party cohesion. In votes where the EP has the most power – those held under the so-called co-decision procedure – MEPs participate more and are more party-cohesive. In our opinion, this unique empirical analysis provides grounds for justifying a generalization of the co-decision procedure.

— *Abdul G. Noury and Gérard Roland*

Economic Policy October 2002 Printed in Great Britain
© CEPR, CES, MSH, 2002.

More power to the European Parliament?

Abdul G. Noury and Gérard Roland

DULBEA and ECARES-ULB, UC Berkeley, ECARES, CEPR and WDI

1. INTRODUCTION

Proposals to give the European Parliament (EP) more power have triggered debates at the highest levels of European politics. As German Foreign Minister Joschka Fischer argued persuasively: 'Today, the EU is no longer a mere union of states, but more and more a union of citizens. Nevertheless, European decisions are still taken almost exclusively by the states. The role of the elected European Parliament as a source of direct legitimisation is underdeveloped. This role has to be further strengthened if we are to overcome the democratic deficit of the Union . . .' Such proposals are also central to various reforms being considered by the European Convention. The exact reforms under consideration are manifold, but they typically include calls for boosting the European Parliament's legislative and budgetary powers.

How would a more powerful EP affect decision-making in an enlarged EU? Answering this critical question conclusively is too vast an undertaking for any single article, however any sensible answer must surely be based on a clear understanding of how the EP has functioned in the past. This is especially important since astonishingly little seems to be known about how the EP operates in practice. The *Financial*

We acknowledge financial support from an ACE grant from the European Union and ARC project from the Communauté française de Belgique. Vincenzo Verardi, Elsa Roland, Iman Chaara and Christophe Piette provided very useful help in assembling the data. Special thanks go to George Destrée who gave invaluable computer assistance. We also thank Simon Hix, Thomas Piketty and Thierry Verdier for their detailed comments on earlier drafts.

The Managing Editor in charge of this paper was Richard Baldwin.

Times, for example, wrote that the EP was 'rarely decisive, barely coherent and often overruled' (10/4/2002) – a comment that we shall show is almost exactly wrong.

Drawing on a unique data set that covers all recorded votes by Members of the European Parliament (MEPs) between 1989 and 1999, we are able to concisely document how the EP has op▾rated.[1] During this period, the Maastricht and Amsterdam Treaties increased the powers of the EP in important ways and EU membership was enlarged. Thus our data, which consists of several million individual votes, allows us to cast light on how the EP may react to the two most critical challenges in its future – receiving more power and adjusting to a near doubling of EU member states.

1.1. The key question

A crucial question in understanding the impact of giving the EP more power is whether coalitions are formed on the basis of country coalitions or on the basis of the traditional left–right divide. If coalitions form along left–right lines, giving the EP more power should encourage European-wide political debates and strengthen cohesion of pan-European party groups. If coalitions are based mostly on national interests, increasing the Parliament's power may not have much effect. The point is that most EU legislation must be approved both by the Council of Ministers (where national concerns are clearly dominant) and by the EP, but majority rules are much more stringent in the Council than in the EP. An EP where voting was arranged around country coalitions would thus not have much influence since anything that could get over the Council's majority threshold would also pass in the Parliament, as Bindseil and Hantke (1997) showed.

The question of coalition formation is even more important in the light of the future enlargement of the EU to countries from Central Europe. If the EP votes mostly along ideological party lines, enlargement will increase the size of the EP and possibly affect its ideological composition, but it would not fundamentally threaten its ability to operate. Giving more power to the EP would thus be beneficial for decision-making within the EU because it would mitigate the dangers of paralysis in decision-making that are inherent to enlargement. Baldwin *et al.* (2001) showed that with enlargement to 27 members, the ability of the EU's Council of Ministers to take decisions would clearly deteriorate. A resolute EP with more powers may thus put pressure on the Council to overcome potential paralysis of decision-making. On the other hand, if the Euro-deputies vote mainly on the basis of national interests, more power to the EP may not help in preventing paralysis of decision-making in the EU Council, and could possibly make things even worse.

A second important question concerns the impact of greater power on the EP's behaviour. Under current rules, EU decision-making follows several different procedures,

---

[1] This is part of a larger research project jointly organized with Simon Hix of the London School of Economics to put together a database on voting in the European Parliament from 1979 to 2001.

each of which entails a different degree of parliamentary power. Under some procedures, the EP's role is merely consultative; under others, the EP has veto power. Does the EP act differently on issues where it has more power? Again, the answer to this question will depend on whether the allegiance of MEPs is to their nationality or party ideology. As mentioned earlier, the former should not make much difference, given the Council's higher majority constraint, whereas the latter should encourage greater pan-European cohesion and debates. The final question concerns the behaviour of MEPs from newly admitted nations. Since our data includes the votes of MEPs from Austria, Finland and Sweden during their first term, we can see how their voting patterns differed from those of MEPs from incumbent EU member states. While the MEPs from nations admitted in the next EU enlargement may act differently, determining the impact of the last enlargement is a natural place to start when thinking about how the coming enlargement will affect the EP.

1.2. Our findings

The empirical analysis we have done suggests clear answers to the above questions:

- The data show that MEPs vote more along party lines than country lines. Party cohesion is comparable to that in the US Congress while cohesion of country delegations (MEPs from the same country) is significantly lower and is declining.
- Legislative decisions giving the EP more power exhibit higher MEP participation and party cohesion while reinforcing a visible tendency toward traditional left–right politics typical of national legislatures.
- Under the previous enlargement, MEPs from newly entering countries did not vote less with their European party group than MEPs from existing member states.

These striking results are robust to various specifications.[2] Though caution should obviously be exercised in drawing policy conclusions, the analysis based on this unique database suggests that giving more power to the EP by generalizing the co-decision procedure is likely to reinforce party cohesion and normal parliamentary coalitions on a left–right basis.

1.3. Organization of the paper

Interpreting the data requires some understanding of the EU legislative process and institutional arrangements in the EP, so we first provide some background on this. The following section presents the 'meat' of our analysis; it examines whether Euro-deputies vote primarily according to their ideology or national interest. To do so, we

[2] These results confirm similar results derived from smaller samples of votes, for example Hix (2001), Kreppel and Tsebelis (1999), and Raunio (1997).

measure the cohesion of party and country votes, the voting pattern of individual MEPs, and use regression analysis. We also analyse coalition formation for both party groups and country delegations. After having established the dominance of party-based voting in the EP, the natural question is: 'Why do MEPs vote mainly along party rather than country lines?' Section 4 considers various possible answers. To further evaluate the impact of enlargement and greater powers on EP voting patterns, Section 5 uses regression analysis to examine the effects of increased power and enlargement on voting discipline. Section 6 addresses the policy implication of our analysis and Section 7 concludes.

2. THE EUROPEAN PARLIAMENT: HISTORY AND POWERS

The European Parliament started life as a toothless, consultative body in a Union with just six members. Today, however, it is directly elected by the citizens of all 15 EU members and has a good deal of power. Since almost all of the Parliament's power comes from being able to shape EU legislation, understanding the EP's powers requires a basic comprehension of the EU's legislative process.

EU legislation is formulated under at least five different procedures, each of which is highly complex. For our purposes, however, the EP's role in all the processes can be stylised as follows. The process is begun by a proposal from the European Commission. After a sequence of consultations and amendments involving both the Parliament and the Council of Ministers, the measure is put to a vote. With minor exceptions, all legislation requires explicit approval by the Council. The most important measures – the budget, trade agreements, enlargements, treaty changes, etc. – require the Council's unanimous approval. While important, such legislation is infrequent. Adoption of the most common measures, including legislation concerning the EU's internal market, involve a lower majority threshold in the Council, known as a 'qualified majority'. A qualified majority requires 71% of Council votes but it is important to note that more populous nations have more votes than small nations. Winning 71% of Council votes thus does not require winning approval of 71% of EU member states. In addition to the Council's approval, many types of legislation (currently about 80% of all EU legislation) also require approval by the European Parliament. Typically, EP approval entails a 50% majority of MEPs. Depending on the measure being debated, though, the 50% requirement may be based on the number of MEPs present, or the total number of elected MEPs, present or not.

The EP's power lies in its ability to shape legislation and this, in turn, rests on its ability to reject, or threaten to reject, measures that it does not like. As a consequence, the EP's power varies according to the exact nature of the procedure followed (the nature of the measure determines which procedure is applied). The most common procedure by far – and the procedure under which the EP has the most power – is the so-called 'Co-Decision' procedure (this was established in the Maastricht Treaty and improved in the Amsterdam Treaty).

Box 1. Legislative procedures

Each Procedure involves a very complex sequence of interactions, details of which can be found on http://www.europarl.eu.int/factsheets/default_en.htm. Here, we summarize their main elements as far as EP power is concerned.

The *consultation* procedure provides the EP with the least influence/power. For measures covered by this procedure, the Commission proposes and the Council decides after the EP has provided its opinion on the matter. The only requirement is that the Council 'take note' of the EP's opinion.

The *assent* procedure provides more power than the consultation procedure since it gives the EP veto power. The EP's vote, however, is a simple up-or-down decision; the EP cannot amend the measure.

The *cooperation* procedure provides a similar level of power to the EP; indeed it can be thought of as the co-decision without the conciliation committee. This procedure is rarely used since the Amsterdam Treaty.

The *budgetary* procedure is a mix of the assent procedure and the co-decision procedure. The EP must approve the overall budget but it can only table amendments to 'non-compulsory' expenditures; these account for about half the budget but exclude important elements such as spending on the Common Agricultural Policy (CAP).

The co-decision procedure puts the EP on an equal footing with the Council by only allowing a measure to become law if both bodies approve it. When disagreements arise, a 'conciliation committee' composed of EP and Council representatives is formed in an attempt to carve out a compromise. If a compromise fails, the proposal is rejected. Otherwise, it is adopted provided that it is accepted by the EP (simple majority) and by the Council (qualified majority). The co-decision procedure thus gives effective bargaining power to the EP as it can use its right of rejection to negotiate compromises with the Council. Co-decision now covers a great deal of EU legislation with the important exceptions of EMU, agriculture, fisheries and fiscal harmonization. Moreover, in some co-decision areas (citizenship, mobility of workers, self-employed, culture), unanimity is still required in the Council and this greatly reduces the EP's scope for bargaining.

The four other procedures are briefly described in Box 1.

Voting in the EP can take one of three forms: by show of hand, by electronic vote, or by roll call vote. A roll call vote can be requested if at least 32 MEPs or a political group ask for it. MEPs do not know in advance whether a roll call will be requested or not. Roughly a third of all votes are by roll call but their share has been increasing over time. In 1988, the number of roll call votes per hour of plenary session was about 1.1. In 1998, it was about 1.5.

In our database, 2291 out of 6473 votes, i.e. slightly over 35% of the votes, were legislative and used one of the existing procedures. Among the legislative votes, 46% used the consultation procedure, 27% the cooperation procedure, 25% the co-decision procedure and 1% the assent procedure. Among all the proposals put to vote, 58.7% passed the majority hurdle.

2.1. The organization of MEPs

MEPs are organized in political groups. The seating arrangement in the parliament-ary chamber's hemicycle resembles that of a typical national parliament, with parties ranked from left to right according to their ideology. In the current Parliament, the seating is as follows. At the extreme left, there is the radical left which regroups many of the communist, former communist or extreme left parties plus the Nordic Green Left parties from Scandinavia. Then, from left to right there is the Party of the European Socialists (PES), the Greens and allies, regrouping regional parties mostly from Spain but also from Wales, the liberal ELDR (European Liberal Democrat and Reformists), the mostly Christian Democratic and conservative European People's Party (EPP-ED), Eurosceptic Gaullists, other rightist groups and finally non-affiliated. The names of the groups change over time across legislatures and sometimes within legislatures reflecting defections from some national parties. Table 1 gives the party groups with the denominations they had over time. In subsequent tables, we will use the common abbreviation listed in the second column from the left in Table 1.

It is not by coincidence that MEPs are ranked according to ideology. The party groups to which they belong truly exist and have a structured internal organization. The EP allocates budgets to party groups. Each group has a Chair, a secretariat and

Table 1. Party families in the European Parliament

Party family	Our symbol	Party group names	Size in third parliament	Size in fourth parliament
Party of European Socialists	PES	PES	180 (34.7%)	198 (34.9%)
European People's Party – Christian Democrats and Conservatives	EPP	EPP, ED, EPP-ED	155 (29.9%)	157 (27.7%)
European Liberal, Democrat and Reform Party	ELDR	ELD, ELDR	49 (9.5%)	43 (7.6%)
Greens and allies	GR	RBW, G, G/EFA	30 (5.8%)	23 (4.1%)
Gaullists and allies	GAUL	EPD, EDA, UFE, UEN	20 (3.9%)	53 (9.3%)
Radical Left and Italian Communists and allies	LEFT	COM, LU, EUL/NGL, EUL	42 (8.1%)	28 (4.9%)
Radicals and Regionalists	RAD	ERA	13 (2.5%)	19 (3.4%)
Anti-Europeans	ANTI-EU	EN, I-EN, EDD	17 (3.3%)	19 (3.4%)
Non-attached (Independents)	NA	IND	12 (2.3%)	27 (4.8%)

Notes: Some MEPs changed affiliation during the period considered. In that case, we defined their party affiliation as their last one in the time period considered. This will tend to slightly underestimate our scores for party discipline.

staff working for them. Members of groups meet in Brussels and during plenary sessions in Strasbourg to make joint voting decisions. Groups have 'whips' who check the attendance and voting behaviour of group members even though groups have limited means to sanction their members. Such structures do not exist at all for the country delegations in the EP. These organizational facts alone should lead one to think that MEPs vote more along party lines than along national lines. For more on the development of European party groups and how they are organized see Kreppel (2001).

3. PARTY OR COUNTRY LOYALTY?

Do Members of the European Parliament vote along ideological lines or along national lines? With data on over 6000 roll call votes, this question can be studied in a number of ways. Here we present four distinct approaches.

Our first approach classifies MEPs according to two criteria – party membership and nationality – and then compares the voting-pattern cohesiveness of the two groupings. The idea behind this approach is to see whether we can more naturally account for MEPs' voting behaviour by viewing MEPs as members of a particular party, or as citizens of a particular nation. After comparing these findings to similar results calculated from the roll-call votes of national legislatures, we turn to our second approach. While the first approach focuses on the voting pattern of groups, the second focuses on the voting pattern of individuals. In particular, we use statistical techniques to check whether the average MEP's voting pattern is better explained by his/her nationality or by his/her party affiliation. These two approaches are obviously related and indeed provide similar answers, but they involve different statistical manipulations and thus provide a crosscheck on each other. The third approach relies on case studies. That is, we take a detailed look at votes on particular issues and use more qualitative evidence to evaluate what the outcomes tell us about the motivations of MEPs. The final approach involves a statistical technique that allows us to study the determinants of MEP voting in a more abstract manner.

3.1. Analysis of voting by groups

To compare the cohesiveness of national groups and party groups, we need a way of gauging the similarity among the voting patterns of a group's members. The main measure we use is the so-called cohesion index. To calculate the cohesion index (CI) for a particular group of voters, we first calculate the group's 'position' on each vote in our dataset. This is done mechanically by defining the group's 'position' as 'Yes', 'No' or 'Abstention' according to which of the three received the most votes from group members. The next step is to calculate the difference between the number of votes for and against this position and normalize this by the total number of group votes. For example, if the position on a particular vote is 'Yes' and 83 members voted 'Yes' and 17 voted either 'No' or abstained, then the CI is (83 – 17)/100. After performing this calculation for each vote in our dataset, we take the average over all votes. This is the group's CI.

While no formal measure can perfectly capture a concept as vague as cohesion, the CI does a good job of capturing the general notion. For example, if all the members of a group voted the same way on every issue, the group's cohesion index would be equal to 1. If the group always divided 50% for the position and 50% against it, the group's CI would be equal to 0. A higher CI thus tends to indicate a greater similarity among the voting patterns of a group's members. Zero, however, is not the lowest possible value for the CI. If the group's voting were always split in three equal parts between the Yes, No and Abstention, then the cohesion index would equal $-1/3$. The CI is not the only index of this type and indeed it can be thought of a variant of the more commonly used 'Rice Agreement Index' (Rice 1928), which ignores abstentions.

3.1.1. Party groups are more cohesive than national groups. The top panel of Table 2 presents the CIs that we calculated for parties in the third and fourth parliament. The bottom panel does the same for national groups.

Comparing the figures in the top and bottom panels of Table 2 clearly shows that cohesion is much stronger when we group MEPs by their party affiliation than it is when we group them by their nationality. The cohesion index for parties is on average 84.2% in the third parliament and 82.2% in the fourth parliament while the average for countries is respectively 74.4% and 68.8%. There is thus a 10% point difference in cohesion. This difference is statistically significant.[3]

The standard deviation is lower for parties than for countries showing that the variability in cohesion is much lower for parties than for countries. The cohesion of countries remains generally somewhat higher than that for the EP as a whole (58% in the third parliament and 52% in the fourth parliament). This reflects to a certain extent the fact that one party dominates many country delegations. For example, the first-past-the-post electoral rule allowed Labour to dominate the UK delegations to the EP. The large cohesion for Greece and Luxembourg can also be explained by the fact that they are mainly affiliated to the two largest political groups.

Note that the cohesion index for France is lower than that for the EP. French representatives are thus the most divided country group in the EP, a fact that may run counter to the intuition of many. Note also that cohesion is the highest among the party families reflecting the usual political cleavages in advanced democracies: Socialists (PES), Christian-democrats and Conservatives (EPP), Greens (GR) and Liberals (ELDR).

---

[3] Note that the standard errors of the CIs equal the standard deviations, which are in parentheses in Table 2, divided by the square root of the number of votes (2733 for the third parliament and 3740 for the fourth), so a 10% point difference is enormous. Testing the null hypothesis that the average party cohesion equals the average country cohesion leads to clear rejection for the third parliament (t-stat = 32) and for the fourth parliament (t-stat = 47).

Table 2. Party versus country cohesion, evidence from the third and fourth parliaments

CIs for parties

	PES	EPP	ELDR	GR	GAUL	LEFT	RAD	ANTI-EU	NA	Eur. Parl.
Third	0.87	0.85	0.77	0.82	0.80	0.80	0.83	0.64	0.74	0.58
	(0.21)	(0.22)	(0.29)	(0.24)	(0.29)	(0.33)	(0.35)	(0.4)	(0.36)	(0.32)
Fourth	0.87	0.86	0.80	0.88	0.72	0.74	0.88	0.56	0.51	0.52
	(0.2)	(0.2)	(0.23)	(0.22)	(0.33)	(0.31)	(0.25)	(0.37)	(0.38)	(0.31)

CIs for countries

	F	UK	I	IRL	FIN	S	D	GR	NL	E	B	P	A	DK	L	Eur. Parl.
Third	0.48	0.7	0.63	0.66	–	–	0.62	0.73	0.66	0.73	0.56	0.68	–	0.65	0.79	0.58
	(0.33)	(0.35)	(0.35)	(0.35)			(0.35)	(0.35)	(0.34)	(0.3)	(0.34)	(0.35)		(0.38)	(0.35)	(0.32)
Fourth	0.44	0.76	0.57	0.55	0.57	0.49	0.63	0.62	0.62	0.63	0.52	0.58	0.59	0.52	0.66	0.52
	(0.33)	(0.24)	(0.33)	(0.35)	(0.35)	(0.35)	(0.37)	(0.35)	(0.32)	(0.36)	(0.31)	(0.34)	(0.36)	(0.38)	(0.38)	(0.31)

Notes: Figures in parentheses are standard deviations, not standard errors (the standard errors are by 52.3 for the third parliament and 61.2 for the fourth). See Table 1 for party abbreviations. Country abbreviations are F: France; UK: United Kingdom; I: Italy; IRL: Ireland; FIN: Finland; S: Sweden; D: Germany; GR: Greece; NL: Netherlands; E: Spain; B: Belgium; P: Portugal; A: Austria; DK: Denmark; L: Luxembourg. See text for explanation of the CI. Formally CI for group i equals $[2*\max(Y_j, N_j, A_j) - (Y_j + N_j + A_j)]/(Y_j + N_j + A_j)$ averaged over all votes j; here Y_j, N_j and A_j are the number of group members voting yes, no or abstaining on vote j.

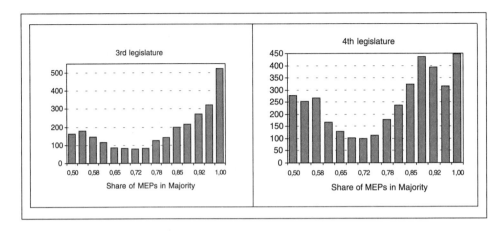

Figure 1. The distribution of majority, third and fourth parliaments

Source: Authors' database.

3.1.1.1. Adjusting group cohesion for near unanimous votes. A fairly large share of votes in the EP are unanimous, or nearly so, as Figure 1 shows. Because the CI is unity for any grouping of voters when a vote is unanimous, the dominance of unanimous and near-unanimous votes tends to dampen the difference between our CI results for party and country groupings. We will therefore adjust for this, but before doing so we comment on the fact itself. Many of these high-majority votes reflect the position of the Parliament relative to Commission proposals or Council decisions or even Parliament initiatives. Indeed, despite representing different ideologies and countries, MEPs generally share the objective of increasing the power of the EP. There is thus a concerted effort in the EP, whenever possible, to appear united in front of the Council and the Commission, especially in cases of institutional conflict. Whatever else it means, we can certainly say that the dominance of high-majority votes can reject the notion, mentioned in the introduction, that the EP is rarely decisive and barely coherent.

To mitigate the effect of unanimity or high majority votes on our average cohesion index, we calculated a 'weighted' cohesion index. This is the usual cohesion index divided by the observed majority in the European Parliament multiplied by two. Thus, a vote with a narrow majority of 50% gets a weight of one, a unanimity vote gets a weight of $1/2$ and weights decrease as the size of the majority increases. When computing the average of those weighted cohesion indices, we divide them by the average index a perfectly cohesive party would obtain so that a perfectly cohesive group would still get an average of 100%.

Using this modified CI, we find that the difference between the cohesion of parties is more pronounced than that of countries. Moreover, in contrast to Table 2, the cohesion of parties tends to be stronger in the fourth parliament as compared with the third parliament. For countries, the opposite can be observed. The lower cohesion for countries shows that the latter picks up the effect of high-majority votes that has declined in the fourth parliament. This reinforces our basic result that voting is along party lines and not country lines. A detailed presentation of the weighted CI for parties and countries can be found in the Web Appendix (see http://www.economic-policy.org).

3.1.1.2. Group cohesion on divided votes.   Still another way of analysing the same issue is to evaluate how cohesion changes with the size of the majority. Table 3 shows the results of party and country CIs calculated according to majority size.

In this case the results are quite striking. The cohesion of parties falls very little as the majority size diminishes. For example, in the third parliament, cohesion of MEPs in the Socialist group (PES) falls from 0.87 to 0.79 while the cohesion of German MEPs falls from 0.62 to just 0.17. The same pattern is found in the fourth parliament but the cohesion of countries falls even more sharply. What this suggests is that much of the cohesion of country groups that we saw in Table 2 was due to the sort of 'strategic unanimity' voting that the EP often engages in. When issues are truly divisive, MEPs tend to vote along party lines rather than national lines. Detailed results for a finer division of majority thresholds are shown in the Web Appendix.

3.1.1.3. Group cohesion by issue.   A final cut at the group cohesion data focuses on the type of issue being voted on. One might imagine, for example, that MEPs voted on an ideological basis on some issues, but according to nationality on others. To explore this possibility, we classified the votes into 11 large categories, using the title of the vote as reported in the minutes of the plenary sessions. We then recalculated a separate party and country cohesion index for votes on each issue.

Table 4 lists the resulting CI's for the third parliament. The figures show that there is no striking difference in cohesion when dividing votes according to issues. The table nonetheless tends to indicate that while socialists (PES) become more cohesive on 'Human beings' issues (human rights, refugees, etc.), conservatives (EPP) and liberals (ELDR) are cohesive on security issues and greens and leftists are cohesive on nature and environmental issues. For the fourth parliament, the above findings remain true for conservatives, greens and radicals but not for socialists and liberals who have also become more cohesive on 'Services' (see the Web Appendix for the fourth parliament figures). Note that the mean cohesion index is the lowest for 'Drugs' and the 'Legal System' whereas it is the highest for 'Services' and 'Security'.

3.1.2. Analysis of voting by coalitions of parties.   Given that the EU is not a parliamentary system, there is no coalition government. We should therefore not expect the typical pattern of legislative voting of parliamentary systems where parties of the coalition vote together against the unified votes of the opposition parties. Coalitions, in the EP, form on a vote-by-vote basis. Nevertheless, as parties are

Table 3. Party and country cohesion indices by majority size, third and fourth parliaments

	Third parliament						Fourth parliament					
	Majority less than or equal to:											
	100% Mean	Std Dev	80% Mean	Std Dev	65% Mean	Std Dev	100% Mean	Std Dev	80% Mean	Std Dev	65% Mean	Std Dev
PES	0.867	0.21	0.760	0.28	0.791	0.26	0.867	0.20	0.787	0.25	0.841	0.23
EPP	0.845	0.22	0.757	0.26	0.806	0.23	0.862	0.19	0.796	0.23	0.834	0.20
ELDR	0.770	0.29	0.651	0.30	0.657	0.29	0.798	0.23	0.723	0.25	0.732	0.24
GR	0.817	0.24	0.802	0.23	0.798	0.23	0.884	0.22	0.898	0.20	0.910	0.19
GAUL	0.798	0.29	0.738	0.30	0.748	0.29	0.717	0.33	0.690	0.32	0.720	0.31
LEFT	0.801	0.33	0.767	0.35	0.780	0.33	0.739	0.31	0.748	0.30	0.771	0.30
RAD	0.830	0.35	0.791	0.37	0.788	0.38	0.876	0.25	0.846	0.27	0.856	0.27
ANTI-EU	0.640	0.40	0.623	0.41	0.630	0.42	0.556	0.37	0.503	0.36	0.502	0.36
NA	0.739	0.36	0.711	0.37	0.704	0.37	0.513	0.38	0.495	0.38	0.515	0.39
F	0.485	0.33	0.289	0.25	0.256	0.24	0.437	0.33	0.332	0.29	0.299	0.28
UK	0.696	0.35	0.405	0.32	0.338	0.29	0.760	0.24	0.590	0.20	0.569	0.16
I	0.626	0.35	0.362	0.29	0.305	0.26	0.571	0.33	0.339	0.28	0.255	0.23
IRE	0.659	0.35	0.504	0.33	0.528	0.33	0.550	0.35	0.407	0.30	0.413	0.30
FIN	—		—		—		0.570	0.35	0.361	0.29	0.337	0.27
SW	—		—		—		0.493	0.35	0.361	0.29	0.367	0.28
D	0.620	0.35	0.289	0.28	0.171	0.19	0.635	0.37	0.301	0.32	0.152	0.19
GR	0.734	0.35	0.456	0.36	0.368	0.33	0.625	0.35	0.359	0.32	0.252	0.27
NL	0.660	0.34	0.370	0.30	0.267	0.24	0.619	0.32	0.392	0.27	0.339	0.22
E	0.733	0.29	0.468	0.27	0.357	0.22	0.634	0.36	0.337	0.32	0.209	0.25
B	0.565	0.34	0.303	0.28	0.228	0.25	0.516	0.31	0.285	0.24	0.231	0.21
P	0.682	0.35	0.433	0.32	0.374	0.30	0.576	0.34	0.342	0.29	0.280	0.26
A	—		—		—		0.591	0.36	0.338	0.29	0.264	0.25
DK	0.650	0.38	0.510	0.38	0.468	0.38	0.520	0.38	0.390	0.35	0.391	0.35
L	0.790	0.41	0.596	0.41	0.517	0.40	0.664	0.38	0.403	0.37	0.316	0.33

Notes: See Table 1 for party abbreviations and Table 2 for country abbreviations and the formal definition of the CI.

Table 4. Cohesion per issue in the third parliament

	Foreign Policy	Internal Functioning	Agro-fish	Industry and Technology	Banking and Finance	Drugs	Services	Human Beings	Security	Nature	Legal System
PES	0.842	0.882	0.836	0.847	0.834	0.855	0.904	0.919	0.865	0.898	0.827
EPP	0.855	0.868	0.801	0.832	0.828	0.754	0.894	0.865	0.908	0.808	0.845
ELDR	0.795	0.799	0.704	0.748	0.757	0.676	0.855	0.787	0.835	0.718	0.769
GR	0.777	0.798	0.797	0.853	0.798	0.856	0.860	0.851	0.843	0.884	0.806
GAUL	0.776	0.783	0.849	0.797	0.848	0.764	0.892	0.807	0.777	0.306	0.757
LEFT	0.787	0.785	0.759	0.754	0.749	0.891	0.874	0.842	0.873	0.881	0.788
RAD	0.799	0.762	0.803	0.882	0.842	0.881	0.955	0.891	0.936	0.866	0.962
ANTI-EU	0.610	0.630	0.621	0.576	0.699	0.653	0.499	0.676	0.779	0.656	0.608
NA	0.732	0.717	0.753	0.762	0.794	0.791	0.690	0.724	0.839	0.725	0.726
Mean CI	0.818	0.835	0.803	0.813	0.819	0.799	0.872	0.859	0.867	0.830	0.776
Countries											
F	0.446	0.506	0.470	0.489	0.468	0.474	0.584	0.471	0.486	0.533	0.511
UK	0.666	0.765	0.717	0.590	0.741	0.644	0.689	0.648	0.699	0.711	0.656
I	0.546	0.701	0.646	0.566	0.611	0.537	0.729	0.605	0.693	0.654	0.520
IRE	0.631	0.672	0.633	0.654	0.744	0.622	0.825	0.633	0.718	0.634	0.676
D	0.564	0.684	0.618	0.532	0.583	0.596	0.674	0.563	0.718	0.724	0.603
GR	0.684	0.771	0.802	0.724	0.672	0.746	0.852	0.687	0.776	0.750	0.726
NL	0.654	0.700	0.656	0.596	0.620	0.565	0.649	0.643	0.746	0.718	0.603
E	0.713	0.767	0.749	0.684	0.726	0.685	0.788	0.692	0.796	0.755	0.745
B	0.527	0.593	0.621	0.506	0.545	0.463	0.672	0.546	0.602	0.612	0.540
P	0.646	0.700	0.725	0.668	0.636	0.678	0.751	0.632	0.751	0.755	0.640
DK	0.643	0.611	0.680	0.626	0.674	0.671	0.680	0.654	0.754	0.707	0.634
L	0.813	0.785	0.843	0.843	0.731	0.758	0.819	0.744	0.820	0.756	0.800

Notes: Mean CI is the average cohesion index weighted by party size.

cohesive, it is interesting to see which parties vote together more often. In particular, is there a left–right pattern in coalition formation across votes? If so, then votes of left-wing parties should be positively correlated with each other and negatively correlated with right-wing parties. To check for this, we measured, for each vote, the intensity of support within a party group for a majority decision (the percentage of members who voted in favour of a particular decision when it was adopted and when a majority of the group voted in favour). We call this the intensity of support.

What we find is a clear pattern of positive correlation coefficients between left-wing parties, between right-wing parties, and no correlation or negative correlation across the ideological spectrum. In the third parliament, votes of PES are mostly correlated with those of the LEFT and RAD and so are the votes of GR. Votes of EPP are mostly correlated with those of ELDR and two other right-wing political groups, GAUL and ANTI-EU. There seems to be a broad left (socialists, Greens, left and radicals) on the one side and a broad right on the other (conservatives, Gaullists, liberals and nationalists). Note, however, the very centrist role of the liberals whose votes are correlated to those of socialists but not to the other more left-wing parties. A similar picture emerges in the fourth parliament, except that the votes of PES are more strongly correlated with the votes of GR and less with the LEFT. This reflects recent tendencies of socialist parties to move from labour parties to 'rainbow-style' parties.

The finding that EP party groups seem to co-ordinate in a manner that would be expected in a 'normal' parliament provides additional support for the notion that the EP operates along traditional party lines. Further details on these findings are provided in the Web Appendix.

3.2. Comparing the EP to national legislatures

It is useful to compare these results to those obtained for a national parliament where both ideology and regional identity play a role. Among national parliaments, the Belgian Parliament is probably the most comparable to the EP because there are two communities or 'nations' and several political families.

3.2.1. The Belgian Parliament. In Belgium, there are distinct regional Flemish and French-speaking Socialist, Christian Democratic, Liberal and Green parties and there is no single national party. The 'socialist family' is thus composed of two distinct regional socialist parties. Party families in Belgium are thus conceptually close to party groups in the EP. Like party groups in the EP, these political families also include different tendencies going from left to right as well as regionalists parties. Of course, the Belgian parliament is much smaller than the EP. Moreover, unlike the European Union, Belgium has a genuine parliamentary system. Cohesion of party families should reflect cohesion of government coalitions since coalitions are based

Table 5. Cohesion index in the Belgian Parliament (30/6/1995 to 18/12/1997)

Part family	Parties	Mean	Std Dev	Size (No. of MPs)
Parties				
1 Christian Democrats	CVP, PSC	0.987	0.08	41
2 Socialists	SP, PS	0.978	0.10	43
3 Liberals	VLD, PRL	0.730	0.38	39
4 Regional parties	VU	0.953	0.16	5
5 Green	ECOLO, AGALEV	0.983	0.09	10
6 Extreme right	VB, FN	0.953	0.11	12
Average		0.931	0.15	25
Regions				
1 F	Flemish	0.315	0.29	92
2 W	Francophone	0.422	0.31	59
Average		0.315	0.29	92
Parliament				
CI (all Parliament)		0.356	0.28	150

Notes: Number of roll call votes is 2080. Party abbreviations are: CVP Christelijke Volkspartij, AGALEV Anders gaan arbeiden, leven en vrijen, VLD Vlaamse liberalen en democraten, VU Volskunie, VB Vlaams Blok, SP Socialistische Partij, PSC Parti social-chrétien, ECOLO Ecolo, PRL Parti réformateur libéral, FN Front national, PS Parti socialiste.

on party families, never on parties only.[4] According to recent theories of political regimes, parties forming a coalition in parliamentary regimes are predicted to be very cohesive (Huber, 1996; Diermeier and Feddersen, 1998, Persson *et al.*, 2000).

We collected more than 2000 roll call votes from the Belgian parliament during the 49th legislature (i.e. from 30/6/1995 to 18/12/1997).[5] Our summary results are listed in Table 5. We can immediately see that party cohesion is very much stronger among Belgian party families than among the party families in the EP, confirming the prediction about cohesion of coalition partners in parliamentary systems. Except for the Liberals who were in the opposition, all other party families have a cohesion index ranging from 95% to more than 98%. The average cohesion index is 93%. The very strong party cohesion stands in stark contrast to the cohesion on a regional or linguistic basis, which is very low. The average cohesion index for regions is one-third of that found for political families. Note, however, the lower cohesion of the Parliament compared to the EP. Compared to Belgium, the EP has a lower party cohesion and higher country cohesion. It is safe to believe that in other countries cohesion of 'regions' would be even much lower than for Belgium.

Table 6 compares the Belgian Parliament and the EP on several key criteria. As the first column shows, the average Belgian parliamentarian votes 'Yes' about 40%

[4] Thus for example, if the Flemish Greens are in the coalition, the French-speaking Greens must also be part of it even though they could be dispensed with to form a minimum-winning coalition, which is the case today. Cohesion of families consists mainly of that commitment to participate together in a coalition or otherwise to be in the opposition.

[5] Surprisingly, it is very difficult if not impossible to collect roll call votes for national Parliaments like Germany or France. Such data are more readily available in newer democracies such as Poland and the Czech republic. See e.g. Noury *et al.* (1999) and Mielcova and Noury (1998).

Table 6. Average abstention and presence in the Belgian and European Parliament

	Belgian Parliament 1995–97	European Parliament 1996–99
Yes votes	40.11	36.73
No votes	43.09	27.08
Abstentions	6.98	2.28
Absences	9.77	34.19
TOTAL	100	100

Note: Figures show the percentage of the number of representatives.

of the time, 'No' about 40% of the time, and the remaining 10% is divided between abstention and absence. In the EP, by contrast, the share of yes-votes is comparable, while the share of no-votes is substantially lower, roughly 30%. The most striking difference is the high absentee rate in the EP. Looking a bit further, we compared the percentage of proposals put to vote that were accepted and rejected. We found an acceptance rate of 40% in the Belgian Parliament compared to 58.7% in the EP. Surprisingly this fact contradicts the view one can easily derive from game-theoretic models that only votes that are likely to pass are put forward. This is not true in the EP, but even less true in Belgium that is a full-fledged parliamentary system.

3.2.2. EP compared to the US Congress. We also compared cohesion in the EP with cohesion in the US Congress. The comparison with the US is especially relevant because the US is a presidential system. The theories of democratic political regimes predict that elected representatives in a presidential system vote less cohesively than in a parliamentary system. Since the EU is not a parliamentary system (but not a presidential system either), its cohesion is not predicted to be as high as in parliamentary systems.

Specifically, we calculated the CIs for democrats and republicans between 1991 and 2000. We found that the cohesion among parties in the US Congress was lower than that of party groups in the EP. Indeed party cohesion indices for most Congresses (each Congress sits for a two-year term) was in the 70% range while it is in the 80% range for most EP party groups, and above 85% for the two main parties, the PES and EPP. However, votes are also much more polarized in the US Congress. If one looks at the 'relative' cohesion indices (i.e. cohesion of parties relative to the cohesion of the legislature), then one finds that cohesion of parties in the US Congress is somewhat higher. On average it was above 1.7 in the US, whereas the PES and EPP have, respectively, relative cohesion indices of 1.43 and 1.4 for the third Parliament and 1.57 and 1.56 for the fourth Parliament. However, cohesion has been increasing in the EP whereas in the US Congress, it has been declining since 1996 and has reached levels comparable to those of PES and EPP for the fourth EP (see the Web Appendix for more detail on this comparison). Cohesion in the EP and in the US

Congress are thus quite comparable and it is reassuring to see that party cohesion in the EP is comparable to that of the most mature presidential system in the world.

3.3. Analysis of voting by individuals

Overall, our analysis of voting patterns by groups suggests that party cohesion in the EP is relatively strong and is getting stronger over time while cohesion among countries is not strong and tends to be weak on the most divisive votes. We now turn to a complementary view of our dataset that focuses on individuals rather than groups.

3.3.1 The Discipline Index. Our first approach to studying individual voting behaviour is to compute a 'discipline index' for each MEP. This measures the frequency of votes of a parliamentarian with his or her party group. The discipline index is different from the cohesion index in that it focuses on the voting behaviour of individuals rather than groups. It provides more disaggregated data as it separates individuals according to both their party and country affiliation. Table 7 gives the average frequency of vote of a MEP from a given country with his or her party in the Fourth Parliament. The last column of the table looks at the average frequency of votes with the country delegation. This allows us to compare the relative loyalty of MEPs to their party and to their country group.

One can immediately see that in general party loyalty is stronger than country loyalty. The discipline index also allows us to see whether MEPs from the latest accession behaved differently from other MEPs. Table 7 shows that MEPs from Finland, Sweden and Austria who entered in 1995 do not behave in a less disciplined way than parliamentarians from other countries. Finnish socialists and liberals are among the most disciplined in their group. Swedish socialists are less disciplined than the other socialists but only slightly so and Swedish conservatives are very disciplined. Austrian MEPs are not less disciplined than the others.

More importantly, new entrants' discipline with their respective country delegations is significantly lower than their discipline with their party groups. Moreover, the country discipline of the new entrants is not higher than for other countries. It is even among the lowest of all. This tends to strongly suggest that new entrants quickly follow the discipline of their party group and do not follow country discipline more than other MEPs. Note that France has the lowest national discipline index. The highest country discipline index is the one for the UK. It must be noted, however, that over half of the British MEPs were Labour MEPs and that this explains to a great extent the greater cohesion. Notice that Table 7 also shows the party distribution of MEPs across countries.

The evidence from Table 7 is encouraging in that it shows that new entrants do not display a different voting behaviour than MEPs from other EU countries. In other words, the Parliament is capable of absorbing new members and integrating them quickly into party groups. Of course, one must be careful in drawing strong

Table 7. Discipline indices for MEPs in the fourth parliament

	PES	EPP	ELDR	GR	GAUL	LEFT	RAD	ANTI-EU	NA	Country delegation
F	92.18	88.2	51.19	97.02	93.78	94.04	96.46	87.18	88.26	76.2
	37	20	12	18	31	8	14	15	14	170
UK	95	93.52	96.2	–	–	–	92.33	72.44	72.16	89.64
	69	39	2	0	0	0	3	1	1	115
I	95.46	93.32	90.44	92.9	82.7	92.82	93.06	–	69.65	80.08
	25	44	6	11	25	12	3	0	17	144
IRL	97.33	95.1	98.15	96.38	89.87	100	–	–	–	83.95
	2	4	2	3	11	2	0	0	0	24
FIN	97.36	93.43	92.31	97	–	83.57	–	–	–	78.14
	6	9	10	1	0	4	0	0	0	30
S	90.47	96.21	87.57	89.17	–	79.81	–	–	–	78.55
	16	7	4	4	0	4	0	0	0	35
D	95.64	97.57	90.08	98.36	–	–	–	n.r*	n.r*	84.18
	53	61	6	17	0	0	0	5	1	143
GR	94.14	96	–	–	87.25	93.52	–	–	–	84.59
	18	16	0	0	2	5	0	0	0	41
NL	97.54	96.37	95.72	98.04	83.22	–	–	76.04	–	82.71
	11	12	11	3	2	0	0	3	0	42
E	95.62	93.87	85.09	84.09	n.r*	95.72	94.43	–	n.r*	83.04
	32	42	6	5	1	11	4	0	1	102
B	94.25	95.63	90.32	99.45	–	–	92.13	–	86.72	79.89
	12	10	10	4	0	0	2	0	3	41
P	95.91	88.81	78.27	n.r*	86.87	94.99	–	–	–	84.09
	20	11	6	1	5	6	0	0	0	49
A	93.16	93.7	93.99	97.44	–	–	–	–	79.13	79.38
	11	12	2	1	0	0	0	0	12	38
DK	91.12	97.73	94.98	n.r*	–	80.87	–	71.03	–	78.06
	5	6	8	1	0	1	0	4	0	25
L	95.43	96.32	91.53	–	–	–	89.4	–	–	82.12
	3	3	3	0	0	0	1	0	0	10

Notes: The average frequency of vote of a MEP with party group or national delegation is listed first with the number of MEPs shown below each discipline index. A 'n.r*' indicates MEP never voted Yes or No on any issue (either mostly absent or abstained).

extrapolations from such an exercise. The future accession countries do not have the same economic, cultural and historical background as the countries from the previous enlargement. Moreover, the number of entrants in the future enlargement will be much higher than in the previous one. Nevertheless, countries from the previous enlargement did have distinct characteristics from the EU. Two out of three were Nordic countries and all had a richer economy than the EU average. Despite this, their MEPs showed strong party discipline.

3.3.1.1. Voting on cohesion and structural funds issues. It is also useful to look at the discipline index for various issues. Table 8 looks at discipline on all votes related to cohesion and structural funds. Here, we would expect that the poorer countries of the EU (Spain, Portugal, Ireland and Greece) would tend to vote more with their country groups than with their party group. One can unambiguously see that MEPs

Table 8. Discipline index for votes on cohesion and structural funds

	PES	EPP	ELDR	GR	GAUL	LEFT	RAD	ANTI-EU	NA	Country delegation
F	91.77	87.81	81.85	100	97.47	92.55	97.95	90.37	82.2	76.33
	35	19	10	16	29	9	14	14	13	
UK	94.67	80.41	100	–	–	–	94.93	70.18	71.43	82.32
	72	38	2	0	0	0	3	1	1	
I	96.7	90.78	95.32	96.45	82.59	87.71	95.5	–	60.95	83.42
	33	42	7	11	24	14	3	0	16	
IRL	95.45	88.62	95.55	86.73	91.61	96.15	–	–	–	80.23
	2	4	2	3	11	2	0	0	0	
FIN	96.28	97.47	91.67	82.05	–	50.67	–	–	–	85.38
	6	9	9	1	0	3	0	0	0	
S	92.05	92.63	82.54	70.64	–	46.13	–	–	–	78.26
	9	5	3	4	0	3	0	0	0	
D	85.28	93.9	92.5	97.11	–	–	–	86.06	100	81.68
	54	62	6	17	0	0	0	5	1	
GR	92.59	89.28	–	–	86.48	92.7	–	–	–	85.63
	21	17	0	0	3	5	0	0	0	
NL	87.57	92.97	89.03	98.85	80	–	–	72.19	–	79.95
	12	12	11	3	2	0	0	3	0	
E	95.95	84.05	95.62	76.19	100	91.34	97.5	–	50	84.82
	35	42	8	5	1	10	4	0	3	
B	97.24	94.01	98.94	99.43	–	–	92.5	–	78.06	81.4
	12	10	9	4	0	0	2	0	3	
P	88.79	78.67	88.24	85	98.11	88.89	–	–	–	86.2
	16	11	6	1	4	7	0	0	0	
A	79.42	94	100	97.62	–	–	–	–	83.09	87.81
	8	11	2	1	0	0	0	0	10	
DK	98.5	95.54	96.37	0	–	–	–	64.4	0	79.72
	5	7	8	1	0	0	0	4	1	
L	98.15	98.67	100	–	–	–	100	–	–	80.85
	3	3	3	0	0	0	1	0	0	

Notes: The average frequency of vote of a MEP with party group or national delegation is listed first with the number of MEPs shown below each discipline index. A 'n.r*' indicates MEP never voted Yes or No on any issue (either mostly absent or abstained).

from Ireland, Portugal, Spain and Greece do not have lower party discipline than MEPs from the other countries on this particular set of issues. Party discipline thus tends to dominate even on issues where country interests would seem to take the upper hand. Accession countries will all be poorer than Portugal, with the exception of Slovenia. Again, one should be cautious in extrapolating but the results of Table 7 suggest that MEPs from accession countries will not necessarily vote with their country even on issues such as structural funds and cohesion. We looked further at the discipline of MEPs on different issues. We found that in general, across issues, party discipline remained stronger than country discipline with a few exceptions (see the tables in the Web Appendix).

3.3.2. Regression analysis of individual votes.
Our second approach to studying individual voting patterns is to use statistical tools to disentangle the impact of

Table 9. Estimates of voting patterns based on party and country affiliation

Period	Party	Country	N	Adjusted R-squared
Third parliament	0.8416	0.1733	230	0.51
(Std Dev.)	(0.21)	(0.24)	(84)	(0.28)
Fourth parliament	0.9732	0.0173	368	0.57
(Std Dev.)	(0.08)	(0.14)	(105)	(0.27)

Notes: The table entries are averages of about 2700 estimated coefficients. Standard deviations are in parentheses. N is the average number of 'yes' and 'no' votes; abstentions of all kind are discarded from the regression analysis. These estimates are from the following equation: $V_j = \alpha\, Party_j + \beta\, Country_j + \varepsilon_j$ where V_j is a dummy variable indicating the 'yes' vote of legislator j, $Party_j$ ($Country_j$) is the proportion of MEP j's party (country) members voting 'yes', and ε_j is the error term. Since V_j is a binary variable, the regression model is also called 'linear probability model'. It is well known that the estimates of V_j by linear probability model may not belong to the admissible range $[0,1]$. This, however, is not a major concern here given that we are primarily interested in the relative importance of *party* versus *country* on voting behavior, not on the predicted values of V_j. The linear probability model has the advantage compared to standard probit (or logit) analysis that coefficients are directly interpretable. To avoid the problem of endogeneity we excluded MEP j's vote from the right-hand side variables. We did not constrain the coefficients to be positive or to add to one. On average, they are both positive and their sum is approximately equal to 1.

party affiliation and nationality on voting behaviour. In particular, we try to explain how the probability that a given legislator will vote 'Yes' depends upon the share of his/her party group that votes 'Yes' and the share of his/her national delegation that votes 'Yes'.

Table 9 shows the average coefficients for the third and fourth parliament. Three important findings can be observed. First, the average *party* coefficient is always greater than the average *country* coefficient. Second, while party effect increases over time, country effect decreases. Third, standard deviations become smaller, meaning that estimates become more precise. In addition, not only the number of 'yes' and 'no' votes (N), but also the fit of the model increased over time. The regression results thus show that party vote is a much better predictor of an individual's vote than country vote.

Figure 2 clearly shows the dynamics of the evolution of average coefficients for batches of 200 votes.

As illustrated in the diagram, the average country coefficient (on the left vertical scale) decreases over time and converges toward zero whereas the party coefficient (on the right vertical scale) increases and converges towards 1. As a result, we conclude that MEPs vote increasingly in accordance with party groups and less and less with their country.

3.3.3. Spatial analysis.   The analytic methods we have applied so far imposed a good deal of structure on the voting behaviour of MEPs. For instance, the regression analysis *assumed* that MEPs' voting patterns depended on party voting and/or national delegation voting. While this statistical method is absolutely standard, it may hide important aspects of voting patterns. If, to take an example, MEPs' voting were marked by an important urban/rural distinction, the method applied above would have missed it.

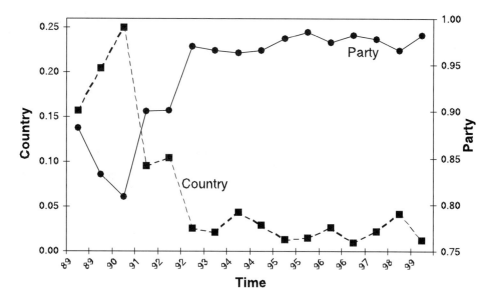

Figure 2. Dynamics of average party and country coefficients

Note: Each point is an average over 200 coefficients. The horizontal axis presents the approximate year. Before computing the averages we excluded unreasonable estimates (negative R-squared, extremely large as well as negative coefficients) as well as votes with small numbers of participants, (i.e. $N < 250$).

Fortunately, there is an analytic technique that allows us to explore the data in a less structured way. The technique – called 'spatial model of voting' – is straightforward, but takes a bit of explaining.[6] Consider the example of Belgian national parliamentarians. Surely Belgian MPs evaluate each issue along a number of dimensions: 'Does it suit my left-right politics?' 'Does it serve Walloon or Flemish interests?' 'Is it good for the environment?' In this example, the MPs' preferences over issues are said to be multi-dimensional, in particular, three-dimensional (left-right, Walloon-Flemish, green). It is also clear that not all dimensions come into play on all issues. Indeed it may be that one can explain almost all of a given MP's votes based on a single dimension (say, left-right), but some votes just make no sense unless one considers other dimensions (say, Walloon-Flemish).

The great merit of spatial analysis is that it does not require us to assume in advance which dimensions are important in determining voting patterns. Indeed, given the vast quantity of data – for the fourth parliament, for example, we have over 2.3 million individual roll call votes – it is possible to determine both how many dimensions matter and where each MEP's preference lies along each dimension. The actual statistical procedure is somewhat involved (see the Web Appendix), but the results are easily interpreted.

As Noury (2002) shows, there are at least two dimensions to the EU policy space. The first dimension, which correctly predicts about 90% of MEP votes, can easily be

---

[6] See also Downs (1957), Poole and Rosenthal (1997) and Heckman and Snyder (1997).

interpreted as the traditional left-right dimension. MEPs that belong to left-wing parties (PES, GR, LEFT) are estimated to have preferences that are located on the left-hand side of the space, whereas those belonging to right-wing parties (EPP, ELDR, GAUL) are on the opposite side. The second dimension adds only 2% more correct vote prediction and can also easily be interpreted as related to attitudes towards further European integration. MEPs belonging to parties that are tradition-ally viewed as favourable to European integration are located on the upper part of the space whereas anti-Europeans are located on the lower part (a schematic repres-entation of this policy space is reproduced in the Web Appendix).

Higher dimensions explain a negligible fraction of votes and are not easily inter-pretable. This is particularly the case for the third parliament. For the fourth par-liament however, Noury (2002) finds third and fourth dimensions with sensible interpretations, although these seems to explain only a minor share of votes. In these dimensions, MEPs from Nordic countries tend to be in opposition with Southern European MEPs. The projection for the third parliament does not show any par-ticular sorting of MEPs in the North–South dimension. Thus, enlargement to Nordic countries did lead to the crystallization of a North–South dimension. This dimension is, however, very modest compared to the left–right dimension. While the latter correctly predicts 90% of votes, the former adds a mere 1.2% to the fit measured by correct classification scores.

The results from the spatial model once again suggest that legislators in the EP vote predominantly according to their European political group affiliations, mostly along the traditional left–right divide but also along the dimension of European integration. The presence of this dimension makes voting somewhat more complex than traditional legislative politics but positions on European integration are more clearly defined across parties than across countries even though support for integra-tion clearly varies across countries. By considering the dynamics of voting over time, Noury (2002) shows that in a multi-dimensional space, members of the European Parliament vote more and more according to party affiliation. The results of the spatial model further indicate that the two main dimensions of conflict are very stable across time. The third and fourth dimensions are highly unstable.

The results of the spatial model thus confirm our previous findings that political parties are the main players of the policy-making game in the European Parliament.

3.4 Examples of votes

Statistical analysis gives a comprehensive picture that is more accurate than the inferences one may draw from looking at specific votes. It is nevertheless useful to complement the statistical analysis by specific examples to get a feel of coalition formation and cohesion with particular votes or voting sequences. Even here, how-ever, we cannot go into details because of the large number of votes and amendments on single bills and the different political stakes of each amendment.

We looked at the debates on the 1999 budget that was approved by a large majority. The EP has limited power in changing the budget proposals of the Commission. Nevertheless, our impression is that it uses the little power it has to focus on issues like employment, education, the environment, regional development and convergence rather than on agriculture or fishing. Corbett *et al.* (2000), who are intimate insiders to the EP, make similar observations. Thus, the EP would tend to care more for expenditures that benefit larger groups rather than targeted interest groups. It seems also that the EP acts more as a check on the Commission's spending plans rather than as a big cash-spender. Various spending items get sent back to the Commission to ask for clarification before getting the EP's approval.

We also looked in detail at many particular events of voting sequences that we only briefly report here. We looked at important votes in 1998 on cohesion funds, reform of Common Agricultural Policy (CAP), structural funds and fisheries. None of these votes were about radical changes to existing policies. They tended to be consensual and were most often the results of compromises worked out between the important party groups after discarding amendments proposed by the smaller parties. Many votes also concern the particular formulation of sentences and are hardly consequential. Quite a few votes have a low party and country cohesion, especially in the area of CAP. This impression is, however, not validated by the broader statistical analysis. Another casual impression is that MEPs tend to amend Commission proposals by adding pro-environment sentences, and emphasizing general goals like employment creation and other social objectives. This reinforces the impression that the EP pays particular attention to aspects of legislation that are relevant to broad groups of the population rather than narrow interest groups.

In the Web Appendix, we provide a detailed account of some of the most dramatic votes in the EP that were given wide publicity in the European media. For example, we looked at the attempt to bring down the Commission by a vote of censure in the context of the scandal around commissioners Cresson and Marin. These votes show a rather clear division along party lines with the PES and RAD trying to defend the commissioners, GR and ELDR in favour of censure and the EPP split. Even though voting was mostly along party lines, one also detects some voting along country lines. MEPs from Italy and Spain tended to vote against censure while the French MEPs were very divided along party lines in this episode.

Another particularly heated debate took place in the EP when a Renault plant was closed in Vilvoorde in Belgium to be relocated in France. In this case some of the workers came to the EP to protest. Apart from the staunch support for the workers on the left and the outright hostility on the right of the hemisphere, the EP considered a resolution recommending that the Commission propose legislation on job transfers by multinational enterprises and asking for an evaluation of EU directives on collective redundancies. Several right wing amendments to the initial resolution were voted down. Moderate amendments were accepted with GR, RAD and LEFT voting against. The final resolution was supported by the left and opposed by the right. The EPP voted for the resolution with a 10% defection in its ranks. Most votes in this episode were clearly on the left–right dimension and parties showed relative cohesion. No precise pattern could be detected in the country votes.

4. WHY DO MEPS VOTE ALONG PARTY LINES?

There are two main potential explanations for the voting behaviour of legislators: (1) policy preferences; and (2) career incentives. Those who emphasize policy preferences assume that individual legislators simply follow their preferences when voting. It follows that members of a party vote cohesively because they have similar preferences. Those who emphasize career incentives assume that legislators vote so as to maximize their probability of re-election and to further their career within their party. While the first potential explanation requires no elaboration, understanding the second requires the knowledge of some facts on how MEPs are elected.

Party groups are composed of elected representatives of national parties and all EU countries are parliamentary democracies where party discipline is strong. National parties thus have obvious instruments to discipline MEPs. They can choose not to put them in a favourable place on the list for the election of the next EP. Moreover, national parties may affect the future careers of MEPs in their own country by denying them eligibility for country elections or denying them other public mandates. Party groups in the EP are also organized in a similar way to party fractions in national parliaments. There are group 'whips' who round up MEPs to vote in a particular way on bills. Presence at EP sessions is rather low. In the third parliament, an average of 17.6% of the MEPs were absent and 35.5% were present in the Parliament but did not vote (for the fourth parliament the figures are 16.8% and 21.6% respectively). Rewards for party loyalty are therefore lower in the EP than in national parliaments, but they are still important. If career incentives are dominant, party cohesion is brought about because legislators have the incentives to vote together with their party because of the rewards associated to party loyalty.

It is very difficult to dissociate in practice the two motivations. On the one hand, if one assumes that legislators are driven solely by policy preferences, a French socialist ought to vote more like a German socialist rather than a French conservative. On the other hand, if one assumes that legislators are driven solely by personal career incentives, then party cohesion is explained only by institutional factors. Within the EP, party groups, and not country delegations, have the power to punish or reward MEPs, by favouring special committee membership, for instance. It follows that MEPs are influenced more directly by their parties than by their national delegations. This effect is reinforced be the grouping of parliamentarians according to party affiliation rather than nationality.[7]

---

[7] In addition one may argue that cultural and/or historical factors explain MEPs voting behaviour (see Hix *et al.*, 2002).

4.1. The role of the Council and EP majority hurdles

The above explanations, inspired mostly by studies of the US Congress, assume implicitly that legislation is decided in the assembly. This may be a good approximation for the US Congress but certainly not for the EP. A good explanation of MEP behaviour must take into account the whole legislative process. This is done in the theoretical literature on the EU (Tsebelis, 1994; Crombez, 1996). However, in that literature, the EP is usually modelled as a single actor with specific preferences. The literature therefore does not explain why MEPs vote along party lines and not along country lines.

Here we suggest a simple explanation based on the fact that the majority hurdle in the Council is higher than the EP's majority hurdle (qualified majority or unanimity versus simple majority most of the time). Assume for simplicity's sake that policymakers' preferences over EU legislation have just two dimensions (a country dimension and a left–right dimension). Moreover, assume that we can approximate the actual EU legislative procedure with the stylization that we introduced in Section 2. Namely, that the Commission formulates legislative proposals but these only become law if both the Council of Ministers and the EP approve them. To get a bill approved in the Council, the measure must attract at least 71% of country votes, keeping in mind the fact that big nations have more votes than small nations. To pass in the EP, the measure must attract the support of at least half of MEPs (there is one vote per MEP, but large nations have more MEPs than small ones).

In this set-up, the EP and the Council have power in the sense that they can veto any Commission proposal that does not suit their preferences. To avoid such vetoes, the Commission crafts the proposals in a manner that it believes will please at least 50% of MEPs, and nations with at least 71% of Council votes. The crux of our argument relies on the fact that the distribution of MEPs per nation in the EP is similar to the distribution of votes per nation in the Council (Baldwin *et al.*, 2001: p. 28). Given this, it is reasonable to assume that if MEPs were to vote solely along country lines, the EP would have no influence. Any proposal by the Commission that can attract 71% of Council votes would also attract at least 50% of MEP votes. To put it differently, if MEPs voted on purely national lines, the Commission could entirely ignore the preferences of MEPs – any proposal that pleased enough Council members to pass the 71% hurdle, would also pass the 50% hurdle in the EP.

By contrast, suppose the opposite extreme, namely that Council members voted on purely national lines, but MEPs voted on purely party lines. In this case, there will be instances in which the MEPs have real power in the sense that the Commission will have to modify their proposals in ways that take account of MEPs' preferences. This reasoning suggests that the EP can influence the EU legislative process when coalitions are formed along party lines rather than along country lines.

Note that this very simple reasoning is consistent with a high occurrence of unanimity voting in the EP. MEPs form coalitions so as to weigh in the decision-making process via the majorities that form on precise bills. The reasoning also suggests that party cohesion should be stronger in cases where the EP has legislative power compared to the votes where it can exercise no power. In other words, national party delegations have an incentive to create cohesive supranational party groups to mobilize MEPs to vote according to agreed party lines. If MEPs vote purely according to their policy preferences, voting behaviour should not be necessarily more cohesive in cases where the EP has legislative powers. We will test this prediction in the next section.

If the above reasoning is true, does it mean that in the absence of a higher majority hurdle in the Council, the EP might vote along country lines? If this were the case, we conjecture that we should observe MEPs voting along country lines in cases where the EP has no power. Since the votes where the EP has real power are less numerous than the others, our results that party cohesion is stronger than country cohesion suggest that ideological divisions in the EP are deeper than divisions between countries.

We conclude that both policy preferences and the desire to weigh in the legislative process along the left-right dimension appear to be reasonable explanations of why MEPs vote mainly along party lines.

5. THE IMPACT OF POWERS AND ENLARGEMENT ON PARTY COHESION

We now investigate via regression analysis the effect of increased powers and of enlargement on the voting behaviour of MEPs. The analysis focuses on party cohesion. Essentially, we ask whether more power and a larger parliament size lead to larger cohesion.

5.1. Determinants of party cohesion

We estimate the cohesion index (CI) for each political group on each vote. We thus have a 'time-series' of over 6000 observations for each political group. The main exogenous variables of interest are:

- RELPRES, measuring the relative presence of a party group with respect to other groups. A high value for RELPRES should indicate that the issue voted on is relatively more important for that party group. We can thus expect tighter control over voting behaviour and thus higher cohesion.
- ENLARGE, a dummy variable taking a value of 1 for votes taking place after enlargement to Austria, Finland and Sweden.
- CO-DECISION, a dummy variable taking a value of 1 if the voting procedure is co-decision, the one giving the most power to the parliament.

We also include a large number of control variables:

- QM, a dummy taking a value of 1 if the vote is by qualified majority;
- LEG4, a dummy to differentiate between the third and the fourth parliament;
- PCT-GVT, measures the percentage of national parties of a group that are in government in their respective countries (we used the data from Müller and Strøm, 2000). The idea is to test whether representation of a party in the Council via the national governments has a positive or a negative effect on the cohesion of the MEPs of the same party;
- 11 dummies indicating the vote's policy issues as follows (with abbreviations in parentheses): foreign policy (FORPOL); internal functioning of the EU (INTERNAL); agriculture, fishing and food (AGROFISH); industries and technology (INDUSTRY); banking system and finance (BANK); drugs and dangerous substances (DRUG); services; human beings (HUMANS); security; nature; legal system (LEGAL).

The results of the regression analysis are reported in Table 10. Each column shows the estimates for a given political group. The results show that RELPRES is statistically significant with a positive sign in all cases. This finding indicates that more participation leads to more party discipline, thus showing that the channel for more discipline is indeed the 'rounding up' effect. The dummy for the fourth parliament is positive for a majority of political groups. However, neither the ENLARGE nor the CO-DECISION variables are significant. Note also that presence in national governments of the same party does not affect cohesion. The main effect on cohesion is thus via party mobilization.

5.2. Determinants of MEP attendance

The physical presence of MEPs at EP sessions is clearly not exogenous. We thus also estimated an equation aimed at explaining the presence of party members of a given group (we call this variable PRES). We used the same explanatory variables as above and added closeness of the votes in the estimation of the presence equation, assuming that whips can mobilize their group more effectively in case of a close vote. The results are shown in Table 11.

The results of the PRES equation show that participation in the EP increases with the EP's power. The estimated coefficient of the LEG4 variable is significant with a positive sign meaning that there is less absence in the fourth parliament as compared with the third. The increase in participation over time can be explained, at least in part, by the decision (in 1996) to modify the rules governing reimbursement for attendance in Strasbourg. It is nevertheless compelling evidence for the increase in power of the parliament. The results also show that CO-DECISION is significantly positive, thus showing that the co-decision procedure mobilizes a larger number of legislators. Thus in the areas where the EP has more power, all political groups become more active. This result indicates that giving more power to the parliament has an unambiguously positive effect on participation. Note that this increase in

Table 10. Results of the estimation of the weighted cohesion equation

Dependent variable: Relative Cohesion Index

	PES	EPP	ELDR	GR	GAUL	LEFT	RAD	ANTI-EU
PCT_GVT	-0.021 (0.20)	0.035 (0.56)	-0.093 (0.55)	-0.146 (1.61)	0.110 (1.98)*	-0.281 (2.50)*	—	—
RELPRES	0.294 (2.35)*	0.610 (4.96)**	1.364 (3.67)**	2.190 (6.75)**	1.074 (2.27)*	1.330 (2.40)*	-3.605 (3.42)**	-8.117 (9.27)**
ENLARGE	-0.036 (0.73)	-0.015 (0.37)	-0.057 (0.81)	-0.009 (0.15)	0.115 (1.97)*	-0.018 (0.31)	-0.031 (0.51)	-0.150 (1.97)*
CO-DECISION	-0.033 (1.59)	-0.028 (1.38)	-0.016 (0.73)	0.013 (0.57)	0.033 (1.20)	-0.021 (0.75)	0.011 (0.39)	-0.140 (4.40)**
QM	0.043 (2.23)*	-0.022 (1.13)	0.026 (1.26)	0.056 (2.55)*	0.002 (0.09)	0.100 (3.79)**	0.040 (1.54)	-0.009 (0.32)
LEG4	0.113 (2.37)*	0.093 (2.20)*	0.123 (2.21)*	0.221 (3.89)**	-0.236 (3.68)**	-(0.002) (0.04)	0.148 (2.38)*	0.119 (1.56)
FORPOL	0.002 (0.10)	0.028 (1.12)	0.093 (3.54)**	-0.047 (1.69)	-0.074 (2.32)*	-0.059 (1.76)	-0.064 (1.89)	-0.086 (2.25)*
INTERNAL	-0.023 (1.01)	-0.013 (0.56)	0.006 (0.24)	-0.091 (3.61)**	-0.105 (3.59)**	-0.150 (4.91)**	-0.021 (0.70)	-0.031 (0.89)
AGROFISH	0.005 (0.21)	0.011 (0.46)	0.016 (0.64)	0.054 (2.03)*	-0.029 (0.94)	-0.021 (0.64)	0.012 (0.37)	-0.026 (0.71)
INDUSTRY	0.029 (1.11)	0.091 (3.51)**	0.073 (2.62)**	0.113 (3.83)**	0.011 (0.31)	-0.028 (0.79)	0.041 (1.16)	-0.105 (2.58)**
BANK	-0.033 (1.09)	0.004 (0.12)	0.037 (1.13)	-0.055 (1.61)	0.006 (0.16)	-0.147 (3.55)**	-0.025 (0.58)	-0.040 (0.85)
DRUG	-0.011 (0.31)	0.016 (0.45)	-0.062 (1.65)	0.025 (0.63)	0.053 (1.16)	-0.058 (1.19)	0.087 (1.80)	-0.069 (1.28)
SERVICES	0.119 (2.72)**	0.099 (2.31)*	0.114 (2.42)*	-0.017 (0.34)	0.058 (1.01)	-0.037 (0.61)	0.085 (1.41)	-0.105 (1.51)
HUMANS	0.059 (2.37)*	0.043 (1.76)	0.050 (1.89)	0.045 (1.61)	-0.040 (1.25)	0.027 (0.81)	0.014 (0.41)	-0.037 (0.96)
SECURITY	-0.020 (0.71)	0.068 (2.41)*	0.045 (1.51)	-0.065 (2.03)*	-0.191 (5.19)**	-0.074 (1.93)	-0.020 (0.51)	0.011 (0.26)
NATURE	0.005 (0.17)	-0.013 (0.48)	-0.002 (0.08)	0.073 (2.33)*	-0.013 (0.37)	0.037 (0.95)	0.019 (0.50)	-0.053 (1.24)
LEGAL	-0.033 (0.96)	0.024 (0.70)	-0.014 (0.37)	0.011 (0.28)	-0.066 (1.48)	-0.026 (0.55)	0.142 (2.94)**	-0.081 (1.51)
Constant	0.978 (11.64)**	0.828 (13.66)**	0.895 (10.44)**	0.901 (25.01)**	0.987 (23.17)**	1.057 (29.13)**	1.111 (32.95)**	1.046 (25.61)**
N	6444	6443	6430	6426	6349	6311	5788	6179
No. of days	479	479	479	478	476	476	454	472
Chi²(19)	61	91	82	261	102	123	68	141
P-value	0.000	0.000	0.000	0.000	0.000	0.000	0.000	0.000

Notes: Absolute value of z statistics in parentheses, * significant at 5%; ** significant at 1%. See Table 1 for Party abbreviations and the text for other abbreviations. Estimation by random-effects technique. Also, since many unobservable factors matter, a day-specific dummy was included. To account for the fact that CI is bounded by 1 and heavily concentrated around 1, we used our weighted index as the dependent variable (see Section 3.1.1). The un-weighted CI was also estimated with Tobit; the results are not fundamentally different from the ones reported here.

Table 11. Results of the estimation of the PRES equation

Dependent variable: Presence

	PES	EPP	ELDR	GR	GAUL	LEFT	RAD	ANTI-EU
CLOSE	49.036 (3.59)**	33.255 (3.04)**	8.589 (3.07)**	7.232 (3.40)**	5.727 (1.99)*	11.125 (5.22)**	4.138 (3.59)**	3.658 (2.82)**
ENLARGE	21.855 (2.46)*	11.442 (1.60)	8.409 (4.68)**	4.535 (3.88)**	1.232 (0.65)	4.069 (3.08)**	1.817 (2.35)*	2.827 (3.35)**
CO-DECISION	9.270 (6.18)**	5.718 (4.75)**	0.664 (2.16)*	1.163 (4.89)**	1.639 (5.18)**	0.213 (0.90)	0.689 (5.44)**	0.712 (4.99)**
QM	13.728 (9.86)**	12.125 (10.86)**	2.681 (9.39)**	1.154 (5.22)**	2.599 (8.85)**	0.824 (3.77)**	0.635 (5.41)**	0.400 (3.02)**
LEG4	19.927 (2.24)*	31.008 (4.34)**	3.241 (1.81)	-3.523 (3.01)**	14.634 (7.72)**	3.887 (2.94)**	4.904 (6.34)**	2.065 (2.45)*
FORPOL	4.120 (2.28)*	2.604 (1.80)	0.882 (2.38)*	0.877 (3.06)**	0.941 (2.47)*	1.060 (3.74)**	0.818 (5.37)**	0.413 (2.40)*
INTERNAL	24.187 (14.71)**	18.748 (14.21)**	4.101 (12.16)**	2.025 (7.76)**	4.356 (12.55)**	2.291 (8.88)**	1.665 (11.99)**	1.676 (10.71)**
AGROFISH	10.995 (6.26)**	6.678 (4.74)**	1.741 (4.83)**	1.197 (4.30)**	3.516 (9.48)**	0.479 (1.74)	0.764 (5.15)**	0.955 (5.71)**
INDUSTRY	4.817 (2.45)*	0.424 (0.27)	0.143 (0.36)	0.510 (1.64)	1.564 (3.78)**	-0.500 (1.62)	0.378 (2.28)*	0.241 (1.29)
BANK	13.735 (6.18)**	12.376 (6.94)**	1.810 (3.97)**	0.547 (1.55)	2.956 (6.30)**	0.823 (2.36)*	0.607 (3.24)**	0.753 (3.56)**
DRUG	1.848 (0.70)	-2.592 (1.23)	0.007 (0.01)	0.202 (0.49)	0.330 (0.60)	-1.818 (4.42)**	-0.279 (1.26)	0.020 (0.08)
SERVICES	7.249 (2.12)*	2.736 (1.00)	1.124 (1.61)	0.225 (0.42)	0.706 (0.98)	-1.657 (3.10)**	-0.198 (0.69)	-0.447 (1.38)
HUMANS	3.243 (1.77)	-2.546 (1.73)	0.057 (0.15)	0.141 (0.49)	-0.063 (0.16)	0.432 (1.50)	0.361 (2.34)*	-0.059 (0.34)
SECURITY	12.554 (6.06)**	8.328 (5.01)**	2.358 (5.55)**	1.886 (5.74)**	1.655 (3.79)**	1.284 (3.95)**	0.844 (4.83)**	1.078 (5.47)**
NATURE	7.731 (3.82)**	5.440 (3.35)**	1.183 (2.85)**	1.286 (4.01)**	3.145 (7.37)**	0.228 (0.72)	1.117 (6.54)**	1.208 (6.28)**
LEGAL	11.684 (4.66)**	7.515 (3.74)**	2.585 (5.03)**	1.217 (3.06)**	1.690 (3.20)**	0.480 (1.22)	1.206 (5.70)**	1.327 (5.57)**
Constant	67.232 (17.66)**	56.836 (18.57)**	10.641 (13.72)**	11.730 (21.09)**	3.104 (3.84)**	3.462 (5.94)**	-0.317	2.148 (5.93)**
N	5967	5967	5967	5967	5967	5967	5967	5967
No. of days	421	421	421	421	421	421	421	421
Chi²(17)	786	1007	761	235	1068	506	862	586
P-value	0.000	0.000	0.000	0.000	0.000	0.000	0.000	0.000

Notes: Absolute value of z statistics in parentheses, * significant at 5%; ** significant at 1%. See notes to Table 9 for abbreviations and statistical issues. Closeness (close) is instrumented by lagged closeness.

participation is not an artefact of the absolute majority requirement (which is the case for a large number of co-decision votes), since we explicitly control for the qualified majority requirement. The votes with a qualified majority indeed increase participation. Finally the enlargement estimates are either statistically positive (in six cases out of eight) or non-significant, but they never take a negative sign. Interestingly, this finding indicates that enlargement does not reduce but increases participation. Against popular opinion, enlargement does not seem to imply more free-riding and more chaotic voting behaviour.

Note that the joint estimation of our cohesion and presence equations produced qualitatively similar results. These results did not change when we excluded from the sample the fully lopsided votes (i.e. when all MEPs voted in the same way).

The results of the two equations show that empowerment of the European Parliament has a direct and positive effect on the cohesion and party discipline of political groups, as well as an *indirect* effect via a higher presence which leads to greater cohesion.

6. POLICY IMPLICATIONS OF OUR ANALYSIS

What policy conclusions can we draw from our analysis? On the basis of our empirical analysis, we can conclude that an increase in the power of the EP would, everything else equal, reinforce participation of MEPs in votes and thus cohesion of party groups. This result clearly comes out of our regression analysis and also makes intuitive sense. When votes carry no consequence, MEPs have less incentive to participate in EP debates and votes. Even when they vote, they will have no incentive to be cohesive because the majority decision will not matter. Individual MEPs will prefer to stick as closely as possible to the interests of their constituency and to express their individual opinions through their vote. This is not a new idea. It is well known that less powerful assemblies tend to behave in a more chaotic way. When votes are consequential, however, then party groups will actively try to mobilize the MEPs of their group to vote in a disciplined way in order to weigh effectively on decision-making.

What does one mean, however, by 'more power to the EP'? What we have in mind, and what comes naturally out of our analysis, is increasing the power of the EP via a generalization of the co-decision procedure as the normal legislative procedure in the EU, or at least, its generalization to all decisions that require qualified majority voting in the Council. Our analysis of the EP shows that MEPs have behaved more cohesively under the co-decision procedure. There is thus little to fear on that front from generalization of co-decision. Another argument for a generalization of co-decision is that simplification of legislative procedure by the adoption of a standard procedure will make the functioning of the EU seem less Byzantine and complex and more transparent to EU citizens. This is certainly very important in terms of enhancing legitimacy of the EU to European citizens, especially in the light of the ongoing

European Convention chaired by former French President Valéry Giscard d'Estaing that will make recommendations for changes to the current Treaties.

Our empirical analysis suggests that left–right politics is the dominant motive for coalition formation in the EP. A more powerful and visible EP may contribute to enhance European-wide debates along the left–right dimension while the Council continues to play the role of guardian of country interests.

Some words of caution are necessary, however. The mobilization effect of EU party groups may have more to do with closeness of preferences among members of a same party than with the disciplining power of the European party groups. If important tensions arose in the future between, say, French and German social democrats on a given issue, it is doubtful whether the EP party group will be able to force them to vote cohesively; whereas we are quite confident that the French and German party would impose cohesion on their members. In order to ensure stronger discipline of EP party groups, one would need to give the latter the power to establish the electoral lists for the EP in the various member country districts (power that is currently entirely in the hands of the national parties). Another reason for caution is that our results do not allow us to say how the EP would vote if the role of the Council were strongly reduced. In the extreme, if the role of the Council were abolished, would coalition formation in the EP still be based on left–right politics rather than on country interests? Maybe not. Our results are based on the – plausible – assumption that the Council will keep its current powers and thus its role of guardian of country interests. Legislative projects in the EU go through two 'filters': the 'left-right filter' of the EP and the 'country filter' of the Council. It is important to have and keep those two filters.

A less safe conclusion that can be drawn from our analysis is related to the effect of the coming enlargement on voting behaviour in the EP. Our analysis of the previous enlargement suggests that party cohesion may not be negatively affected and may even be positively affected. This conclusion is, however, only based on the experience of past enlargement. It is a big logical leap to conclude that the next enlargement will have similar effects. Although we cannot be certain, there are grounds to be optimistic in that respect. Indeed, even if party cohesion drops dramatically after enlargement, there will be competitive forces driving party groups in that direction. A cohesive party will realize that it can weigh more in decision-making when its role is pivotal. Cohesion will make votes of the group more predictable. This in turn will make it easier for a cohesive group to negotiate compromises with other groups. Less cohesive groups will thus have an incentive to become more cohesive.

7. CONCLUSION

In this paper, we have used a unique database to analyse the voting behaviour of individual MEPs in the European Parliament for the third and fourth parliament (1989–94 and 1994–99). We found that the cohesion of party groups was strong and increasing over time, even if the size of majorities in the EP has declined during that time period. Cohesion in the EP is comparable to cohesion in the US Congress but remains smaller than in the one parliamentary democracy we looked at, namely Belgium. In contrast, country cohesion is low and generally not higher than cohesion of the EP as a whole. These findings are valid for a wide range of policy issues, something we did not necessarily expect.

Our empirical analysis shows that the major dimension of coalition formation is ideology. In other words, party groups of the left tend to vote together against party groups of the right. However, the left–right dimension is not the only one. There are other dimensions at play like pro- versus anti-European integration and Northern versus Southern country interests. These additional dimensions, however, are much less important than the left–right dimension.

We found that the channel for increased party cohesion works via the mobilization of MEPs by their party group to come and vote. Participation, we found, is stronger when the EP exercises more power through the co decision procedure. The last wave of enlargement had a positive effect on participation and thus on cohesion. We also found that MEPs from newly entering countries are not less disciplined than those from other countries. Discipline across issues is strong for all countries.

Our empirical analysis provides grounds for justifying a generalization of the co-decision procedure in the EP.

Discussion

Thomas Piketty
CEPREMAP, Paris

This paper asks whether giving more power to the European Parliament will generate chaotic coalitions and paralyse decision-making or will lead to stable coalitions and efficient decision-making. This is obviously a key policy question for the future of Europe (arguably the most important question), and Noury and Roland rightly point out that there has been very little research on these issues. Their analysis relies on a unique data base using all roll call votes from individual deputies in the EP between 1989 and 1999 (third and fourth legislatures), which allows them to analyse voting patterns by country and party origin, coalition formation, the impact of new entrants, etc. As such, this paper is a very useful contribution to knowledge. It should stimulate both policy debates and future academic research.

My main criticism is that the authors might be a little bit too optimistic in their conclusions. Noury and Roland find that European MPs are voting more and more along party lines (rather than on the basis of country origin), and conclude that giving 'more power to the European Parliament' is a relatively safe option. I see two limits with their argument.

First of all, it is not entirely straightforward how one should interpret the cohesion index estimates given in the paper. For instance, Noury and Roland find that cohesion is much stronger for MEPs from a given party than for MEPs from a given country, and country cohesion tends to decline relative to party cohesion. In order to go beyond this qualitative conclusion and to better understand what these numbers mean, it would be useful to know what similar indexes would look like for MPs in national parliaments. Presumably, the cohesion index for national MPs from the same region (say, French MPs from Burgundy, or German MPs from Saxony) is fairly small in most countries. Comparing regional loyalty in national parliaments and country loyalty in the European parliament would give a way to measure how far we've got in terms of political integration.

In that respect, the figures computed by Noury and Roland for the Belgian Parliament are a bit frightening. They find that the cohesion index for the Flemish and Francophone parts of Belgium are around 30–40%, i.e. twice as low as the country cohesion indexes observed in the European Parliament (around 70%). Given that Belgium can hardly be viewed as an ideal point (Belgium is generally considered as a country that is deeply divided along community lines, and regional cohesion indexes would probably be much lower than 30–40% in countries like France or Germany), this suggests that Europe has still a long way to go. Unfortunately, Noury and Roland were not able to compute similar figures for other countries. Surprisingly enough, there seems to exist no systematic database on roll call votes in most European countries. This shows how useful the EP database constructed by Noury and Roland really is. Their pioneering work should be complemented by similar research on national parliaments.

Next, and most importantly, one limit of the analysis is that we don't really know what MEPs are voting upon. Noury and Roland do use some classification of roll call votes based on broad issues (agriculture, foreign affairs, etc.), but it is hard to know how important these votes are. Many observers assume (maybe wrongly) that MEPs have no real power and vote for the most part on secondary issues, so that it's hard to predict how they will behave when they will vote on real budgets. Noury and Roland use an indirect indicator of how important a vote is (i.e. whether or not the co-decision procedure is used), but they find that it has no direct impact on cohesion (it only has impact on participation). Ideally, one would like to weight each vote by the amount the money at stake, but it is unfortunately very hard to construct such data.

Another way to reply to this criticism would be to give more concrete examples of real votes and coalition formation on important issues, for instance for votes where one would have expected country loyalty to be dominant and where party loyalty turns out be more important. In that respect, the detailed analysis of the Cresson–Marin crisis (when two socialist Commissioners were accused by the EP of mismanagement and diversion of funds) offered by Noury and Roland is not fully convincing. The fact that there was little cohesion among French MEPs at that time is hardly surprising. Cresson had been a very unpopular socialist Prime Minister several years before, and it would have been very strange if right-wing French MPs had voted in favour of Cresson during the crisis (even the French left-wing press was against Cresson at the time of the vote). There is no way one can infer from this vote that country cohesion would remain low in case MEPs were voting on real issues. If MEPs were asked to vote on agricultural subsidies, country cohesion would probably be much stronger than party cohesion (especially among French MEPs). As suggested by Noury and Roland, the 'filtering' role of the European Council and of EP factions is probably needed to make sure that MEPs do not vote on issues that are too divisive on a country basis. Whether it will remain so in the future is very much an open issue at this stage.

Thierry Verdier
DELTA, Paris

This is a very timely and useful paper for several reasons. First, given the present policy debates on the so-called 'democratic deficit' of European institutions and the perspective of future enlargement of the EU to countries from Central Europe, investigating the functioning of the European Parliament (EP) and the voting pattern of European MPs is obviously crucial for European policymaking. Second, this paper undertakes a very useful task to the profession as it brings together an impressive new database on roll call votes of European MPs during the third and fourth EPs. Without doubt, this will trigger a host of quantitative research on legislative politics.

The paper addresses two sets of questions. First, it investigates how voting coalitions within the EP are likely to form. In particular, do MEPs vote along ideological lines or more along a 'national interest' line? The second set of questions considers some kind of comparative statics exercise. What are the effects of increased powers to the EP on the cohesiveness of MEPs and what are the effects of European Union enlargement on the voting behaviour of MEPs? The answers are surprising and provocative. MEPs seem to have more 'party' loyalty than 'country' loyalty, party cohesion and participation are stronger when the MEPs have more power, and MEPs from the new entrants are just as party oriented as MEPs from incumbent nations.

From these findings, the authors derive important policy implications for reforms of the European institutions. As right–left politics is the main game in the EP, the EP seems to function then more or less like a national Parliament. In such a context, giving more power to the EP seems to be particularly appropriate. This is appropriate because more power to the EP will in a sense countervail the nationalistic tendency of the Council's politics. Therefore, by making European politics more representative of the average European citizen, it will reduce the democratic deficit of European institutions. According to the authors, empowerment of the EP is also good in the context of the coming enlargement, as, they argue, it will facilitate decision-making. Contrary to what happens at the level of the Council and the Commission, bringing new countries in the EP will basically just increase the number of MPs reorganizing themselves along the right–left divide line, without much affecting the complexity of political coalitions in decision-making.

I would like first to discuss one of the authors' discussion main points, namely the degree and nature of cohesiveness of MEPs. Then I will turn to the policy implications derived in their conclusions.

On the issue of party-versus-country issue, let me say that while I do share overall their views, there are still a few points to be cleared up. My first concern stems from how political cohesiveness is measured. The authors' cohesion index (CI) reduces information in some particular way, as is the case with all indices. In particular, a given value of the CI can correspond to very diverse types of voting patterns. Consider two different voting situations. In situation 1, there are 50 Yes votes, 50 No votes and 0 abstentions. In situation 2 there are 50 Yes, 25 No and 25 abstentions. It is easy to see that the CI gives the same value (zero) for both situations. Intuitively though, I would have found it more natural to say that situation 1 is less cohesive than situation 2. It is easy to show that this simple example can be further generalized and to see that there may be a continuum of different voting patterns associated with the same value of the cohesion index. Though certainly common to all studies using indexes, one may then wonder about the degree of robustness of higher party cohesiveness to changes on the measure of cohesiveness.

Another aspect comes from the fact that all votes in the EP are somehow considered equal in the statistical analysis. But are they all equally important in MEPs' eyes? Given that MEPs vote on so many things, many of them of little importance, it may be that there exists a few 'important' votes for which 'country loyalty' appears to be crucial, while for most other non-consequential votes, MEPs are happy to follow their party line. In such a situation, one would see a high degree of party cohesiveness on average. Still, for the few votes that matter, MEPs could exhibit a strong degree of country cohesiveness.

A related issue is the fact that one may observe votes in the EP organized along 'party' lines simply because, by construction, the EP actually does not have to vote decisively on issues with a strong country-specific component. MEPs may be happy to vote according to party lines because their vote does not imply much at stake for their own countries. For instance, I am quite surprised to see in the spatial analysis of voting behaviour of the authors that the EU integration dimension explains so little of the voting pattern of MEPs. After all, one would expect the EP to be quite concerned with European integration questions. One way to understand this paradox perhaps is to note that a number of important European policy areas (like foreign policy or CAP) are not covered by the co-decision procedure. These areas have obvious country-specific redistributive aspects and the EP has little effective power on them. The explanatory weakness of the EU integration dimension may then simply be reflect the fact that many important European policy dimensions are not decided within the EP and therefore that MEPs are just content to signal their party royalty at no real cost for their own country's interest. Typically, though, the authors find

French representatives to be among the least disciplined in terms of nationality. I cannot help thinking, as a Frenchman myself, that things would be rather different if the EP had effective powers on the CAP!

This brings me to a final caveat of the authors' analysis, namely the fact that the voting pattern is explained, taking as given what happens inside the Commission and the Council. Clearly, in order to understand the voting behaviour of the EP, one would want to take explicitly into account the strategic interactions with the other two institutions, the Council and the Commission. Building up a structural model of the functioning of the whole set of European institutions would then be the natural (and daunting) route to follow. While I understand perfectly that this task is beyond the scope of the present paper, I also think that without such a framework, the comparative statistical conclusions of EP's empowerment and EU enlargement on the voting behavior of the MEPs have to be taken with a grain of salt. Indeed any reform that positively affects the power structure of the EP will also affect negatively the power structure of at least one of the other two institutions. This in turn will affect their political behaviour and the outcome they can achieve. If MEPs do in fact integrate these changes in their behaviour, then explaining MEPs' voting patterns, taking the Council and the Commission actions as given, may provide misleading predictions on the final outcome reached by the EP.

This observation leads me then directly to the policy implications of the paper. Should we give more power to the EP? According to the authors, yes. Yes, because it increases the participation of MEPs, brings the functioning of European Institutions closer to what happens within individual national states and thereby reduces their democratic deficit. Yes, also because it will make EU enlargement easier in terms of the functioning of European institutions. While both assertions follow logically from the paper's analysis, I would be a bit less enthusiastic than the authors to reach these conclusions so quickly.

First, and as emphasized before in my discussion, the effect of more power on the voting pattern is obtained by taking implicitly as fixed what happens in the other institutions. In other words, bringing in new issues with strong country-specific interests in the realm of the decision-making power of the EP, may indeed affect dramatically the voting behaviour of MEPs, internalizing how these changes have implications on the outcomes reached by the other two institutions. In such a context, 'party loyalty' may be more difficult to preserve than what this paper predicts. Second, I also think that the authors somehow underestimate the impact of EU enlargement on the EP's functioning. The likely impact of EU enlargement to central Europe is extrapolated from the voting of MEPs from Austria, Sweden and Finland. Given that MEPs from Central Europe do not necessarily share the same political culture as those from Scandinavia, one may wonder how far one can go with this extrapolation.

Clearly, the issue, from a policy point of view, is to understand when there might or might not be a structural break in voting behaviour after integration. Again, my own feeling is that a good answer to that question will require the elaboration of a full-fledged structural model of the functioning of the whole set of European institutions. This paper, by bringing together and discussing an impressive data set on the EP's voting patterns over 10 years, hopefully paves the way for a whole line of research in that direction.

Panel discussion

Ray Rees thought that the results of the paper might be biased in favour of cohesion of party groups for the European Parliament because its members are held accountable by their constituencies to a smaller extent than national members of parliament. In response, Gérard Roland emphasized that the members of the European Parliament are elected through a list system so that parties can put pressure on them along the party line. This is not possible with respect to the country dimension.

Xavier Vives mentioned that cohesion of party groups rather than country cohesion is not necessarily desirable if preferences are relatively heterogeneous across countries.

Charles Goodhart thought that it would be necessary to control for the number of party seats per country. Otherwise, the effects of party concentration and cohesion would be confused because countries with a big majority of one party have a high index of country cohesion. Moreover, the study should adjust for the size of a country. Gérard Roland agreed, but pointed out that without the bias introduced by party concentration the main result on party cohesion should be even stronger.

Rafael Repullo agreed with the discussion of Thomas Piketty that the results on declining country and increasing party cohesion are emphasized too much in the paper, in particular, because the standard deviations of the reported means are wide. He suggested to weigh important votes relatively more to reduce the noise of the estimates. He put forward participation in the votes as a suitable weight. Gérard Roland replied that the authors wanted to follow this suggestion and he was confident that the main results would be robust to this extension. Concerning the time trend he agreed that the time trend might not be significant. He stressed that the most important result of the paper is not the time trend, but that cohesion is much stronger for the party than for the country dimension.

Referring to the German example with two chambers, *Bundestag* and *Bundesrat*, George de Ménil was not sure that giving more power to the European Parliament increases the efficiency of decision-making. If two chambers could stop legislation, the decision-making process would become less efficient. He thought a justification assigning more power to the European Parliament could be democracy, i.e., the control of the executive power, the European Commission.

Phillip Lane pointed out that country cohesion might vary over time depending on how close elections were and how pro-European a country would be. He suggested looking at individual representatives and following how their voting behaviour changes over time. Moreover, he thought that the voting behaviour of members of parliament of new EU member countries might become more pro-European over time as countries become more integrated.

Several panellists questioned the fact that the dataset contained only roll call votes. Abdul Noury agreed that roll call votes are only a fraction of all votes in the European Parliament. He pointed out, however, that roll call votes are the most important votes.

In reply to the discussions of Thomas Piketty and Thierry Verdier, Gérard Roland noted that they had done various robustness tests such as using different measures for cohesion, various weights such as size of the majority and performing a truncation analysis. Moreover, Abdul Noury replied to Thierry Verdier that the authors had experimented with an alternative cohesion measure that would address the problem of symmetric treatment of Yes-votes, No-votes and abstentions. The main result that party membership is most important for coalition formation turns out to be very robust.

WEB APPENDIX

This may be downloaded free from http://www.economic-policy.org

REFERENCES

Baldwin, R., E. Berglöf, F. Giavazzi and M. Widgrén (2001). 'Nice try: Should the Treaty of Nice be ratified'? *Monitoring European Integration*, 11 (MEI), London: CEPR.
Bindseil, U. and C. Hantke (1997). 'The power distribution in decision making among EU member states', *European Journal of Political Economy*.
Corbett, R., F. Jacobs and M. Shackleton (2000). *The European Parliament*, London: Harper.
Crombez, Ch. (1996). 'Legislative procedures in the European Community', *British Journal of Political Science*.
Diermeier, D. and T. Feddersen (1998). 'Cohesion in legislatures and the vote of confidence procedure', *American Political Science Review*.
Downs, A. (1957). *An Economic Theory of Democracy*, New York: Harper and Row.
Heckman, J. and J. Snyder (1997). 'Linear probability models of the demand for attributes with an empirical application to estimating the preferences of legislators', *Rand Journal of Economics*.
Hix, S. (2001). 'Legislative behavior and party competition in the EP', *Journal of Common Market Studies*.
Hix S., A. Kreppel and A. Noury (2002). 'The party system in the European Parliament: Collusive or competitive?', *Journal of Common Market Studies*, forthcoming.
Huber, J. (1996). 'The vote of confidence in parliamentary democracies', *American Political Science Review*.
Kreppel A. (2001). *The European Parliament and Supranational Party System*, Cambridge: Cambridge University Press.
Kreppel A. and G. Tsebelis (1999). 'Coalition Formation in the European Parliament', *Comparative Political Studies*.
Mielcova, E. and A. Noury (1998). 'Roll call voting in a multi-party parliament: The case of the Czech Republic', CERGE-EI Discussion Paper.
Müller, W.C. and K. Strøm (eds) (2000). *Coalition Governments in Western Europe*, Oxford: Oxford University Press.
Noury, A. (2002). 'Ideology, nationality and Euro-parliamentarians', *European Union Politics*.

Noury, A., W. Dobrowolski and M. Mazurkiewicz (1999). 'Voting behavior in the Polish Parliament' mimeo, Free University of Brussels.

Persson T., G. Roland and G. Tabellini (2000). 'Comparative politics and public finance', *Journal of Political Economy*.

Poole, K. and H. Rosenthal (1997). *Congress: A Political-Economic History of Roll Call Voting*, Oxford: Oxford University Press.

Raunio, T. (1997). *The European Perspective: Transnational Party Groups in the 1989–1994 European Parliament*, London: Ashgate.

Rice, S. (1928). *Quantitative Methods in Politics*, New York, Knopf.

Tsebelis G. (1994). 'The power of the European Parliament as a conditional agenda setter', *American Political Science Review*.

Delocation and European integration

Is structural spending justified?

SUMMARY

How is European integration changing the location of industry? And what part are national and EU aids to industry playing in this process? We show that states and regions are becoming more specialized within the EU, but this process is very slow. While there is no evidence of polarization occurring at the national level, some regions are losing out. National state aids to industry appear to have little effect for either good or ill, since their effectiveness at attracting economic activity and employment is limited. European Structural Funds expenditure, by contrast, does have an effect on the location of industry, notably by attracting industries that are intensive in research and development. However, this effect has mostly been acting counter to states' comparative advantage – R&D-intensive industries have been encouraged by these aids to locate in countries and regions that have low endowments of skilled labour. Only in Ireland, where Structural Funds reinforced rather than offset comparative advantage, have poor regions been enabled systematically to catch up with the EU average.

— *Karen Helene Midelfart-Knarvik and Henry G. Overman*

Economic Policy October 2002 Printed in Great Britain
© CEPR, CES, MSH, 2002.

Delocation and European integration: is structural spending justified?

Karen Helene Midelfart-Knarvik and Henry G. Overman

Norwegian School of Economics and Business Administration and CEPR; London School of Economics and Political Science and CEPR

1. INTRODUCTION

Deepening EU integration – the completion of the Single Market and the introduction of the Euro – is expected to deliver large economic benefits. Both member states and the European Commission recognize that realizing these gains will involve structural changes in the economies involved. The fact that structural change underpins many of the potential gains raises two serious policy concerns. First, national policies may prevent these structural adjustments from occurring. Of particular concern here is the proliferation of state aids, which may replace barriers to trade removed as part of the integration process. Second, the gains from these changes may be distributed unevenly across member states. This uneven distribution of gains may work directly against the EU's aim of achieving greater economic and social cohesion.

The EU has responded to these concerns in two ways. The first is that it has taken steps to monitor and reduce overall levels of state aids. The process of monitoring

We would like to thank Tony Venables and Steve Redding, our co-authors on two earlier related pieces. We would also like to thank Gilles Duranton, Andres Rodriguez-Pose, Helen Simpson, seminar participants at the LSE and Stockholm University for comments on earlier versions of the paper. Finally, comments from our two discussants, members of the panel and the editors have resulted in substantial improvements to the paper.
The Managing Editor in charge of this paper was Paul Seabright.

began with the adoption of the First Survey on State Aids in the European Community in 1988. Attempts to reduce state aid have been reflected in the rigorous application of Commission powers under Articles 92–93 of the EEC Treaty. The second key element to the EU response has been an increasing emphasis on the role of EU interventions under the auspices of the Structural Funds (SFs). These interventions are targeted at economies either lagging behind, or undergoing substantial structural change. This two-pronged strategy reflects an important working assumption, that most state aid is inconsistent with realizing the full potential of the single market, while EU aid is a vital component in achieving that potential.

The EU uses a three-part scheme to classify interventions as horizontal, sectoral or regional. Horizontal aid is assistance to certain types of activity (small and medium-size enterprises, R&D) that is independent of sector and location of the firm. Shipbuilding, steel and motor vehicle production are the main recipients of sectoral aid. Regional aid is assistance to specific locations. These often take the form of infrastructure investments or training and unemployment initiatives. In all categories the EU considers the aid element for a wide range of expenditures when estimating totals. In addition to its general view on the desirability of state versus EU aid, the Commission also makes assumptions on the desirability of these different types of interventions. Sector specific aid is generally assumed to be undesirable, unless it reflects help with restructuring. Regional aid is assumed to be desirable if it reflects EU objectives as laid out in Articles 92(3)a and 92(3)c, but undesirable otherwise. For example, most SF interventions require matching funding from member states that would be deemed desirable. Finally, it is assumed that funding for horizontal objectives is often in the community interest, but may sometimes be undesirable if it has a negative impact on competition.

In this paper we analyse the validity of this two-pronged approach by studying the patterns of location and relocation of EU industry. We begin by assessing how location patterns have changed over time to see whether we can detect the kinds of structural change that are expected to deliver gains from the integration process. We find that structural change is occurring, but this change is slow and the process is not uniform across different economies. This finding raises the possibility that government and community actions may be hampering the process of industrial restructuring. This is an even bigger possibility at the regional level where changes in specialization are much less pronounced. To assess what role, if any, is played by policy, we examine the factors that determine changes in location patterns. *A priori* we would expect industrial relocation to be driven by deeper integration and changes in factor endowments. However, our results suggest EU industrial relocation only weakly reflects these developments.

Does policy play a role in mitigating the economic forces at work? Our results suggest that this is indeed the case. The direct impacts of SF expenditures are counter to economic determinants, thereby possibly impeding an efficient allocation of resources. EU expenditures appear to be more distortionary than state aids. More detailed investigations suggest that the Commission's assumption about the benign effects of horizontal aid is probably correct, although the results here might prove disappointing to governments that think they can provide aid to 'attract' desirable industries. For example, countries that spend a lot on horizontal aid targeted at innovation do not attract additional R&D-intensive activities. Our results also indicate that the 'pay off' from sector specific national state aid in terms of sustaining or reinforcing a particular industry is insignificant.

Put together, our results emphasize the importance of EU attempts to coordinate and regulate state aids. However, they also pose a challenge to the EU policy process itself. SF expenditure is partly distorting the efficient relocation of economic activity, which will prevent us from realizing the gains from closer integration. Such a policy may be justified if it delivers the EU's goal of economic cohesion. However, the results that we present here urge considerable caution, because current expenditure patterns do not seem to be doing so. In fact, we will argue that some elements of policy may directly work against this objective.

The organization of the paper is as follows. Section 2 briefly outlines the theoretical framework that we use for thinking about the impact of integration and the role played by community interventions and state aid. Section 3 provides descriptive evidence on specialization and industrial location in the EU. Section 4 briefly describes the size and structure of state aid and SF expenditure. Section 5 reports our main empirical results on the determinants of the relocation of industrial activity. Section 6 concludes and spells out implications for policy.

2. THE THEORY OF INDUSTRIAL LOCATION, ECONOMIC INTEGRATION, AND WELFARE

Economists identify two key sources of potential gains from deeper EU integration. First, integration may cause the restructuring of industry, thereby providing a more efficient allocation of resources. Second, integration may encourage the accumulation of additional resources (see Baldwin, 1994). In this paper we concentrate on the first source of gains by analysing the processes driving structural change. To help us organize and interpret our evidence, this section provides a theoretical framework that addresses a set of key questions: What are the potential forces determining industry location? What are the channels through which integration could affect industrial location? What are the possible outcomes of integration? What are the implications for welfare? How might policy affect the outcome?

To think systematically about these issues we need to take into account the forces that interact in determining industrial location. We will think of industrial location patterns as the outcome of two opposing forces:

- agglomeration forces that encourage firms to concentrate geographically as a result of localized external economies of scale;

- dispersion forces that encourage economic activity to spread out because production uses natural resources and other immobile factors of production.

Both types of forces may work between and/or within industries. The strength of agglomeration and dispersion forces will be affected by the degree to which goods and factors of production are mobile. If factors are immobile, and barriers prevent trade, then production must take place locally, regardless of differences in factor prices or potential gains from agglomeration. If, however, either goods or factors are mobile, the forces for dispersion and agglomeration come into play. Changing good and factor mobility is precisely the mechanism through which we expect integration to change the structure of EU production.

2.1. Agglomeration forces

The New Economic Geography literature identifies two agglomeration forces that are expected to influence industrial location across EU countries and regions:

- Access to customers: If it is costly to transport goods firms will want to locate near to their customers.
- Access to suppliers: If it is costly to transport intermediate inputs firms will want to locate near to their suppliers.

See Fujita, Krugman and Venables (1999) for details, and Ottaviano and Puga (1998) for a survey.

2.2. Dispersion forces

As production concentrates the prices of immobile factors will rise relative to locations where production does not take place. Again see Fujita Krugman and Venables (1999) or Ottaviano and Puga (1998) for more details.

2.3. The role of EU integration

Agglomeration and dispersion forces interact to determine the location of industry. However, these forces are not exogenous to the integration process. Both their absolute and relative strength will be affected by integration because integration may affect both trade costs and the mobility of factors. If integration has a larger impact on trade costs than on mobility, the geographical distribution of factors will work as a force for dispersion (see Norman and Venables, 1995). This will then provide a finite limit to the degree of geographical concentration of industrial activity that integration may bring about.

What do we expect to happen to industrial location as the EU becomes more integrated? Will the outcome be a desirable one in terms of higher welfare and convergence, or are there reasons to worry about the direction taken by market forces?

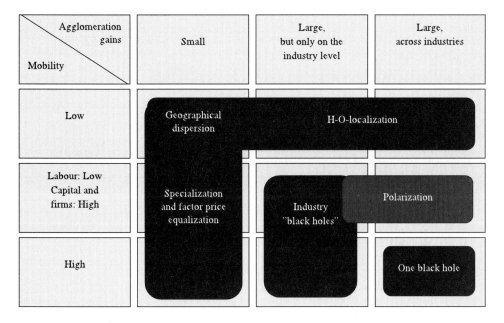

Figure 1. The possible outcomes of European integration

Source: Norman (2000).

Figure 1 shows the possible outcomes of closer integration as a function of the gains from agglomeration and the mobility of factors. Factor mobility increases as we work down the rows of the table, while the gains from, and nature of, agglomeration forces change as we move across the columns of the table. Since integration may affect both the strength of agglomeration forces and factor mobility it is clear that we may move both across the columns and down the rows of the matrix.

The first row of the matrix in Figure 1 assumes low factor mobility, the second high firm and capital mobility, but low worker mobility, and the third high mobility of all factors. The first column assumes that gains from agglomeration are small, the second that they are strong within particular sectors, and the third that they are strong across sectors. Each element of the matrix then outlines the expected outcome of closer integration. If factors are immobile then we expect integration to lead to specialization. If all factors are mobile, then the extent of agglomeration reflects the nature of linkages. When gains from agglomeration are small, we might still get specialization. If linkages are strong within sectors, but weak between sectors, then we might expect concentration of specific industries ('industry black holes'). Finally, if linkages are strong across sectors then we expect one large agglomeration in the core region ('one black hole'). These outcomes have in common that integration leads to higher welfare for the whole EU population.

To finish our classification of possible outcomes, we examine the impact of integration when firms and capital are mobile, but labour is immobile. Small gains from

agglomeration lead to specialization and factor price equalization. With strong linkages within sectors, we see the same tendency towards industrial concentration as we
saw with mobile workers. However, in this case, some countries may see larger gains
if particular industry black holes deliver greater returns than others. If all factors were
mobile, factor migration would have ensured that this would not be the case. There
is one important additional difference from the previous two cases if firm linkages
are strong across sectors. Then it is possible that we again see overall geographical
agglomeration of industrial activity. This agglomeration appears similar to the case
with mobile workers but there are very stark contrasts in terms of welfare outcomes.
In the mobile workers' case, workers move to live in the core region, so all benefit from
the agglomeration. Now, however, industry and capital owners move but workers do
not follow. This implies that welfare outcomes can be very polarized with increased
inequality between core and periphery.

How might policy interventions affect the outcome of the integration process? We
can identify three possible channels. First, policy can affect the geographical distribution of factors. This should impact on the elements of location patterns driven by
comparative advantage. Second, policy can directly affect the forces for agglomeration (see Martin and Rogers, 1995). For example, infrastructure investment can affect
the transportation costs between economies. Finally, policy may target particular
sectors or locations so as to prevent or encourage relocation. Obvious examples here
are direct state aids to particular sectors and EU expenditures in particular countries.

When is intervention justified? Intervention may be justified from an equity or an
efficiency perspective, if the direction taken by market forces is an undesirable one.
From an equity perspective, the polarization outcome that we described above is
clearly not desirable given the EU's cohesion objectives. More subtly, the industry
black hole outcome may be undesirable from a welfare perspective if some industries
are more valuable than others. From an efficiency perspective, the industry black hole
outcome may be undesirable if agglomeration forces run counter to, rather than
reinforce, comparative advantage.

We shall argue that at the national level the empirical evidence points to the
gradual emergence of industry black holes. Thus, if there is a justification for EU
intervention, then it must be because

1. industry black holes occur in the 'wrong' places and thus impede an efficient
    allocation of resources; or
2. market forces imply an uneven distribution of the more valuable industry black
    holes across countries.

This is clearly a very difficult issue to assess, but we will provide evidence suggesting that certain EU interventions may be leaving countries worse off than they would
have been if the economic forces had been allowed to run their course. We reach a
similar conclusion for regional intervention, but here the inappropriateness of some
EU interventions is even more serious given the fact that regional outcomes appear

to be characterized by polarization rather than the emergence of industry black holes. Our arguments are spelt out in more detail in the three sections that follow.

3. INDUSTRIAL LOCATION IN THE EU

What has happened to specialization and industrial location over the last few decades? Has integration led to more specialization? Are changes dramatic or gradual? In terms of the possible outcomes described in the previous section, where has integration brought us and in what direction are we heading? What does the evidence suggest about the forces at work, and about the impact of national and EU policy? We will answer these questions by considering the relocation of industry in response to closer integration at two spatial scales – national and regional. Data Appendix A provides details on the exact sources and definitions.

3.1. Specialization and concentration

The industrial structure of EU countries is changing:

- States and, to a lesser extent, regions have become more specialized, but the process of structural change is slow.
- The distribution of overall manufacturing activity has remained constant at the national level, but at the regional level has become more concentrated.
- Evidence on industrial concentration and the distribution of aggregate activity suggests that at the national level agglomeration gains mainly occur within and not across industries. The strength of these agglomeration forces appears to vary by industry.
- In contrast, at the regional level, the evidence suggests agglomeration gains may occur across, rather than within, industries.

3.1.1. Countries becoming more specialized.   Table 1 shows that from the early 1980s onwards all countries except the Netherlands became more specialized (see Midelfart-Knarvik *et al.*, 2000a). The table reports the Krugman specialization index for each country. This index allows us to compare each country's industrial structure with that of the average of the rest of the EU. It takes value zero if country i has an industrial structure identical to the rest of the EU, and takes maximum value two if it has no industries in common with the rest of the EU. For details on how to calculate the measure see Krugman (1991) or the Web Appendix on http://www.economic-policy.org. Figure 2 shows that despite the fact that trade between these countries had been liberalized by previous agreements, the much deeper integration implied by joining the EU has consistently led to an increase in specialization for new members. These findings of increased specialization are consistent with previous studies using different descriptive measures (each with their own inherent advantages and disadvantages), see for example Amiti (1999) and Brülhart (2001).

Table 1. Countries are becoming more specialized: evidence from the Krugman specialization index

	1970–73	1980–83	1985–88	1990–93	1994–97
Austria	0.307	**0.268**	0.280	0.288	0.340
Belgium	**0.314**	0.340	0.356	0.378	0.431
Denmark	0.554	**0.545**	0.582	0.578	0.578
Spain	0.416	**0.269**	0.294	0.323	0.317
Finland	0.591	**0.501**	0.513	0.522	0.582
France	0.169	**0.156**	0.175	0.170	0.166
UK	0.192	**0.160**	0.168	0.197	0.177
Germany	0.225	**0.224**	0.259	0.252	0.257
Greece	**0.527**	0.574	0.619	0.666	0.700
Ireland	0.698	**0.619**	0.661	0.673	0.769
Italy	0.307	0.305	**0.296**	0.322	0.380
Netherlands	**0.487**	0.543	0.533	0.505	0.495
Portugal	0.532	**0.473**	0.562	0.586	0.560
Sweden	0.409	**0.381**	0.389	0.386	0.480
Average	0.409	**0.383**	0.406	0.418	0.445

Note: Krugman specialization indices calculated for four-year averages. Bold figures indicate the minimum value of the index for each country.

Source: Midelfart-Knarvik *et al.* (2000a).

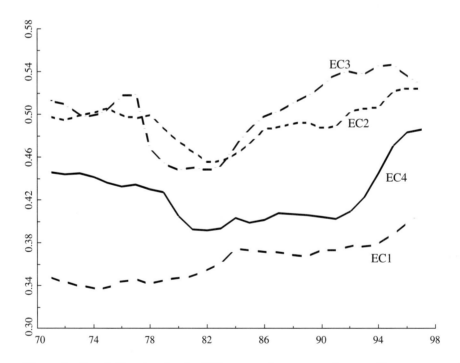

Figure 2. Specialization in the EU: countries grouped according to entry date

Notes: The figure plots two-year moving averages of the Krugman specialization index for countries grouped according to entry date. Definitions of groups are as follows:
EC1 Belgium, France, Germany, Italy, Luxembourg, the Netherlands   EC3 Greece, Portugal, Spain
EC2 Denmark, Ireland, UK   EC4 Austria, Finland, Sweden.

Source: Midelfart-Knarvik *et al.* (2000a).

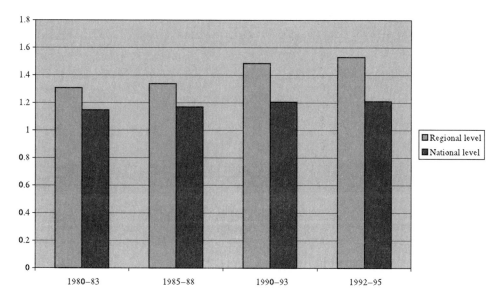

Figure 3. The geographical concentration of manufacturing activity

Notes: Coefficient of variation for four-year averages of shares in total EU manufacturing.
Source: Authors' own calculations.

3.1.2. A mixed picture for regional specialization.   Disaggregated industrial data are not available at the regional level for Austria, Finland, Greece and Sweden. For the remaining countries, there has been little overall change in regional specialization between 1980 and 1995: 53% of regions got more specialized, while the remaining 47% got less specialized. On average we only find a tiny increase in specialization.

3.1.3. Distribution of aggregate industrial activity – stability for nations, concentration for regions.   Has the concentration of the manufacturing sector increased or decreased? To illustrate the development in concentration, Figure 3 reports the coefficient of variation for the distribution of manufacturing activity across states and regions. The pattern of overall manufacturing concentration across states has been remarkably stable (Table 1 in the Web Appendix shows that the same is also true for individual country shares in aggregate manufacturing). However, once we move down to the regional level, we make two important observations. First, manufacturing activity is more concentrated across regions than across states. Second, activity has become more concentrated over the last two decades.

3.1.4. Industrial concentration.   There is no general trend with respect to the concentration of individual industries (see Midelfart-Knarvik *et al.*, 2000a): during the process of integration, some industries have become more concentrated, others have become less, while the remainder have kept a fairly fixed pattern. These differing patterns across industries reflect the fact that the relative strength of agglomeration and dispersion forces varies across industries depending on technology and intensities.

A comparison of the industries that have become more concentrated versus less concentrated provides more detailed insight. Labour intensive industries like textiles, wearing apparel and leather industries, have become more concentrated over the last two decades as they have agglomerated in southern Europe. In contrast, high-tech industries such as office and computing machinery, radio, TV and communication, and professional instruments have become less concentrated. Both these developments appear to be driven by countries specializing according to comparative advantage but with the result being distinctly different in terms of industrial concentration. To the extent that agglomeration forces are at work in these industries, they have reinforced the patterns of specialization for labour intensive industries, but been dominated by dispersion forces (presumably factor market considerations) in the high-tech industries.

3.2. Nation states and industry black holes?

To understand where we are, and where further integration might take us, we need to consider both industrial structure and factor mobility. There is a substantial literature on factor mobility in the EU summarized and discussed by Braunerhjelm *et al.* (2000). They conclude that (1) total cross-border flows of real capital investments have increased substantially in recent years; and (2) EU labour mobility is limited both with respect to past levels and relative to that in the United States.

Our descriptive evidence on the distribution of aggregate activity and individual industries suggests that at the national level agglomeration forces tend to be industry specific. Coupled with the evidence on mobility this suggests that integration is fostering a pattern of industrial location determined by comparative advantage and agglomeration forces working at the industry level, and that we may expect increased specialization and eventually the emergence of 'industry black holes' (see Section 2). However, the evidence suggests that we still have a long period of industrial restructuring ahead.

3.3. Regional polarization?

The picture looks different, and worrying, at the regional level. Changing industrial structures are characterized by a lack of specialization, while industrial activity is becoming more geographically concentrated. The pattern for incomes is similar – over the last two decades income inequality *across* member states has decreased, while regional inequality *within* member states has increased (see e.g. Braunerhjelm *et al.*, 2000). Couple this divergence with the evidence that capital is, if anything, more mobile between national regions than internationally and we cannot rule out the possibility of a polarization of industrial activity at the regional level.

Our analysis so far allows us to make a couple of important observations, while it also raises a number of questions. From the theory outlined above we know that agglomeration forces working across industries, if combined with lack of worker mobility, may be responsible for less desirable outcomes of integration. These types of forces do not appear to play any significant role in determining industry location across member states. However, at the sub-national level, the signs of polarization and a lack of specialisation suggest that these types of forces may play a significant role. Our analysis does not allow us to conclude why agglomeration forces differ in their impact at national versus sub-national levels, i.e. whether this is market or policy driven. But our results communicate one important message: to the extent that EU policy initiatives have sought to counteract less desirable outcomes of integration, they may have been successful on the national level, but definitely less so on the sub-national level. Despite the fact that the EU has spent around 35% of its budget on regional objectives, we observe increasing regional inequality.

4. NATIONAL STATE AID AND COMMUNITY AID PROGRAMMES

The process of specialization is slow at the national level – and even more so at the regional level. As a result, the gains from EU integration will be realized later rather than sooner. What are the reasons for this slow process? Have national policy interventions hampered the process of structural change through industry specific aid programmes? Have EU policy initiatives prevented polarization and divergence or just impeded greater specialization and a more efficient resource allocation? To answer these questions, we need a more systematic study of both the economic determinants of industrial relocation and the role played by policy. In this section we briefly describe national state aid and community aid programmes, before turning to consider their impact in Section 5.

Data on the size of interventions is published in the EU's periodic reports on state aids. These reports also provide some details on the nature of the interventions by classifying state aid as either horizontal, sectoral or regional. Assessing the size and nature of interventions is not an easy task and the data should be treated with caution.

4.1. Nation state aids counter EU interventions

As discussed earlier, attempts to monitor state aids reflects two concerns. First, that nation states are intervening to prevent structural adjustment. Second, that the size of these interventions tends to overshadow community expenditures that are intended to foster economic and social cohesion. Figure 4 illustrates the data that underlies this second concern. The figure plots nation-state and EU aid per capita. Nation-state aid is restricted to aid to manufacturing. EU aid is the sum of social, regional and cohesion funds, but excludes any aid to agriculture and fisheries since our empirical analysis focuses purely on manufacturing. We use the same definitions in the

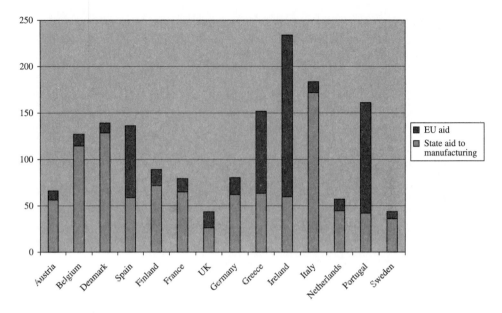

Figure 4. EU aid and state aid to manufacturing, 1994–96

Notes: Calculations are based on annual average 1994–96 in ECU per capita. State aid includes all national aid to manufacturing, while EU aid includes social fund, regional fund and cohesion fund expenditure.

Source: European Commission (1995, 1998).

econometric section below. The negative relationship between EU and state aid is clear. The correlation coefficient between the two types of aid is -0.25.

4.2. Nations have different state aid priorities

Ideally we want to clearly identify recipients of state aids. Information provided by the European Commission allows us to distinguish differences across states in the type of aid provided. We consider the six classifications illustrated in Figure 5. The figure clearly shows that nation states can vary quite considerably in the nature of the state aid that they give to manufacturing.

We now turn to consider the role that national and EU policy interventions play in shaping the location of activity.

5. WHAT DETERMINES INDUSTRIAL RELOCATION IN THE EU?

In this section we develop an empirical model to analyse the forces that drive industrial relocation in the EU to allow us to assess the role played by policy. To do this, we build on earlier work where we focused purely on the economic determinants of industrial location (Midelfart-Knarvik *et al.*, 2000a and 2000b). The text develops the intuition behind our empirical specification. Technical details can be found in Appendix B.

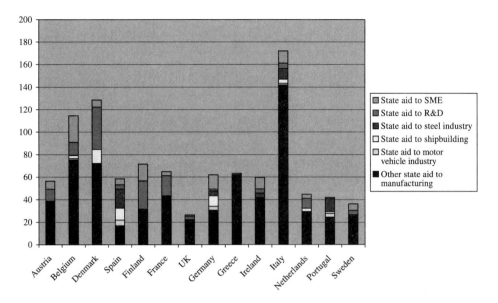

Figure 5. The distribution of state aid to manufacturing according to objectives and sectors, 1994–96

Notes: Calculations are based on annual average 1994–96 in million ECU per capita.

Source: European Commission (1995, 1998).

5.1. An empirical model of industrial relocation

According to the theory outlined in Section 2, in the absence of government intervention, location patterns will be driven by the interplay between agglomeration and dispersion forces. Integration itself is expected to allow economic forces to play a greater role in determining industry location, while it may also change the balance of agglomeration and dispersion forces.

In Section 2, we suggested that two types of agglomeration forces may play a key role in determining the location of EU industrial activity – access to customers and access to suppliers. Their impact on industrial location will depend on two factors. First, how much locations differ with respect to their market size in terms of access to customers and suppliers. Second, whether agglomeration gains are predominantly within or between industries. If gains are strongest within industries, then the impact of these agglomeration forces on different industries will reflect differing internal economies of scale in production and differences in the use of intermediates.

Dispersion forces reflect the comparative advantages of member states. We consider four factors as sources of comparative advantage: land, and low, medium and high-skilled labour (we exclude capital from the analysis on the grounds that it is internationally mobile). Their impact will again depend on two factors. How much locations differ with respect to their endowments and whether agglomeration forces counteract or reinforce comparative advantage. Unless agglomeration forces counteract comparative advantage, industrial location will reflect differing factor intensities and relative endowments.

In the absence of government and community intervention, an industrial structure determined by agglomeration and dispersion forces should have the following characteristics:

- Country size: larger countries will have larger shares in all sectors.
- Differences in transaction costs: firms that sell a larger share of output to other firms may locate differently from firms that sell a larger share of output to final consumers. This will be the case if these two types of firms face different transaction costs, and thus vary in their responsiveness to market access.
- Access to suppliers: a country with relatively good access to intermediate good suppliers, will have a larger share in industries that use large amounts of intermediate goods.
- Access to customers: a country with relatively good market access to customers will have a larger share in industries that are subject to increasing returns to scale.
- Agricultural endowment: a country with relatively high agricultural output will have a larger share in industries that use a lot of agricultural products.
- Labour endowments: a country relatively well endowed with a particular type of labour will have a larger share in industries that use a lot of that type of labour.

Of course, the opposite should also hold. For example, countries with relatively small amounts of a particular type of labour will have relatively small shares in industries that use a lot of that type of labour. There are three reasons why the industrial structure may not have these characteristics:

- Agglomeration forces work between industries rather than within industries. In this case, we would expect agglomeration forces to have no differential impact across industries. Factor endowments could still play some role if industries are agglomerated in a number of core locations.
- Agglomeration forces work within industries but counter to comparative advantage. In this case, we would expect agglomeration forces to have differential impacts across industries but factor endowments should play no role.
- Agglomeration forces and dispersion forces do not determine the industrial structure. Instead, the structure is determined by non-economic factors.

In the absence of government and community intervention, this reasoning gives us an estimation equation of the form:

Share of a country in an industry = f(Size of the country, Country characteristics, Industry characteristics).

This is the equation that we estimated in Midelfart-Knarvik *et al.* (2000a and 2000b) (shown as equation B1 in Appendix B.) Estimation of this equation implies:

- Including countries' share of population and of total manufacturing to capture the country size effect.
- Including country and industry characteristics both separately and interacted with one another in line with the reasoning above.

How can we extend this equation to take into account the role of policy? In Section 2 we identified three possible roles for policy. Policy can:

1. change endowments;
2. change the balance and strength of agglomeration and dispersion forces by facilitating deeper integration;
3. directly affect the location of particular sectors through aid programmes.

It should be obvious that we will indirectly capture the impact of (1) if we allow country characteristics to change over time. We can capture the impact of (2) if we allow the coefficients on country and industry characteristics to change over time. However, to allow for (3) we need to extend the estimation equation to assume that:

Share of a country in an industry = f(*Size of the country, Country characteristics, Industry characteristics, Total aid from EU, Total state aid*).

See Equation B2 in Appendix B for the detailed specification.

To capture the direct impact of aid we make some stylized assumptions about the role of this type of intervention. Broadly, we think of this type of intervention as either seeking to protect jobs or to attract new types of activity. Spending to protect jobs usually involves subsidies to protect large employers in heavy manufacturing. Spending to attract new types of activities tends to take two broad forms. First, spending to attract high value-added industries that employ more skilled workers. Second, spending to attract R&D-intensive and other 'innovative' activities. Thus, in terms of our classification of industries, we assume both government and EU expenditure have sought to affect three types of activities: those that have increasing returns to scale, are medium skill intensive or are R&D intensive.

To capture these effects, we need detailed data on the targets for EU and state aid. We can get this for state aid. As we saw in Section 4, we can get data on the amount of state aid that goes to steel, motor vehicles and shipbuilding. We assume that this aid targets those industries specifically (we enter the amount of aid per capita interacted with a dummy for those industries). We can also get a breakdown of horizontal aid by objective. We focus on two categories of horizontal aid – to R&D innovation and to small and medium-size enterprises (SMEs). These horizontal aids can be clearly related to the industry characteristics that we are using. We assume that aid to R&D will target R&D-intensive activities and that aid to SMEs will target industries with low returns to scale (we enter the amount of aid per capita interacted with the relevant industry characteristics). We cannot get such details for the type of EU expenditure by country, so we use a more aggregate approach. For EU aid we interact the quantity of aid per capita by country with the characteristics of each industry with respect to scale, skill intensity and R&D. A positive coefficient on the EU aid interaction variables informs us that a country with high levels of aid has increased its share in industries that are relatively scale intensive, medium skill intensive, or R&D intensive.

For both countries and regions data limitations stop us from estimating the resulting specification directly. In the remainder of this section we focus on the national level data, consider a number of data and econometric issues, and derive the two specifications that we will estimate in Section 5.2. We deal with the regional level analysis in Section 5.3.

5.1.1. Data.   Appendix A gives details of the production data that we use to construct the left-hand side variable, which are the same as the production data that we used for the descriptive exercises in Section 3. Appendix C provides details on data available to construct the right-hand side variables. The latter are somewhat limited. First, it is not possible to get endowment data for all years that are comparable across countries. Instead, we have four cross-sections of endowment data for 1980, 1985, 1990 and 1994. A second, and more severe restriction, is that we cannot get information on the stocks of EU and state aid (i.e. the total amount received over, say, the last two decades). Instead, we only observe flows for all countries in the last time period for which we have data.

To get round the restriction placed on us by the availability of aid data we study *changes* in production structure between two periods: 1990–93 and 1994–97. We shall refer to these two time periods as Periods 1 and 2. We use four-year time averages to remove fluctuations due to differential timing of country and sector business cycles. Policy impacts on changes between these two time periods will be driven by flows of aid (for which we have data) rather than stocks of aid (for which we have no data).

5.1.2. Econometric issues.   At its most general such a specification would allow changes in production structure to be driven by changing endowments, the changing balance of agglomeration and dispersion forces, and policy interventions targeted at particular sectors or activities. Unfortunately if we allow for all three effects at the same time we run into a common econometric problem – multi-collinearity prevents us from separating out the effects of different variables. To get round these problems we conduct two exercises that impose one of the following assumptions about how EU and state aid might be affecting location.

- Assumption 1: Aid has a direct effect on location as do changing endowments, but closer integration is not significantly changing the balance and strength of agglomeration forces (i.e. we ignore policy effect 2 and the impact of non-policy factors on the balance between agglomeration and dispersion forces).

- Assumption 2: Aid has a direct effect on location as has closer integration, but changes in endowments are unimportant (i.e. we ignore policy effect 1 and the impact of non-policy factors on changing endowments).

The exact specifications that result from imposing each of these assumptions in turn are provided as Equations B3 and B4 in Appendix B. By ignoring one effect in turn, we can derive specifications that can be estimated with the data that are available. Specification 1 captures the impact of changing endowments and aid programmes, while Specification 2 captures the impact of integration on the forces that determine location, as well as the impact of aid. Fortunately, our results from imposing either assumption are similar, allowing us to reach some tentative conclusions about the role of policy interventions in the EU.[1]

Problems may arise in estimating the two resulting specifications if the aid variables are endogenous. That is, if changes in industrial shares in particular industries lead to changes in flows of aid, rather than the other way round. It is clear that this is potentially a problem for flows of state aid to particular sectors (e.g. steel) where governments are able to respond quickly to downturns in those sectors. For example, the EU allowed state aid to the steel industry to increase dramatically between 1994 and 1996 as part of a restructuring process. Thus countries may have spent a lot precisely because their share was changing dramatically. This reverse causality can cause OLS estimates to be inconsistent. *A priori* this reverse causality represents less of a problem for the flows of EU aid. The EU uses five-year plans for its allocation of aid across EU countries and regions. Thus, the decisions on the amount of aid to make available to different countries and regions will have been made prior to the changes in individual sectors' production structure that we observe here. It is still possible for EU aid flows to be endogenous, however, if the amount of EU aid countries actually spend in any given period is related to changes in production structure for individual industries. Thus, timing of EU expenditures may be related to changes in production structure even if total aid ceilings did not take account of those changes. Although this cause of endogeneity is less likely, we still want to ensure that our results are robust to this type of reasoning. To get round endogeneity problems relating to both state and EU aid we will present additional results from two-stage least squares (2SLS) using lagged values of production, endowments and aid variables as instruments. As we show below, neither instrumenting, nor a number of other robustness checks change our overall results.

---

[1] There is a third possible assumption that we adopted in Midelfart-Knarvik *et al.* (2000a and 2000b). There, we assumed that policy had no direct impact on the location of industry, but only played a role through changing endowments and changing the balance and strength of agglomeration forces. The advantage of that approach was that it allowed us to use all four cross-sections of data and gets round the fact that we do not have data on stocks of aid. The disadvantage is that *if* policy does play an indirect role, we have omitted a variable from our empirical specification. If, as is likely, this omitted variable is correlated with the included variables our estimates on country and industry characteristics may be biased.

5.1.3. Reporting results.   In what follows, we will concentrate on the aid variables which tell us the role of aid in determining location and on the interaction variables for the economic variables which inform us about the sensitivity of location patterns to country and industry characteristics. The results for nations are reported in Section 5.2 while Section 5.3 reports results for regions. Table D1 in the appendix reports beta coefficients for the ordinary least squares (OLS) results. These coefficients give the percentage increase in the share of a location for a one standard deviation increase in both the location and industry characteristics.

5.2. Explaining relocation at the national level in the EU

In this section we outline our results for relocation at the national level. The first subsection imposes Assumption 1 to capture the impact of changing endowments and aid programmes, while the second imposes Assumption 2 to capture both the impact of aid and the impact of integration on the forces that determine location.

5.2.1. Specification 1: The role of changing endowments and policy.   We impose Assumption 1 to give an estimating equation of the form:

Change in share of a country in an industry = f(*Change in size of the country, Change in country characteristics, Industry characteristics, Flow of EU aid, Flow of state aid*).

The exact specification is given as Equation B3 in Appendix B. Technically, we assume that the coefficients are constant over time and first difference the specification given in Equation B2 of Appendix B. The results are reported in Tables 2 and D1.

For the moment, consider the first column of Table 2, where we ignore the possibility that aid is endogenous. For the economic variables, we report results for changes in the interaction terms. Remember that our data on industry characteristics do not vary over time, so these interactions capture the impact of changing endowments on changes in industrial structure. For example, a positive coefficient on the interaction between endowment of medium-skilled labour and medium-skilled intensity tells us that countries that have seen a relative increase in their endowment of medium-skilled labour have attracted industries that are relatively intensive in the use of medium-skilled labour. The aid interaction variables capture the direct impact of aid on production structures in a similar fashion. For example, a positive coefficient on the interaction between EU aid and R&D intensity tells us that countries that receive a lot of EU aid have been relatively successful in attracting R&D-intensive activities.

5.2.1.1. Results.   The results show that there is no strong link between changing endowments and changing industrial structure. There are only two significant effects. First, countries that have seen a relative increase in their centrality have seen some decrease in their share of firms selling high proportions of their output to industry. Second, countries that have seen a relative increase in their endowments of high-skilled workers

Table 2. The determinants of industrial relocation, Specification 1

Dependent variable	OLS Change in share of a country in an industry between Period 1 and 2	2SLS Change in share of a country in an industry between Period 1 and 2
Δ Share of a country in EU population	−11.867*** (4.225)	−12.400*** (4.958)
Δ Share of a country in total EU manufacturing	0.839*** (0.137)	0.979*** (0.269)
(A) Δ General market access * Sales to industry	−1.045*** (0.375)	−0.851 (0.648)
(B) Δ Market access to suppliers * Use of intermediates	12.118 (10.746)	18.334 (17.219)
(C) Δ General market access * Economies of scale	−0.218 (0.357)	−0.386 (0.703)
(D) Δ Agricultural production * Use of agricultural inputs	0.041 (0.484)	−0.788 (1.115)
(E) Δ Medium skilled labour * Use of skilled labour	0.052 (1.949)	3.865 (4.167)
(F) Δ High skilled labour * R&D intensity	21.893* (12.126)	22.408* (11.944)
EU aid * Economies of scale	0.008 (0.017)	−0.018 (0.026)
EU aid * Use of skilled labour	−0.209** (0.105)	−0.491 (0.522)
EU aid * R&D intensity	1.010** (0.488)	3.933** (1.994)
State aid to shipbuilding	−0.009 (0.008)	−0.239 (0.224)
State aid to steel industry	−0.002 (0.004)	0.002 (0.012)
State aid to motor industry	−0.001 (0.021)	0.736 (1.119)
State aid to R&D + innovation	−0.073 (0.131)	0.301 (0.216)
State aid to SMEs	−0.130 (0.218)	−0.432 (0.454)
R squared	0.22	
Number of observations	456	456

Notes: ***, ** and * denote coefficient significantly different from zero with 1%, 5% and 10% confidence level respectively. Two-sided tests applied to all coefficients.

have been relatively successful at attracting R&D-intensive activities. Note, however, that changes in comparative advantage with respect to low and medium-skilled labour are not driving changes in production structure. This suggests that changes in endowments do not necessarily translate into changes in industrial structure, meaning that policy interventions in this area will have little effect on industrial relocation. We return to this, when we discuss policy issues further below. Two key results emerge on the role of aid. First, the direct impact of EU aid is to help countries attract R&D-intensive industries, but at the expense of medium-skilled industries (the coefficient on the R&D interaction is positive, that on the skilled labour interaction negative). Second, targeted state aid, to specific sectors or to specific types of activity does not attract that sector or activity. Before proceeding, we consider a number of robustness issues.

5.2.1.2. Robustness issues.   In Section 5.1 we discussed the possibility that changes in aid might be partly driven by changes in production structure rather than vice-versa. If this is the case, we can use past values of endowments and aid (which by construc-tion cannot be driven by current changes in production structure) to instrument for current values of aid. A Durbin–Wu–Haussman (DWH) test using these instruments suggests that we can reject the null hypothesis that our coefficient estimates are consistent. This tells us that aid is sufficiently endogenous so as to affect the consist-ency of our OLS results. Column 2 of Table 2 presents results when we instrument all aid variables using past values of endowments and aid. Several key aspects of the results that we highlighted above are robust to this instrumenting. First, EU aid helps attract investment in R&D-intensive activities. Second changes in the endow-ments of high-skilled workers feed through to changes in production structure, but low and medium-skilled endowments play no role. Third, the effect of state aids is insignificant. Once we instrument, however, we can no longer detect a negative impact of aid on medium-skilled industries. Note that, when discussing policy recom-mendations in Section 6, we focus on the implications of the findings that are robust to instrumenting.

There are a number of other robustness issues that we need to consider. First, our five-way classification of state aid represents highly varying proportions of total state aid by country (from a low of 3% in Greece, to a high of 70% in Spain). By far the largest 'missing' aid category is regional aid. Once we allow for regional aid, we can characterize at least 65% of aid for all countries. There is a potential problem if this regional aid is being targeted at R&D or SME activities but being classified as regional (this should not happen for aid to specific industries). To check this, we have to re-run our analysis assuming that regional state aid is spent purely on horizontal objectives in the same proportions as state aid that is actually identified as horizontal. Doing this does not change our results. As an additional check, we have included all unidentified state aid interacted with the same three industry characteristics as EU aid. None of these additional interaction terms are significant. Finally, the results on the impact of EU aid are not driven by any specific country. In particular the impact is still positive if we drop Ireland (a country which has attracted a lot of R&D-intensive industry and a lot of EU expenditure). We report results from a number of these robustness checks in Table 2 of the Web Appendix.

This implies that if integration is having no effect on relocation then:

- changing endowments of low and medium-skilled labour does not feed into changes in production structure;
- changing endowments of high-skilled labour do imply changes in production structure;

- EU aid helps recipients attract R&D-intensive industries;
- horizontal and sectoral state aids do not positively affect production shares.

5.2.2. Specification 2: The role of economic integration and policy. We now turn away from changes in relocation of industry driven by changing endowments and instead focus on the impact of integration. As outlined in Equation B4 in Appendix B, we do this by regressing the change in production on endowments and aid holding endowments fixed over time. That is, we estimate:

Change in share of a country in an industry = f(*Size of the country, Country characteristics, Industry characteristics, Flow of aid*).

The results are presented in the first and second columns of Tables 3 and D1. A significant coefficient on an interaction tells us that integration has impacted on that determinant and that this has resulted in changes in production structure.

5.2.2.1. Results. The first columns in Table 3 present the results when we continue to ignore the possibility that aid is endogenous. The results show that, once we condition out the effect of aid:

- market access has become less important for firms that sell a relatively high proportion of their output to industry (and thus more important for firms that sell a relatively high proportion of their output to final consumers);
- access to suppliers has become more important;
- access to agriculture inputs has become more important;
- the role of endowments of high-skilled workers has increased, but that of low and medium-skilled endowments remains unchanged.

These results highlight the extent to which changes in production patterns do not seem to reflect the impact of integration. In particular, despite deepening integration, the impact of comparative advantage in low and medium-skilled labour is unchanged. This reinforces our results from Specification 1 on the weak role of comparative advantage in determining structural change in Europe. In fact, the results we present below using instrumental variables are even stronger, as they suggest a declining role for comparative advantage in low and medium-skilled industries. Results for the aid variables are exactly in line with those from Specification 1. EU aid has a significant impact on the location of R&D-intensive activities, while state aid plays no direct role in influencing the location of production.

5.2.2.2. Robustness issues. Results from the DWH test suggest that aid is again sufficiently endogenous that our OLS results may be inconsistent. Column 2 of Table 3 shows that if we instrument for the aid variables, our results on the role of EU aid and high-skilled endowments go through as before. As mentioned above, our 2SLS

Table 3. The determinants of industrial relocation, Specification 2

Dependent variable	OLS Change in share of a country in an industry between Period 1 and 2	2SLS Change in share of a country in an industry between Period 1 and 2
Share of a country in EU population	−0.205** (0.107)	−0.228 (0.129)
Share of a country in total EU manufacturing	0.228** (0.110)	0.251*** (0.190)
(A) General market access * Sales to industry	−0.075* (0.042)	−0.019 (0.064)
(B) Market access to suppliers * Use of intermediates	4.184*** (1.593)	1.812 (2.947)
(C) General market access * Economies of scale	−0.039 (0.046)	−0.168* (0.100)
(D) Agricultural production * Use of agricultural inputs	0.710*** (0.256)	0.404 (0.277)
(E) Medium skilled labour * Use of skilled labour	−1.612 (1.924)	−5.896* (3.264)
(F) High skilled labour * R&D intensity	7.634* (4.724)	17.952*** (5.734)
EU aid * Economies of scale	0.034 (0.077)	−0.183 (0.165)
EU aid * Use of skilled labour	0.094 (0.590)	−1.174 (1.523)
EU aid * R&D intensity	3.646* (2.174)	9.886* (5.526)
State aid to shipbuilding	0.002 (0.012)	−0.008 (0.023)
State aid to steel industry	−0.007 (0.007)	0.002 (0.012)
State aid to motor industry	0.041 (0.028)	0.986 (0.689)
State aid to R&D + innovation	0.052 (0.112)	0.157 (0.160)
State aid to SMEs	0.243 (0.389)	−0.077 (0.692)
R squared	0.23	
Number of observations	456	456

Notes: ***, ** and * denote coefficient significantly different from zero with 1%, 5% and 10% confidence level respectively. Two-sided tests applied to all coefficients.

results suggest that the role of low and medium-skilled endowments may even have decreased somewhat. However, given that a number of coefficients on economic variables change when we instrument, we think that this result should be treated with caution. As before, our results on the impact of EU aid and the role of high-skilled endowments are robust with respect to the following: (1) rescaling aid; (2) including residual aid; and (3) the exclusion of any given country (including Ireland). We report results from a number of these robustness checks in Table 3 of the Web Appendix.

This implies that, if integration is affecting relocation then:

- There appears to be no change in the role of low and medium-unskilled endowments. If anything, their role may have actually decreased.
- The role of high-skilled endowments in determining industry location is increasing.
- EU aid helps recipients attract R&D-intensive industries.
- Horizontal and sectoral state aids do not positively affect production shares.

We return to the policy implications of these findings below, but before that we consider the relocation of economic activity and the role of aid programmes at the sub-national level.

5.3. Explaining relocation at the regional level in the EU

This section provides a brief analysis of the factors determining relocation at the regional level. Our analysis is restricted by the availability of production, endowment and aid data. We exclude Austria, Finland, Greece and Sweden because we have no regional production data. Getting comparable endowment data for all EU regions is only possible for the mid 1990s, so we have no data on changing endowments. The production data also finish two years earlier than the state data. Finally, we can only get data on EU regional aid and matching government expenditure. We cannot get a detailed breakdown of state aid. All these restrictions mean that we consider only Specification 2 for a subset of regions between 1985–88 (Period 1) and 1992–95 (Period 2).

The results are reported in Tables 4 and D1. As above, a significant coefficient tells us that integration has impacted on the role of that determinant, resulting in changes in production structure. From the results, it is clear that we cannot detect a significant impact of integration on any of the economic determinants. With respect to the impact of aid, the results from the regional analysis are very much in line with what we found when analysing relocation at the national level. EU expenditures help regions to attract R&D-intensive industries. Moreover, we find, that EU aid actually increases regional shares in low returns to scale activities (it decreases their share of increasing returns to scale activities).

5.3.1. Robustness issues. Due to data limitations we are not able to carry out the same number of robustness checks as in the analysis of relocation using national data. In particular, our data set does not provide us with suitable instruments. One important robustness check does show that our results are again robust to the exclusion of any given country including Ireland.

Table 4. Determinants of regional relocation

Dependent variable	OLS Change in share of a region in an industry between period 1 and 2
Share of a region	0.002
in EU population	(0.012)
Share of a region	−0.083**
in total EU manufacturing	(0.042)
(A) General market access	−0.141
* Sales to industry	(0.156)
(B) Market access to suppliers	−0.623
* Use of intermediates	(0.475)
(C) General market access	−0.002
* Economies of scale	(0.005)
(D) Agricultural production	−0.114
* Use of agricultural inputs	(0.160)
(E) Medium skilled labour	0.745
* Use of skilled labour	(1.913)
(F) High skilled labour	4.733
* R&D intensity	(4.687)
EU aid	−0.001***
* Economies of scale	(0.000)
EU aid	0.000
* Use of skilled labour	(0.001)
EU aid	0.014***
* R&D intensity	(0.005)
R squared	0.13
Number of observations	1040

Notes: ***, ** and * denote coefficient significantly different from zero with 1%, 5% and 10% confidence level respectively. Two-sided tests applied to all coefficients.

6. EU INTEGRATION, INDUSTRIAL RELOCATION AND LESSONS FOR POLICY

6.1. EU structural change

6.1.1. Nation states and industry black holes. As integration has proceeded, nation states have become more specialized. This process has been gradual. Our descriptive and empirical evidence suggests that location patterns may be slowly evolving towards industry black holes. Although agglomeration forces and comparative advantage appear to play some role in determining the patterns of specialization and concentration in the EU (see Midelfart-Knarvik *et al.*, 2000), the recent structural changes are not so clearly market driven. In particular there are signs that (1) changes in industrial structure are only weakly related to changes in endowments, and (2) the role of comparative advantage – differences in endowments – has not increased markedly as a result of integration. This problem is reinforced by EU policy interventions that attract R&D-intensive industries to locations without large endowments of high-skilled labour – an issue to which we return below.

6.1.2. Regional polarization.   Our evidence on regional relocation tells a different story, suggesting that emerging location patterns may be characterized by the idea of polarization. Specialization patterns across regions have remained stable while industrial activity has become more concentrated. This concentration has occurred in regions that already had large industrial shares. We find that integration has not facilitated an increased impact of agglomeration and dispersion forces in determining industrial location. At the same time, EU aid programmes attract R&D-intensive industries to regions receiving relatively high amounts of aid, but which are not abundantly endowed with high-skilled labour. Couple the results from the empirical analysis with those from the descriptive analysis, and this indicates that regional structural change may primarily be driven by agglomeration forces working *between* industries, as well as by policy interventions (see the discussion in Section 5.1).

6.2. What is the effect of policy?

EU expenditure partly distorts the relationship between changing endowments and changing industrial structure. The direct impact of EU expenditures is to attract high-skilled industries. Once we control for the effect of intervention, changes in the location of R&D-intensive industries reflect changes in country's endowments of high-skilled workers. The same is not true of low and medium-skilled endowments. If we take into account the impact of integration, we again see a similar story: Endowment of high-skilled workers has become more important for attracting R&D-intensive industries, while the direct impact of EU expenditures is also to attract high-skilled industries. Our findings at the regional level confirm the results based on national data: EU aid distorts the location of R&D-intensive industries.

Thus, for both regions and countries, EU expenditure has a particularly large positive impact on the location of R&D-intensive activities. To see why this expenditure is distortionary, consider Figure 6, which plots relative endowments of high-skilled workers and per capita EU expenditure for each country. The figure makes it clear that EU expenditure is attracting R&D industries to countries without the right endowments of high-skilled workers. We reach exactly the same conclusions when studying the impact of EU expenditure at the regional level.

The effects of national state aids are much less clearly identified. We cannot detect any specific effects of nation-state interventions. In particular, state aids targeted at R&D have no effect on the location of R&D-intensive activities. Our evidence suggests that given the overall patterns of aid expenditure, worries about state aid grossly distorting the location of specific industrial activities may be unwarranted.

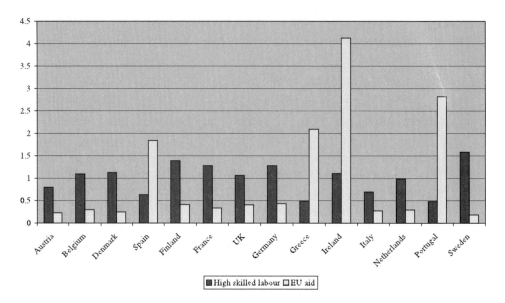

Figure 6. Endowment of high-skilled labour and provision of aid relative to the EU average

Notes: High-skilled labour is measured as share of a country's labour force using the average for 1993 and 1995. Aid is measured per capita and is based on the annual average 1994–96. EU aid includes social fund, regional fund and cohesion fund expenditure. All figures are relative to the EU average.

Source: European Commission (1995, 1998).

6.3. Lessons for policy

6.3.1. EU policy affects restructuring despite state aids.
Our evidence suggests that SF expenditure has had an impact on relocation patterns despite the fact that richer nations have high state aid expenditures that could potentially offset the effect of EU expenditure. This is true at both the national and the regional level. In particular, EU policy has affected the location of R&D-intensive activities.

6.3.2. The EU may still be right to emphasize overall reductions in state aids.
The EU argues for reductions in state aid because they distort restructuring and counter attempts to foster cohesion. Our findings do not provide much evidence for either of these arguments. This would appear to weaken the case for monitoring and reducing state aids. However, we would argue that member states should still welcome this effort. Countries believe that they can attract or retain industries by targeting them with state aid. Our findings suggest that this is not the case, given that everyone else is trying to do exactly the same thing. In particular, horizontal state aid to R&D does not help nation states attract additional R&D-intensive industries – the so-called high value-added industries. Unless there are other reasons to give state aids to these activities, countries should welcome attempts by the EU to coordinate reductions in overall expenditures.

6.3.3. Both vertical and horizontal aid may be distortionary. On average, EU intervention distorts the location of economic activity away from the patterns that would result if the underlying economic forces had played out. This distortion occurs despite the fact that all EU aid is effectively horizontal. Despite Commission assumptions to the contrary, horizontal aid can also distort adjustment even if it is targeted at activities rather than being sector specific, because industries vary with respect to the intensity with which they benefit from this aid.

6.3.4. Why Ireland's high-tech policy 'worked'. Our results on state aid suggest that the success of Ireland's high-tech policy relates to their substantial investment in education over the last decades. The evidence in Figure 6 shows that Ireland has many more high-skilled workers than the other Cohesion countries. Our analysis allows us to calculate what industrial structure would have been in the absence of aid. To do this, we take the results from our two specifications and predict shares in industries with the amount of EU aid set to zero and with the amount of EU aid at its actual level. We then use these two sets of predicted shares to recalculate the Krugman specialization index that we used in Section 3.[2] These calculations suggest that Ireland is the only Cohesion country that has become more specialized as a result of state and EU expenditures than it would have been without them. This suggests that Ireland's policy 'worked' because state and EU expenditures reinforced its comparative advantage and encouraged appropriate structural change rather than inhibiting it.

6.3.5. Is structural spending justified? EU aid is acting counter to market forces and distorting industrial restructuring. Of course, this is exactly what the Commission intended! If EU aid was supposed only to do what market forces would have done anyway, one might wonder what would be the point of EU aid at all. Deciding whether or not EU policy is justified involves resolving two tricky questions. First, is some sort of intervention justified? Second, is current EU policy the right sort of intervention? We will address each of these issues in turn.

Some sort of intervention is justified if market forces are taking us in a direction that is not desirable in terms of either efficiency or welfare. Given the EU's objectives on cohesion the evidence of polarization at the regional level presented in Section 3 would justify intervention on welfare grounds. But despite substantial intervention, with a significant and distortionary effect, the current SF programme is not preventing regional polarization.

There is no evidence of polarization at the national level. Both descriptive and empirical analysis indicates that agglomeration forces are stronger within than between industries. Couple this with the evidence on international mobility of

---

[2] Note that we use *predicted* shares with and without aid to make this comparison. Comparing actual shares to predicted shares without aid would bias our results because our regressions cannot explain all of the cross-country differences in industrial shares, so we would expect actual shares automatically to suggest higher specialization.

workers, firms and capital in the EU, and according to the theory in Section 2, we may expect a gradual emergence of industry black holes. Despite this, EU intervention could still be justified on efficiency and welfare grounds if the distribution of these black holes across locations is undesirable. The evidence on determinants of industry location and relocation suggests that this is not the case from an efficiency perspective, as comparative advantage is not found to be dominated by agglomeration forces. So what about the welfare argument that some black holes give higher returns? Economists have a natural aversion to policies based on this line of reasoning because they understand that the concept of 'high value-added' industries is fraught with difficulties. Most importantly the value-added for an industry will be a function of where that industry locates. In particular, industrial agglomeration in line with comparative advantage delivers the highest returns.

To summarize, there is a strong case for intervention at the regional level, but a much weaker case for intervention at the national level. The results presented in this paper provide some initial evidence that this may reflect differences in the role of market forces at the two spatial scales. However, our current understanding of industrial restructuring is such that we cannot rule out the possibility that part of the explanation may lie with the fact that policy interventions have been more successful at the national level but failed at the regional level. Regardless, our finding of regional polarization suggests that current interventions may not be doing the right thing to counter that polarization.

As we pointed out above, the EU's interventions in Ireland have helped Ireland to become more specialized. Interventions in the remaining three Cohesion countries have made these countries less specialized. One might counter that Ireland became specialized in the 'right sort of things'. But EU expenditure helped these other countries attract these types of activities (remember, our results go through if we drop Ireland from the regressions). This suggests that the payoff to this sort of policy was so much higher in Ireland because it tended to reinforce rather than counter comparative advantage. We would argue that the EU wants to refocus its interventions towards activities that better reflect and reinforce the comparative advantages of locations. In particular, we should be worrying about why relatively large increases in medium-skilled endowments are not translating into increases in production shares in medium-skilled industries. This matters because the poorer countries in the EU are precisely those that are seeing larger increases (the correlation coefficient between EU aid and changing medium-skill endowment is 0.34). Part of the problem is that the EU aid is so targeted at R&D-intensive activities that it is, at best, having no impact on medium-skilled industries. At worst, it is actually having a negative impact.

We reach a similar conclusion at the regional level. Despite interventions, our evidence suggests increased polarization at the regional level. Among the 30 Objective 1 regions, 20 have decreased their share in total EU value-added. This polarization has occurred at the very time that EU expenditures on regional intervention have increased dramatically. However, looking at the 10 better performing regions is very illuminating. Among the 10 regions that gained share, eight became more specialized. This suggests that policy should be refocused on encouraging specialization according to comparative advantage. There are two reasons why this is not occurring within countries. The first is that regional spending by the Commission is encouraging relocation counter to comparative advantage. The second is that regional comparative advantage (as opposed to national) is severely restricted by the fact that factor price returns tend to be equalized within nation states due to the centralized nature of wage setting.

This suggests that if the European Commission wants to advantage inhabitants in the poorest regions in Europe it needs to do three things. First, focus EU aid on helping regions change their endowments and specialize according to the resulting comparative advantage. Second, encourage member states to remove the factor price distortions that prevent dispersion as a result of differences in comparative advantage. Third, remove barriers to, or even encourage, internal mobility to achieve the most favourable outcome of a concentration of workers, capital and firms.

Polarization at the regional level calls for an urgent rethink on the way the EU operates its Structural Funds. Currently, too much emphasis is put on attracting 'high-tech clusters' of industries to poorer regions and countries. Instead, the Commission should be worrying about why changes in endowments are not feeding through to changes in production structure, and what it should be doing about this.

Discussion

Philip R. Lane
IIS, Trinity College Dublin and CEPR

This paper fits very well the aims of this journal by addressing a topic of major importance to European policy-makers. EU and national aid expenditures are motivated by a range of economic and political factors, and it is instructive to ask whether the outcomes of these aid programmes match any of the stated objectives. This study is also quite timely, in that a review of these funds feeds naturally into the debate stimulated by the accession process and the current Convention examining the future direction of the EU.

In their econometric work, the authors seek to explain the role of EU and national aid expenditures in determining changes in the share of industry i that is located in country j. Of course, this captures only a narrow part of the potential total impact of aid. For instance, the impact of aid on the growth of the services sector is not included in the study, nor is the impact of aid on the overall share of manufacturing in the total economy. The latter is noteworthy since the results in Tables 2–3 show that a country's share in total EU manufacturing is the most important single indicator of its share in any individual sector.

Due to data constraints, the authors are forced to examine industrial relocation over a narrow window: the change between 1990–93 and 1994–97 as a function of average aid flows over 1994–96. In the presence of adjustment costs, this interval is surely far too short to fully reflect the impact of aid on relocation patterns. Indeed, the descriptive statistics in Table 1 show that industrial structures change only very gradually.

Moreover, a more comprehensive dynamic structure is necessary to account properly for the impact of aid. On the one side, aid expenditures on education or physical infrastructure may only influence location choices with a substantial lag. On the other side, projections of future aid flows may also be important in determining some location decisions. Non-linearities are also potentially important: for instance, aid that is spent on enhancing infrastructure may have a high return if infrastructure quality is low, but will have little marginal impact once a threshold level is reached.

More data would also allow some key empirical questions to be addressed: for instance, does EU aid accelerate convergence to some equilibrium long-run pattern of industrial structures (which is not addressed by the authors here)? For these reasons, the results obtained here should be considered as extremely provisional in nature: once a longer span of data is available, a more conclusive study will be possible. In this regard, the provision by the European Commission of a comprehensive and up-to-date dataset on aid expenditures would be very welcome.

To avoid multi-collinearity problems, the authors offer two alternative regression specifications that underlie Tables 2 and 3. Each can be viewed as a restricted version of a more general model that cannot be feasibly estimated due to the lack of data. For this reason, at least one (or possibly both) of the regressions must be mis-specified: they cannot both be correct. Again, this reinforces the feeling that the results here are at best suggestive.

That said, the authors do find some interesting results. A potentially important finding is that high levels of aid are associated with an increasing share in the location of R&D-intensive industries. However, with a multi-stage production process, it is not automatic that the arrival of an R&D-intensive industry into a country implies an increase in R&D activity: the R&D may take place elsewhere, with only the final assembly or marketing stages migrating. Again, this is a feature of the Irish experience: the R&D score for the general computer or pharmaceuticals sectors overstates the amount of such activities being located in Ireland.

The authors calculate that Ireland is the only Cohesion country to show a positive relation between EU aid and increased specialization. However, my view is that there may not be any causal link: an alternative explanation for the rise in specialization is that there was a strategic decision in Ireland in the 1980s to target its domestic industrial policy efforts at attracting just two sectors (electronics and pharmaceuticals). Understanding why this 'picking winners' policy paid off so successfully would be an interesting case study in the growing literature on the determinants of industrial location.

More generally, the authors make the important point that EU and national policy interventions should be jointly studied: the fundamental issue is how all branches of government can influence the pattern of economic activity. This extends beyond direct aid expenditures: public spending on education, basic research and infrastructure, plus regulatory and procurement policies are all potentially important influences (see Brülhart and Trionfetti, 2000, on the latter). Studying the effectiveness of these various policies remains a high priority for those interested in the ongoing dynamics of the economic geography of Europe.

Jean-Marie Viaene
Erasmus University, CESifo and Tinbergen Institute

The appeal of the 'New Economic Geography' lies in its potential for throwing light on changing economic patterns across space as a result of policy. This is especially relevant in Europe where the moves towards deeper economic integration of existing member countries raise fears that small countries and those in the periphery may de-industrialize.

The objective of the paper is to look at the patterns of location, and relocation of EU industry as a result of government intervention. As structural changes seem to occur slowly the main empirical hypothesis of the paper is to verify whether interventions by member states and/or EU intervention schemes through Structural Funds altered the equilibrium pattern of location of industrial activity. The answer is yes, and it turns out that EU expenditures appear to be more distortionary than state aid.

Given the distortionary nature of government polices, one of the conclusions of the authors is that the EU and member countries should make attempts to reduce overall expenditures. However, there is no indication as to whether all forms of government intervention should be abolished. The economic literature has identified a number of arguments in favour of intervention, four of which are outlined below in decreasing order of importance. First, political economy considerations weigh heavily in favour of selective interventionism. Manufacturing is a small activity sector whose employment has declined in the last decades in all EU countries except Ireland. In 2000, for example, 14.5% of total employment in the Netherlands was working in manufacturing compared to 3.2% in agriculture, 6.0% in construction and 75.7% in services. In Greece, the share of the working force employed in manufacturing (14.1%) was lower than that in agriculture (17.0%). This declining role of manufacturing in economic activity is likely to affect the weighting of manufacturing producers relative to other groups in the welfare function of elected officials. Second, endogenous growth theory has shown how government activities turn out to have effects on long-run growth rates. An example of such a public good is the knowledge that governments create by sponsoring research. Public services of this kind have a positive effect on capital's marginal product. However, as there is the adverse impact of distorting taxation, the optimal provision is non-zero but finite. Third, government policy is inherent to economic geographic models because of the possibility of multiple equilibria: for given levels of transport costs, both agglomeration and diversification are possible. As these equilibria have a clear welfare ranking, policy in these models has an important role in selecting which equilibrium prevails. Fourth, we can also invoke the strategic trade argument. As most manufacturing industries are large exporters, also to non-EU countries, a small production subsidy in industries enjoying large market shares may be better than none. In the case of imperfect competition, however, there is first and foremost the issue of robustness.

In this paper, there is no attempt to derive plausible tests of the economic geography models against real alternatives. That is, the results of Tables 2 and 3 are given an interpretation in that sense, but they could possibly be derived from alternative theories. It is possible to derive an estimation equation of the form employed by the authors but using other frameworks. For example, assuming neoclassical production functions that are similar across countries and international capital mobility, we obtain that each region's share in industry output and share in physical capital stock is equal to the region's share in the stock of human capital. While a propensity to agglomerate in economic geography models requires increasing returns and transport costs, this result rests simply on the assumption of constant returns to scale and capital mobility. This alternative specification gives a role to (1) foreign direct investment from non-EU countries and (2) strategic education policies to foster local human capital in order to increase the marginal product of physical capital and thereby increase its share in the integrated economy's output.

The model and the empirical estimations typically assume that EU expenditures and state aid are independent observations. Crowding out of national aid as a result of EU intervention is therefore excluded though the authors have obtained a correlation coefficient between EU and state aids of −0.25. This result is a first indication of crowding out in the aggregate though there are too few data points to perform significance tests. However, the database of this research is rich enough to estimate crowding out parameters for each EU country and see whether this could be a cause of the lack for effectiveness of EU interventions in some regions.

Panel discussion

Karen Helene Midelfart-Knarvik and Henry Overman agreed with Philip Lane that data limitations meant caution was appropriate before drawing strong conclusions from their results. They agreed with Jean-Marie Viaene that the manufacturing sector is only a small part of the economy, but pointed out that no data with industry characteristics are available for the service sector across countries. They also suggested that the manufacturing sector might be considered a catalyst for other changes in the economy.

Carol Propper expressed concern about the endogeneity of aid, especially since poor countries lobby for aid. Henry Overman replied that it was unsurprising that aid did not show up as strongly endogenous in the results, since for endogeneity to matter a shock in the share of an individual sector needs to affect the aggregate amount of aid. The only industry for which a long-lasting decline indeed seems to have increased aid is the automobile sector.

Fiona Scott-Morton did not think that the fact that some of the regions were not richer after receiving aid could be taken as evidence that providing aid was not efficient. The counterfactual could very well be that these regions would have performed even worse otherwise.

Michael Devereux questioned the econometric specification. He expected increasing specialization to depend on what industries are already present in a region. He was also unsurprised by the apparent lack of impact of endowment changes, since the data covered too short a time period to expect substantial changes in skill.

Philip Lane wondered whether the apparent result that regions were attracting R&D-intensive industries might instead be driven by a feature of fast growing industries in general, namely that new entrants are more mobile than established firms.

Tito Boeri emphasized that EU aid and state aid represented two different kinds of policy. Whereas state aid tended be targeted more towards restructuring, EU aid served much more redistributive purposes. Jean-Marie Viaene stressed that it would depend on the objective function of the EU whether the policy of providing EU aid could be considered successful.

APPENDIX A: DATA

Our national level analysis is based on data for 14 EU member states (the EU 15 excluding Luxembourg). Our main data source is the OECD STAN database. This provides production data (gross value of output) for 13 EU countries and 36 industries, from 1970 to 1997. We combine this with production data for Ireland from the UN UNIDO database. UNIDO splits manufacturing into 27 industries, and the classification has been adjusted to be consistent with the STAN database. For more details on the data set see Midelfart-Knarvik et al. (2000a).

Our regional analysis is based on gross value-added data for ten EU countries. Regional disaggregated industry data are not available for Sweden, Finland, Austria and Greece. For the remaining countries we use NUTS 2 level data, for the period 1980–95 from Eurostat which splits the manufacturing sector into nine industries. Data on German regions has been estimated using national employment data. See Hallet (2000) for details.

National aid: Aid data is from the Fourth and Sixth Surveys on State Aid in the European Union (European Commission (1995, 1998). The data we use are averages for the years 1994–96 in million ECU per capita. State aid refers to total state aid to manufacturing, while EU aid refers to the sum of regional fund, social fund and cohesion fund expenditures.

Regional aid: Aid data is from European Commission (1997). EU aid refers to the sum of regional fund, social fund and cohesion fund expenditures in Objective 1 regions only. The data is the total sum for the years 1989–93 in million ECU per capita.

APPENDIX B: ECONOMETRIC SPECIFICATION

The equation estimated in Midelfart-Knarvik *et al.* (2000a) is:

$$\ln(s_i^k) = \alpha \ln(pop_i) + \beta \ln(man_i) + \sum_j \beta[j](y[j]_i - \gamma[j])(z[j]^k - \kappa[j]) \tag{B1}$$

Where s_i^k is the share of industry k in country i; pop_i is the share of population living in country i; man_i is the share of total manufacturing located in country i; $y[j]_i$ is the level of country characteristic j in country i; $z[j]^k$ is the industry k characteristic that we interact with country characteristic j. Finally α, β, $\beta[j]$, $\gamma[j]$ and $\kappa[j]$ are coefficients. We do not estimate our specification directly, but instead expand the relationship to give the estimating equation:

$$\ln(s_i^k) = \alpha \ln(pop_i) + \beta \ln(man_i) + \sum_j (\beta[j]y[j]_i z[j]^k - \beta[j]y[j]_i\kappa[j] - \beta[j]\gamma[j]z[j]^k)$$

For each time period, we estimate using OLS, pooling across industries. The left-hand side, population and manufacturing are four-year averages. Further details on the right-hand side variables, i.e. country, region and industry characteristics are provided in Appendix C.

We omit three sectors – petroleum refineries, petroleum and coal products, and manufacturing not elsewhere classified (essentially a residual component). There are potentially two important sources of heteroscedasticity – both across countries and across industries so we report White's heteroscedastic consistent standard errors. We use these consistent standard errors for all hypothesis testing.

To account for the role of policy we need to extend the estimation Equation B) to

$$\ln(s_i^k) = \alpha \ln(pop_i) + \beta \Delta \ln(man_i) + \sum_j \beta[j](y[j]_i - \gamma[j])(z[j]^k - \kappa[j])$$
$$+ \sum_p \beta[p](y[p]_i - \gamma[p])(z[p]^k - \kappa[p]) \tag{B2}$$

where $y[p]_i$ is the aid programme of type p in country i; $z[p]^k$ is the industry k characteristic that we interact with aid programme p.

Specification 1: The role of changing endowments and policy, is given by

$$\Delta\ln(s_i^k) = \alpha\Delta \ln(pop_i) + \beta \Delta \ln(man_i) + \sum_j \beta[j](\Delta y[j]_i - \gamma[j])(z[j]^k - \kappa[j])$$
$$+ \sum_p \beta[p](\Delta y[p]_i - \gamma[p])(z[p]^k - \kappa[p]) \tag{B3}$$

Specification 2: The role of economic integration and policy, is given by

$$\Delta\ln(s_i^k) = \Delta\alpha \ln(pop_i) + \Delta\beta \ln(man_i) + \sum_j \Delta\beta[j](y[j]_i - \gamma[j])(z[j]^k - \kappa[j])$$
$$+ \sum_p \beta[p](\Delta y[p]_i - \gamma[p])(z[p]^k - \kappa[p]) \tag{B4}$$

APPENDIX C: COUNTRY AND INDUSTRY CHARACTERISTICS

Industry characteristics

Because available data on industry characteristics is not very extensive we therefore have to rely on information that is not time varying.

A. Sales to industry: Percentage of domestic sales to domestic manufacturing as intermediate and capital goods.** Source: Input-output tables, OECD.

B.   Use of intermediates: Total use of intermediates as a share of gross value of output.**
     Source: Input-output tables, OECD.

C.   Economies of scale: Engineering estimates of increasing returns to scale. Source: Pratten
     (1988).

D.   Use of agricultural inputs: Use of agricultural inputs (incl. fishery and forestry) as share of
     gross value of output:** Source: Input-output tables, OECD.

E.   Use of skilled labour: Share of non-manual workers in workforce.* Share of labour com-
     pensation in gross value of output. Source: STAN, OECD, and COMPET, Eurostat.

F.   R&D intensity: R&D expenditures as share of gross value of output.* Source: ANBERD
     and STAN, OECD.

Notes:

*   As industry intensities are assumed to be equal across countries R&D shares of gross value
     of output are calculated as weighted averages. We use data for Denmark, Finland, France,
     Germany (former FRG), Italy, Netherlands, Spain, Sweden and the UK for the year 1990.

**   We use a weighted average of 1990 Input-output tables for Denmark, France, Germany
     and the UK to calculate intermediate input shares and the destination of final output
     (intermediate usage versus final usage). Intermediates include both domestically purchased
     and imported inputs. The data needed to calculate the industry intensities were in general
     not available for the 36 sectors disaggregation, so intensities calculated at a cruder level of
     disaggregation were mapped into the 36 sectors classification.

Country and region characteristics

Data on country characteristics are time varying. They are calculated for the same four-year
averages (1990–93 and 1994–97) as the production data where continuous time series were
available. If not, we use data for a year as close as possible to the beginning of the respective
time periods.

A. and C.   General market access: Indicator of economic potential based on gross value
            added. Source: Midelfart-Knarvik *et al.* (2000b).

B.   Market access to suppliers: Indicator of economic potential based on gross value-
            added and individual industries sales to manufacturing. Source: Midelfart-
            Knarvik *et al.* (2000b).

D.   Agricultural production: Gross value-added of agriculture, forestry and fishery
            products as a percentage of all branches. Source: Eurostat.

E.   Low and medium-skilled labour: National level: Share of population aged 25–59
            with at least secondary education. Source: Eurostat Yearbooks (levels for 1996–97),
            and Barro and Lee (1993) (for growth rates used to calculate other year values);
            Regional level: Share of population aged 25–59 with upper secondary education.
            Source: Table E14 in Eurostat (1997).

F.   High-skilled labour: National level: Researchers per 10 000 labour force. Source:
            OECD Science, Technology and Industry Scoreboard 1999. Regional level: Share
            of population aged 25–59 with more than upper secondary education. Source as
            above.

APPENDIX D: BETA COEFFICIENTS

Table D1 reports beta coefficients from OLS estimation of the specifications in Sections 5.2 and 5.3.

Table D1. The determinants of industrial relocation, Beta coefficients

Dependent variable	OLS	OLS	OLS
	National level analysis Specification 1	National level analysis Specification 2	Regional level analysis
	Change in share of a country in an industry between Period 1 and 2	Change in share of a country in an industry between Period 1 and 2	Change in share of a region in an industry between Period 1 and 2
Share of a location in EU population	−0.271***	−0.674**	0.004
Share of a location in total EU manufacturing	0.290***	0.833**	−0.274**
(A) General market access * Sales to industry	−0.245***	−0.227*	−0.363
(B) Market access to suppliers * Use of intermediates	0.364	1.985***	−0.907
(C) General market access * Economies of scale	−0.058	−0.145	−0.124
(D) Agricultural production * Use of agricultural inputs	0.003	0.621***	−0.033
(E) Medium skilled labour * Use of skilled labour	0.003	−0.239	0.227
(F) High skilled labour * R&D intensity	0.373*	0.339*	0.254
EU aid * Economies of scale	0.033	0.140	−0.426***
EU aid * Use of skilled labour	−0.138**	0.062	0.009
EU aid * R&D intensity	0.184**	0.664*	0.174***
State aid to shipbuilding	−0.028	0.007	
State aid to steel industry	−0.006	−0.025	
State aid to motor industry	−0.001	0.045	
State aid to R&D + innovation	−0.049	0.036	
State aid to SMEs	−0.038	0.071	
R squared	0.22	0.23	0.13
Number of observations	456	456	1040

Notes: Column 1 is for changes in variables A–F as per specification 1. Columns 2 and 3 are levels of variables A–F as per specification 2. ***, ** and * denote coefficient significantly different from zero with 1%, 5% and 10% confidence level respectively. Two-sided tests applied to all coefficients.

WEB APPENDIX

This may be downloaded free from http://www.economic-policy.org

REFERENCES

Amiti, M. (1999). 'Specialization patterns in Europe', *Weltwirtschaftliches Archiv*, 135, 1–21.

Baldwin, R. (1994). *Towards an Integrated Europe*, London: Centre for Economic Policy Research.

Barro, R.J. and J.W. Lee (1993). 'International Comparisons of Educational Attainment', *Journal of Monetary Economics*, 32(3), 363–94.

Braunerhjelm, P., R. Faini, V.D. Norman, F. Ruane and P. Seabright (2000). Integration and the regions of Europe: How the right policies can prevent polarization, *Monitoring European Integration* 10, Centre for Economic Policy Research, London.

Brülhart, M. (2001). 'Growing alike or growing apart? Industrial specialisation of EU countries', in C. Wyplosz (ed.), *The Impact of EMU on Europe and the Developing Countries*, Oxford: Oxford University Press.

Brülhart, M. and F. Trionfetti (2000). 'Public expenditure and international specialisation', DEEP Working Papers, No. 0023, University of Lausanne.

European Commission (1995). Fourth survey on state aid in the European Union in the manufacturing and certain other sectors. Luxembourg: Office for Official Publications of the European Communities.

European Commission (1997). The impact of structural policies on economic and social cohesion in the Union 1989–99. Luxembourg: Office for Official Publications of the European Communities.

European Commission (1998). Sixth survey on state aid in the European Union in the manufacturing and certain other sectors. Luxembourg: Office for Official Publications of the European Communities.

Eurostat (1997). Education across the European Union: Statistics and Indicators 1996. Luxembourg: Office for Official Publications of the European Communities.

Fujita, M., P.R. Krugman and A.J. Venables (1999). *The Spatial Economy: Cities, Regions and International Trade*, Cambridge, MA: MIT Press.

Hallet, M. (2000). 'Regional specialization and concentration in the EU', Economic papers No. 141 March 2000, European Commission, Brussels.

Krugman, P.R. (1991). *Geography and Trade*, Cambridge: MIT Press.

Krugman, P.R. and A.J. Venables (1990). 'Integration and the competitiveness of peripheral industries', in C. Bliss and C. de Macedo (eds), *Unity with Diversity in the European Community*, Cambridge: Cambridge University Press.

Martin, P. and C.A. Rogers (1995). 'Industrial location and public infrastructure', *Journal of International Economics*, 39.

Midelfart-Knarvik, K.H., H.G. Overman, S. Redding and A.J. Venables (2000a). 'The location of European industry', report prepared for the Directorate General for Economic and Financial Affairs, European Commission, Economic papers No. 142. April 2000. European Commission, Brussels.

Midelfart-Knarvik, K.H., H.G. Overman and A.J. Venables (2000b). 'Comparative advantage and economic geography: estimating the determinants of industrial location in the EU', CEPR Discussion Paper No. 2618.

Norman, V.D. (2000). Unpublished notes on trade and location.

Norman, V.D. and A.J. Venables (1995). 'International trade, factor mobility and trade costs', *Economic Journal*, 105.

Ottaviano, G.I.P. and D. Puga (1998). 'Agglomeration in the global economy: a survey of the new economic geography', *World Economy*, 21.

Pratten, C. (1988). 'A survey of the economies of scale', in *Commission of the European Communities: Research on the 'Cost of non-Europe'. II. Studies on Economic Integration*, Luxembourg: Office for Official Publications of the European Communities.

Union density
The economic roles of unions and institutions

SUMMARY

We study the evolution of union density in 14 European countries over the postwar period in light of theoretical rationales for union membership. Unions offer not only wage bargaining strength, but also protection against uninsurable labour market risks, and similar protection may also be offered by labour market institutions. Empirically, such institutions as job security legislation and wage indexation do appear to crowd out unions. Conversely, institutional features that make it easier for unions to function (such as workplace representation and centralized wage bargaining) are empirically associated with higher unionization.

— Daniele Checchi and Claudio Lucifora

Economic Policy October 2002 Printed in Great Britain
© CEPR, CES, MSH, 2002.

Unions and labour market institutions in Europe

Daniele Checchi and Claudio Lucifora

Università di Milano; Università Cattolica del Sacro Cuore, Milano

1. INTRODUCTION

Many workers are union members, pay union dues, let their pay be set by collective contracts, and participate in strikes and other forms of collective action. Trade unions exist since the industrial revolution, and economists typically take unions as a historically given feature when investigating how they affect labour market performance (Nickell, 1997; Nickell and Layard 1999; Blanchard and Wolfers, 2000). Unionization rates, however, have evolved rather sharply over the postwar period, and quite differently across countries. Are unions doomed in an environment of deeper integration and more intense competition? How do institutional reforms interact with union activities, and are reforms envisaged at the European Union level likely to affect the role and relevance of unions?

To answer, we first need to understand what motivates individuals to join unions. In this paper, we view unions as economic agents that supply private and collective services to their members, are financed by their members' contributions, and can be effective only if their membership is large. We go beyond the traditional view of

The Managing Editors, the discussants Tito Boeri and Jan van Ours, an anonymous referee, and panel participants provided very helpful comments. We also thank Giacomo Corneo and Robin Naylor for valuable suggestions, and Steve Nickell, Jelle Visser and the OECD for making data available to us. This paper has been written while Claudio Lucifora was visiting RSSS at the Australian National University whose hospitality is gratefully acknowledged. Financial support from CNR is also gratefully acknowledged. The usual disclaimers apply.
The Managing Editor for this paper was Giuseppe Bertola.

unions as rent-seeking entities, and consider an alternative view whereby unions can perform useful roles, not fulfilled by markets or government institutions, in a complex reality characterized by uninsurable risk, imperfect competition, and extensive government intervention. Then, we empirically investigate the competing hypotheses and discuss alternative scenarios in light of the economic and institutional characteristics of the countries and periods we consider. We focus our analysis, in particular, on the evolution of the share of union members among dependent workers, or union density, for which abundant comparable cross-country data is available.

1.1. Two views of unions

Unions can thrive and exist only if workers choose to be their members, and economic incentives to do so should be quite relevant in determining union density. In the traditional literature the main incentive to join the union lies in the appropriation of employer rents originating in the product market and in their distribution to members. In this context, unions – like any other monopolist – by controlling the labour supply end up distorting relative prices, reducing employment, and generating efficiency losses and poor economic performance (Boeri et al., 2001a). We shall refer to this as the 'bad view' of unionism.

However, individual union membership can also be motivated by inadequate insurance against unemployment and labour income risks (Agell, 1999, 2000). Then, unions play a useful role in an imperfect world, and in this 'good view' unions benefit risk adverse individuals whose demand for insurance is not satisfied by imperfect markets or by government intervention.

The two competing views of unionism have different empirical and policy implications. For example, from the 'bad' viewpoint product market regulation and protection from international competition should be associated with higher rents and higher unionization levels (Peoples, 1998; Blanchard and Giavazzi, 2001). We include in our regressions some variables meant to capture the existence of rents in the economy (Scarpetta, 2002); in particular, since the most regulated and protected employment is in the public sector, the rents associated with public sector jobs should empirically increase unionization (Freeman, 1984; Algan et al., 2002). From the 'good' viewpoint, conversely, it should be increasing exposure to international shocks to increase unionization, by raising the perception of job insecurity among the workers (Ebbinghaus and Visser 2000).

Not only the structure of economic interactions, but also institutions can affect the value of union membership and unionization patterns. Costs and benefits of union membership depend on whether the market or the state already provides similar services to workers. Empirically, institutions and economic conditions that make it more desirable or easier for unions to provide insurance should be associated with higher union density. Conversely, union density should be lower when insurance is already provided by a country's legislative framework, or less needed. State-provided unemployment insurance, employment protection legislation, and wage indexation can reduce labour market risks, and make unions redundant. Conversely, institutions such as workplace representation or centralization of bargaining make it easier for unions to perform their economic role, and should foster union membership. In either case, the interaction between 'substitute' and 'complementary' (to union activity) institutions makes it impossible to treat unionization as given, independently of other institutional features. Both the 'bad' view of unions, and the 'good' view, should lead researchers to consider unionization as variable to be explained by economic and institutional factors. We discuss these interactions in detail below, and we bring them to bear on empirical analysis including in our regressions a standard set of time-varying institutional variables.

The contrast between the two views and empirical results can offer useful policy insights. To the extent that the 'good' view of unions is empirically relevant, 'complementary' institutions that make it easier for unions to operate are to be considered beneficial, as they lower the costs of setting up institutions dealing with market failures. Similarly, the finding that unions are crowded out by 'substitutable' institutions introduced by benevolent governments (as much as the development of suitable insurance markets, or macroeconomic stability, might as well be desirable) would just confirm the view that unions play a welfare-enhancing role. If the alternative 'bad' view is correct, of course, 'complementary' institutions (such as workplace representation or centralization of bargaining) have more dubious policy appeal, since making it easier for unions to restrict labour supply has the same detrimental effects on efficiency losses as any other restriction to competition. Such policies may benefit union members and employed workers as a group, but impose even bigger losses on other economic agents. And 'substitutable' institutions may also be undesirable if they simply replace unions with similarly inefficient minimum wage and other constraints.

1.2. What we find

Demand for protection from labour market risks is likely to coexist with rent-seeking behaviour, and theory and empirical analysis can help us to assess the relative relevance of the 'good' and the 'bad' views. Empirically, we find that labour market institutions are important in explaining the differences in unionization patterns. Policies such as employment protection legislation, wage indexation, and statutory minimum wages appear to crowd out unions. Conversely, institutional features that make it easier for unions to function, such as workplace representation, and centralization of bargaining, have a positive effect. The results are less clear as regards the 'bad' view of unions. On the one hand, it appears that unions have been very successful in extracting rents and increasing membership in public sector jobs. On the other hand, the effects of decreasing rents on falling membership, as implied by product market deregulation and increasing openness of the economy, does not receive empirical support.

As always, empirical results have to be interpreted with care, and the question of whether unions may be able to provide security more efficiently than markets or state intervention is beyond the scope of our analysis in this paper. Similarly, we admit that institutions themselves might be endogenous in the long run, but the issue cannot be studied with available data. Still, our focus on individual workers' motivation to join unions does offer interesting insights into such deeper issues. Optimality of labour market institutions vis-à-vis the role of unions is not easy to assess in an imperfect world, and unions may or may not be beneficial for economic performance. Nevertheless, in the context of the ongoing debate concerning the flexibilization of European labour markets and the role of institutions which have been or are being designed to regulate the functioning of both product and labour markets – such as the Economic Monetary Union (EMU) process, the European Social Charter (ESC) and more generally the system of welfare provisions – we believe that our results offer implications both for the design of European institutions as well as for the future of trade unions in Europe.

In the next section we discuss in more detail theoretical reasons why union membership can be influenced by the institutional context and we review the relevant literature. Section 3 presents the data and the stylized facts concerning unionization patterns in postwar Europe. Section 4 reports the main set of results of the empirical analysis, Section 5 discusses different patterns across countries, and Section 6 discusses the policy implications of the results. A formal theoretical model, data and variable descriptions, and detailed econometric results are reported in the Web Appendix on http://www.economic-policy.org.

2. WHY DO UNIONS EXIST?

More than a century ago, Sidney and Beatrice Webb wrote: 'A trade union, as we understand the term, is a continuous association of wage earners for the purpose of improving the conditions of their employment' (Webb and Webb, 1894: p. 1). This definition already conveyed the modern view of unions as a coalition of workers meant to strengthen their hand in bargaining with their counterparts. However, different types of unionism have developed under different institutional settings. Remarkable differences can be observed between North America and Europe (especially Continental Europe). In the former, firms become unionized only after 30% of workers have signed a petition calling for an election and half of the workers have voted in a ballot for union admission (Kremer and Olken, 2001). Thus workers can choose between union and non-union workplaces (or, using a Tiebout analogy, choose to become members with their feet), and self-sorting of workers makes it difficult to assess the effects of union presence (Card, 1998; Farber, 2001). While in 'closed shop' systems, employment by a unionized firm entails union membership; in Europe unions provide mostly public goods, since collective contracts are (mandatorily, or *de facto*) extended to all workers regardless of union membership. In such an 'open shop' context, it is not easy to account for union membership in terms of self-interested behaviour (see Box 1 for alternative explanations). Unions, however, provide not only collective bargaining services, but also such excludable benefits as legal and pension advice, grievance and promotion procedures, preferential manning and shift-work negotiation, subsidized access to medical aid, pension and insurance schemes (Booth and Chatterji, 1995).

2.1. 'Bad' versus 'good' unions

As mentioned, labour economists typically adopt a 'bad' view of unions as collusive organizations engaged in rent extraction. If higher wages reduce labour demand, unions have monopoly power, and collective bargaining makes it possible to obtain higher wages and (despite employment losses, which are small when demand is not very responsive to wages) a higher wage bill. There is, however, an alternative 'good' view of unionism, as provider of (second best) redistribution against uninsurable risk (Agell, 2000). This has received less attention in the literature, and deserves to be discussed in more detail.

Consider a situation where all markets exist and are perfectly competitive. Then, there will be no rents, resources will be efficiently allocated across heterogeneous agents: for example, individuals who are more risk averse or more exposed to job loss will buy more insurance against inflation or unemployment, older agents will save less for retirement, and so on. Of course, a coalition of agents could collude and try to exploit monopoly power by forming a union. However, the pressure of competition could easily prevent credibility of the coalition pact, since individual workers would generally benefit from increasing their labour supply. And if the benefits of collusion accrue to workers regardless of their participation in union activities (as is the case of 'open shop' arrangements), then 'free riding' considerations cast further doubts on the feasibility of monopolistic union behaviour in such a context.

In reality, of course, competition is not perfect, and there exist product market rents. Then, it is desirable and may be possible for workers to appropriate part of

---

Box 1. Theoretical literature on union density

The literature proposes several models of union membership. If the collective benefits of union activity are available to all workers at no cost, individual workers would obviously prefer others to pay the costs of union activity, and unions should have no members. To escape from this free-riding paradox, one line of research follows the so-called *social custom approach*. The membership of unions that yield collective benefits can be positive in equilibrium if unions also grant their members a 'good societal values' reputation, and a reputation to, for example, be caring and supportive is privately valued by workers (Booth,

1985). Union density and bargained real wages can be determined in equilibrium, with threshold effects, if different workers assign different values to social
reputation; and pro-union legislation and lower membership costs increase
union density in that equilibrium (Naylor and Cripps, 1993). Employers and
union activists obviously have opposite objectives in strategic interactions, and
the size of the workers' surplus and the degree of bargaining centralization
can be shown to affect equilibrium union density (Naylor and Raaum, 1993;
Corneo, 1995). And if the value of reputation depends on the number of
'believers' (Akerlof, 1980), equilibrium density can be higher or lower depending
on whether 'conformist' or 'elitist' attitudes prevail in the worker population
(Corneo, 1997).

An alternative line of research considers provision of *private goods* to union
members. If unions can obtain preferential treatment for their members in,
e.g., layoff procedures, then workers join the union in order to obtain some
insurance against unemployment, and non-members (the first to be laid off)
are excluded from the benefits of union activity. Again, a variety of modelling
features can affect equilibrium union density in this framework. If workers
have different attitudes towards the risk of unemployment, the more risk-averse
become union members, and higher unemployment risk tends to increase
union density (Booth, 1984). Of course, wage, unemployment and union density are jointly determined in equilibrium, and membership can be a decreasing
function of unemployment if union bargaining power and labour supply
play a role in equilibrium (Booth and Chatterji, 1995). But an exogenous
increase of employment probabilities lowers the value of union insurance, and
union density, thus decreasing the expected gain of becoming a union member (Jones and McKenna, 1994). If employers follow a last-in first-out rule in
layoffs, and seniority also plays a role in union voting, membership increases
with past employment (Burda, 1990; Grossman, 1983). If unions increase on-
the-job training rather than job security, less skilled workers are more likely to
unionize (Acemoglu *et al.*, 2000), and in general if unions offer other exclusive
services to their members (such as financial advice and legal support) union
density is an increasing function of the quality of such services provided (Booth
and Chatterji, 1995).

Both strands of the literature provide testable predictions. Union membership should be positively correlated with solidarity values, with labour productivity (since it increases available surplus), and with bargaining centralization
according to the first theoretical perspective; and with unemployment risk
(with possibly different signs at different levels of aggregation) and employment
rates (in light of last-in-first-out layoffs procedures) according to the second
theoretical perspective. Both approaches predict that more costly or less effective union activity should reduce membership.

those rents (Blanchard and Giavazzi, 2001). Government policies could of course accomplish redistribution from profit to wages (i.e. through appropriate fiscal policy), but political lobbying may well be more costly and cumbersome than unionized labour market bargaining. Further, there may be missing markets for risk and insurance. Again, government intervention may be desirable: for example, the absence of appropriate markets can justify state provision of unemployment insurance and pension schemes, and firing restrictions could also enhance efficiency in such a context (Aghion and Hermalin, 1990). If not the government, then coalitions of economic agents (like unions) can perform a similarly useful role in an imperfect world, addressing income and employment risks and other market failures.

So, why unions rather than political parties? Unions are likely to be better informed than political parties as regards labour market imperfections, and they cooperate with employers in running training programmes (in Germany) or with the state in running unemployment schemes (in the Ghent countries). And, in comparison to political parties that have to mediate with other social groups, unions are more directly representative of workers' interests. Monitoring of union leaders by union members (and vice versa) may reduce the scope for opportunistic behaviour and foster accountability, and an individual seeking insurance against income or unemployment risk may well join a union and 'buy' a well-defined protection package through membership fees, rather than vote for a political party whose policy package holds similar promise but may or may not be implemented once in power.

2.2. Theoretical interactions

This perspective on union activities can be made precise in the context of a labour market where individuals are risk averse and heterogeneous with respect to employment probability. One may think of differences in job search (ability or intensity), or in retention probability.[1] Unions act as monopolist wage setters and maximize the utility of the median member, so that the negotiated wage will not necessarily coincide with that preferred by the median worker. Since employers cannot discriminate, the negotiated wage is the same for both members and non-members, and gives no incentives to join the union. However, if unions can increase their members' employment probability (by supplying information on job opportunities, opposition to firing, and off-the-job training) then the cost of union dues can be offset by the benefit of higher employment probability. Note that without this excludable good – since wages are the same for members and non-members – free riding would drive membership to zero, and wages to the competitive level. Individuals with low employment

[1] We follow the model proposed by Booth (1984), in which workers are heterogeneous with respect to the alternative wage in the non-union sector (due to their different degree in risk aversion). Firms follow discriminatory rules for hiring (unions members are hired first), as would be the case in a closed shop environment. In a different context, Jones and McKenna (1994) model union membership dues as an insurance premium to reduce the impact of random shocks on job security.

probability benefit more from union membership, which therefore includes a well-defined subset of the heterogeneous worker population. Workers at the margin of this subset are indifferent to joining the union, since the expected benefits of membership are equal to its costs.[2]

In this context, higher risk or more pronounced risk aversion raise the net benefit of membership, and imply higher union density (see the Web Appendix for a formal model). Labour market institutions can play straightforward roles in such a framework. For example, other things equal, an increase in the ability of the union to provide employment protection or income insurance increases the value of membership, and implies higher union density. Conversely, higher employment or income protection reduces risks for incumbent workers, makes union-supplied protection less valuable, and reduces membership. In the case of employment protection, labour market institutions that are 'complementary' to union activity, like the right to be defended by union officers in legal litigation, tend to increase union membership. Conversely, institutions that, independently from union membership status, operate so as to reduce workers' need to be protected by the unions (e.g., reducing the overall risk of unemployment for incumbent workers), by acting as 'substitutes' to union activity determine a reduction in union membership.

A similar argument applies to unemployment benefit schemes, and details of their administration offer a particularly clear example. When unemployment benefits are paid by the state, higher unemployment can be expected to reduce union membership, since unemployed workers have no reason to pay union membership fees. However, in the so-called 'Ghent' system (currently observed in Finland, Belgium, Sweden and Denmark) unemployment insurance schemes are run by trade unions, and partially subsidized by the state. Hence, higher unemployment increases the value of union membership, and can imply a positive relationship between unemployment and union density. In other words, the association between labour market performance and unionization depends on the scope and design of the institutional setting – in this case unemployment insurance schemes – which might be seen as 'complementing' (i.e. under the 'Ghent' system) or 'substituting' (i.e. when paid by the state) the insurance role of unions.

As to the real wage protection granted by the unions through collective bargaining, its relevance also depends on institutional features. Higher inflation may increase the value of union bargaining activity as an insurance device against reductions in purchasing power, but institutions may work as a 'substitute' to union bargaining activity (i.e. when wage indexation mechanism are in place), or a 'complement' if real wage protection is easily extended to all workers (i.e. when wages are bargained centrally or mandatory provision for collective contract exist).

---

[2] Similarly, Acemoglu *et al.* (2000) assume that less skilled workers have an incentive to become union members because under firing restrictions firms find it convenient to train them.

If union membership is associated with a higher expected income (because unions offer unemployment insurance schemes, as in Ghent countries), workers with higher unemployment risks are more likely to join the union.[3] Conversely, when unemployment benefits are provided unconditionally, union unemployment insurance schemes lose value and membership declines. More generally it can be argued that labour market institutions providing unconditional protection for the unemployed – *ceteris paribus* – will reduce the incentive to join the union, while insurance schemes that exclude non-members increase the expected gain from unionization. Alternatively, with respect to income insurance, it could be argued that risk averse workers are prepared to pay a premium (i.e. union dues) to be insured against (real) income variability.[4] If union members rely on renegotiation of wages to obtain some insurance, union membership is valuable. However, when automatic indexation clauses are introduced, the benefit of renegotiation declines, and so does membership.[5] Hence, any kind of automatic wage indexation mechanism – *ceteris paribus* – reduces the scope for union activity, thus making union membership less valuable. The value of any insurance mechanism, however, is higher in periods of high turbulence (e.g. those of the oil shocks) and, for any given level of institution, also the value of union bargaining depends on its effectiveness to reduce income variability.

Finally, consider the supply of union activity. Unions collect membership dues to pay for staff and equipment, and use such factors to deliver protection to their members. The 'technology' for doing that is in many ways influenced by institutional features such as the right to workplace representation, strikes regulations, procedures for workers' recruitment and payment of union dues, and protection of union activists from discriminatory dismissals. Allowing the presence of union representatives in each workplace and protecting them from dismissal reduces the cost of union services and/or increases their effectiveness.[6] Thus we can derive a prediction that labour market institution directed at lowering the cost of organizing a union have – *ceteris paribus* – a positive effect on membership.

Of course, the role of other institutions is not as easy to analyse in the simple stylized framework outlined above, and cultural and historical factors may also be quite relevant in determining union membership. As to welfare effects, it is difficult

[3] Blanchflower *et al.* (1990) find that local unemployment is a significant predictor of regional membership (in Great Britain in 1984), and explain this effect as a consequence of union status reducing the risk of lay-off. A similar explanation is invoked for a similar result by Andrews and Naylor (1994) (who referred to the 1980–84 period in Great Britain).

[4] Similarly, real wage fluctuations could be induced by productivity fluctuations (technological shocks, variation in intermediate input supplies, etc.) in a context of nominal wage setting.

[5] The Italian experience provides a paramount example of this phenomenon. In 1983 the Italian government reduced the coverage of the indexation mechanism (*scala mobile*) that had been operating since 1958. While a referendum was called for to re-establish the indexation mechanism, Italian trade unions (CISL, UIL and a fraction within the biggest confederation of unions, the CGIL) opposed this choice, on the ground that full indexation was reducing unions' scope in wage bargaining. The referendum was then held in 1984, and expressed against the re-establishment of the old system.

[6] There is empirical evidence of favourable effect of the institutional context onto union membership: Freeman and Pelletier (1990) show the significance of a 'legal index' measuring the attitudes towards the unions of the government in place; Pehkonen and Tanninen (1997) use a step-variable measuring the change in the pro-union attitude of the government; Checchi and Corneo (2000) use a step-variable to control for the introduction of a worker charter favouring unionization at workplaces.

to evaluate whether unions are superior to state-provided insurance in offering unemployment/inflation insurance schemes. On the one hand, worker-level organization implies better monitoring of individual behaviour (for example in the effort of job search), with beneficial effects whenever information problems (moral hazard, adverse selection) can be detrimental to a good functioning of the scheme. On the other side, unions historically represent dependent employees and therefore have problems in granting universal coverage, whereas state-provided schemes are more likely to extend coverage to other segments of labour force. On the whole it is hard to say whether state bureaucracy with extended universalism is better than union provision with limited coverage.

3. UNIONIZATION IN EUROPE: DATA AND STYLIZED FACTS

Our analysis is constrained by limited availability of institutional information, which is scarce and often restricted to some point in time. We were able, however, to collect and organize consistently an extensive data set, covering 14 European countries over the postwar period.[7]

3.1. Data availability and existing empirical studies

The most widely used measures of union presence are union membership, union coverage and strike activity. Membership, the number of workers who pay union dues, is a good measure of demand for union representation: for members, unions deliver more economic value than the dues they pay. Union coverage refers to the number of workers paid according to collective contracts, regardless of whether they are union members, and is relevant to the unions' bargaining power as well as to the degree of universalism in union claims. Finally, strike activity proxies the potential effectiveness of union threat.

In light of our theoretical framework, membership is determined by demand for insurance that fails to be satisfied by markets or government policies. Accordingly, we analyse union density, the ratio of gainfully employed union members (excluding unemployed and retired members) to employment. Attention must be paid to changes, over time in some countries, in the definition of membership. We have data on union density for the 1950–98 period in most countries (except Belgium, 1950–95; Denmark and Italy, 1950–97; and Spain, 1981–97). Information on time-varying institutions is available from the 1960s onwards, and restricts the sample available for econometric analysis. Data definitions and sources are fully described in the Web Appendix.

---

[7] The countries are: Austria, Belgium, Denmark, Finland, France, Great Britain, Ireland, Italy, the Netherlands, Norway, Spain, Sweden, Switzerland and Germany (West Germany until 1989). The data range from the 1950s to the end of the 1990s.

Similar, but smaller samples have already been analysed by Western (1997), Lange and Scrugg (1999), Oskarsson (2001) and Checchi and Visser (2001). This literature typically controls for unemployment schemes administration ('Ghent' or not) and workplace representation. We expand the set of institutions potentially affecting union density, by including several others indicators, such as employment protection, unemployment benefit (both replacement rate and benefit duration), minimum wage legislation, mandatory extension of contracts, bargaining structure, tax wedge and product market regulation.

The literature has proposed alternative explanations for the dynamics of union density, which can be roughly grouped into different categories. First, *business cycle factors* typically include unemployment and inflation rates. Second, *compositional effects* such as sectoral employment shares, age, gender and skill composition of the labour force. Third, selected *institutional variables* like Ghent-like unemployment subsidies and workplace representation (Freeman and Pelletier, 1990; Oskarsson, 2001), the degree of wage setting centralisation (Ebbinghaus and Visser, 1999), the degree of financial openness and political attitude of governments (Lange and Scrugg, 1999). While taking into account economic factors and compositional effects, in the remainder of the paper we shall focus on the effects of a wider set of labour market institutions on union density.

3.2. The effects of institutions on union density

Given our focus on the effects of institutions on the incentives for individual workers to join a union, we briefly review existing information on labour market institutions in the recent economic and industrial relations literature. We restrict our attention to explicit and quantifiable measures of institutional forces, in order to be able to measure their impact on union density. Restricting the scope in this way avoids excessive arbitrariness in defining the relevant institutions.

In the economic literature some institutional indicators have proved capable of explaining a great deal of differences in the structure and dynamics of wages and (un)employment across countries.[8] Similarly, the industrial relations literature has stressed the importance of institutional arrangements in the rise or the decline of unions in Western countries.[9] While reviewing this extensive literature is beyond the scope of the present paper, we discuss some results that are relevant to our research. The other aspects, related to employment/unemployment and wage setting, are reported in Box 2. We group existing institutions under different headings, as reported in Table 1.

---

[8] See, among others, Bertola (1990), Layard *et al.* (1991), Grubb and Wells (1993), Nickell (1997), Gregg and Manning (1997), Nickell and Layard (1999), OECD (1999), Garibaldi and Mauro (1999), Blanchard and Wolfers (2000), Belot and van Ours (2000), Boeri *et al.* (2000), Bertola *et al.* (2001).

[9] See Hancké (1993), Visser (1993), Western (1997), Golden *et al.* (1997), Waddington and Whitston (1997), Lange and Scrugg (1999), Ebbinghaus and Visser (1999), Checchi and Visser (2001), Oskarsson (2001), Lipset and Katchanovski (2001), Traxler *et al.* (2001).

Table 1. Classification of labour market institutions

Labour market institutions	Effect on employment	Effect on wages	Expected effect on density
Employment protection: * advanced notice for dismissal * protection against unfair dismissal * regulation of fixed term contract * temporary work agency * working time regulation	Limited effect on unemployment level Significant effect on (un)employment composition and on net job creation	Increases bargaining power ↓ Increases bargained wage	Substitute for union protection ↓ Less incentives to join the union
Unemployment benefit: * replacement rate * benefit duration * administrative responsibility on unions	Increases unemployment	Increases outside option ↓ Increases bargained wage	Reduces job insecurity *but* reward unions if they have administrative responsibility
Extension of bargaining outcomes: * wage indexation * coverage * mandatory extension * minimum wages	Increases unemployment (sometimes in combination with union density)	Lowers impact of unemployment on bargaining power ↓ Increases bargained wage	Incentive to free-ride on union outcomes ↓ Less incentives to join the union
Employee rights: * representation rights * work council * voting rights	No effect on unemployment levels	Increases bargaining power ↓ Increases bargained wage (and sometimes productivity)	Stricter contact with union representatives ↓ Reduces the cost of unionizing workers
Bargaining structure: * coordination among unions * coordination with employer representatives * centralization	Reduces unemployment (possibly in a non-linear way)	Internalizes adverse effect of high wages ↓ Reduces bargained wage	Lowers managerial opposition and inter-union competition ↓ Reduces the cost of unionizing workers
Tax wedge: * payroll taxes * income taxation * consumption taxation	Increases unemployment if higher labour costs are required to sustain welfare provision	Higher wage pressure under real wage resistance	Stronger demand for union protection *but* Higher provision of welfare benefits
Product market regulation: * entry regulation * state intervention * barriers to trade and investment	Reduced firm competition increases unemployment (higher rents and lower competitiveness)	Higher rents increases bargained wage	Higher rents may trigger union formation in order to boost wage share
Wage compression: * decile ratios in earnings distribution * sectoral wage differential	Increases unemployment for less skilled workers	Reduces pay flexibility ↓ Increases bargained wage	Increased unionization among low skilled *but* declines among high skilled workers

Box 2. Employment and wage effect of labour market institutions

Theory and evidence suggest that employment protection *per se* does not raises unemployment, but may lower employment rates, job creation and unemployment turnover, thus increasing the share of long-term unemployed people (Grubb and Wells, 1993; Bertola, 1990; Nickell, 1997; Nickell and Layard, 1999; OECD, 1999; Garibaldi and Mauro, 1999; Blanchard and Wolfers, 2000). However, Bertola *et al.* (2001) show a positive effect of employment protection on unemployment when it is interacted with different types of shocks (wage share, real interest rate, total factor productivity, change in inflation and youth population share). Some aspects of employment protection have also some impact on price setting inertia and unemployment hysteresis (Layard *et al.*, 1991: p. 417).

With respect to the second group of institutions measuring the extent of subsidization of unemployed, the consensus among economists is that they increase unemployment because they lower search intensity (Nickell, 1997; Nickell and Layard, 1999; Blanchard and Wolfers, 2000). Similarly, mandatory extension of wage bargaining and/or legislated minimum wages could have a positive impact on unemployment because of the effect on the average wage level and downward flexibility of wages (especially among unskilled workers and first job seekers – see Dolado *et al.* 1996; Bertola *et al.*, 2001). These institutions increase both the bargained wage (through a reduced effect of unemployment onto wage) and its persistence, thus raising unemployment hysteresis. In addition, indexation schemes reduce stickiness of nominal wages, and thus increase real rigidity, even without affecting the NAIRU (Layard *et al.*, 1991).

Employee rights are often measured together with employment protection (Nickell and Layard, 1999). While there are no strong theoretical arguments to expect direct effects on unemployment, some impact can be detected in wage setting, when proxied by employment share in firms with less than 100 employees: a higher share of employees in small size firms induces more wage flexibility and therefore less unemployment and hysteresis (Layard *et al.*, 1991). The (mandated) existence of work councils in most countries may improve cooperative attitudes among the workers, and therefore productivity (Rogers and Streeck, 1995).

With respect to institutional aspects of wage bargining, starting from the seminal paper by Calmfors and Driffill (1988), it has gone uncontested that centralized bargaining induces less unemployment via wage moderation (alternative channels of influence are discussed in Calmfors, 1993). Evidence of positive effect on unemployment of alternative measures of centralized wage setting is reported in several papers (Nickell, 1997; Nickell and Layard, 1999; OECD, 1999; Bertola *et al.*, 2001). With respect to wage setting, bargaining centralization and inter-union/inter-firm coordination work in the same direction, by raising wage elasticity to unemployment and reducing the NAIRU (Layard *et al.*, 1991: p. 418).

Labour taxation has more or less obvious negative effects on employment rates (Nickell, 1997; Nickell and Layard, 1999; OECD, 1999; Garibaldi and Mauro, 1999; Bertola *et al.*, 2001), which can be attenuated by centralized wage setting (Daveri and Tabellini, 2000). With respect to wage setting, the higher is the real wage resistance, the higher will be labour costs and the related employment loss (Layard *et al.*, 1991).

In the first group we consider different aspects of *employment protection*. If unions act as substitutes for employment protection, a negative impact is anticipated on union density: the stricter is labour market regulation vis-à-vis dismissals, the lower the risk of unemployment for currently employed members, the lower will be the demand for union protection.[10] However, if union shop stewards are at risk of being fired then employment protection, by lowering the cost of union activity in the workplace, may mitigate the negative impact of those measures on union density.

A second group of institutions include variables measuring *unemployment subsidies,* while in the third we consider *mandatory extension of collective contracts* (usually measured through union coverage[11]) and *statutory minimum wages*. The effect of these two groups of institutional measures on union density can be ambiguous. On the one hand, unemployment benefits can be taken as an indicator of pro-labour attitudes of governments (effectively proxying for welfare provisions – see Checchi and Visser, 2001),[12] on the other hand, several authors have stressed the importance of a voluntary but publicly supported scheme of unemployment insurance directly administered by the unions or simply dominated by the union (Ghent system type of arrangements – see Lange and Scrugg, 1999; Ebbinghaus and Visser, 1999; Checchi and Visser, 2001; Oskarsson, 2001; Lipset and Katchanovski, 2001).[13] However, if a compulsory system is administered by government agencies then demand for insurance provided by unions is expected to be lower.

[10] This may not necessarily be true when the risk of dismissal is unevenly distributed in the population (Saint-Paul, 1996). In such a case, the effect on density could be reversed.

[11] The extent of union coverage is usually tested in combination with a measure of union density (Nickell, 1997; Nickell and Layard, 1999, Blanchard and Wolfers, 2000, Bertola *et al.*, 2001), but the two variables are hardly jointly significant.

[12] On the account that 'historical experience suggests that union movements have grown where unions control unemployment benefits, the labour market is centrally organised and social democratic parties with close ties to organised labour have been in power . . .' (Western, 1997: pp. 87–88), some authors include left voting (or left share in Parliament seats) among the explanatory variables for union density (Western, 1997; Lipset and Katchanovski, 2001 – also Oskarsson, 2001 includes left voting without finding any statistically significant effect). Similarly, some authors (Western, 1997, Checchi and Corneo, 2000) make use of strike activity as an explanatory variable for union density. Since we consider these variables as potentially endogenous, we use it only as additional controls in Appendix D.

[13] See Holmlund and Lundborg (1999) for discussion of this issue.

The fourth group of variables measures *employee rights*, such as establishment-level workplace representatives. This feature is sometimes pooled with employment protection and other measures (see Nickell and Layard, 1999), but there is evidence suggesting that workplace representation *per se* can be very effective in raising membership (Hancké, 1993),[14] since it ensures that union services are available only to union members (Booth and Chatterji, 1995). With respect to union density, it has been argued that it is the combination of bargaining and locally strong unions that can exert positive influence on the union density level, hence showing positive effects of (alternative) measures of workplace representation (Lange and Scrugg, 1999; Ebbinghaus and Visser, 1999; Oskarsson, 2001).

The fifth group relates to institutional features of *wage bargaining*. As far as union density is concerned, a centrally organized union gains new members because of reduced managerial opposition, increased public recognition and easier access to sites and business. Evidence of positive effect of centralization on density are reported in Western (1997) (associated with Left-party representation in government), Lange and Scrugg (1999) (in combination with workplace access and Ghent-type unemployment benefits, yielding a single measure of 'union compatible institutions'), Ebbinghaus and Visser (1999), Checchi and Visser (2001) (where the measure of centralization combines the distribution of bargaining authority, vertical coordination, with the distribution of members, horizontal coordination), and Oskarsson (2001) (who combines indices of organizational inter-union coordination with measures of centralization of wage bargaining).

The sixth group of institutions concerns *labour taxation*. Its effects on union density are less clear-cut from a theoretical point of view. To the extent that taxes on labour serve to finance public welfare provisions, by redistributing resources to marginal workers may reduce the insurance and risk-reducing role unions (Moore *et al.*, 1989), in this respect union density could be expected to be negatively correlated with taxes. However, labour taxes may also imply a higher tax wedge and lower net wages, which may push workers to call for stronger union protection (Daveri and Tabellini, 2000).[15]

The seventh group of institutions is related to *product market regulation*. Standard theoretical analysis suggests that increased competition among firms in the national market (Blanchard and Giavazzi, 2001) and the removal of barriers to external competition, by reducing the available economic rents, lowers bargained wages and raises – in the long run – employment prospects. Alternatively, since higher external exposure may induce higher economic volatility and uncertainty, a risk-reducing role by government redistribution or union protection might be desirable (Rodrik, 1998). Empirical evidence also suggests that countries with highly regulated product market

---

[14] A thorough discussion of the relevance of recruiting methods is provided in Waddington and Whitston (1997).

[15] High taxes are more likely to be found in social-democratic (pro-worker) political environments and, to the extent that our measures of 'complementary' institutions do not appropriately control for pro-union policies, can be associated with higher union density.

(mostly Mediterranean countries) also exhibit higher unemployment and a larger share of self-employment (Boeri *et al.*, 2000; Nicoletti *et al.*, 2000, Nicoletti and Scarpetta, 2001). Since product and labour market regulations strengthen each other, it may be hard to disentangle the relative (net) contribution of each variable for unionization patterns. On the basis of the above discussion, there are no clear-cut predictions about the effect of market regulation and openness on union density. To the extent that market regulation raises the available surplus and unions are perceived by workers as rent seekers (at the expenses of outsiders), it will benefit union formation. Alternatively, if the lowering of product market regulations and/or barriers to external competition is associated with higher labour market risks, the value of union protection can (positively) affect the demand for unions.

An additional feature, which has received little attention mainly due to lack of data, is *wage compression* that can be correlated with both unemployment and union density. In recent papers, Kahn (2000) and Bertola *et al.* (2001) have drawn attention to wage compression as a potential factor explaining the different unemployment performance of the United States *vis-à-vis* Europe. In that framework, downward rigidity of low wages would translate in lower employment opportunities for low-skill workers.[16] One problem with this explanation is that wage dispersion is endogenous and tightly associated with other labour market features, and this makes it difficult to disentangle the empirical roles of minimum wages, mandated extension of wage bargaining, and direct union activity (DiNardo *et al.*, 1996).

3.3. The facts

In Figure 1 we plot the evolution of (aggregate) unionisation for 14 European countries since the postwar period. The solid line shows the employment weighted average of net union density, and the two dotted lines report variation of national union density levels around the average. Unionization patterns exhibit first a moderate decline, from an average of 45% in the early 1950s, followed by a rapid increase throughout all the 1970s and a steady decline from the 1980s onwards.[17] The dotted lines suggest the existence of a significant dispersion – which has been increasing over time – across countries, from 12% in France to more than 80% in Sweden in the mid 1990s.[18]

---

[16] Card (1998) has raised doubts on this traditional explanation on the basis of self-selection among potential union members.

[17] We tested the existence of different growth rates across the three periods (1950–65, 1966–80, 1981–98) by running a simple regression in first differences with period dummies and testing the null of similar coefficients within periods. We could not reject the hypothesis at the 5% level for the first two periods and at the 10% level for the last period.

[18] As a measure of variability we computed the standard deviation of country unionization rates over the sample period. The inclusion of Spain in the last decade of the sample period partly contributes to the observed increase in dispersion. However, the exclusion of Spain from the sample reduces only marginally (less than 5%) the standard deviation of unionization rates. The turning point at the end of the 1970s is mainly attributable to Italy and Great Britain's union density: see Figure C1 in Appendix C.

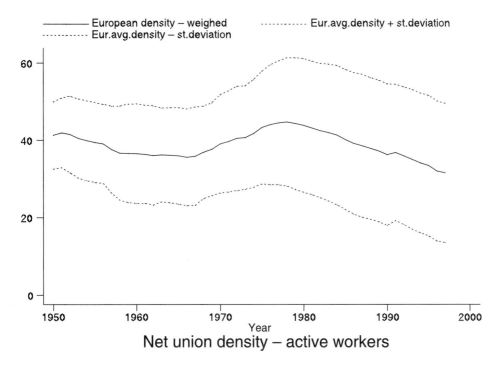

Figure 1. Union density in Europe (14 countries, employment weighted average, 1950–98)

To highlight different patterns in European countries, in Figure 2 we report the evolution separately by country. Levels and evolutions are quite different across countries, but the pattern of increasing unionization in the 1970s followed by gradual decline is common to all. The differences in long-run growth rates in some cases are substantial. As shown in Table 2, most Nordic countries (Finland, Sweden and Denmark) experienced in the postwar period a rapid increase in unionization rates, while the opposite occurred in some other countries in continental Europe (France, Netherlands and Austria). A common feature shared by most countries is the high-density rate observed in the public services.

The differences in growth rates, however, have not substantially modified the ranking of countries according to their immediate postwar unionization rates (the rank correlation between beginning and end of sample is $\rho_{rk} = 0.80$). If we compare union density rates across countries in the mid 1960s and the mid 1990s, as we do in Figure 3, most countries lie near the 45° line, thus suggesting that the structure of unionization rates has remained relatively constant over time.[19] Along the 45° line, the countries

---

[19] In Figure 3, we report the estimated country-time fixed effects, obtained by regressing union density levels against country fixed effect interacted with a three time effect dummies (i.e. for the sub-periods 1950–65, 1966–75, 1976–95). Only extreme points are reported in the figure to reflect unionization rates by countries between 1950–65 and 1976–95.

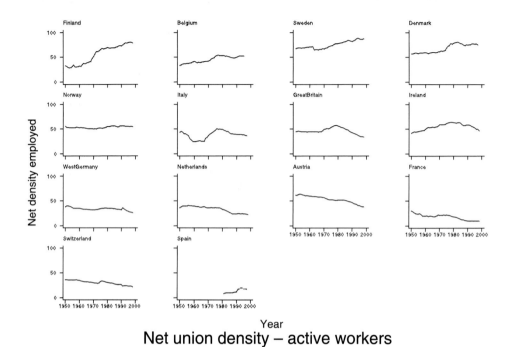

Net union density – active workers

Figure 2. Evolution of net union density in Europe (1950–98)

Table 2. Net union density rates

	1960–65	1975–80	1990–95	Difference (9095–6065)	Density rate in public services (1995)
Finland	32.5	57.7	74.0 ·	41.5	n.a.
Denmark	58.4	66.9	77.2	18.8	n.a.
Sweden	68.7	71.1	83.9	15.3	60.0
Belgium	38.1	47.7	51.2	13.1	47.8
Ireland	48.1	59.7	57.3	9.3	n.a.
Italy	32.7	41.4	41.0	8.2	52.1
Norway	52.8	51.7	55.5	2.7	88.3
Great Britain	44.8	51.3	44.2	−0.6	88.3*
(West) Germany	35.8	33.5	32.3	−3.6	84.2
Switzerland	34.6	31.0	25.9	−8.7	56.7
France	22.8	20.8	12.2	−10.6	17.5**
Netherlands	39.2	36.3	25.9	−13.3	64.9**
Austria	60.8	54.3	46.4	−14.4	99.6
Spain	–	–	13.5	–	36.2

Note: *data refer to 1987 for selected branches; **data refer to 1993 for only some sectors.

featuring the most different permanent unionization are France and Sweden, while Finland and Austria have experienced the largest changes in union density (moving, respectively, from the 5th to the 12th and from the 12th to the 8th position in the ranking).

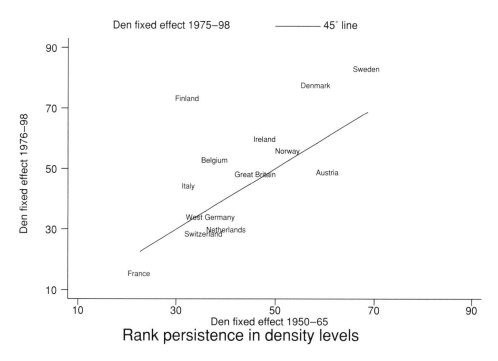

Figure 3. Union density patterns in Europe (1950–65 versus 1976–98)

While some common shocks can explain the common trends over time, the heterogeneity of individual country experiences both in the levels and in the long-run trends of unionization calls for an explanation. The theories reviewed above suggest that unemployment and inflation rates may explain unionization patterns. As a first step, we explore the patterns in terms of country-specific and time-specific effects in unionization and further investigate the behaviour of the residual component. We regress union density, unemployment, and inflation rates on country and time effects,

$$x_{it} = C_i + T_t + \varepsilon_{it} \tag{1}$$

where x_{it} stands for union density, or unemployment, or inflation rates; i indicates the ith country in period t; C is a country fixed effect; T is a common time effect; and ε_{it} is the residual term. This decomposition allows us to get a general idea of the general patterns of unionization in Europe, under the maintained assumption of time invariant country effects and common time effects. As an example take two countries, Finland and France: estimating Equation (1) we find that the country effects are, respectively, 54 and 16%, while the (common) time effect for 1990–95 period is 2.8%. Hence the predicted unionization rates, for the final period, are 56.8 and 18.8%, respectively for Finland and France. Comparing the predicted with the actual rates (76.2 for Finland and 10.2 for France, in 1990–95) we find that union density was 19.7 percentage points above what would have implied a 'common' behaviour in

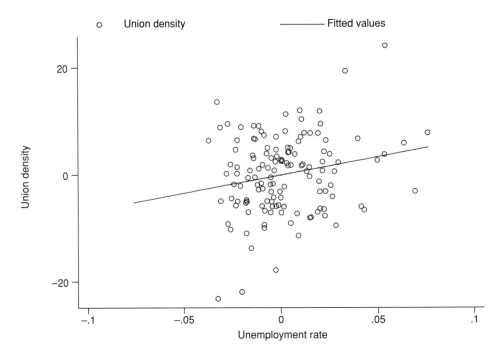

Figure 4. Union density and unemployment in Europe

Europe, while France was 8.6% below. How can we explain this residual? In other words, can the exceptionally low (high) unionization rates observed in France (Finland), as opposed to the pattern predicted by our simple model, be explained by equally low (high) patterns in unemployment or inflation? Estimating equations in the form (1) for unemployment and inflation rates, we can plot in Figures 4 and 5 union density deviations against unemployment and inflation deviations (from countries- and time-effect estimates).

A positive relationship is apparent in both Figures 4 and 5, and provides some support to the idea that unexpected economic shocks (in unemployment and/or inflation) have affected demand for union protection.[20] The pairwise relationship between unionization and unemployment residuals is strong and significant (but is weaker if Finland is excluded from the sample); it is positive, but only weakly significant, between unionization and inflation residuals.[21] To give a more direct intuition of the economic implication of this (linear) trade-off consider that an increase of one percentage point in inflation determines a 0.66 point increase in union

---

[20] In both graphs Finland's residuals are significantly dispersed. This can probably be attributed to the critical economic circumstances that occurred in the aftermath of the 'fall of the Berlin Wall'. The profound restructuring process that occurred in Finland and in most Eastern European countries had a major impact on the structure of these economies, which is unlikely to be explained by our simple dummy variables specification.

[21] The estimated coefficient of regression line reported in Figure 4 is obtained from a univariate regression of union density residuals on unemployment residuals is 0.68 with a *t*-stat of 2.42. Conversely the coefficient from a regression of union density residuals on inflation residuals is 0.677 with a *t*-stat of 1.77.

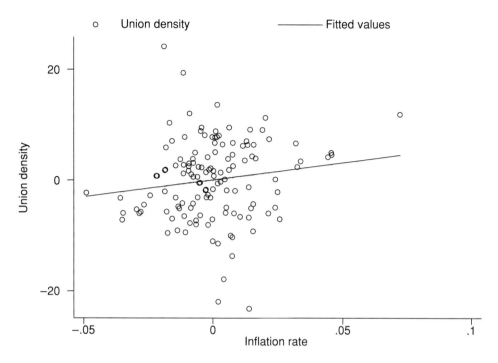

Figure 5. Union density and inflation in Europe

density. Obviously, these exercises only aim at providing some descriptive evidence on correlations between variables leaving open the issue of the direction of causality.[22]

It is also evident that there is much more to be explained in terms of the evolution of union density across countries than a simple decomposition can achieve.[23] Furthermore, the exercises seem to suggest that the explanatory contribution of economic shocks, affecting an individual's decision to join the union is only marginal and that there ought to be other factors which are potentially relevant to explain both the differences across countries and over time. In the Web Appendix we report information about existing measures for labour market institutions and we repeat the same exercise for each measure (see Figure A.3.2). There is statistically significant evidence of positive correlation of union density with benefit replacement rate, mandatory extension, Kaitz index, workplace presence and tax wedge, and negative correlation

---

[22] Empirical evidence on reverse regressions suggest a similar picture, that is a regression of unemployment residuals on union density residuals shows a coefficient of 0.061 (2.42), while inflation residuals show a coefficient of 0.061 (1.77).

[23] We estimated an alternative specification where country-specific effects (C) were also interacted with a time trend ($trend$): $x_{it} = C_i + C_i \cdot trend_t + \varepsilon_{it}$ where C_i is a country fixed effect and $C_i \cdot trend_t$ is a country-specific trend. In this way, unionization patterns can be decomposed in country-specific 'levels' and 'trends'. The estimated country-specific trends in union density reveal a significant heterogeneity across countries. Moreover, simple pairwise correlations between estimated country-specific trends in union density, respectively, with unemployment ($\rho_{den,une} = 0.04$) and inflation ($\rho_{den,inf} = 0.21$) show low correlations and statistically insignificant coefficients. In other words, it seems that long-run trends in unemployment and inflation have little explanatory power on unionization patterns.

with wage indexation. However, as pointed out by Belot and van Ours (2000), it is the combination of institutions that matters for labour market performance, and therefore we have to resort to multivariate analysis.

Ideally, we would have liked to account also for wage compression effects, however, a number of important limitations prevented us from formally including wage compression among our explanatory variables. First, data availability is limited to recent years; second, the direction of causation is not straightforward and reverse causation should be a main concern. We did explore the issue, computing correlations and fitting regressions using data for restricted periods (see Figure A.3.3 in the Web Appendix). Results seem to suggest that union density is negatively related to wage inequality at both ends of the earnings distribution. This provides additional support to the hypothesis that unions aim at reducing wage dispersion and particularly so for low-wage workers.

3.4. The data

In Table 3 we report descriptive statistics for the entire dataset.[24] Our union variable is the density rate among active workers. We account for compositional effects in the workforce controlling for the share of Male, Manual workers in the Manufacturing sector (the so-called triple 'M' workers, who are the typical union members in a Fordist society). Economic shocks are captured by inflation and unemployment rates. Other variables account for the main features characterizing the labour market institutional setting, namely: replacement rates and duration of unemployment benefits, employment protection measures, minimum wage and tax wedge. Further indicators of the environment in which unions operate are mandatory extension of collective agreement, workplace representation, centralization of bargaining and multiple-union competition. Information on union dues would be very relevant, but no data are available. The significance of strike activity is less than fully clear: it can represent commitment to be a union member, or alternatively it can measure the relevance of a social custom, as a way to conform to a behavioural norm (Checchi and Corneo, 2000), or even be an indirect measure of the degree of social conflict and management opposition. Product market rents are proxied by several variables: share of public sector employment, indicators of market regulation, degree of openness to international trade, wage share on the gross domestic product. Finally, the share of left voting in general elections captures the political orientation of the government.

Given the emphasis placed on the long-term determinants of unionism, to remove excessive cyclical fluctuation in economic variables and in order to match relevant institutional data, the variables have been averaged over five-year periods. Most of the institutional variables are only available from the 1960s, and therefore we shall restrict our sample period to 1960–98, thus implying eight observations per country. Since

---

[24] A more detailed description of data sources is reported in Appendix B, and country means are reported in Appendix C. A data set and sample program are available on the *Economic Policy* website, http://www.economic-policy.org.

Table 3. Descriptive statistics (14 countries – unweighted averages)

Variable definition	Var name	Obs	Mean	Std. dev	Min	Max
Union (net) density rate for active dependent employment	DEN	649	45.77	17.69	8.30	88.60
Share of male dependent employment in industry on total employment	MMM	668	0.25	0.07	0.02	0.41
Unemployment rate	UNE	686	0.07	0.05	0.00	0.25
Inflation rate (yearly change) in consumer price index	INFL	686	0.05	0.04	−0.05	0.28
Unemployment benefit replacement rate	BRR	504	0.40	0.21	0.00	0.88
Index of unemployment benefit duration	BD	504	0.40	0.31	0.00	1.00
Index of employment protection	EP	504	1.13	0.56	0.00	2.00
Index of centralization/coordination	CENTR	659	0.35	0.21	0.06	0.74
Ghent system (i.e. Union administered unemployment benefit)	GHENT	686	0.28	0.45	0.00	1.00
Taw wedge	TW	495	0.50	0.12	0.17	0.83
Workplace representation	WORK	655	0.63	0.29	0.20	1.00
Kaitz index (minimum wage/average wage)	KAITZ	686	0.54	0.10	0.32	0.71
Mandatory extension of collective agreements	MANDAT	686	0.76	0.24	0.18	1.00
Share of governmental employment in dependent employment	PA	629	0.19	0.07	0.07	0.37
Index of product market regulation (overall)	MKREG	686	1.56	0.48	0.50	2.30
Index of product market regulation (7 sectors, time varying)	MKREGD	686	5.00	0.74	1.00	6.00
Herfindahl index (over six main unions)	HERF	582	0.62	0.24	0.21	1.00
Degree of openness to international trade (export + import/gdp)	OPEN	476	0.67	0.27	0.22	1.56
Wage share on value added (private sector)	WAGESH	406	0.57	0.07	0.39	0.77
Share of left voting in general elections	LEFTV	597	0.39	0.09	0.12	0.56
Workers involved in strike on dependent employment	STRIKE	615	0.07	0.14	0.00	1.00

Notes: Variable names as reported in the tables in the Web Appendixes. Self-explanatory names have been used in the tables reported in the main text.

unionization data for Spain are available only from 1981 onwards, the country has been excluded from the empirical analysis, though included in the descriptive analysis.

4. EMPIRICAL ANALYSIS

In this section we sketch the main features of the empirical analysis and discuss the main set of results. We assume that observed unionization rates are determined both by economic factors, as well as by institutional arrangements. Economic circumstances may affect the desire of workers to be insured against labour market risks by unions or to share rents through collective bargaining, while labour or product market regulations and welfare provisions may alter unionization patterns by either favouring or providing suitable alternatives to union activity. We focus on union density as an indicator of unionization. Denoting S_{it} as union density in the ith country at time t, we run regressions in the form

$$S_{it} = \varphi(X_{it}, R_{it}, \mu_i, \lambda_t) \tag{2}$$

where X_{it} is a vector of economic factors that can affect unionization rates; R_{it} is a (country-specific, time-varying) set of institutional features; and μ_i and λ_t are country and time fixed effects. The specification of Equation (2) with the unemployment rate in the X_{it} vector can be thought of as one of the structural equations to be estimated in order to assess the impact of (endogenous) union density on unemployment. The standard literature on the effect of unions on economic performance usually focuses on a specification with the total (or long-term) unemployment as a dependent variable and union density (as well as coverage and other unionization indicators) on the right-hand side, considering the latter exogenously determined (Nickell, 1997, 1999; Blanchard and Wolfers, 2000). Here, we find it interesting to reverse the standard order of causation and investigate the impact of economic factors on union density.[25]

Our specifications include the following variables: a proxy for compositional effects (i.e. demographic, industry and other structural employment features), economic shocks (i.e. inflation, unemployment and product market rents) and various institutional arrangements (i.e. employment protection, unemployment benefits, structure of collective contracts, indexation clauses, local workplace representatives, mandatory extension of collective contracts, minimum wages, tax wedge, product market regulation and public employment).

In the standard framework, the evolution of union density – net of composition effects and controlling for country and time fixed effects – should be entirely explained by countries' long-run economic factors and there should be no (residual) role for institutional factors to play. But union density rates can also depend on whether labour market institutions are more or less union 'friendly'. Hence, we have proceeded in two steps. First, we have run basic specifications including controls for composition effects and economic factors only. Then, we introduced our set of institutional variables, initially as time invariant (as it is often done in the literature) and also as time varying components (to capture for relevant changes occurring over time). When the specification allowed for it, we also included specific time dummies and country fixed effects. In order to improve the efficiency of the estimates, we used generalized least squares (GLS) methods using both a robust estimator (Huber–White

---

[25] We investigate the impact of macroeconomic shocks and institutional arrangements on unionization patterns, but union density may in turn affect unemployment and inflation, as well as some of the institutional variables. While *a priori* it is not evident why the causation should go in that direction – as maintained by most studies on the effect of institutions (Nickell, 1999; Blanchard and Wolfers, 2000; Bertola *et al.*, 2001) – we are aware of the potential endogeneity problems that may affect our estimates. Given the lack of appropriate instruments and the restricted degrees of freedom available, in the analysis we only present simple OLS estimates. However, following the above-mentioned literature on the effects of labour market institution on unemployment, we also experimented an unemployment equation with union density among the explanatory variables and instrumented it with the variable measuring worker representation rights. With OLS and time-invariant institutions we obtain an impact of union density onto unemployment equal to 0.069 (3.36), whereas when endogeneity of union density is accounted for the estimated coefficient declines to 0.054 (2.20). This implies that neglecting the role of labour market institutions estimates of the effect of union presence onto unemployment might be biased. We are grateful to Ian van Ours for drawing our attention on this point.

procedure) as well as allowing correlation of errors within countries (but independent across countries). It should be noted right at the start that the real test for the relevance of institutions to explain unionization patterns in Europe is in terms of the evolution over time of a country's specific institutional feature, which is what we do in our final step where we estimate a full fledged model with both country-specific economic and institutional (time varying) factors, as well as the relevant interactions among them.

4.1. Unionization, economic shocks and institutions

We start by investigating the impact of economic factors on their own, controlling for compositional factors (proxied by the employment share attributable to men employed in manufacturing, which is commonly thought to be the 'core' of union membership) and relegating to the country fixed effects and to the common time effects the role played by institutional forces. In all estimated equations compositional effects are insignificant, as they are likely to be absorbed by fixed effects. Conversely, both unemployment and inflation show a positive impact on unionization (see Table A.4.1 in the Web Appendix). In order to address the potential endogeneity of unemployment rates, we also estimate a model where unemployment is a (lagged) predetermined variable. In general, results seem not to be significantly affected by the introduction of lagged unemployment, while the coefficient itself is smaller and statistically insignificant.[26]

While reverse causation cannot be completely ruled out, the estimates are consistent with increasing union density in the face of adverse shocks to workers' welfare, at least as measured by inflation and unemployment rates.[27] Part of the effect of the unemployment level as a proxy of the risk of job loss can be captured by a 3-year moving standard deviation of the unemployment rate, which is positively significant when considered as an alternative to unemployment rate. The estimated coefficient on inflation suggests a strong and statistically significant impact on union density rates: an increase of 1% in inflation rate commands an almost equal increase in density rates.[28] Inflation variability (3-year moving standard deviation of the inflation rate) is found to be not statistically significant. In order to capture the relevance of a more complex relationship between unemployment and inflation (as opposed to the linear one implied by the so-called 'misery index' – see Okun, 1981, Bruno and Sachs, 1985),[29] we also experimented an interaction term which never turned to be

---

[26] Also, given the choice of focusing on a long-run relationship by using quinquennial averages, a five-year lag in unemployment does not have an obvious interpretation. In the rest of the analysis we restrict our attention to the current unemployment rate.

[27] On British data Booth (1983) and Carruth and Disney (1988) find a negative impact of unemployment rates whereas Freeman and Pelletier (1990) find a positive one for the same country. A positive sign for the unemployment rate is also found for Finland (Pehkonen and Tanninen, 1997) and for West Germany in the long-term (Carruth and Schnabel, 1990), whereas a negative sign is obtained for Italy (Checchi and Corneo, 2000, via the definition of worker surplus) and the Netherlands (van Ours, 1992). In the latter papers unemployment has a negative impact both in the short and in the long run (via a cointegrating vector).

[28] The estimated coefficient is, however, statistically different from one in most equations.

[29] The so-called 'misery index' captures adverse shifts (outwards) in the inflation-unemployment trade-off (or Phillips curve).

significant. On the whole it appears that economic shocks, affecting both employment probability and purchasing power of wages, raise the demand for unionism after controlling for country characteristics.

The above results highlight the potentially relevant but rather limited role of economic factors in explaining the evolution of unionization as well as cross-country differences in Europe. To account for, and better interpret, the substantial variation captured by (unobserved) country fixed effects in the previous estimations, we initially replaced country fixed effect with (time invariant) measures of institutions. While this imposes that all (time invariant) differences in union density be accounted by differences in institutions, it also implicitly assumes that no major changes have occurred in the institutional setting over the period considered. Since treating institutions as time invariant country attributes is excessively reductive – for the institutional setting has experienced significant changes over the time period considered – we will not place too much emphasis on these estimates. In practice, as time invariant institutions we have used the country mean value of each variable over the time period considered. There is, however, an advantage in doing so because for some important institutional arrangements no time varying information is currently available in a comparable way.

The results (see Table A.4.2 in the Web Appendix) suggest that to the extent that institutional arrangements reinforce the role and the bargaining power of unions on the labour market (i.e. wage floor levels, workplace representation, functions in administering benefits and centralization in bargaining), their impact is likely to be positive; conversely when the effect of the institution weakens the relevance of the services offered by the unions (i.e. duration and coverage of benefits, wage indexation clauses, employment protection measures and mandatory extension of collective contracts) the impact is expected to be negative. When we abstract from economic and compositional effects (only captured in their common trends by time dummies), labour market institutions can be divided into two groups. On one side, some institutional features raise union density, and can therefore be labelled as *complementary institutions*, since they favour union activity, either by reinforcing bargaining power or by raising the net benefit of unionization: minimum wages (as measured by the Kaitz index), workers representation rights, 'Ghent' administrative system of insurance schemes (providing unemployment benefit to union members only) and centralization of collective bargaining. Conversely, a negative impact on union density rates is found on the duration of unemployment benefits, employment protection legislation, indexation clauses, mandatory extension of collective contracts. The above institutions seem to be perceived by workers as a substitute for union income and job-insurance activity, and therefore we will label these institutions as *substitute institutions*. In general these results are unchanged when country-specific economic factors are introduced, the statistical significance of the latter, however, falls when also common time effects are considered. The same classifications carry over almost unchanged when time varying measures of institutions are allowed to replace time invariant ones.

However, some institutional variables do not conform to our theoretical expectations. One is the unemployment replacement rate, which we would expect to rank among 'substitute' institutions, on the ground that the higher replacement rate of the benefit, the lower is the value attached to union protection. The time invariant measure for this variable changes sign and is often insignificant. The other is the tax wedge variable that does not conform to our expectations. Since labour taxes are less distortionary in more centralized (i.e. more unionized) labour markets, we would anticipate a positive association with union density (Summers *et al.*, 1993). This is the effect we find when time varying measures are considered, whereas for time invariant values a negative and statistically significant correlation emerges.[30]

Finally, the 'bad view' of unions as coalition of rent-seekers finds some support in the data. The share of public employment is positively associated with union density (for the lower managerial opposition and ease of securing public rents), and also product market regulation in the private sector works in the same direction. This is consistent with the idea that the more regulated (and/or closed to foreign competition) is the internal market, the higher are firms' rents and the stronger are the incentive to join a union in order to obtain a larger share of these rents (Blanchard and Giavazzi, 2001). While the proxy for market regulation is positively correlated with union density, the degree of openness seem to point more in the direction of protection from external risk, showing a negative and statistically significant sign.

4.2. Main findings

To accommodate the changes that the institutional setting has undergone over the postwar period, when information is available, we allow for institutional variables to change over time. Table 4 reports the main set of results. In addition to a constant and dummies to account for changes in the definition of the dependent variable, all estimated equations control for time dummies and – when only time varying institutions are included – also country dummies. In this context, the effect of the variables should be interpreted as the impact of within country changes. When we investigated the effects of the Kaitz index and mandatory extension of collective contracts – for which we do not have time varying information – country dummies are to be excluded (see columns 2, 4 and 6). Without country fixed effects – and to the extent that the time invariant institutions included cannot fully account for time invariant observed (and unobserved attributes) – estimates pick up also some cross-country variation and thus might be interpreted differently. Of course, the two-way fixed effect

---

[30] The effect can be ambiguous as opposing forces can be at work: on the one hand, the effect of the wedge by raising the cost of labour may negatively affect employment and ultimately unionization rates; alternatively, workers' fear that employers may pass onto wages the effect of taxes may induce workers to join the union to seek protection against wage cuts (Daveri and Tabellini, 2000). In this light we expect the compositional effect (i.e. the between effect) of the tax wedge to show up when time invariant institutions are considered, while the incentive effect to join the union to dominate in time varying fixed effects regression (i.e. the within effect).

Table 4. Union density, economic shocks and time varying institutions (13 countries, 1960–2000)

Model	1	2	3	4	5	6
Labour market institutions						
ben.replac. ratio	0.008	0.063	−0.042	−0.088		−0.006
	(0.15)	(1.14)	(−0.95)	(−1.81)		(−0.11)
ben.durat.	−0.177	−0.189	−0.112	−0.187		−0.244
	(−4.89)	(−4.14)	(−2.88)	(−4.27)		(−7.46)
empl.prot.	−0.088	−0.179	−0.088	−0.104		−0.092
	(−2.85)	(−6.62)	(−3.42)	(−3.28)		(−3.85)
bargaining centr/coord	−0.123	0.209	−0.092	0.201		−0.023
	(−1.66)	(3.81)	(−1.53)	(3.95)		(−0.36)
wage indexation	−0.050	−0.033	−0.034	−0.055		−0.067
	(−2.19)	(−1.27)	(−1.61)	(−2.60)		(−3.75)
workplace represent.	0.240	0.355	0.187	0.222		0.170
	(3.72)	(8.99)	(4.05)	(4.09)		(3.17)
tax wedge	0.641	0.394	0.425	0.366		0.416
	(4.14)	(2.91)	(3.03)	(3.68)		(4.35)
ghent system		0.177		0.226		0.290
		(8.35)		(8.97)		(10.42)
kaitz index		1.324		2.045		1.917
		(4.94)		(8.10)		(9.04)
mandatory ext. of contr.		−0.464		−0.773		−0.606
		(−5.50)		(−7.85)		(−7.89)
Product market regulation						
public sect. employm.			1.213	1.191	1.832	0.812
			(4.90)	(4.74)	(6.80)	(4.26)
wage share					−0.309	−0.030
					(−1.77)	(−0.21)
prod.market regulation					0.010	−0.037
					(0.48)	(−2.99)
trade openness					6.739	10.744
					(0.68)	(2.81)
herfindhal index (unions)					0.144	0.164
					(1.24)	(3.55)
Economic factors						
unemployment			−0.212	−1.194	−0.047	−0.927
			(−0.71)	(−3.70)	(−0.15)	(−2.96)
inflation			0.539	−0.447	0.779	0.121
			(2.13)	(−1.17)	(3.12)	(0.38)
male empl. manufactur.			0.504	0.280	0.564	0.484
			(2.87)	(1.61)	(2.44)	(2.42)
Constant	Yes	Yes	Yes	Yes	Yes	Yes
Change-def.	Yes	Yes	Yes	Yes	Yes	Yes
Country dum.	Yes	Yes	Yes	Yes	Yes	Yes
Year dum.	Yes	Yes	Yes	Yes	Yes	Yes
R^2	0.939	0.839	0.964	0.899	0.948	0.929
N. obs :	104	104	104	104	104	104

Notes: Robust *t*-statistics in parentheses; variable description as in Table 3.

specification chosen – and reported in Table 4 in columns 1, 3 and 5 – represents the hardest test for our empirical model.

Our composition factor – i.e. the 'male, manual, manufacturing' share in the employee workforce – has positive impact on unionism, indicating that demographic and structural changes in the workforce may have played a relevant role in unionization patterns. Both economic factors – unemployment and inflation – appear less robust once compositional effects, time varying institutions and country and time dummies are included. Coming to the role of institutions, we find that benefit duration (and in some cases the benefit replacement rate as well) has a strong negative impact on unionization. Similarly, employment protection regulation, indexation clauses and mandatory extension provision, all report a negative impact thus confirming a 'substitute' role for union activities. Conversely, the presence of workers' representation rights, responsibilities in administering benefits, the existence of a wage floor and a large tax wedge all contribute to the rise of unions, thus validating a 'complementary' role for unions. In the latter group the centralization variable is sometimes wrongly signed and statistically insignificant. However, in the last two columns we introduce an alternative measure for union organizational set-up. If the success of union organizational activity also depends on the existence of economies of scale and lack of fragmentation across different trade unions, an index proxying for inter-union competition should exert a negative impact. Coherently with this theoretical expectation, the Herfindahl index computed on membership shares indicates that the more fragmented is the membership across competing unions, the lower is total membership.

The specifications reported in columns 5 and 6 of Table 4 assess the empirical relevance of the 'bad' view. A protected, highly regulated sector where unions can extract rents at little (or no) employment cost, proxied by the share of public sector employment, shows a strong and statistically significant impact on union density. This indicates that the success of the unions indeed requires both economic rents and reduced product market competition – with the public sector offering an extreme example. Other variables proxying for product market regulation in the private sector and external competitiveness do not perform as well showing a different sign, as compared to theoretical expectations, and in some specifications, lack of statistical significance. In interpreting the openness variable, however, it cannot be excluded that the dominating effect is the risk-reducing role played by the unions (Rodrik, 1998).[31] We also experimented with the wage share in value added, which also exhibits an odd sign. Even abstracting from labour market institutions and focusing exclusively onto variables accounting for the 'bad' view of unions (as we do in column 5), those variables are mostly statistically insignificant.

---

[31] In order to disentangle the price and quantity effects of foreign trade, we have tried to use the standard deviation of terms of trade, without finding any significant effect. We thank Thierry Verdier for raising this point during the discussion.

We have performed a number of sensitivity tests to check the robustness of our results.[32] In general our preferred specifications proved highly robust to most of the sensitivity checks performed maintaining signs and (in almost all cases) statistical significance. If we look at the predictive power of the model, our preferred specification with time varying institutions and country fixed effects (column 3 in Table 4) proves quite accurate in explaining differences in the evolution of unionization patterns across countries. In Figure 6 we plot both actual and fitted union density rates from 1960–65 to 1990–95. In general, the fit is good and the model does a good job tracking the major changes that occurred in unionization across Europe. In addition, since the effect of some institutions might be better captured when interacted with the economic factor they have been designed for – for example, Ghent system with unemployment, indexation clauses with inflation, unemployment subsidy with unemployment – we also experimented several specifications with interaction effects (the statistically significant interactions are reported in Table A.4.3 in the Web Appendix, which builds on the specification reported in column 4 of Table 4).[33] Results indicate that some institutional variables are correctly signed and statistically significant. In particular, the unemployment variable in the 'Ghent' countries (Finland, Sweden, Denmark and Belgium) is positive, indicating that the value of being a union member is higher when unemployment benefits are directly administered by unions themselves and the risk of losing the job is also high. Similarly, the substitute effect played by employment protection is stronger in countries where unemployment is high, suggesting the presence of insider effects replacing union membership. Finally, the higher is the generosity of unemployment subsidies in countries where unemployment is high, the lower is the incentive to 'buy' union protection.

5. ACCOUNTING FOR DIFFERENCES

We can now return to Table 1's list of labour market institutions and assess empirically the effects of institutional factors, identifying institutions that act as 'union

---

[32] Since misspecification or measurement error could bias our estimates, we experimented with different specifications, different definitions for the variables and sensitivity to the inclusion of a different set of countries (see Appendix D for a more detailed discussion). We first investigated whether results were significantly affected by the inclusion (exclusion) of any of the countries considered. We then experimented by excluding one institutional feature at a time, or alternatively by introducing each institution on its own affected results. Finally, in order to evaluate the impact of other variables on unionization patterns, not included in our reference specification, we also checked alternative specifications: we introduced country size to capture the incentive to form a union; we experimented a large set of other controls (which never achieved statistical significance) such as real wages, D5/D1 deciles range, long-run growth rates, capital controls, etc; finally we also included the level of 'activism' proxied by the average number of workers involved in a strike. However, the interpretation of a strike variable in our specification is not straightforward, as it might be the case that strike activity (particularly when measured, as in our case, by strike participation) is significantly influenced by union density itself. Also, the issue of whether strikes should be considered as an indicator of strong (or weak) bargaining power is much debated in the literature. For the above reasons we refrain from entering the strike variable in our preferred specification.

[33] To save on degrees on freedom, we also experimented a non-linear model – as in Blanchard and Wolfers (2000) – in which the whole set of institutions is interacted with either time effects or country-specific economic factors. The model did not perform well and most of the interactions turned out to be non-significant. The main reason for this is probably due to the fact that the impact of institutions and economic factors on unionization, is not of a general form but only works through selected effects of the relevant institutional features on economic shocks.

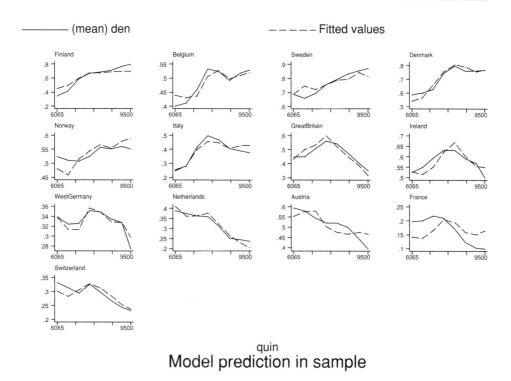

Figure 6. Actual and predicted union density rates in Europe (1960–65 to 1995–2000, 13 countries)

complements' (either lowering the cost of unionizing or providing private incentive goods to members) and institutions that operate as 'union substitutes' (by reducing income/employment variability and lowering the implicit demand for union protection). Table 5 reports the results of our preferred specification when country fixed effects are excluded (Table 4, column 4). Signs and statistical significance, however, have proved robust under alternative specifications for most of the variables included.

It is particularly interesting to find that employment protection legislation 'substitutes' demand for union services. Unions might have promoted the introduction and extension of employment protection norms in most countries, but such policies (in the longer run) appear to have weakened union membership. Similarly, mandatory extension and wage indexation strengthening the incentive to free-ride have proved detrimental to union membership. Unemployment subsidies, replacement rate and benefit duration also seem to reduce the incentive to join the unions, and not surprisingly so if they make the outside option less risky.

On the contrary, some institutions seem to have a positive effect on union density. For example, workplace representation and union centralization affect membership by lowering the cost of membership, while direct administration of unemployment benefit (though publicly subsidized) provides a privately appropriable benefit to members. High minimum wage (relative to average wages) seem favourable to unions: in

Table 5. Summary results and institution classification

Labour market institutions	Estimated coefficient 4th column of Table 4	Union substitutes	Union complements	Rent seeking
Employment protection (EP)	−0.104**			
Unemployment benefit replacement rate (BRR)	−0.088*			
Unemployment benefit duration (BD)	−0.186**			
Wage indexation (INDEX)	−0.054**			
Mandatory extension (MANDAT)	−0.773**			
Unempl. benefit administered by unions (GHENT)	0.226**			
Minimum wages (KAITZ)	2.044**			
Workplace representation rights (WORK)	0.221**			
Bargaining centralization (CENTR)	0.200**			
Tax wedge (TW)	0.365**			
Governmental employment (PA)	1.191**			

Notes: * significant at 5% level; ** significant at 1% level.

this case, the lower is dispersion in the lower tail of the wage distribution, the higher is solidarity among workers and stronger the cohesiveness in collective bargaining and industrial action. While the presence of a wage floor often goes hand in hand with the existence of employment protection legislation (Bertola, 1999), still the two features seem to impact differently on union density. Finally, the tax wedge resulted to exert a positive impact (with time-varying institutions), thus corroborating the hypothesis that unions gain credit in protecting (net) wages and find a more favourable environment in a centralized bargaining setting. The positive impact of the share of public sector employment on union density shows that unions as rent-seekers are more successful in an economic context where rents are high and market competition is limited.

To illustrate better our results and provide a clearer interpretation, we report for each country the (average) predicted unionization levels and the contribution of each set of variables. In practice, in order to assess the relative importance of each factor in explaining unionization patterns (over the entire period), we computed the overall effects using estimated coefficients and (average) characteristics of right-hand side variables in each country. Results reported in Table 6 are obtained using our preferred specification that includes time varying institutions with compositional and economic factors, as well as country and time fixed effects (as reported in column 3 of Table 4). In the table, the numbers in columns 3–8 are the contribution (in density points) of each group of variables to explaining empirical union density patterns. For comparison purposes in the first column we also report the (average) actual density. When we look at the average unionization level over the whole period, the compositional and economic factors account on average for almost 20% of the

Table 6. Predicted (average) union density level and contribution of economic and institutional factors, 13 countries, 1960–2000

	Actual density	Predicted density	Country fixed effects	Compositional factors	Economic factors	Institutional factors (substitute)	Institutional factors (complement)	Rent seeking
Finland	0.559	0.622	0.086	0.107	0.036	−0.162	0.312	0.244
Belgium	0.461	0.484	0.070	0.129	0.022	−0.233	0.247	0.249
Sweden	0.753	0.768	0.049	0.120	0.037	−0.131	0.344	0.351
Denmark	0.681	0.705	0.052	0.156	0.034	−0.188	0.312	0.339
Norway	0.535	0.536	−0.062	0.112	0.034	−0.201	0.335	0.318
Italy	0.383	0.386	−0.029	0.112	0.045	−0.207	0.293	0.172
Great Britain	0.464	0.467	−0.091	0.129	0.040	−0.103	0.246	0.246
Ireland	0.549	0.574	0.094	0.142	0.040	−0.108	0.162	0.243
West Germany	0.337	0.328	−0.065	0.151	0.017	−0.185	0.236	0.175
Netherlands	0.332	0.317	−0.037	0.154	0.023	−0.191	0.197	0.171
Austria	0.533	0.511	0.044	0.186	0.024	−0.143	0.236	0.166
France	0.181	0.165	−0.431	0.122	0.031	−0.144	0.262	0.326
Switzerland	0.302	0.288	−0.076	0.136	0.021	−0.096	0.132	0.170
Full sample	0.457	0.473	−0.031	0.135	0.031	−0.161	0.255	0.244

Notes: 'Compositional' includes male industrial employment share (MMM); 'economic' includes inflation rate (INFL) and unemployment rate (UNE); 'substitute' institutions includes duration (BRR) and coverage (BRR) of benefits, wage indexation clauses (INDEX) and employment protection (EP); 'complement' institutions includes centralization in bargaining (CENTR), workplace representation (WORK) and tax wedge (TW); 'rent seeking' includes public employment share (PA).

predicted levels, while the rest is accounted by institutional factors and fixed effects.[34] Labour market institutions jointly explain a significant portion of density variation (with opposite signs and a prevailing role played by union complement measures) and the remaining variation can be attributed to rent seeking behaviours.

The relevance of economic and institutional factors is quite different across countries, and the combination of complement and substitute (to union activities) institutional arrangements adds further heterogeneity in the overall picture. For example, we can compare two countries, choosing one with high predicted union density, such as Sweden, and one with a relatively low density level, such as the Netherlands. To explain the different outcome in predicted union density it can be noted that while both countries experienced similar dynamics in compositional and economic factors, the effects of product market rents and institutional change have been significantly different. On the one hand, in the Netherlands both lower rents and a weaker impact of union-complement institutions seem to account for the progressive decline of union density. On the other hand in Sweden over the same period a significant growth in public sector rents, as well as the introduction of union-complement institutions, contributed to a significant rise in membership. Comparing Great Britain and Italy can provide a further example. In terms of institutional settings, the long-run union density level in Great Britain is the result of both lower than average 'complement' and 'substitute' factors, while in Italy the contribution of 'complement' institutional factors is higher than average, but the latter is more than compensated by a very generous set of protection measures ('union-substitute') which, on average, seem to have weakened the effectiveness of unions.

We also use our model to construct a number of counterfactual experiments: what would the long-term level of unionization have been in Sweden under the set of institutions prevalent, over the entire period, in the Netherlands? The average union density level that would have prevailed in Sweden, under Dutch institutions, is 0.371 rather than the 0.753 actually observed. The Dutch combination of lower rents and less favourable union environment would have reduced by a half the postwar unionization rate in Sweden. Conversely, the Netherlands under Swedish institutions would be predicted to feature at the long-run unionization rate of 0.678, rather than 0.332.[35]

Given that each country has its own specific features and institutions evolve in clusters, a point worth further investigation would be try to characterize how labour market institutions interact among them. That is, we wonder whether we can identify some common institutional patterns across countries and over time that help explaining how institutions interacted and evolved over time in the countries considered. In

---

[34] Note that fixed effects are also likely to capture the effect of some (time invariant) institutional features not included here, such as the Ghent system, Kaitz index and mandatory extension, as well as others.

[35] We have performed similar computations for France and the UK. Quite interestingly, if UK institutional features prevailed in France union density would be even lower there (0.123 rather than 0.181), while French institutions in the UK would slightly increase union density (to 0.483 rather than 0.463).

order to explore the possibility of institutional clustering, we applied factor analysis to union density and to our set of time varying labour market institutions (principal component method – see Table A.4.7 in the Web Appendix). The two first components extracted account for over 80% of total variance, and the variable contribution can be interpreted along the complement-substitute institutional divide. The first component bears a positive correlation between union density and workplace representation, centralization and tax wedge; the second component displays a negative correlation between density and both employment protection and wage indexation.[36] We interpret the first component as the impact of 'union-complement' institutions, whereas the second captures mainly 'union-substitute' institutions. For each country and for each time period we computed the score attached to each component, and plotted them in Figure 7(a) and (b). The graphs report on the axes the (average) scores associated to the two factors. The scattered points represent the 'gravity' centres (for countries in Figure 7(a) and for years in Figure 7(b)) with respect to the contribution of the complement-substitute components. They can be interpreted as a synthetic measure of the institutional environment affecting individual decisions with respect to union membership decisions, either across countries or over time). The south-east quadrant of the figures is the best environment for the prosperity of unions, as it combines low 'substitute' with high 'complements' institutions, while in the north-west quadrant unions have to face strong employment protection and lower union rights for workers – implying that workers have low incentive to demand union protection, and unions have limited ability to deliver it.

Figure 7(a) portrays country location along the complement-substitute dimensions. The cluster of Nordic countries, characterized by the highest density rates in the sample, score highest on the complementary dimension, without being reduced by excessive employment protection. Mediterranean countries (Italy, France but also Spain, being possible to predict its components for the last decade only) exhibit high values on the substitute axis, as if they were providing excessive guarantees to the workers, thus depressing the incentive to join a union.[37] Great Britain and Ireland, where labour standards are low, are located at the opposite extreme. Austria and Belgium come out as the countries with the closest institutional mix to the European average.

As to evolution over time, Figure 7(b) shows that until the end of the 1970s institutions evolved so as to create a favourable union environment (shifting along the 'complement' axis) in European countries. In this period unions gained considerable importance in collective bargaining, worker representation and strike rights. It was then that landmark legislation such as the Italian *Statuto dei Lavoratori* (possibly the

---

[36] Unemployment benefit duration and replacement are rather independent, since they load on the third component.

[37] Actually Italy and France are a case on their own, as they combine at the time a very different set of institutions, such as low unemployment benefit and high employment protection (Italy) or relatively generous benefit with a rather decentralized bargaining structure and low representation rights (France).

(a)

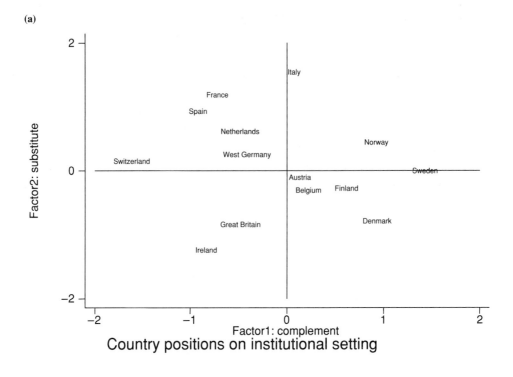

Country positions on institutional setting

(b)

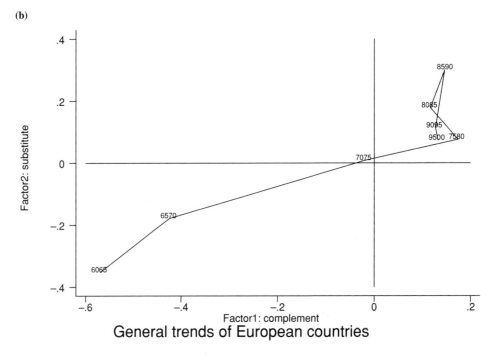

General trends of European countries

Figure 7. (a) Country averages for two first components; (b) Year averages for two first components

most favourable work legislation among European countries) and the British 'closed shop' law were implemented. Later, and until the end of the 1980s, generous welfare systems and employment protection measures were introduced in most countries (an upward rise along the 'substitute' axis). Recently, observations shift down along the same axis. Labour market deregulation, lower employment protection, decentralization of collective bargaining, increasing use of temporary contracts, reforms of unemployment benefit schemes, as well as (only in some cases) diminished representation rights lie behind this development. Examples are Mrs Thatcher's labour market reforms (abolition of 'closed shop' rules and reduction of strike rights), the abolition of the *scala mobile* in Italy, and the widespread 'welfare to workfare' move in European labour market reforms.

The evolution along both complement-substitute dimensions, which to some extent compensate each other, explains why a significant union density decline (North American style) has been confined to selected countries only. Indeed only Great Britain and, to some extent, the Netherlands move towards the north-west quadrant. The case of France is also quite interesting since, for most of the period considered, it can be depicted as a case where the legislator provides most services and allows a generalized extension of collective contracts (strong upward movement in the complement-substitute space). By so doing, it renders the unions almost totally superfluous; only the presence of a large public sector (and the associated economic rents) prevent the unions from disappearing in that country. In the same vein, Italy is characterized by high scores on the 'substitute' axis (see Figure A.4.1 in the Web Appendix). The recent attempt of the Italian government to weaken the legislation on employment protection (thus increasing the possibility for employers to dismiss employees) would imply a downward shift, and support for Italian unions (as indicated by the successful general strike of March 2002).

6. POLICY ISSUES AND CONCLUDING REMARKS

There is no generalized downward trend in European union density. Aggregate figures show a progressive decline, but conceal a highly heterogeneous picture where countries with high and growing membership coexist with others where unionization is low and declining. Our theoretical and empirical analysis highlights factors behind this heterogeneity. A 'bad' view, seeing monopolistic behaviour and rent-seeking activities in highly protected sectors as the main objectives of unions, finds some support in the empirical relevance of public employment. And a 'good' view of unions as a provider of insurance against labour market risks is supported by the empirical role in determining union density not only of inflation and unemployment, but also of institutional features: employment protection legislation, wage indexation, statutory minimum wages appear to crowd out unions. Finally, it is comforting to find that workplace representation and centralization of bargaining have a positive effect on unionization, by making it easier for unions to perform their ('bad' or 'good') role.

These results have interesting implications for topical policy reform issues. The 'good' role of unions in protecting workers against labour market risk is more relevant the higher is the risk, and the lower is the universal insurance offered by state-provided schemes. Hence, the future role of unions is likely to depend very much on the design of the policy mix concerning deregulation, privatization and reduced welfare provisions that are currently in the policy agenda of European countries. To the extent that reforms contribute to a diffuse feeling of reduced protection and more insecurity, workers might be more inclined to seek protection in unions, and increase their membership. And, while government schemes are in general meant to benefit all individuals, union practices have often been directed to the benefit of the 'insiders' (current members) at the expense of the 'outsiders' (potential members).

However, the ability of unions to provide services is conditioned by the 'friendliness' of the institutional environment in which unions operate. Restrictions to organizational activity, increasing fragmentation of bargaining, and reduced coverage of negotiated agreement can significantly increase the costs and reduce the membership of unions. Policies directed to the reduction of public sector expenditures and public sector employment can also have important effects. A smaller public sector means reduced rents to be extracted and thus reduced membership among public sector workers; however, to the extent that public sector jobs crowd out private sector jobs and increase unemployment, a countervailing effect on overall membership can be expected. The effects of rent extraction on membership outside the public sector are more controversial: increased competition and growing openness to international trade, while reducing the scope for rent seeking behaviour, also increase exposure to internal and external economic risks.

Along these lines, it is likely that the stability pact for those countries within the EMU, by reducing the significance of inflationary shocks but not necessarily that of unemployment shocks, would adversely impact on unionization patterns. Less immediately, the Amsterdam treaty and the European Social Charter invoke common standard across European countries with respect to welfare provision as well as worker rights. The net effect on unionization is likely to depend on the relative effect of the two. And while the process of convergence towards a common set of institutional measures might be expected to foster convergence in union densities across European countries, high heterogeneity of industrial relations systems, and restricted degrees of freedom in responding to idiosyncratic shocks, still leave a lot of uncertainty as to possible future evolutions.

Finally, while the paper has focused on the behaviour of a union's 'customers' (potential members), the results offer intriguing insights into the possible attitudes of union leaders towards labour market reforms. If the viability of unions depends on the size of their membership and the institutional environment in which they operate, union leaders might be expected to oppose reforms that in the long run would drive out unions, and to favour institutions that are complementary to their activity. From this point of view, it is puzzling to witness resistance by European union leaders against attempts of governments to reduce labour market regulation. Perhaps union leaders realize that such institutions may reduce union membership and their individual power and visibility, but do satisfy their customers' protection needs. Or perhaps union leaders represent 'insiders' (members and non-members alike) rather than all potential workers, or are myopic enough to neglect long-term effects unfolding after the end of their term in office. Conversely, unions should obviously favour workplace representation (such as European work councils), recommended by the European Social Charter as a means of building trust between workers and managers. In general, when designing institutional changes, it should be borne in mind that altering the balance between institutions that are complements or substitutes to union activities can have complex feedbacks on union presence and influence.

Discussion

Tito Boeri
Università Bocconi

This is a careful empirical paper on the determinants of union density in Europe, contributing an assessment of the empirical relevance for a number of potential interactions between union membership and labour market institutions. I have only two remarks to make.

First, a key finding of the paper is that union density declines with the strictness of legislated employment protection (EPL). If high density benefits unions, this result is at odds with the strong resistance of unions across Europe to reforms reducing EPL. However, union leaders may aim at maximizing coverage of collective agreements signed by the unions, rather than membership. Indeed, union coverage and EPL are positively related in cross-section (the correlation coefficient is 0.63: see the figure below, which uses the same data as the paper). And the positive effect of EPL on coverage proved robust in multivariate regressions of excess coverage, the difference between the coverage of collective bargaining as tabulated by OECD (1997) and Nickell *et al.* (2001) and union density measured according to the same data source of Checchi and Lucifora, over the 1990–98 period and across 14 OECD countries. With excess coverage as the dependent variable, there are significant effects of employment protection legislation and of the generosity of unemployment benefits (the OECD summary measure of the replacement rates over the first two years of an unemployment spell). However, in the countries with the strictest EPL provisions (mainly Southern Europe) higher unemployment generosity is associated with less excess coverage, perhaps because strict provisions can only be enforced by union militancy. When protection against labour market risk can be provided in an excludable fashion, as in the so-called Ghent countries where unions administer unemployment benefit systems, as discussed by Checchi and Lucifora, it actually reduces excess coverage.

bargaining coverage and epl strictness

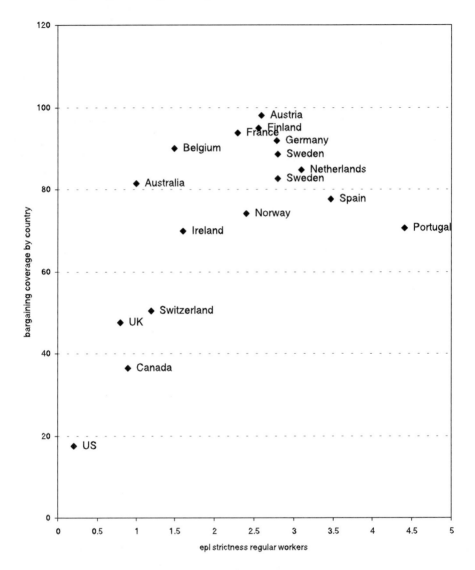

The fact that membership is a declining function of legislated employment protection is quite consistent with the idea that state-provided insurance against job loss competes with the social insurance provided by unions. This leads me to the second remark. The paper's 'good' view of unions is based on their provision of services to members. However, the fact that unions provide some services to workers (e.g., social insurance or tax advising) does not imply automatically that unions are welfare enhancing. Rather, to the extent that unions' provision of a given service is a substitute for state's provision, one should also show that unions can be more efficient than the state in this function. For instance, there are important risk-sharing and risk-pooling arguments for state-provided unemployment insurance, and simplification of tax rules may be preferable on these grounds to the provision of tax advising by the unions.

Jan C. van Ours
Tilburg University

Differences in unemployment rates across countries are often explained by differences in union density or union coverage and other labour market institutions. In their overview of the relationship between labour market institutions and labour market performance, Nickell and Layard (1999) conclude that worrying about strict labour market regulations, employment protection, and minimum wages is probably a waste of time: in order to bring unemployment down the policy focus should be on social security systems and on unions, which have a 'bad' effect on labour markets because they engage in inefficient rent extraction. Social security benefit reforms should foster active labour market policies to move people from welfare to work, while the influence of unions can be reduced by encouraging product market competition.

The paper by Checchi and Lucifora presents a mirror image where differences in union density are explained by differences in institutions and unemployment rates. The authors entertain the possibility that unions are 'good' as providers of insurance against labour market risks. Their paper is a pleasure to read, their analysis of the relationship between unions and labour market institutions is interesting, and the empirical work is neatly done with a lot of sensitivity analyses and robustness checks. Their main claim is that unions and certain labour market institutions (like employment protection legislation, wage indexation and statutory minimum wages) are substitutes, in the sense that strict regulations crowd out unions. My main comments concern some peculiarities of the analysis.

One of the conclusions of the paper is that there is no generalized downward trend in union density in Europe. As Table 2 shows, it is true that since the late 1970s there are five countries that have experienced an increase in union density, while in eight countries union density went down. However, this dichotomy is largely due to the difference between Ghent and non-Ghent countries. Density went up in all 'Ghent' countries, where unemployment benefit schemes are administered by unions. In all non-Ghent countries, except Norway, union density went down. Now, in the Ghent countries union membership is determined more by institutional rules than by economic factors. Therefore, one could conclude that in almost all countries in which unions behave like an economic agent union density went down over the past decades. And, empirically, it is not clear that both types of countries can be treated in the same way.

Checchi and Lucifora use their results to present some simulations. They show that if the Netherlands had Swedish institutions their union density would go up from 33% to 68%, while if the Swedes had Dutch institutions their union density would go down from 75% to 37%. The exercise is nice, and shows that institutions can make a lot of difference to unionization. But the results are hard to believe: the simulation experiment does not entail particularly dramatic institutional changes (since the Dutch and Swedish labour market structure is more similar than that of many other pairs of countries), yet union density in the Netherlands would be at its all time high, and union density in Sweden would be at an unprecedented low. Maybe the result is driven by the Ghent non-Ghent difference. However, whether a country has a Ghent system or not is not what I would call a major difference in institution. It is merely a difference in set-up of unemployment benefit administration, on the basis of which one would hardly except any influence on the functioning of the labour market.

One of the main points in the paper is that union activity and institutional government interventions interact, because both have a risk-reducing role. Hence, institutional change can have a negative effect on union density, and for example if unions succeed in achieving strict firing regulations they would also create a disincentive for workers to join unions. If this were correct it would imply that there is a hump-shape relationship between worker power (through unions) and union density. If unions don't have a lot of influence, union density will be low because workers do not have an incentive to joint unions. If workers (through unions) have a lot of political influence, they will manage to get strict labour market regulations, and again union density will be low. Only in the intermediate range union density will be high, and low union density can be an indicator of both weak and strong worker power. In this respect there is a clear analogy with the non-linear influence of the level of wage bargaining (Calmfors and Driffill, 1988), and cross-country unemployment differences should be explained by a composite variable consisting of both union density and other labour market institutions.

From a broader perspective the question is whether the paper is just informative about unions and in particular the determinants of unionization or whether there is a broader perspective. The evidence on the role of institutions is largely consistent with the 'good' view of unions, but does the study change the perspective of unions as 'bad'? I don't think so. The study shows that the influence of unions can be reduced if regulations concerning employment protection are introduced. However, it does not address the issue of whether unions are relevant when it comes to the determination of unemployment, hence cannot quite change one's view on that issue.

Panel discussion

Responding to Tito Boeri's discussion, the authors mentioned that coverage measures are not available for the whole sample. Thierry Verdier pointed out that aggregate union density hides important within-country variation, because unions are particularly concentrated in certain sectors, and that labour market institutions and union density are jointly determined, especially in the long time span analysed in the paper.

He thought it might be useful to try and disentangle the 'good' and 'bad' effects of unions using terms-of-trade volatility as well as openness as explanatory variables. While higher uncertainty implies a larger protective role for unions along the lines of Rodrik (1998), openness increases competition and diminishes the rent-extraction role of unions.

Thomas Piketty would have liked the paper to address normative issues. Depending on whether the 'good' or 'bad' view of unions prevails, it could be optimal to, for example, tighten employment protection legislation in order to decrease union power.

Georges de Ménil found surprising the decrease of UK union density as labour markets become more flexible. Ray Rees pointed out that while in the paper union membership is a matter of choice in the UK 'closed shop' institutional environment membership is compulsory. Rafael Repullo asked why five-year averages are used instead of annual data. The authors replied that changes of complementary institutions (such as strike rights and workplace representation) explain the evolution of UK membership, where 'closed shop' rules were abolished by Mrs Thatcher to imply that, as in other European countries, union membership is chosen by individual workers; and that, while five-year averages usefully smooth out noisy fluctuation, results were very similar using annual data.

WEB APPENDIX

This may be downloaded free from http://www.economic-policy.org

REFERENCES

Acemoglou, D., P. Aghion and G. Violante (2000). 'Deunionisation, technical change and inequality', mimeo.

Agell, J. (1999). 'On the benefits from rigid labour markets: Norms, market failures and social insurance', *Economic Journal*, 109, F143–F164.

Agell, J. (2000). 'On the determinants of labour market institutions: Rent sharing versus social insurance', CESifo working paper No. 384.

Aghion, P. and B. Hermalin (1990). 'Legal restrictions on private contracts can enhance efficiency', *Journal of Law, Economics and Organization*, 2: 381–409.

Akerlof, G. (1980). 'A theory of social custom, of which unemployment may be one consequence'. *Quarterly Journal of Economics*, 95: 749–75.

Algan, Y., P. Cahuc and A. Zylberberg (2002). 'Public employment: Does it increase employment?', *Economic Policy*, 7–66.

Andrews, M. and R. Naylor (1994). 'Declining union density in the 1980s: What do panel data tell us?', *British Journal of Industrial Relations*, 32(3): 413–31.

Belot, M. and J.C. van Ours (2000). 'Does the recent success of some OECD countries in lowering their unemployment rates lie in the clever design of their labour market reforms?', CEPR working paper 2492.

Bertola, G. (1990). 'Job security, employment and wages', *European Economic Review*, 6: 851–86.

Bertola, G. (1999). 'Microeconomic perspectives on aggregate labour markets', in O. Ashenfelter and D. Card, *Handbook of Labor Economics*, North-Holland, 3c: 55–74.

Bertola, G., F. Blau and L. Kahn (2001). 'Comparative analysis of labour market outcomes: Lessons for the US from international long-run evidence', NBER working paper No. 8256.

Blanchard, O. and F. Giavazzi (2001). 'Macroeconomic effects of regulation and deregulation in goods and labour markets', NBER working paper No. 8120.

Blanchard, O. and J. Wolfers (2000). 'The role of shocks and institutions in the rise of European unemployment: The aggregate evidence', *Economic Journal*, 110/462: C1–C33.

Blanchflower, D., R. Crouchley, S. Estrin and A. Oswald (1990). 'Unemployment and the
demand for unions', NBER working paper No. 3251, May.

Boeri, T., A. Brugiavini and L. Calmfors (eds), with A. Booth, M. Burda, D. Checchi, B.
Ebbinghaus, R. Freeman, P. Garibaldi, B. Holmlund, R. Naylor, M. Schludi, T. Verdier,
and J. Visser (2001a). *The Future of Collective Bargaining in Europe*, Oxford: Oxford University
Press.

Boeri, T., G. Nicoletti and S. Scarpetta (2000). 'Regulation and labour market performance',
CEPR working paper 2420.

Boeri, T., G. Garibaldi and M. Macis (2001b). 'Adaptability of labour markets: A tentative
definition and a synthetic indicator', Fondazione DeBenedetti, mimeo.

Booth, A. (1983). 'A reconsideration of trade union growth in the United Kingdom', *British
Journal of Industrial Relations*, 21: 379–93.

Booth, A. (1984). 'A public choice model of trade union behaviour and membership', *Economic
Journal*, 94: 883–98.

Booth, A. (1985). 'The free rider problem and a social custom model of trade union membership', *Quarterly Journal of Economics*, 100: 253–61.

Booth, A. (1995). *The Economics of the Trade Union*, Cambridge: Cambridge University Press.

Booth, A. and M. Chatterji (1995). 'Union membership and wage bargaining when membership is not compulsory', *Economic Journal*, 105: 345–60.

Braun, A.R. (1976). 'Indexation of wages and salaries in developed economies', *Staff Papers
IMF*, 23/1: 226–71.

Bruno, M., and J. Sachs (1985). *Economics of Worldwide Stagflation*, Oxford: Basic Blackwell.

Burda, M. (1990). 'Membership, seniority and wage-setting in democratic labour unions',
Economica, 57/228: 455–66.

Calmfors, L. (1993). 'Centralisation of wage bargaining and macroeconomic performance:
A survey', OECD working papers No.13.

Calmfors, L., and J. Driffill (1988). 'Centralisation of wage bargaining and macroeconomic
performance', *Economic Policy*, 6: 13–61.

Card, D. (1998). 'Falling union membership and rising wage inequality: What is the connection?', NBER working paper 6520, April.

Carruth, A. and C. Schnabel (1990). 'Empirical modelling of trade union growth in Germany,
1956–1986: Traditional versus cointegration and error correction methods', *Weltwirtschaftliches
Archiv-Review of World Economics*, 126/2: 326–46.

Carruth, A. and R. Disney (1988). 'Where have two million trade union members gone?',
Economica, 55, 1–19.

Checchi, D. and G. Corneo (2000). 'Trade union membership: Theory and evidence for Italy',
Lavoro e Relazioni Industriali, 2: 1–36.

Checchi, D. and J. Visser (2001). 'Pattern persistence in European trade union density', University of Amsterdam-AIAS working paper No. 4.

Corneo, G. (1995). 'Social custom, management opposition, and trade union membership',
European Economic Review, 39: 275–92.

Corneo, G. (1997). 'The theory of the open shop trade union reconsidered', *Labour Economics*,
4: 71–84.

Daveri, F., and G. Tabellini (2000). 'Unemployment, growth and taxation in industrial countries', *Economic Policy*, 30: 49–104.

DiNardo, J., N. Fortin and T. Lemieux (1996). 'Labour market institutions and the distribution
of wages, 1973–1992: A semiparametric approach', *Econometrica*, 64(5): 1001–44.

Dolado, J., F. Kramarz, S. Machin, A. Manning, D. Margolis and C. Teulings (1996). 'The
economic impact of minimum wage in Europe', *Economic Policy*, 23: 317–72.

Ebbinghaus, B. and J. Visser (1999). 'When institutions matter: Union growth and decline in
Western Europe, 1950–1995', *European Sociological Review*, 15(2).

Ebbinghaus, B. and J. Visser (2000). *Trade Unions in Western Europe since 1945*, Basingstoke:
MacMillan.

Farber, H. (2001). 'Notes on the economics of labor unions', Princeton University – Industrial
Relations section working paper No. 452.

Flora, P., F. Kraus and W. Pfenning (1987). *State, Economy and Society in Western Europe 1815–
1975*, Basingstoke: MacMillan.

Freeman, R. (1984). 'Unionism comes to the public sector', *Journal of Economic Literature*, 1–41.

Freeman, R. and J. Pelletier (1990). 'The impact of industrial relations legislation on British union density', *British Journal of Industrial Relations*, 28/2, 141–64.

Garibaldi, P. and P. Mauro (1999). 'Deconstructing job creation', IMF working paper 99/109.

Golden, M., P. Lange and M. Wallerstein (1997). Union centralization among advanced industrial societies: an empirical study (data downloaded at http://www.shelley.polisci.ucla.edu/data on 3 April 2001).

Gregg, P. and A. Manning (1997). 'Labour market regulation and unemployment', in D. Snower and G. de la Dehesa (eds), *Unemployment Policy: Government Options for the Labour Market*, Cambridge: Cambridge University Press.

Grossman, G. (1983). 'Union wages, temporary layoffs, and seniority', *American Economic Review*, 73/3: 277–90.

Grubb, D. and W. Wells (1993). 'Employment regulation and patterns of work in EC countries', *OECD Economic Studies*, 21.

Hancké, B. (1993). 'Trade union membership in Europe, 1960–1990: Rediscovering local unions', *British Journal of Industrial Relations*, 31(4): 593–613.

Holmlund, B. and P. Lundborg (1999). 'Wage bargaining, union membership, and the organization of unemployment insurance', *Labour Economics*, 6(3): 397–415.

Jones, S. and C.J. McKenna (1994). 'A dynamic model of union membership and employment', *Economica*, 61/242: 179–89.

Kahn, L. (2000). 'Wage inequality, collective bargaining and relative employment from 1985 to 1994: Evidence from 15 OECD countries', *The Review of Economics and Statistics*, 82(4), 564–79.

Kremer, M. and B. Olken (2001). 'A biological model of unions'. NBER working paper No. 8257.

Lange, P. and L. Scrugg (1999). 'Where have all members gone? Union density in an era of globalization', *Stato e Mercato*, 55: 39–75.

Layard, R., S. Nickell and R. Jackman (1991). *Unemployment: Macroeconomic Performance and the Labour Market*, Oxford: Oxford University Press.

Lazear, E. (1990). 'Job security provisions and employment', *Quarterly Journal of Economics*, August, 699–726.

Lipset, S. and I. Katchanovski (2001). 'Corporatism, left government and union density in advanced Western countries', mimeo.

Mackie, T. and R. Rose (1974). *International Almanac of Electoral History*, reported in 'Codebook for 18-nation pooled time-series data set: Strength of political parties by ideological group in advanced capitalist democracies' by Duan Swank (downloaded at http://www.marquette.edu/polisci/p5095code.htm on 5 July 2001).

Moore, W., R. Newman and L. Scott (1989). 'Welfare expenditure and the decline of unions', *Review of Economics and Statistics*, 71(3): 538–42.

Naylor, R. and M. Cripps (1993). 'An economic theory of the open shop trade union', *European Economic Review*, 37: 1599–1620.

Naylor, R. and O. Raaum (1993). 'The open shop union, wages and management opposition', *Oxford Economic Papers*, 45: 589–604.

Nickell, S. (1997). 'Employment and labor market rigidities: Europe versus North America', *Journal of Economic Perspectives*, 11(3): 55–74.

Nickell, S. and R. Layard (1999). 'Labour market institutions and economic performance', in O. Ashenfelter and D. Card, *Handbook of Labor Economics*, North-Holland, 3c: 3029–84.

Nickell, S., L. Nunziata, W. Ochel and G. Quintini (2001). The Beveridge curve, unemployment and wages in the OECD from the 1960s to the 1990s. LSE-CEP, mimeo, July.

Nicoletti, G. and S. Scarpetta (2001). 'Interactions between product and labour market regulations: do they affect employment? Evidence from OECD countries', forthcoming as OECD Economic Department working paper.

Nicoletti, G., S. Scarpetta and O. Boylaud (2000). 'Summary indicators of product market regulation with an extension to employment protection legislation', OECD working paper no. 226.

OECD (1997). *Employment Outlook*, Paris: OECD.

OECD (1999). *Employment Outlook*, Paris: OECD (Ch. 2: Employment protection and labour market performance).

OECD (2001). *Employment Outlook*, Paris: OECD (Ch. 4: Eligibility criteria for unemployment benefits, by D. Grubb).

Okun, A. (1981). *Prices and Quantities: A Macroeconomic Analysis*, Washington: Brookings Institution.

Oskarsson, S. (2001). 'Class struggle in the wake of globalization: Union organization in an era of economic integration', in L. Magnussen and J. Ottosson (eds), *Europe: One Labour Market?*, Brussels.

Pehkonen, J. and H. Tanninen (1997). 'Institutions, Incentives and trade union membership', *Labour*, 11(3): 579–98.

Peoples, J. (1998). 'Deregulation and the labor market', *Journal of Economic Perspectives*, 12(3): 111–30.

Rodrik, D. (1998). 'Why do more open economies have bigger governments?', *Journal of Political Economy*, 196(5): 997–1032.

Rogers, J. and W. Streeck (1995). *Works Councils: Consultation, Representation and Cooperation in Industrial Relations*, Chicago: University of Chicago Press.

Saint-Paul, G. (1996). 'Exploring the political economy of the labour market institutions', *Economic Policy*, 23: 263–317.

Scarpetta, S. (2002). 'Regulation, productivity and employment: An international comparison and the challenge for Italy', mimeo.

Scharpf, F. and V. Schmidt (eds) (2000). *Welfare and Work in the Open Economy* (vol.1), Oxford: Oxford University Press.

Summers, L., J. Gruber and R. Vergara (1993). 'Taxation and the structure of labor markets: the case of corporatism', *Quarterly Journal of Economics*, 108(2), 385–411.

Traxler, F., S. Blaschke and B. Kittel (2001). *National Labour Relations in Internationalized markets: A Comparative Study of Institutions, Change and Performance*, Oxford: Oxford University Press.

van Ours, J.C. (1992). 'Union growth in the Netherlands 1961–1989', *Applied Economics*, 24: 1059–66.

Visser, J. (1993). 'Union organisation: Why countries differ', *The International Journal of Comparative Labour Law and Industrial Relations*, 9.

Waddington, J. and C. Whitston (1997). 'Why do people join unions in a period of membership decline?', *British Journal of Industrial Relations*, 35(4), 515–46.

Webb, S. and B. Webb (1894). *The History of Trade Unionism*, London.

Western, B. (1997). *Between Class and Market: Postwar Unionization in the Capitalist Democracy*, Princeton: Princeton University Press.

Active policy evaluation
Problems, methods and results

SUMMARY

European countries with poorly performing labour markets and labour market institutions conducive to high unemployment also feature considerable expenditures on active labour market policy, and such policies are emphasized by the European Union's employment strategy. However, the practice of these programmes' evaluation is much less well developed in Europe than in the United States. We outline key issues facing such evaluation and offer a review and formal assessment of European evaluation studies over the last three decades. We find that programme effects are very heterogeneous across types of interventions and target groups, that training and job search assistance can be effective, and that the young among the unemployed are typically difficult to assist.

— *Jochen Kluve and Christoph M. Schmidt*

Economic Policy October 2002 Printed in Great Britain
© CEPR, CES, MSH, 2002.

Can training and employment subsidies combat European unemployment?

Jochen Kluve and Christoph M. Schmidt

University of California, Berkeley and Universität Heidelberg; Universität Heidelberg and IZA

1. INTRODUCTION

A growing literature has documented the contrast between European and US labour market performance, emphasizing in particular high rates of overall and long-term unemployment and wage compression in Europe, and low unemployment and high wage dispersion in the US. Possible causes of the observed differences between European economies and the US have been discussed, and identified most prominently with labour taxation, employment protection, trade union activity, and systems of unemployment support.[1] An aspect receiving relatively less attention in this debate is the differing intensity and character of *active labour market policy* (ALMP), such as job search assistance, provision of training, subsidization of job creation in the private sector, and direct job creation in the public sector. While the US have accumulated

We are grateful to Boris Augurzky, Fe Bundschuh-Schmidt and Marcus Tamm for comments and technical support, and to various researchers, in particular participants of the IZA-CEPR workshop on programme evaluation (Berlin, December 1999) for their discussion and their recent papers. We have benefited from discussions during the Panel meeting and from suggestions by Jan van Ours and the Managing Editors. We are particularly grateful to David Card for his comments and advice, and to the Center for Labor Economics, UC Berkeley for its hospitality. We gratefully acknowledge financial support by the VolkswagenStiftung and IZA.

The Managing Editor for this paper was Giuseppe Bertola.

[1] See in particular Nickell (1997), Ljungqvist and Sargent (1998), Bertola (1999), Machin and Manning (1999), Mortensen and Pissarides (1999b), Nickell and Layard (1999).

extensive experience in the design and implementation of public sector programmes targeted at economically disadvantaged individuals, expenditures for these programmes have nevertheless remained small in the US, and their principal aim has been the improvement of earnings prospects of programme participants, rather than combating unemployment. Since US programmes have been accompanied by methodologically rigorous evaluation studies for a long time, the empirical knowledge about their (limited) potential is considerable (see for instance Stanley *et al.*, 1999). It has been realized, in particular, that their effects and their cost effectiveness differ across types of interventions and target groups. Generally, their moderate impact and their limited scale imply that their operation is not crucial for the overall stance of the US labour market.

By contrast, many European economies spend notable shares of their budgets on labour market interventions targeted at specific groups of workers. These policy measures in the European context typically aim at mitigating negative employment consequences for the least fortunate, under the existing set of rules and regulations. Specifically, realizing that unemployment is typically far from a transient state for European workers suffering job loss, ALMP measures mostly target long-term unemployed individuals. The recent formulation of a joint *European Employment Strategy* places remarkable emphasis on the need for identification of potent ALMP measures and calls for utilization of such measures, as identified by cross-country comparison of policy practices.

Unfortunately, European countries can draw neither from a comparatively long experience with ALMP as the US, nor from a reliable and extensive body of empirical evaluation results regarding their impact or cost effectiveness. Yet the sobering results of US evaluation studies on the impact of targeted labour market interventions suggest that even well-intended, carefully designed and generously funded programmes might not alter the labour market prospects of programme participants. Throughout the last decades, the literature in labour economics and applied econometrics has developed the appropriate methodological framework for dealing with this type of question (Heckman *et al.*, 1999). This literature emphasizes the heterogeneity of individual participants and of the effects that treatment under the programme exerts on them, and places central attention to the necessity to construct genuinely comparable comparison groups for the purpose of gauging average programme effects.

This article elucidates the conclusions that *can* be drawn regarding ALMP effectiveness in Europe on the basis of state-of-the-art evaluation research. Current knowledge on ALMP measures in Europe is limited by lack not only of comprehensive data, but of co-operation between those designing and implementing these interventions and those analysing them. However, methodological advances and increasing (if still scattered) awareness of comparability issues and data requirements among policy-makers foster growth of a micro-econometric literature addressing these concerns.

On balance, the evidence suggests that well-targeted programmes with considerable training content do have the potential to improve the labour market outcomes of those targeted, and that well-designed financial incentives might also raise employment at lower cost. By contrast, direct job creation in the public sector is usually less effective. Overall, ALMP programmes display a limited potential to alter the economic prospects of the individuals they intend to help, making it indispensable to place considerable further effort on the thorough evaluation of each specific intervention.

Section 2 contrasts the labour market performance of the major European economies with that of the US. We discuss discrepancies in labour market institutions, then focus on the role of ALMP in European economies, and characterize the emerging European Employment Strategy embodied in the Luxembourg Process. Section 3 outlines the methodological issues involved in programme evaluation and contrasts the current practice of ALMP evaluation in the US and Europe. Section 4 discusses the findings from European programme evaluation, illustrated by a quantitative analysis of evaluation studies from the last three decades. Section 5 concludes with a discussion of the general lessons for economic policy that arise from the available evidence.

2. EMPLOYMENT PERFORMANCE AND ALMP: EUROPE AND THE US

2.1. The role of labour market institutions

Western European economies have experienced high and persistent unemployment rates only since the 1980s or 1990s. Figure 1 depicts the development of unemployment rates since 1966 for countries of the European Union (EU, formerly EEC), transition countries of Central and Eastern Europe (CEE), the US, and the total of OECD countries. While EU unemployment had been slightly below or around the OECD average until 1981, since then it has persistently exceeded the OECD average, and since 1984 this difference has always exceeded two percentage points. US unemployment displays an opposite development: whereas the unemployment rate was above the OECD average until the early 1980s, it has been decreasing substantially since then, lying below the OECD total most of the years, and always since 1993. Similarly, the formerly socialist countries of Central and Eastern Europe did not have to address large-scale *open* unemployment before the demise of the socialist regimes. Figure 1 documents how for European transition countries in the early 1990s unemployment rates skyrocketed to levels clearly above the OECD average.

It has therefore been only over the last two decades that combating high unemployment has become one of the most urgent policy issues across Europe. Unemployment, however, is not an equitable phenomenon. At all states of the cycle, it tends to afflict more heavily groups outside the 'core' of the labour force, i.e. women, the young, the old, the less skilled, and immigrants and ethnic minorities. A combination

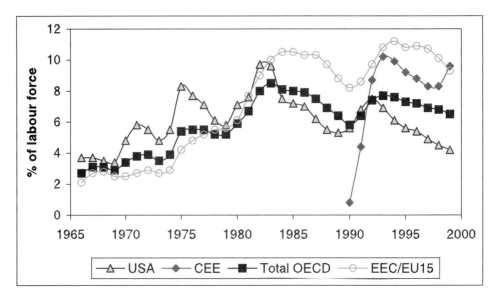

Figure 1. Unemployment rates 1966–99

Notes: OECD total = unweighted average, CEE = Hungary, Poland, Czech Republic, for 1990 and 1991 Czech Republic only.

Source: OECD (2000c, 1998, 1991).

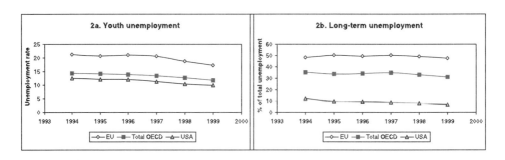

Figure 2. The structure of unemployment

Source: OECD (2000b: Tables C, G); OECD (1998: Tables B, C, G).

of two or more of these characteristics seems to be particularly detrimental. In addition to discrepancies in average employment performance, some groups suffer to a disproportional extent when the economic cycle deteriorates. For instance, Schmidt (2000b) documents substantial excess cyclical volatility of unemployment for young workers in Germany.

Panels a and b of Figure 2 underscore the difference between US and European labour markets in illustrating that youth (15–24 years old) and especially long-term unemployment (more than 12 months) is far less of a problem in the US. The high incidence of long-term unemployment is widely regarded as one of the distinct and most serious problems of European labour markets (Machin and Manning, 1999).

In our account we use the 'EU' synonymously for the general idea of 'Western Europe' (thus including Norway and Switzerland), in contrast with the US, since this classification is the most relevant one for ALMP measures and their evaluation. As Nickell (1997) and Nickell and Layard (1999) emphasize, however, for many purposes it is inappropriate to restrict the discussion to European aggregate figures, since European unemployment experiences and labour market institutions are quite diverse. The simple call for more 'labour market flexibility' to improve matters is too coarse to yield insight into the causes for the lacking average European labour market performance, or to lead to the formulation of possible remedies. Instead, there is a consensus that one has to look at the level of individual economies and specific labour market institutions to detect traces of how their interplay determines labour market outcomes. Following this idea, the relevant literature identifies several major institutional differences which could be responsible for the divergence in economic performance.

In line with cross-country studies on the labour market institutions-employment performance nexus,[2] the first column of Table 1 reports the results of a simple cross-country regression for 20 OECD countries of the proportion of the unemployed in long-term unemployment on indicators of labour market rigidities. The other columns are discussed in Section 2.2.3. Specifically, the explanatory factors included are the tax wedge between the real consumption wages received by workers and the real cost of a worker for the employer, an indicator for high employment protection, union density and an indicator for high union coverage, the unemployment benefit replacement ratio, and two indicators for the duration of unemployment benefit eligibility, one for benefit duration exceeding one year, the other for indefinite benefit duration.

Neither employment protection nor labour taxation display a significant correlation with a high share of long-term unemployment. *Employment protection* as an institutional characteristic receives considerable prominence in discussions of the performance of European labour markets. Bertola (1999) discusses how job security provisions seem to be responsible for lower employment variability, and their association with the relatively high wage growth underlying the relatively moderate average European employment growth. Regarding *labour taxation*, Nickell and Layard (1999) observe a wide variation in levels of taxation, with high rates being prevalent in the continental European economies, where expenditures on social security and unemployment benefits are correspondingly high as well. Ljungqvist and Sargent (1998) argue on the basis of a general equilibrium search model that the high levels of income taxation and generous welfare benefits in Europe tend to distort workers' labour supply decisions in a way that makes them responsible for a large part of the dismal European labour market performance.

---

[2] E.g. Nickell (1997), Nickell and Layard (1999), Blanchard and Wolfers (2000), Nickell and van Ours (2000).

Table 1. Labour market institutions, long-term unemployment, and expenditures on active labour market policies

	Long-term unemployed	Expenditures on ALMP	
Constant	13.864	−43.607**	−43.862**
	(0.63)	(3.35)	(3.38)
Tax wedge (%)	0.365	0.550**	0.549**
	(0.93)	(2.38)	(2.38)
Indicator (1/0) for high	2.102	10.143*	7.040
employment protection	(0.24)	(1.96)	(1.77)
Union density (%)	−0.323*	0.326**	0.307**
	(1.82)	(3.12)	(3.00)
Indicator for high union	25.060**	−6.174	–
coverage	(2.25)	(0.94)	
Replacement ratio (%)	0.026	0.319**	0.316**
	(0.115)	(2.38)	(2.37)
Indicator for benefit	−14.769	−8.998	−11.804*
duration > 1 year	(1.35)	(1.39)	(2.07)
Indicator for indefinite	26.249**	12.409	13.918*
benefit duration	(2.21)	(1.77)	(2.05)
Observations	20		
Adj. R-squared	0.4042	0.5987	0.6023

Notes: Absolute *t*-ratios are reported in parentheses, a * indicates significance at the 10%-level, and ** indicates significance at the 5%-level, respectively (two-sided test). Regressions involve the proportion of unemployed who are long-term (out of work for more than 1 year) in 1995 (Machin and Manning 1999, Table 1 col. (2)) and expenditures on active labour market policy expressed as a percentage of GDP divided by unemployment 1991 (Nickell and Layard, 1999, Table 10 col. (3)), respectively. Explanatory factors are all taken from Nickell and Layard, 1999 (indicator variables are constructed accordingly), specifically the tax wedge 1989–1994 (Table 5 col. (2)), an indicator for high employment protection (index > 10) 1990 (Table 6 col. (2)), union density 1988–1994 (Table 7 col. (1)), an indicator for high union coverage (index > 2) 1988–1994 (Table 7 col. (2)), the benefit replacement ratio 1989–1994 (Table 10 col. (1)), and indicators for unemployment benefit duration exceeding 1 year and for indefinite benefit duration, respectively, 1989–1994 (Table 10 col. (2)). Countries involved in the regression are Australia, Austria, Belgium, Canada, Denmark, Finland, France, Germany, Ireland, Italy, Japan, the Netherlands, New Zealand, Norway, Portugal, Spain, Sweden, Switzerland, the UK and the US.

This second aspect regarding the generosity of systems of *unemployment support* is one of the key institutional features discussed in the literature on European and US labour market differences. The degree of generosity of the benefit system can be expressed using the benefit replacement rate and the duration of benefit payments. European countries display considerable variation with respect to these two attributes. In our data set, the replacement rate ranges from 20% for Italy to 90% for Sweden, and the benefit duration ranges from 6 months for Italy up to 'indefinite' duration, i.e. 4 years or more, for a set of countries, including Belgium, Germany, Ireland and the UK. Whereas our results do not indicate a strong correlation between high replacement rates and high long-term unemployment, there seems to be a clear positive association between indefinite availability of unemployment benefit payments and a high share of long-term unemployed.

Traditionally, the extent of *trade union activity* and ensuing comprehensiveness of systems of minimum wages are also central to any debate of European labour market performance (Calmfors and Driffill, 1988; Dolado *et al.*, 1996). The wages of most European workers are affected by collective bargaining, and there are clear indications that this is important for employment performance. For instance, in an equilibrium unemployment model with search and recruitment frictions, the wage decides how the quasi-rents associated with any job-worker match are shared between workers and employers. If wage determination is the result of union bargaining, unemployment incidence is lower and expected unemployment duration is higher than under a corresponding competitive regime of wage determination (Mortensen and Pissarides, 1999a). Comparatively high average duration and low incidence are precisely the characteristics of European unemployment when compared to the US (Cohen *et al.*, 1997; Schmidt, 2000a). Our results support the importance of the degree of union activity. While union density displays a negative partial correlation with the proportion of long-term unemployed, we find a clear indication that a high coverage rate by union contracts – which we observe for most European countries, except Switzerland and the UK – is positively associated with high shares of long-term unemployed.

2.2. Active labour market policies in Europe

Notwithstanding the accumulated critique of European labour market institutions, it would be quite unrealistic to expect that any comprehensive policy reform aimed at challenging their operation, or even abolishing them, will be pursued by European governments in the foreseeable future. After all, these institutions were implemented with the intention to protect the jobs of the employed and the living standards of the unemployed, and while they might indeed discourage search, hamper job creation, and prevent efficient reallocation across sectors, they will nonetheless remain largely untouchable as a political reality. Consequently, implementing countervailing policies instead of pursuing comprehensive reform might be a feasible alternative in order to improve labour market performance.

2.2.1. Expenditures on ALMP by European economies.   Within 'active' labour market policies, it is useful to distinguish *training programmes*, such as classroom training, on-the-job training, work experience, or job search assistance; *wage subsidies* to the private sector, i.e. subsidies to employers or financial incentives to workers; and *provision of jobs* in the public sector. Frequently, the latter two are subsumed under the heading 'employment subsidies'. These policies entail aspects that qualify as 'carrots', encouraging desirable behaviour, and 'sticks', sanctioning undesirable behaviour. In practice the sanctioning elements receive relatively little attention.

Panels a to c of Figure 3 depict time series of the GDP share that the US, the EU, the CEE countries, and the total OECD, respectively, allocated to (a) unemployment compensation, (b) active measures in general, (c) labour market training in particular. For the unemployment benefit allocation in the EU, Figure 3a shows a more or less stagnant series until 1990, then a steep incline until 1993, followed by a substantial decline until 1997 almost back down to mid-1980s level. This shape is congruent with the development of the unemployment rate shown in Figure 1. While the curve for

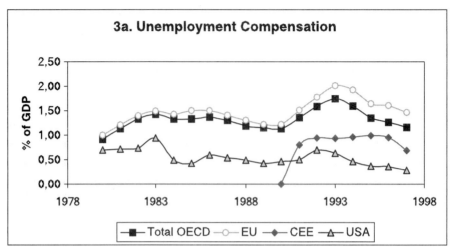

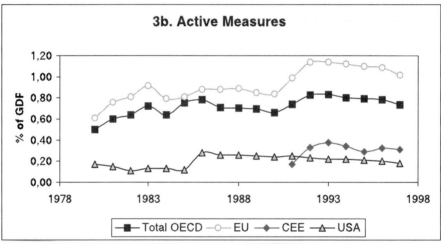

Figure 3. Public spending 1980–97

Source: OECD (2000a).

the OECD average is very close to the EU series at a lower level, the US series varies less, although it displays a similar behaviour for the 1990s – this, however, at a substantially lower (relative) level.

In terms of active measures (Figure 3b) the EU has seen a more or less steady increase since 1980, also including a more pronounced increase between 1990 and 1992, followed by a slow decrease since. The OECD average shows similar though less pronounced developments. The US has spent a substantially lower GDP share on active measures than the OECD total, decreasing very little but steadily ever since a short increase between 1985 and 1986. The series for labour market training in Figure 3c display similar shapes, although the EU high of 1992 is followed by a short steep decline, a steady increase until 1996 and another dip in 1997. For the US, the 1986 high is also more pronounced, as is the steady and substantial decrease up to a stagnant series from 1993 on.

Figure 4 illustrates the development of public spending on (a) unemployment compensation, (b) active measures, and (c) labour market training for the years 1985, 1991, 1997 for selected European countries (see Martin, 2000 for the composition of total spending on the various measures). Countries are ordered by 1997 expenditure from left to right, including bars for the EU average and OECD total to the far right. Unsurprisingly, Sweden and Denmark can be found to the right in all panels, with Sweden leading expenditure on active measures, and Denmark on labour market training. These two countries are similar in terms of their 1997 spending on unemployment compensation. However, whereas in Sweden this implies a strong increase, the figures highlight Denmark as the prime example among European countries performing the transition from a benefit system of passive measures to one of active measures.

Instead, the UK has reduced public spending on active measures (Figure 4b) and has strongly reduced spending on benefits (Figure 4a), which results in a position to the far left. Countries like Germany and France display relatively little change, noteworthy being France increasing its spending on active measures (Figure 4b) and Germany temporarily devoting large budget shares to labour market training in 1991. The latter is due to the provision of labour market training to large numbers of newly unemployed from the Eastern *Länder* succeeding reunification (see Lechner, 2000). Ireland managed to reduce unemployment compensation payments (Figure 4a), and largely reduced spending on labour market training (Figure 4c). The Netherlands allocate a large share of GDP to benefits (Figure 4a). Public spending of a substantial amount on both passive and active measures is a very recent phenomenon in Switzerland, where significant unemployment is also only observed in recent years. OECD and EU averages display relatively little change.

2.2.2. Theoretical justifications for the provision of ALMP. The consequences of long-term unemployment are a matter of serious concern, for equity and efficiency reasons. *Equity* reasons are one part of the argument justifying the provision of

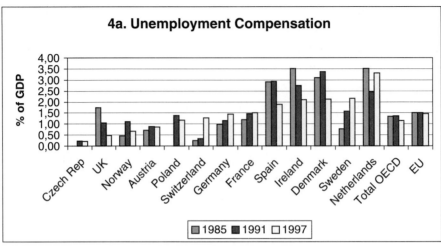

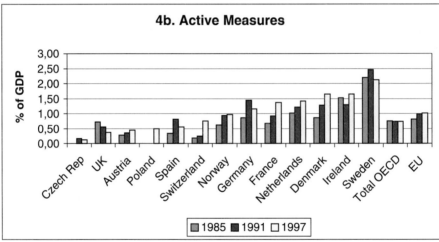

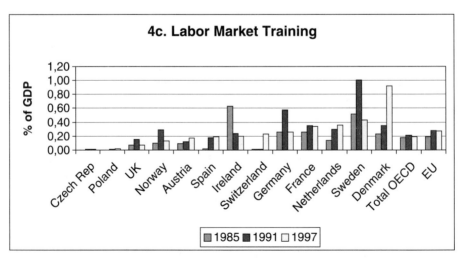

Figure 4. Public spending by countries

Source: OECD (2000a).

directly targeted policies. Both the long-term unemployed and the less skilled are typically among the poorest and most disadvantaged workers, so that one should target them for redistributive reasons alone. Machin and Manning (1999) emphasize that one of the major pathways to poverty in Europe seems to be a persistent lack of work. Consequently, the high relevance of long-term unemployment implies that this experience might be concentrated on a smaller group of individuals, particularly if long-term unemployment hits the same individuals recurrently, who become heavily disadvantaged compared to other workers.

Any *efficiency* argument for directly targeted policies must be based on some presumed inefficiency in the operation of labour markets in the absence of such policies, i.e. some form of externality. The one externality that Machin and Manning (1999) discuss more directly is a negative externality on wage pressure, arising from a high share of long-term unemployed among the jobless. Similarly, Calmfors (1994, 1995) argues that ALMP might exert positive effects on the labour force, in the sense that they might maintain the size of the effective labour force during times of high unemployment, thereby providing *competition* for insiders.

In addition, ALMP might also raise the *productivity* of targeted workers more generally, and more specifically lead to increased effectiveness of the *matching* process. This effect might be induced most directly by facilitating a fast *re-allocation* of labour across sectors or by aiding in a process of *screening* workers for their job suitability. This argument is also one of three main policy directions identified by the *Manpower and Social Affairs Committee* of the OECD. In its original account, ALMPs are viewed as improving the trade-off between inflation and unemployment by stabilizing employment during the cyclical downswing and by removing labour market bottlenecks during the upswing (OECD, 1990). To the extent that labour market interventions aim at improving an economy's employment performance by fostering competition among workers, they should at least increase employment rates among the target group.

Any labour market intervention might carry sizeable deadweight and substitution effects. *Deadweight loss* implies that there is no net job creation, since the targeted workers would have found employment also without the programme, while *substitution* captures the possibility that the support of targeted workers leads to the displacement of other workers, or to expanding employment at subsidized firms at the expense of employment in other firms. Another caveat acknowledged in the literature is *locking-in*, i.e. the search activity of programme participants tends to be reduced while on the programme (see e.g. Carling *et al.*, 1996). Consequently, Calmfors (1994) emphasizes that the assessment of the impact of any active labour market intervention needs to proceed net of so-called bookkeeping effects.

Depending on the nature and extent of their direct and indirect – on workers outside the target group – effects taken together, ALMP programmes might or might not be advocated on efficiency grounds. While the need for an assessment of their impact at the macroeconomic level is indisputable, it seems fair to argue that at least a central, if not decisive aspect for this question is the effect of programmes on the programme participants themselves. Under most conceivable circumstances, interventions that fail to improve labour market outcomes for their intended target group can hardly command a positive net effect on the economy. Correspondingly, in many European countries the current discussion of the impact of ALMP mainly regards possible consequences for the employment situation of the workers targeted by these programmes.

2.2.3. Correlates of ALMP expenditures. The second and third column of Table 1 document the results of regressions of ALMP expenditures, expressed as a percentage of GDP divided by unemployment, on factors capturing the presence and extent of various labour market institutions. These factors are the same as described above (but the union coverage indicator, a relatively coarse measure, is excluded in column 3). In a structural model, of course, the intensity and character (active versus passive) of labour market interventions would be explained by economic and political interactions. Hence, the partial correlations reported in Table 1 are purely descriptive. Still, a clear and interesting pattern emerges from these regressions. Countries characterized by exactly those labour market institutions which have been associated with high long-term unemployment also tend to utilize ALMP more heavily. In particular, a high tax wedge, considerable employment protection policies, and a high union density tend to be positively correlated with a heavy use of ALMP measures. Similarly, a high unemployment benefit replacement rate is typical for countries with intense ALMP in operation. Most interestingly, while countries with a benefit system guaranteeing unemployment support for more than one year do not heavily rely on active measures, this pattern is reversed for those countries which feature indefinite duration of unemployment benefits.

These regressions add emphasis to the distinction we draw between ALMP practice in the US and Europe. In the US targeted programmes intend either to relieve the income situation of the disadvantaged who are usually working at low wages, or to provide incentives for recipients of welfare benefits to take up work. This is in stark contrast to the European perspective where it is unemployment that is the major source of concern. European systems of poverty relief are generally felt to be working very successfully, and it is the lacking contribution to overall activity by the recipients of generous welfare and unemployment support, less the failure of poverty alleviation, which apparently represents the motivation for the intense utilization of active measures in European labour markets.

2.3. The Luxembourg Process

Against the background of an unsatisfactory European employment performance, in 1997 the EU Commission started what has become known as the *Luxembourg Process*.

The Amsterdam Treaty introduced a new Employment Title and, thus, for the first time gave explicit recognition to the fact that employment issues have a status equal to that of other key aspects of EU economic policy. This is regarded as a crucial step in the European Employment Strategy. While the Amsterdam Treaty recognizes that the primary responsibility for design and implementation of employment policies resides at member state level, it emphasizes that 'member states [. . .] shall regard promoting employment as a matter of common concern and shall co-ordinate their actions' (Article 2). Furthermore, in the Treaty the Union commits itself to a high level of employment as an explicit goal 'in the formulation and implementation of Community policies and activities' (Article 3).

The corresponding Luxembourg Process started at the Luxembourg Jobs summit in November 1997 when member states decided that this European Employment Strategy should be built on thematic grounds, grouped in four *pillars* – employability, entrepreneurship, adaptability, equal opportunities – and described in *Employment Guidelines*. The procedure is as follows: each year, the Commission and the Council formulate employment guidelines within each pillar. The guidelines are translated into National Action Plans (NAPs) for employment by the member states. In turn, these NAPs, along with labour market developments in each country over the year, are then analysed by the Commission and the Council and result in an annual Joint Employment Report (JER). The findings of the JER constitute the basis for reshaping the guidelines and country-specific recommendations for member states' employment policies for the following year.

For instance, regarding the 'employability' pillar, the initial 1998 *Employment Guidelines* focus on tackling youth and long-term unemployment by ALMP, as well as more generally on the restructuring of the benefit system in moving from passive to active measures (European Commission, 1997). Since then, the *Employment Guidelines* have remained more or less the same. While there has been almost no further specification of concrete targets, it seems that the initial guideline formulations have been softened further in order to accommodate individual member states' desire (or necessity) to possibly deviate from the stated objectives. But even if many objectives remain vague, the basic feedback set-up of guidelines leading to NAPs, NAPs and actual developments leading to JERs, which in turn lead to revised guidelines for the next year etc., does seem promising.

In particular the JERs give a clear – even if not always concise – account of problems that have been addressed and problems that need further attention (e.g. European Commission, 1998, 2000). Indeed, the Report's 'Identification of Good Practice' might help to identify those policy measures across countries that actually work. However, a major problem in this feedback set-up remains: 'Systematic evaluation of employment and labour market policies is still not common practice in many Member States' (European Commission, 1998). How else would it be possible to judge the performance of any employment policy? It remains strikingly odd that only few member states turn to independent scientific evaluation in order to achieve the desired monitoring of progress and learn about the desired effectiveness of policy mix (Council of the European Union, 2001).

Since the net effect of ALMP is so difficult to assess, and since the central ingredient is the direct effect they exert on targeted workers, thorough programme evaluation is indispensable. If the Luxembourg Process intends to properly pursue its goals, it needs a stronger connection to scientific evaluation practice in order to make the feedback structure and 'identification of good practice' meaningful. Ideally, our study would review evidence on ALMP programmes implemented after the beginning of the Luxembourg Process. This is not yet possible, however, and therefore almost all available results refer to programmes at least initiated before the introduction of EU *Employment Guidelines*. Still, these results can indicate how existing policies should be continued, adjusted or abolished, and hence which of them should play a further role in the Luxembourg Process.

3. PROGRAMME EVALUATION: METHODOLOGY AND IMPLEMENTATION

Labour economists and econometricians have developed appropriate methods for programme evaluation (for an exhaustive overview see Heckman *et al.*, 1999). This literature emphasizes the heterogeneity of individual participants and of the effects that treatment under the programme exerts on them, and places central attention on the necessity to construct comparison groups which are genuinely comparable for the purpose of assessing average programme effects. Yet, the current practice of programme evaluation is quite different across the Atlantic. We argue below that the 'evaluation culture' is best developed in the US, and that Europe needs to catch up in many regards.

3.1. Methodology and data requirements

While complete assessment of general equilibrium effects would be highly desirable (see below), most of the literature on programme evaluation is concerned with the evaluation of partial equilibrium effects. Specifically, the objective is the identification of the effect of programme participation for the participant population. The 'mean effect of treatment on the treated' is assessed by measuring an outcome variable that captures labour market performance – either employment probability or earnings *post-treatment*. The causal connection of interest is between treatment and associated outcome. Since it is possible to measure the outcome for participants, the crucial question one needs to answer is: What outcome would programme participants have had if they had not participated in the programme? Once an answer is found to this counterfactual question, the causal effect of the programme can be computed as the difference of outcome variables between participation and non-participation state (for participants). Of course, it is impossible to observe individuals in two different states of nature at the same time and place. Yet, a comparison between these two states is necessary to identify the causal effect of treatment on the treated. Thus, finding a credible estimate for the counterfactual state of nature is the principal task of any evaluation study. This is the so-called *evaluation problem*, to which Box 1 offers a basic introduction.

Randomized experiments provide the easiest solution to recovering the desired counterfactual. If individuals eligible for programme participation are randomly assigned to a treatment and control group, these two groups differ from each other (on average) neither in observable nor in unobservable characteristics. Since the control group can therefore be considered 'identical' to the treatment group, the average difference of outcomes between the two groups provides a simple answer to the counterfactual question.[3]

If randomized experiments are not feasible or experimental data is not available, evaluation research has to rely on *non-experimental* (or *observational*) methods. The validity of non-experimental approaches has been a matter of intense discussion ever since the paper by LaLonde (1986) showed that state-of-the-art (at the time) non-experimental econometric methods could not replicate experimental estimates of training effects.

Box 1. The evaluation problem

Let 1 denote the state associated with receiving treatment, and 0 the state associated with not receiving treatment, where 'treatment' comprises a particular programme of ALMP. Receiving treatment is expressed by the indicator variable D_i. Causal inference on the effectiveness of treatment compares two states of the world: What would happen to individual i on the labour market if i did receive treatment ($D_i = 1$) relative to the case in which i did not receive treatment ($D_i = 0$). The causal impact for i is thus given by

$$\Delta_i = Y_{1i} - Y_{0i}, \tag{1}$$

where the variable Y captures post-treatment labour market outcomes (e.g. employment rates). It is the core of the *evaluation problem* that we can never observe Y_{1i} and Y_{0i} – and therefore Δ_i – simultaneously for any given individual, since a worker can either participate in the treatment or not. The essential conceptual point is that nonetheless every individual has two possible outcomes associated with herself, where one realization of the outcome variable can actually be observed for each i, and the other one is a *counterfactual* outcome.

Counterfactual outcomes describe hypothetical states of the world, as it is impossible to observe the probability distribution of the Δ_i in the population.

---

[3] In practice, however, even randomized experiments are not entirely free of complications: see Heckman and Smith (1995) for further discussion of advantages and disadvantages.

The only frequency distributions we can estimate are those of Y_{1i} for participants ($D_i = 1$) and that of Y_{0i} for non-participants ($D_i = 0$), respectively. Moreover, in general we cannot assume that Δ_i is equal for all workers: Some might be better off as a result of treatment, some worse. It is thus impossible to estimate individual gains with confidence. Yet, it might be possible to assess the population average of gains from treatment, as we know that the population averages of the frequency distributions of Y_{1i} and Y_{0i} can be estimated for the $D_i = 1$ and $D_i = 0$ populations, respectively. Interest in programme evaluation is therefore on specific *evaluation parameters*, i.e. values that summarize the individual gains from treatment appropriately. The most prominent evaluation parameter is the *mean effect of treatment on the treated*,

$$M = E(\Delta \,|\, D = 1) = E(Y_1 - Y_0 \,|\, D = 1) = E(Y_1 \,|\, D = 1) - E(Y_0 \,|\, D = 1), \qquad (2)$$

where the expectations operator $E(.)$ denotes population averages, and individual subscripts are dropped to reflect the focus on population averages. The mean effect of treatment on the treated appropriately summarizes the individual gains of those individuals who do receive the treatment, without restricting their heterogeneity.

Clearly, one of the two population averages featured in (2) is identified from observable data, while the other one is not: In principle one can estimate $E(Y_1 \,|\, D = 1)$ with infinite precision from available data on programme participants, but it is impossible to estimate the population average $E(Y_0 \,|\, D = 1)$, since no sample size alleviates the fact that the Y_{0i} are not observed for participants. Ultimately, the evaluation problem is thus the problem of finding an appropriate *identification assumption* that allows replacing the counterfactual population average $E(Y_0 \,|\, D = 1)$ with an entity that is identified from observable data. It is a counterfactual because it indicates what would have happened to participants – on average – if they had not participated in the programme. This problem cannot be solved by more or refined measurement, but only by finding a plausible comparison group.

A common strategy is to estimate the unobservable $E(Y_0 \,|\, D = 1)$ with the observable $E(Y_0 \,|\, D = 1)$, using the non-participation outcomes of the non-participant population. This identification assumption is most likely to hold under *randomization*: a randomized social experiment ensures that treatment and comparison group do not differ systematically from each other in both observable and unobservable characteristics. In an *observational study*, however, this property is more difficult to achieve: Even when one compares comparable individuals for all relevant configurations of observable characteristics and weighs the corresponding means appropriately, there might be unobservable factors that invalidate the comparison. In formal terms, it could be that $E(Y_0 \,|\, D = 1) \neq E(Y_0 \,|\, D = 0)$. This phenomenon is called *selection bias*.

In recent years, *matching* estimators have received substantial attention in the evaluation literature as one way to solve the evaluation problem in a non-experimental context. Matching estimators mimic a randomized experiment *ex post* by constructing a comparison group as similar as possible to the treatment group. The comparison group thus substitutes for an experimental control group. However, even with the most informative data, matching can only control for observable differences between treatment and comparison group, and the method therefore assumes that there is no remaining unobserved heterogeneity between the two groups that could potentially bias the treatment effect estimate. Carefully applied, matching estimators can convincingly answer the counterfactual question of programme evaluation.[4] Alternative approaches for evaluating policy measures are so-called *control function*, or *selection-corrected*, estimators and *instrumental variables* techniques.[5] Classical selection-corrected estimation (Heckman, 1979) typically proceeds along a two-step procedure. First, a 'participation equation' is estimated to account for differences between participants and non-participants and to obtain for each participant a corresponding 'selection-correcting' parameter, an indication of how likely programme participation of participants would have been *a priori*, given their various observable characteristics. As this estimated parameter provides information on any unobserved – to the researcher – characteristics of the participants, it can be used as an explanatory factor in a second-step estimation of the 'outcome equation', in addition to an indicator of programme participation and other control variables. This technique has played a major role in early evaluation research (see e.g. Björklund and Moffitt, 1987), yet it has recently met serious criticism, since in most applications researchers have to proceed under restrictive assumptions on functional forms and statistical distributions (see Vella, 1998).

While most evaluation studies in the US focus on earnings (a continuous variable) as the outcome of interest, the focus of most European studies is on employment success (a discrete variable). In practice, these studies often focus on the length of individual spells of unemployment, with and without treatment under a labour market programme. So-called *duration* models analyze spell length in terms of a series of exit propensities (or hazard rates): at any point in time, exit from unemployment to employment (or possibly out of the labour force) might occur depending on inherent features of unemployment state, which might for example imply negative *duration dependence* (hazard rates tend to decline) due to depreciation of human capital; or on the observed and unobserved characteristics of the worker, the latter typically specified as multiplicative shifts of individual hazard rates (in so-called mixed proportional

---

[4] Building on the LaLonde paper and using the same data set, Dehejia and Wahba (1999) show that their matching algorithm can reproduce the experimental benchmark estimate. However, as Smith and Todd (2002) demonstrate, this result appears to be coincidental. In any case, it looks very much as if the general question, whether matching can reproduce experimental estimates or not, cannot be answered with the (small and uninformative) data set of LaLonde's paper. The current enthusiasm about matching estimators rather seems to find justification in thoughtful applications in which matching algorithm and data are meticulously adapted (see Heckman *et al.*, 1997; Kluve *et al.*, 1999; or Lechner, 2000).

[5] Due to space constraints we omit the discussion of instrumental variables techniques. See Heckman *et al.* (1999) for further details. None of the evaluation studies we assess in Section 4 applies an instrumental variable approach.

hazard models); or on similarly modelled treatment effects of labour market programmes.[6]

3.1.1. General equilibrium effects and cost–benefit analysis.

The macroeconomic literature (e.g. Calmfors, 1994, 1995) concludes that micro-econometric estimates of individual treatment effects merely provide partial information about the full impact of ALMP. However, reliable empirical evidence which considers all direct and indirect effects on programme participants and on workers not targeted by the intervention is very difficult to generate. Any appropriate non-experimental strategy would have to rely on suitably exploiting variation in the extent of ALMP across jurisdictions or across time, or both. Moreover, at the aggregate level expenditures for ALMP tend to be high in bad times: this two-way causality between policy measures and outcomes makes it very difficult to assess the impact of the former on the latter, and reliable evidence from macro studies is limited. One attempt is the analysis of regional Swedish data by Calmfors and Skedinger (1995). Their study explicitly tries to account for a policy response function to mitigate the endogeneity of explanatory factors, but is still lumping together various types of programmes. Overall, efforts to disentangle general equilibrium effects of ALMP programmes empirically have remained scarce, and the results inconclusive. Most existing studies suffer from substantial data and technical difficulties (see Martin, 2000). Moreover, as Heckman *et al.* (1999) emphasize, accounting for *general equilibrium effects* in a convincing way generally requires the construction of a structural model of the labour market. Their discussion indicates that the use of general equilibrium methods can help produce more accurate assessments of the true impact of the programmes. However, the difficulty of assembling all behavioural parameters for a structural general equilibrium model is substantial, and the conclusions from these models remain controversial, so that their relative value compared to the now more traditional 'treatment effect' evaluations continues to be an open research question (see also Smith, 2000).

Apart from research complications it also has to be emphasized that general equilibrium effects play an important role only in certain contexts. For instance, they are more likely to be relevant in the evaluation of a large-scale – relative to the population – policy measure rather than in assessing the impact of a small-scale programme. The crucial insight for programme evaluation is that a programme with no partial equilibrium effects – i.e. no positive individual treatment effect – will likely not have general equilibrium ones either. A training programme that does not enhance the human capital of its participants will not have them displace non-participants in the labour market. It therefore makes sense to begin programme evaluation at its most important point: the assessment of treatment effects on the treated population. Hence, the focus of the evaluation literature on individual

---

[6] See Ham and LaLonde (1996), Magnac (2000), and Abbring and van den Berg (2000) for a comprehensive account of duration methods for estimating treatment effects.

treatment effects appears justified, and a necessary approach in order to learn about programme effectiveness.

Assessing the effects of policies is the most immediate issue for evaluation exercises, but the results also offer essential input to *cost–benefit analysis*. In turn, conducting cost–benefit analyses is important for 'evidence-based' policy-making, based on facts rather than theory or ideology (Smith, 2000). Cost–benefit analysis compares the estimated benefits of a policy to its estimated costs. Assuming that benefits and costs are correctly measured, the policy is justified on efficiency grounds if the former exceed the latter, and should otherwise be abandoned unless other justifications – such as equity reasons – can be found for it. The most important benefits of ALMP are earnings and employment gains in the post-programme period. Furthermore, benefits include the value of the output produced in the programme (if any), and reduced costs on other training and employment programmes. The cost side consists mainly of the direct programme implementation and operation costs. Additional costs include foregone earnings, and costs arising from displacement effects and deadweight loss.

Cost–benefit analyses could be conducted for several of the groups involved in an ALMP measure: programme participants, non-participants, the government, or society as a whole. For programme evaluation as part of an evidence-based policy, the government perspective should be of particular interest. Estimating treatment effects on individual employment probabilities or earnings for the treated population, which is what almost all evaluation studies do, merely covers the benefit side from the viewpoint of programme participants. Whereas these constitute an important factor to the cost–benefit analysis, the cost side is frequently neglected. Indeed, in practice rigorous cost–benefit analyses as part of an evaluation study remain the exception (Heckman *et al.*, 1999). Usually, interest is exclusively focused on identifying whether a programme shows positive effects or not, without relating the results to the costs involved.

3.1.2. Data issues.   State-of-the-art evaluation research holds that the most robust evidence on programme effectiveness will result from social experiments. Indeed, at least for the US, this insight has led to numerous evaluation studies based on randomized experiments (see Section 3.2). Even taking into account various difficulties intrinsic to experimental designs, such as ethical objections, institutional limitations, costly implementation, etc., the case for social experiments remains strong, and the difficulties in methodology or interpretation associated with them are far smaller than those arising in non-experimental settings.[7]

If experimental data is not available, evaluation research has to rely on non-experimental studies. The main challenge for observational studies is to answer the counterfactual question in a convincing fashion – the very question that randomized

---

[7] See Burtless and Orr (1986), Heckman and Smith (1995), Heckman *et al.* (1999), Schmidt (1999) for discussion.

experiments answer by design. Many problems for non-experimental evaluations result from seemingly simple problems, e.g. that only data on participants is available and comparison group data has to be obtained from a different source. If some or all of the resulting difficulties – such as different questionnaires being administered to treatment and comparison group, possibly leading to differing measurement of the outcome variable, or both groups not being placed in the same local labour market, etc. – did not arise, much if not all of the bias in non-experimental estimates could be avoided. In order to be able to 'compare the comparable' (Heckman *et al.*, 1999) in an observational study, treatment and comparison group data must come from the same source, and be sufficiently informative. A good example is a non-experimental evaluation study for Swiss ALMP by Gerfin and Lechner (2000). Using matching estimators, the authors are able to produce credible impact estimates thanks to a solid method applied to highly informative data, which was collected for treatment and comparison group at the same time.

This also shows that, ultimately, the solution to the evaluation problem lies in both the method and the data (Heckman *et al.*, 1999). No particular estimation technique supplies a magic bullet to recovering the desired counterfactual. Randomized experiments can produce reliable treatment effect estimates in a straightforward fashion, and recent advances in non-experimental techniques make credible impact estimates in observational studies possible. This is particularly true for approaches displaying a fine-tuned adjustment of method and data. Most of the evaluation literature has focused on advances in methodology, but even the most sophisticated estimators will fail if applied to poor data, and one should not forget that good, informative data are essential for meaningful evaluation.

3.2. The state of affairs

3.2.1. The US experience.
Evaluation practice and research in the US is not perfect, but it is certainly the most advanced. Ever since early training programmes such as those implemented under the MDTA (Manpower Development and Training Act, enacted 1962) or the CETA (Comprehensive Employment and Training Act, 1975) were started, these programmes have been accompanied by deliberate evaluation efforts. This manifests a certain 'evaluation culture' in which it is without question that any programme should be subject to an assessment of its efficiency.

Programme evaluations are performed by different institutions. Smith (2000) distinguishes four main groups: government employees conducting 'in-house' evaluations, for-profit consulting firms, non-profit consulting firms, and academic researchers. Clearly, each group has specific advantages and disadvantages regarding their knowledge of methodology, their ability to deliver results on time, and their incentives to promote the interests of the programme at the expense of the evaluation. Often different groups collaborate in a large-scale evaluation, combining the virtues of the various actors (Smith, 2000). Also, movements between academia, government and consultants are frequent, strongly increasing the communication between groups and the connection of methodological development and practical application.

This evaluation culture led to the widespread use of evaluations based on randomized social experiments, since researchers found early non-experimental results to differ too strongly to deliver convincing results. For instance, inconclusive evidence from non-experimental evaluations of the MDTA and CETA programmes led to the experimental evaluation of the National JTPA Study (Job Training and Partnership Act, 1982) – see Friedlander *et al.* (1997) for further discussion. In fact, experimental evaluation has come to be an indispensable part of the political process implementing any new social programme. Besides achieving the strong emphasis on social experiments, the close connection between evaluation practice and academic research strongly contributed to recent methodological developments in non-experimental techniques, in particular matching estimators.

Stanley *et al.* (1999) summarize the quantitative evidence available from the evaluation of US labour market programmes. Disadvantaged youth are in general difficult to assist, although some programmes have succeeded in doing so. Programmes for disadvantaged youth under 21 – in particular high school dropouts – have been less successful than programmes for other populations, unless training was highly intensive or quite well implemented. Programmes offering government jobs appear successful in improving employment rates during the subsidy period, but there is little or no evidence on long-term positive effects. The target population of poor adults – especially single parents seeking to leave welfare – appears to respond well to training programmes. Furthermore, programmes aimed at encouraging additional job search assistance for dislocated workers appear to have positive effects.

Job search assistance in general seems to be a measure that reliably speeds up the return to work and saves government money. While earnings impacts tend to be moderate at best, Stanley *et al.* (1999) find the record for these efforts to be 'consistent and clear', as on average they lead to a faster return to work. Among other programme types, earnings supplements, hiring subsidies, and subsidized employment lead to employment gains for the disadvantaged. However, the increase in employment rates mainly occurs during the period when the actual subsidy is offered. On the other hand, if subsidized employment is combined with on-the-job training, adult trainees – but unfortunately not the disadvantaged youth – show higher employment rates and earnings well after the period of subsidized employment is over.

The findings reported by Stanley *et al.* (1999) are congruent with the overall results summarized by Heckman *et al.* (1999). Evidence from both experimental and non-experimental evaluations in the US suggests that government employment and training programmes (1) can improve the economic prosperity of low-skilled persons, and (2) have markedly varying impacts on different demographic and skill groups. Findings reveal that these programmes raise the earnings of economically disadvantaged adult women. For adult men, this impact is often smaller and less consistently positive. The evidence for youths is not encouraging, as neither experimental nor non-experimental evaluations indicate that employment and training programmes help improve US youths' labour market prospects.

The general conclusion regarding ALMP effectiveness in the US is that if there are any positive treatment effects at all, then these will be small (Heckman *et al.*, 1999). Frequently, the individual gains from programmes are not sufficiently large to lift many participants out of poverty (as is the principal goal in many US programmes). The returns to ALMP measures are generally low compared to the substantial costs they involve. Due to these findings it was possible to eliminate ineffective programme components. As a result, ALMP programmes have received less attention by US governments in recent years. Whereas this may not be the most desirable result (clearly, effective programmes would be favoured by everybody), it does emphasize the importance of a healthy evaluation culture. Failure of programmes should not be equated with failure of evaluation practice.

3.2.2. The European experience.   Ever since the first introduction of ALMP into European economies there has been ongoing research on their evaluation. However this research – even after introduction of the Luxembourg Process – is still in its infancy, mainly due to lack of communication between the scientific community and those financing, designing and implementing public sector programmes. The European evaluation culture is lagging behind the US in at least three interrelated aspects.

First, in many European countries it is far from obvious for political practice to have ALMP programmes accompanied by evaluation efforts. Second, even when this is the case, evaluations are often conducted in-house only, or with a large time-lag, or are not accompanied by satisfactory data collection. Third, it remains unclear whether evaluation results will have any impact on future policy.

The first aspect can only be explained with either a general reluctance towards a practice of evidence-based policy, or possibly with the fact that ALMP measures are introduced for political rather than efficiency reasons. It may be convenient for a government to show activity, but not to assess whether the activity actually pays off.[8] This is a question of political incentives and attitude, and may be difficult to change, or will at least take time to do so. Within Europe, the need for evaluation is felt with greatly differing strength across countries' governments. For instance, whereas the Swiss government initiated a large-scale research programme for the evaluation of its active labour market policies (see Lalive *et al.*, 2000; Gerfin and Lechner, 2000), the German government mostly relies on in-house accounting of ALMP measures rather than rigorous evaluation, with no gain in knowledge about their efficiency whatsoever (Schmidt *et al.*, 2001).

---

[8] One political incentive could be that active labour market programmes – implying direct interventions in favour of the unemployed – are much easier to convey to the electorate than comparatively controversial or unpopular measures such as lower unemployment benefits, shorter benefit duration, or less strict employment protection legislation, even though the beneficial effects of the latter on the efficiency of the labour market might be equally large or even larger. Of course, as Calmfors (1995) puts it '[t]here is nothing wrong with this if large-scale active labour market programmes are an efficient way of promoting employment. The problem is if they are not.'

The second aspect concerns evaluation practice. Since neither non-profit nor for-profit consulting firms play a role in evaluating European ALMP, and since in-house evaluations may often both fall behind in terms of methodological knowledge and face strong incentives to produce positive findings (Smith, 2000), an unsatisfactory evaluation practice in Europe seems to be mostly due to a lack of communication between policy-makers and the scientific community. Deliberate evaluation efforts rarely accompany programmes from the first step of their implementation, so that (1) academic researchers are usually excluded from the process of designing and real-izing the programmes, and (2) the data collected during the programme are not sufficiently informative, or not accessible, in many cases. The latter point concerns both experimental and non-experimental data – although it is particularly unfortunate that policy-makers in many European countries remain reluctant to introduce social experiments, even though most academic experts are calling for their introduction and even though experiments have produced the most reliable evidence in the US.

But even non-experimental studies rarely go hand in hand with the programme itself – rather, programmes are often implemented without any thought of whether they will ever be evaluated. High quality data remains the exception, and academic researchers conduct their studies *ex post* without real connection to the programme and possibly without ever being able to communicate their results to policy makers. Hence the uncertainty as to whether evaluation results will have any influence on future policy cannot be surprising.

Clearly, Europe has much to learn from the evaluation culture in the US. But there are signs of hope. First, our assessment of the Luxembourg Process (Section 2.3) has shown that EU policy-makers have started a joint employment strategy entailing the use of ALMP, a strategy redesigned and adapted each year based on a feedback process. In theory, this feedback structure – if it wants to be efficient – implies rigorous programme evaluation, and some day soon perhaps academic researchers will be included in this process.

Second, European researchers have followed US researchers in their development of modern evaluation methods. European academic economists can handle the ana-lytical tools that solve the evaluation problem, and they are ready to use them. The large number of current evaluation studies that we review in the next section (and which in most cases were not attached to the implementation of the programme they analyse) gives proof to this claim. Thus, even though the European evaluation culture must catch up with the US in many respects, recent developments on both the political side and the academic side point to the right direction, and a mere connec-tion of the two sides would imply a large step forward.

4. FINDINGS FROM EUROPEAN PROGRAMME EVALUATION

In many European economies, the sheer scale of ALMP interventions alone implies that macroeconomic repercussions might be considerable: active measures might improve aggregate employment performance through several channels, but programmes might also deliver unintended side effects. Thus, there is high demand for a better understanding of European labour markets and of the impact of ALMP on participants and labour markets at large. An important first step in this endeavour is provided by the growing amount of state-of-the-art evaluation research regarding ALMP effectiveness in Europe, a literature that focuses on treatment effects.

This section discusses the conclusions that *can* be drawn regarding ALMP effectiveness in Europe on the basis of evaluation research. Due to the substantial heterogeneity characterizing European labour markets, it is not entirely clear what any one European country can eventually learn from experiences made in any other country – in an economically integrated Europe it is therefore imperative to collect evidence throughout all its constituent economies. The coarse but crucial juxtaposition of the US and Europe should not be confused with a uniformity of programme effects across European economies. While many of the particular evaluation questions – the emphasis on youth programmes, or the focus on employment instead of earnings – are of a distinct European character, programmes across Europe are quite heterogeneous.

Increasing academic interest in evaluation research finds expression in a large number of evaluation studies. Previous research (on programmes before 1994) has been reviewed in Heckman *et al.* (1999, Table 25). Here, we focus on findings from research since then. Table 2 presents an overview of recent evaluations of ALMP in various European countries. Looking at the *type of programmes*, we find a substantial variety across countries. But even though regulations differ greatly in detail, a broad classification into 'training-type' and 'subsidy-type' programmes seems apt. Many subsidy-type programmes are designed as incentive schemes, directed at potential private sector employers and workers. Other programmes merely subsidize employment in the public sector. One incentive scheme in Switzerland intends to get unemployed into programmes by making unemployment benefit receipt conditional on ALMP participation (Lalive *et al.*, 2000). Some programmes exclusively focus on job search assistance – like the 'Counselling and Monitoring' programme in the Netherlands (van den Berg and van der Klaauw, 2001) – or entail such assistance to a large degree, like the 'New Deal' in the UK (Bell *et al.*, 1999).

Unemployed individuals who either receive unemployment benefits or are at least eligible for the receipt constitute the *target group* of most programmes. Many programmes – in particular in Northern Europe – target the young among the unemployed. Few of the ALMP measures make finer distinctions in targeting, e.g. the Dutch 'Counselling and Monitoring' programme which is aimed at unemployed workers with 'relatively good labour market prospects'.

The evaluation of this programme (van den Berg and van der Klaauw, 2001) is also the only study in our review originating from a *social experiment*. All other papers rely on *non-experimental* data. This reflects the fact that most of the studies were not connected to the political process that decided on, and implemented the programmes. Exceptions are evaluations of Swiss ALMP by Lalive *et al.* (2000) and Gerfin and Lechner (2000), which were part of the same research programme initiated by the Swiss Government. The remaining studies did not accompany the programme, and were thus conducted with (sometimes substantial) time lag, and without certainty as to whether their results will reach policy-makers.

As indicators of *programme effectiveness*, most of the studies analyse treatment effects on either employment (unemployment) rates or employment (unemployment) durations or hazards, respectively. A minority of studies (Bell *et al.*, 1999; Larsson, 2000; Lechner, 2000; Raaum and Torp, 2002; Regnér 2002) also considers wages as outcome variables of interest. With respect to *estimation methods*, most studies apply matching estimators, which – given the prevalence of non-experimental data – try to mimic a randomized experiment *ex post*, as outlined in Section 3.1. Compared to the early European evaluation studies cited in Heckman *et al.* (1999) cross-sectional data has largely disappeared and ALMP research in Europe is now based on much more informative longitudinal data, potentially making the impact estimates more reliable.

4.1. Quantitative analysis

In order to get some insight into the status quo of ALMP evaluation in Europe we begin with a brief quantitative analysis. We combine the information on the first generation of European evaluation studies given in Table 25 of Heckman *et al.* (1999) with the second generation studies from our Table 2. This results in a data set of European evaluation studies in which each observation represents the evaluation of one particular ALMP programme.[9] Since this approach entails the joint statistical analysis of estimated treatment parameters which were derived under a large range of circumstances and with differing methods and, presumably, scientific rigour, our quantitative analysis must remain exploratory. We use as a dependent variable in our analysis an indicator variable (1/0) reflecting whether the study found a significantly positive treatment effect or not. In the data set, 28 of the 53 evaluations report a positive treatment effect.[10]

We employ as our explanatory factors indicator variables for three *treatment types* – subsidy-type schemes (used as a base category), training programmes, and job search assistance – and an indicator variable for programmes in which *young workers* were targeted. Nearly two out of three interventions included in our analysis concerned training programmes, and approximately one out of four were subsidy-type schemes (which comprise wage subsidies to private employers, but also subsidized employment

---

[9] If a study evaluates more than one programme, treatment effect estimates for all different programmes are used. For instance, a study by Payne *et al.* (1996) reported in Table 25 of Heckman *et al.* (1999) evaluates both a training and a subsidized employment programme in the UK. On the other hand, if different studies report essentially identical evaluations (same programme, same time, same result), we consider the result only once.

[10] Among the 33 programme evaluations we extracted from Heckman *et al.* (1999) 20 reported a positive effect, whereas this is the case for 8 out of the 20 programme evaluations we extract from Table 2.

Table 2. Recent European evaluation studies

Study	Country	Measure	Target group	Design	Observation period	Outcome of interest	Estimation method	Results
Larsson (2000)	Sweden	2 programmes: Youth Practice and labour market training	Young unemployed	Non-experimental	1991–1997	Annual earnings, re-employment probability, probability of regular education	Propensity score matching (multi-valued treatment), OLS, Probit	Both programmes: short-run 0 to −, long-run 0 to slightly +; Youth Practice better than Labour market training
Sianesi (2001)	Sweden	Various ALMP measures condensed into one 'treatment'	Unemployed	Non-experimental	1994–1999	Various measures of labour market status, in particular employment probability	Propensity score matching	At best 0 effects (if cycling excluded), and − otherwise
Regnér (2001)	Sweden	Training	Unemployed	Non-experimental	1987–1992	Earnings	Selection models; linear control fct., fixed effects, random growth	0 or − effects
Raaum and Torp (2001)	Norway	Labour market training	Unemployed	Non-experimental	1989–1994	Earnings	Selection models; linear control fct., fixed effects, random growth (2)	+ for the linear control fct. model, other models rejected
Jensen (1999) Jensen et al. (2000)	Denmark	Youth Employment Programme	Unemployed low-educated youth	Non-experimental	1996	Unemployment duration	Competing risks duration model	Sign. increase in transition rate U→S, weaker: U→E
Rosholm (1999)	Denmark	Employment subsidy (public and private sector)	Unemployed (UI benefit eligible)	Non-experimental	1983–1990	Unemployment hazard, employment hazard	Duration models	Private sector: U→E generally +, E→U strongly − Public sector: U→E mostly −, E→U strongly −
Bell, Blundell, van Reenen (1999)	UK	Temporary wage subsidy, training ('New Deal')	Young unemployed	Non-experimental	1997–1998	Productivity = wages	Trend-adjusted difference-in-differences	Productivity effects relatively modest (compared to size of subsidy)

Study	Country	Programme/Measure	Target group	Type	Period	Outcome	Method	Results
van den Berg, van der Klaauw (2000)	Netherlands	Counselling and Monitoring	UI recipients (w/ relatively good labour market prospects)	Social experiment	1998–1999	Unemployment hazard	Duration models, limited dependent variable models	No significant effect on individual transition rate U→E (still: programme is cost effective)
Brodaty, Crépon, Fougère (2001)	France	Youth employment programmes: 'work-place' training prog. (private s.), 'workfare' programmes (public s.)	'The most disadvantaged and unskilled young workers'	Non-experimental	1986–1988	Employment status	Propensity score matching (multi-valued treatment)	On-the-job training in private sector + (due to higher amount of vocational and specific training)
Lechner (2000)	Germany	Training and Retraining	Workers in East Germany	Non-experimental	1990–1994	Employment probability, earnings, career prospects	Partial propensity score matching	Short-term −, long-term 0, 'waste of resources'
Lalive, Zweimüller, van Ours (2000)	Switzerland	Benefit receipt conditional on ALMP participation	Unemployed UI recipients	Non-experimental	1997–1999	Unemployment duration	Duration model	Unemployment duration: men ↑, women ↑
Gerfin, Lechner (2000)	Switzerland	Training (5 types), employment programmes (private and public), temporary wage subsidy	Unemployed UI recipients	Non-experimental	1997–1998	Employment	Propensity score matching (multi-valued treatment)	Temporary wage subsidy ++, employment programmes −, training mixed
Kluve, Lehmann, Schmidt (1999)	Poland	Training, IW (wage subsidies in private sector), PW (public sector employment programme)	Unemployed	Non-experimental	1992–1996	Employment rates, unemployment rates	Exact covariate matching	Training: men and women +, IW: women 0, men −, PW: men −
van Ours (2001)	Slovak Republic	Training, SPJ (Socially purposeful jobs), PUJ (Publicly useful jobs)	Unemployed	Non-experimental	1993–1998	Job finding rate, job separation rate	Duration model	Short-term subs. jobs +, long-term subs. jobs −, training +

Notes: U = unemployment, E = employment, S = schooling, UI = unemployment insurance. Detailed reviews of all studies are available from the authors upon request.

in the public sector). Approximately 10% of the evaluations included here regarded job search assistance programmes. Youth programmes are relatively frequent in Europe, which is evidenced by the high rate of youth programmes (approximately 40%) in the data.

To capture developments in data availability and evaluation methodology, we include an indicator variable for the *study design* reflecting whether the evaluation was performed by way of a randomized experiment (only four of the studies), and indicator variables for the *timing* of the programme, i.e. the 1970s (used as a base category), the 1980s and the 1990s (both comprising nearly one-half of the studies). A finer set of time indicators did not alter the qualitative results of our analysis. Since the treatment types considered in the analysis necessarily subsume relatively diverse interventions under a common heading, even relatively imprecise estimates might be quite indicative of the basic patterns in the data.

Furthermore, we use several aggregate variables to control for the *macroeconomic environment* in which the programmes were implemented. These variables comprise indices for regulation intensity on the labour market, specifically (1) dismissal protection and (2) regulation concerning temporary work (both by country and decade). The indices are taken from Eichhorst *et al.* (2002), and range from 0.8 (UK in the 1980s and 1990s) to 3.1 (the Netherlands in the 1980s and 1990s), and from 0.0 (UK and Ireland in the 1980s and 1990s) to 3.5 (France in the 1980s), respectively.

Furthermore, we include (3) the unemployment rate, (4) government expenditures on ALMP, and (5) real GDP growth (all three by country and time of intervention). The lowest unemployment rate is 1.9% for Sweden in the late 1970s, the highest 16.5% for Ireland in the late 1980s. Government spending on ALMP programmes is expressed as a percentage of GDP, and ranges from 0.3% for the Slovak Republic in the late 1990s to 2.7% for Sweden in the early 1990s. Real GDP growth is lowest for Sweden with 0.12% and highest for Poland with 5.2%, both in the early 1990s.

Table 3 reports the marginal effects, evaluated at the sample mean, in the corresponding probit regression, i.e. the difference in the predicted probability for achieving a positive treatment effect which arises from a marginal change in a continuous explanatory factor (such as the GDP growth rate), or from changing an indicator among the explanatory factors (such as the indicator for experimental study design) from 0 to 1. The results indicate that it is important to control for the timing of the programme implementation and for the macroeconomic environment in which the programme was conducted. The discussion therefore concentrates on our preferred specification, which is reported in column (3).

4.2. What is effective?

Training measures and job search assistance are more likely than subsidy-type schemes to display a positive impact on programme participants. This finding confirms the results reviewed in Table 2, which indicate that programmes with a large

Table 3. Effects of active labour market policies: a quantitative analysis

	(1)	(2)	(3)
Indicators (1/0) for **Type of Treatment** (Base: Subsidy-Type Programme) and **Target Group** (Base: Adult Workers)			
Job search assistance	0.276 (1.16)	0.334 (1.23)	0.436 (1.53)
Training programme	0.179 (1.09)	0.145 (0.83)	0.315* (1.66)
Young workers	0.032 (0.22)	−0.043 (0.28)	−0.296 (1.41)
Indicators (1/0) for **Study Design** (Base: Non-experimental Evaluation) and **Timing** (Base: 1970s)			
Experimental design	–	−0.243 (0.70)	−0.166 (0.39)
Programme implemented in the 1980s	–	−0.093 (0.31)	−0.328 (1.00)
Programme implemented in the 1990s	–	−0.357 (1.25)	−0.666** (2.19)
The **Macroeconomic Environment**			
Index for dismissal protection	–	–	−0.230 (1.63)
Index for temporary work regulation	–	–	0.065 (0.65)
Unemployment rate	–	–	0.074* (1.85)
Expenditures on ALMP (% of GDP)	–	–	−0.154 (0.87)
GDP growth	–	–	−0.054 (0.54)
Observations		53	
Pseudo R-squared	0.0236	0.0856	0.2779

Notes: The dependent variable is an indicator (1/0) variable, reflecting a positive estimate of the programme effect. Table entries document the marginal effect (evaluated at the sample mean) in the corresponding probit regression, i.e. the difference in the predicted probability for achieving a positive treatment effect which arises from a marginal change in a continuous explanatory factor (such as the GDP growth rate) or which arises from changing an indicator among the explanatory factors (such as the indicator of an experimental study design) from 0 to 1. Absolute *t*-ratios of the marginal effects are reported in parentheses, a * indicates significance at the 10%-level, and ** indicates significance at the 5%-level, respectively (two-sided test). Countries involved in the estimation are Austria, Denmark, France, Germany, Ireland, the Netherlands, Norway, Poland, Slovakia, Sweden, Switzerland, and the UK. The indicator for regulation intensity are taken from Eichhorst *et al.* (2002).

training content (the more costly measures) seem to be most likely to improve employment probability (Raaum and Torp, 2002; Brodaty *et al.*, 2001; Kluve *et al.*, 1999; van Ours, 2001). Recent country studies do not unanimously report positive effects (Regnér, 2002; Gerfin and Lechner, 2000); but since both direct job creation and employment subsidies in the public sector almost always seem to fail (Rosholm, 1999; Brodaty *et al.*, 2001; Kluve *et al.*, 1999), in particular if they are only meant to keep unemployed persons off the register (Lechner, 2000), training does appear remarkably effective.

The dismal performance of subsidy schemes, relative to training or job search, appears to be due to ineffective public sector programmes. Indeed, wage subsidy schemes are more often reported to be positive when aimed at the private sector than the public sector (Rosholm, 1999; Gerfin and Lechner, 2000). In general, results on subsidy-type schemes seem to imply that the incentive structure needs to be well-specified in order to make them work. These tentative findings – training is better than employment subsidies, private sector programmes are superior to public sector programmes – add substantial insight to ALMP effectiveness in Europe, in particular since Heckman *et al.* (1999) found no consistent pattern emerging from the first generation of European studies.

The one consistent result from previous European research (that holds for the US alike) was the positive effect of programmes providing job search assistance, a finding borne out by our regression and current research. For instance, positive effects of job search assistance are reported for the 'New Deal' in the UK (Bell *et al.*, 1999), and for the 'Counselling and Monitoring' programme in the Netherlands, where van den Berg and van der Klaauw (2001) conclude that the more intensive the job search assistance, the higher the exit rate from unemployment to work. Furthermore, the negative sign on the coefficient for 'youth' reflects the fact that youth programmes have usually displayed negative effects. Recent evaluation studies (Jensen, 1999; Larsson, 2000) indeed conclude that in Europe, like in the US, it is also true that youths are especially difficult to assist.

The indicator for experimental evaluation does not uncover any noticeable differences, but only four studies were based on a randomized experiment (two of which report a positive effect). Looking at the timing, one might have expected more recent studies to find less optimistic results for reasons of increasing methodological rigour alone. The large (particularly when compared to the marginal effects of the programme-type indicators) and significant negative effect of our indicator for observations from the 1990s is absolutely consistent with this idea. However, this result could also be a reflection of ALMP programmes being more effective in the 1970s or 1980s, when ALMP was used at a somewhat more moderate scale.

Finally, regarding the economic environment, it seems that strict dismissal protection might be associated with non-positive treatment effects, although the effect is not significant at conventional levels. With respect to the unemployment rate it appears that positive programme impacts were mostly found at times when unemployment was high. This may not be so surprising, since e.g. van den Berg and van der Klaauw (2001) conclude that the worse the individual or macroeconomic labour market prospects, the larger is the effect of job search assistance, specifically monitoring, on the exit rate to work.

Further looking at the studies in Table 2, we find two specific results arising from current evaluation research noteworthy. First, the large positive effect of the temporary wage subsidy in Switzerland identified by Gerfin and Lechner (2000) contrasts the pessimistic general assessment of employment subsidies. This programme encourages job seekers to accept job offers that pay less than their unemployment benefit by compensating the difference with additional payments. As the income generated by the scheme is higher than the unemployment benefit for remaining unemployed, it is financially attractive for both the unemployed and the placement office. This seems to be a promising alternative ALMP measure, and it would be interesting to see whether other countries would make similarly positive experiences with it.

Second, we notice that in quite a few cases unemployment benefit regulations seem to be closely connected with programme effects. Two points are relevant. On the one hand, with respect to a tightening of rules it remains unclear whether positive treatment effects can at all be induced by a measure that forces individuals into participation (see Lalive *et al.*, 2000). On the other hand, it seems to be a major distorting factor for treatment effectiveness if programme participation restores benefit receipt eligibility. Then, many unemployed persons engage in a 'cycling' behaviour, i.e. they participate in the ALMP programme after having run out of unemployment benefit eligibility, just to re-enter benefit recipient status after the programme is over (and has restored their eligibility). Given the substantial number of studies providing evidence for this hypothesis – Rosholm (1999), Kluve *et al.* (1999), Sianesi (2001), Regnér (2002) – this appears to be one of the most robust results of current evaluation research. In fact it is surprising that such regulations are still common practice in many European countries, especially since – by a literature discussed above – too generous unemployment benefit systems have frequently been identified as one labour market feature in Europe associated with high unemployment.

In summary, the estimates from recent evaluation studies suggest that treatment effects of European ALMP are rather modest, and probably smaller and less consistently positive than policy-makers would have hoped for. Whereas the cross-country evidence does make out some effective programmes, the number of disappointing results cannot be ignored. The general lessons arising from the recent evidence are approximately in line with the overall findings reported by Heckman *et al.* (1999) for the US. ALMP programmes *can* contribute to improving the employment prospects of unemployed persons, but different programmes are differently effective for different individuals. While we want to emphasize that the results of our crude quantitative analysis have to be taken with caution, we do feel that the exercise appropriately combines previous results on European evaluation research with more recent evidence, and contributes new insight into ALMP effectiveness in Europe. At the very least, the exercise illustrates that (1) training and job search assistance can be useful measures, (2) the youth are difficult to aid effectively, and (3) early evaluation results have been overly optimistic.

5. CONCLUSION

After briefly recalling evidence of poor performance by European labour markets and discussing the link with European labour market institutions, we have argued that on the *policy side* the combination of poor performance and poor institutions has led to increasing expenditure on ALMPs, as well as more recently to the European Employment Strategy and the Luxembourg Process. We have also sketched recent advances in evaluation research, arguing that the *science side* has developed adequate tools to answer evaluation questions on ALMP effectiveness with confidence.

To the extent that policy may be misguided, a closer connection of the two sides would obviously be very beneficial. We have discussed the rationale behind introducing ALMP programmes, and reasons why they might fail to accomplish their goal. From the perspective of evidence-based policy-making, all programmes should be accompanied by an evaluation and a cost–benefit analysis. These, in turn, can be conducted at various levels, and raise different methodological problems. Since impacts at an aggregate level are more difficult to disentangle, most evaluation studies have focused on individual treatment effects. This approach makes sense, since under most circumstances positive effects at the individual level are a necessary condition for positive effects at more aggregate levels. However, they may not be sufficient, and a programme with positive treatment effects need not be cost-effective or welfare-improving. Thus, an ideal complete evaluation would have to take general equilibrium effects into account.

We have proceeded to discuss methodological and data issues that arise in the venture of programme evaluation. In terms of methodology, the evaluation problem can be solved by various approaches. The current state of the art holds that social experiments provide the most credible results. However, recent developments in non-experimental methods have made their results more reliable, and improved data quality (in particular availability of panel data) has played a substantial role, although there remains room for improvement. As our methodological discussion argues, the focus of European programmes and their evaluations is typically not on wage earnings, but on how the employment situation of programme participants is altered by the treatment, necessitating a somewhat different set of statistical approaches.

We have found that the evaluation culture is best developed in the US, and that Europe lags behind with respect to three aspects. First, in Europe it is not self-evident that programmes need to be evaluated. Second, even when an evaluation is carried out, this is often done only in-house, or the data collection accompanying the programme is unsatisfactory. Third, it remains unclear whether evaluation results will have any impact on future policy. This situation could be improved a lot if only policy-makers – who introduce ALMP programmes – and academic researchers – who have the tools to evaluate these programmes – were to communicate more closely.

Even though this situation is not yet optimal, existing research has contributed important evidence. A more consistent pattern emerges from current evaluation research compared to the previous lack of such a pattern in early European evaluation research, and it coincides largely with US findings: the young among the unemployed are typically difficult to assist and job search assistance, in particular intensive monitoring of the low-skilled, is useful. Private sector subsidies fare better than public sector programmes. Most interestingly, though, training programmes can apparently help to improve the labour market prospects of economically disadvantaged individuals in Europe, the somewhat disenchanted view on the effects of training programmes in the US (see Heckman et al., 1999) notwithstanding. Yet, this apparent contrast in results might be smaller than a first glance suggests: while US programmes aim predominantly at poverty alleviation, European training programmes intend to facilitate the transition out of unemployment, operating in labour markets where educational credentials matter considerably. Whether this positive assessment of the potential of well-targeted and well-implemented training programmes survives more intense evaluation efforts remains to be seen, as European labour market programmes by and large are still awaiting the confrontation with experimental study designs.

Can training and employment subsidies combat European unemployment? We think they can, but important caveats apply. First, any programme must be well targeted, and particularly the incentive structure of wage subsidy schemes must be well implemented. Second, the programme must not be connected to renewal of benefit receipt eligibility. Third, even if this is adhered to, one can only expect modest effects, especially if a cost–benefit analysis is conducted. A clear conception *ex ante* of what benefits would be worth which costs is imperative.

Large macroeconomic effects require treatment effects for participants to be substantial. Since individual-level effects seem to be small at best, ALMP can only be one ingredient in a set of possible policy measures aimed at labour market reform. To fulfil even this limited function, their implementation must be pursued with utmost care. As it is set up now, ALMP in Europe threatens to remain solely a device for showing political activism. An improved data collection, an inclusion of academic researchers from programme implementation to evaluation, and an opportunity to communicate expectations and results between policy makers and evaluators would go a long way in shaping a European evaluation culture.

Discussion

Jan C. van Ours
Tilburg University

Unemployment is still a major problem in many European countries and a lot of money is spent to get the unemployed back to work. Therefore, investigating the effectiveness of active labour market policies (ALMP) is very important. Jochen Kluve and Christoph Schmidt give a thorough discussion of a lot of issues involved in evaluating the effects of ALMP. They present a clear overview of empirical evaluation studies, which they use to perform an interesting empirical analysis in which every study is one data point. Finally, their call for additional research based on newly collected data is appealing. Since I basically agree with most or their arguments I will restrict my comments to three elements in the presentation where I have a slightly different opinion or where the authors could have expanded their argumentation a bit. The three comments concern the role of benefit sanctions, the importance of macroeconomic research and the plea for more evaluation by academic researchers.

An important difference between the US and Europe is that in the US financial incentives for unemployed workers to search actively for a job are stronger than in Europe. Therefore, I think that the authors could have given more attention to 'sticks' and not just to 'carrots'. Monitoring search effort of unemployed workers and subsequently imposing benefit sanctions if they fail to meet certain requirements may be an efficient way to bring the unemployed back to work. A system of monitoring and benefit sanctions does not have to be very expensive, since monitoring has to be done anyway. The authors remark that 'in practice the sanctioning elements receive relatively little attention'. I'm not sure about this since in a number of countries there have been studies on benefit sanctions showing that they are very efficient.

The authors stress at various places in the paper that it is important to take the macroeconomic effects into account. Micro-econometric research can only partly answer the relevant policy questions. It can study the effectiveness from the perspective of the individual but not macroeconomic effects such as crowding out, substitution and displacement. The authors state that success at the level of the individual is a necessary ingredient for an overall positive effect of active labour market programmes and that, since a programme that is not effective on the micro level will never be so on the macro level, it is justified to focus on empirical literature on the microeconomic level.

If I were a policy-maker, that approach would not make me too happy. The line of reasoning is that even though positive effects for individual participants may not be a sufficient condition for overall success, they are a necessary one. True as this may be in a lot of cases, it is not true for all programmes. One can easily imagine a programme that is very successful from the individual point of view and completely unsuccessful from a policy point of view. Take for example a programme of monitoring and benefit sanctions. There are two types of effects related to such a programme. The first effect is caused by the imposition of a benefit sanction. Unemployed workers that are confronted with a reduction of their benefits will search harder for a job and thus reduce their unemployment duration. The second effect has to do with the presence of the programme. Even before an individual is confronted with a benefit sanction he or she may search harder to avoid being punished. It is easy to imagine that the second effect is more important than the first. Comparing workers with and without benefit sanctions may reveal that the effect of a sanction is small, because the main effect is that every unemployed worker searches harder because of the threat of getting a sanction imposed. Or, in other words, from a micro perspective it is as if the programme has no effect while from a macro perspective it is highly effective. Therefore, I think the macroeconomic consequences of ALMP should be high on the research agenda as well. As Heckman *et al.* (1999) put it: 'The microeconomic treatment effect literature ignores the effects of programs on the interactions among agents . . . The lessons from the treatment effect literature that ignores social interactions can be quite misleading. The challenge in estimating these general equilibrium effects is the challenge of estimating credible general equilibrium models. However, unless the challenge is met, or the social interactions are documented to be unimportant, the output of micro treatment effect evaluations will provide poor guides to public policy.'

An important recommendation is that academic researchers instead of 'in-house' evaluators or consulting firms should do more evaluation studies. I very much agree with this conclusion. Independent evaluation of new policy initiatives (whether or not they refer to the labour market) should be obligatory in every country. However, the plea for more evaluation studies could have been more convincing. An important question is why policy-makers in Europe are reluctant to use independent researchers to do the evaluation. My guess is that policy-makers have a different methodology to measure the effectiveness of their policy. They look at input. For a politician it may be more important to claim the spending of €100 million on a new policy initiative as a success rather than to really investigate whether this new initiative made any sense. Also, politicians may be mostly interested in reducing open unemployment quickly rather than in long-term effects of policy programmes. Information from the US might have been helpful here. In the US there was a shift from non-experimental to experimental studies. This shift occurred because researchers found the results from non-experimental evaluations in the 1960s and 1970s too widespread. It would have been interesting if the authors had given some illustration of the usefulness of American policy evaluations. That might persuade European policy-makers to think along similar lines as their American colleagues.

All in all, I like the paper very much. I agree with most of the statements and recommendations in the paper, and I am sure it will be useful for both researchers and policy-makers.

Hylke Vandenbussche
Catholic University of Leuven

This is a very relevant paper from an economic policy point of view. It offers a very exhaustive literature review of the effects of active labour market policies (ALMP) in the EU compared to the US. One of the important differences the authors see is that in the EU much more money is spent on ALMP, while at the same time much less effort goes into the design of ALMP and the evaluation of these programmes than in the US.

The authors clearly explain the methodologies that can be used nowadays to evaluate active labour market policies (training, wage subsidies, provision of jobs) which are much more systematic and rigorous than what has been going on in Europe so far. Both existing econometric techniques and the design of social experiments are explained at length. The authors argue in favour of social experiments and support their arguments in favour of this methodology by referring to the long US experience in this area that has been positive.

The experience in the US in terms of measurement and evaluation of ALMP, however, has also revealed that despite a good methodological setup, active labour market programmes do not always yield the desired effect. The return on investment of public sector money in this area, on the evidence that is available, turns out to be poor. In light of Europe's large expenditures on ALMP the discussion of the effectiveness of these programmes, based on US studies, is quite sobering for policy-makers.

From a political point of view, the authors argue that researchers involved in the evaluation of programmes should be involved in the design phase of these programmes, and should have opportunities to present their findings to policy-makers and influence the design of future programmes. A critical note is in order here, however. The authors argue that the effects of ALMP are small, but also that in Europe empirical validation has been lacking and that inappropriate methods or insufficient evaluation have accompanied most public sector programmes. So, while the authors seem to answer the question raised in the title by a 'no', a more appropriate answer should in my opinion be more nuanced: not enough evidence has been systematically collected at this stage to answer that question. Perhaps, the evidence is just too thin to conclude on the effectiveness of ALMPs.

Panel discussion

Thierry Verdier argued that the reluctance of policy-makers in Europe compared to the US to do social experiments resulted from a stronger taste against *ex post* inequality in Europe. Andrew Rose disagreed because this should also apply to medical experimentation, where US and Europe appear very similar. Christoph Schmidt replied that a main factor for lack of policy evaluation might be the unwillingness of policy-makers to admit failure. Paolo Mauro found it unclear why the ALMP in Switzerland mentioned in the paper was successful, and in particular whether it created jobs that would not have been created anyway. Kai Konrad thought that the paper's European policy perspective was interesting, and led him to wonder whether policy spill-overs could justify funding and administration of ALMP at the European Union rather than national level.

REFERENCES

Abbring, J. and G. van den Berg (2000). 'The non-parametric identification of treatment effects in duration models', *mimeo*, Free University Amsterdam.

Bell, B., R. Blundell and J. van Reenen (1999). 'Getting the unemployed back to work: the role of targeted wage subsidies', *International Tax and Public Finance*.

Bertola, G. (1999). 'Microeconomic perspectives on aggregate labor markets', in O. Ashenfelter and D. Card (eds), *Handbook of Labor Economics* 3, Elsevier, Amsterdam.

Björklund, A. and R. Moffitt (1987). 'The estimation of wage gains and welfare gains in self-selection models', *Review of Economics and Statistics*.

Blanchard, O. and J. Wolfers (2000). 'The role of shocks and institutions in the rise of European unemployment: the aggregate evidence', *Economic Journal*.

Brodaty, T., B. Crépon and D. Fougère (2001). 'Using matching estimators to evaluate alternative youth employment programs: evidence from France, 1986–1988', in M. Lechner and F. Pfeiffer (eds), *Econometric Evaluation of Labour Market Policies*, Physica, Heidelberg.

Burtless, G. and L. Orr (1986). 'Are classical experiments needed for manpower policy?', *Journal of Human Resources*.

Calmfors, L. (1994). 'Active labour market policy and unemployment – a framework for the analysis of crucial design features', *OECD Economic Studies* 22.

Calmfors, L. (1995). 'What can we expect from active labour market policy?', *Konjunkturpolitik*.

Calmfors, L. and J. Driffill (1988). 'Centralisation of wage bargaining and macroeconomic performance', *Economic Policy*.

Calmfors, L. and P. Skedinger (1995). 'Does active labour market policy increase employment? – theoretical considerations and some empirical evidence from Sweden', *Oxford Review of Economic Policy*.

Carling, K., P.-A. Edin, A. Harkman and B. Holmlund (1996). 'Unemployment duration, unemployment benefits, and labor market programs in Sweden', *Journal of Public Economics*.

Cohen, D., A. Lefranc and G. Saint-Paul (1997). 'French unemployment: a transatlantic perspective', *Economic Policy*.

Council of the European Union (2001). 'Council Decision of 19 January 2001 on Guidelines for Member States' employment policies for the year 2001', *Official Journal of the European Communities*, L22.

Dehejia, R. and S. Wahba (1999). 'Causal effects in non-experimental studies: re-evaluating the evaluation of training programs', *Journal of the American Statistical Association*.

Dolado, J., F. Kramarz, S. Machin, A. Manning, D. Margolis and C. Teulings (1996). 'Minimum wages: the European experience', *Economic Policy*.

Eichhorst, W., S. Profit and E. Thode (2002). *Benchmarking Deutschland: Arbeitsmarkt und Beschäftigung* [Benchmarking Germany: Labour Market and Employment], Springer, Berlin.

European Commission (1997). *The 1998 Employment Guidelines*, http://europa.eu.int/comm/ employment_social/elm/summit/en/papers/guide2.htm.

European Commission (1998). *Employment Policies in the EU and in the Member States – Joint Report 1998*, European Commission DG V, Brussels.

European Commission (2000). *Joint Employment Report 2000*, European Commission DG V, Brussels.

Friedlander, D., D.H. Greenberg and P.K. Robins (1997). 'Evaluating government training programs for the economically disadvantaged', *Journal of Economic Literature*.

Gerfin, M. and M. Lechner (2000). 'Microeconometric evaluation of the active labour market policy in Switzerland', *IZA Disc. paper* No. 154, IZA: Bonn.

Ham, J.C. and R.J. LaLonde (1996). 'The effect of sample selection and initial conditions in duration models: evidence from experimental data on training', *Econometrica*.

Heckman, J.J. (1979). 'Sample selection bias as a specification error', *Econometrica*.

Heckman, J.J., H. Ishimura and P.E. Todd (1997). 'Matching as an econometric evaluation estimator: evidence from evaluating a job training programme', *Review of Economic Studies*.

Heckman, J.J., R.J. LaLonde and J.A. Smith (1999). 'The economics and econometrics of active labour market programs', in O. Ashenfelter and D. Card (eds), *Handbook of Labor Economics* 3, Elsevier, Amsterdam.

Heckman, J.J. and J.A. Smith (1995). 'Assessing the case for social experiments', *Journal of Economic Perspectives*.

Jensen, P. (1999). 'The Danish youth unemployment programme', *mimeo*, Center for Labour Market and Social Research, Aarhus.

Jensen, P., M. Svarer Nielsen and M. Rosholm (2000). 'The effects of benefits, incentives, and sanctions on youth unemployment', revised version of Working Paper 99-05, Center for Labour Market and Social Research, Aarhus.

Kluve, J., H. Lehmann and C.M. Schmidt (1999). 'Active labour market policies in Poland: human capital enhancement, stigmatization, or benefit churning?', *Journal of Comparative Economics*.

Lalive, R., J. Zweimüller and J.C. van Ours (2000). 'The impact of active labour market programs and benefit entitlement rules on the duration of unemployment', University of Zurich, IEW Working Paper No. 41.

LaLonde, R.J. (1986). 'Evaluating the econometric evaluations of training programs with experimental data', *American Economic Review*.

Larsson, L. (2000). 'Evaluation of Swedish youth labour market programmes', Uppsala University, Department of Economics Working paper 2000-6.

Lechner, M. (2000). 'An evaluation of public sector sponsored continuous vocational training programs in East Germany', *Journal of Human Resources*.

Ljungqvist, L. and T.J. Sargent (1998). 'The European unemployment dilemma', *Journal of Political Economy*.

Machin, S. and A. Manning (1999). 'The causes and consequences of longterm unemployment in Europe', in O. Ashenfelter and D. Card (eds), *Handbook of Labor Economics* 3, Elsevier, Amsterdam.

Magnac, T. (2000). 'Subsidised training and youth employment: distinguishing unobserved heterogeneity from state dependence in labour market histories', *Economic Journal*.

Martin, J.P. (2000). 'What works among active labour market policies: evidence from OECD countries' experience', *OECD Economic Studies* 30.

Mortensen, D.T. and C.A. Pissarides (1999a). 'New developments in models of search in the labor market', in O. Ashenfelter and D. Card (eds), *Handbook of Labor Economics* 3, Elsevier, Amsterdam.

Mortensen, D.T. and C.A. Pissarides (1999b). 'Unemployment responses to "skill-biased" technology shocks: the role of labour market policy', *Economic Journal*.

Nickell, S. (1997). 'Unemployment and labor market rigidities: Europe versus North America', *Journal of Economic Perspectives*.

Nickell, S. and R. Layard (1999). 'Labor market institutions and economic performance', in O. Ashenfelter and D. Card (eds), *Handbook of Labor Economics* 3, Elsevier, Amsterdam.

Nickell, S. and J.C. van Ours (2000). 'The Netherlands and the UK: A European unemployment miracle?', *Economic Policy*.

OECD (1990). *Labour Market Policies for the 1990s*, OECD, Paris.

OECD (1991). *Labour Force Statistics 1969–1989*, OECD, Paris.

OECD (1998). *Labour Force Statistics 1977–1997*, OECD, Paris.

OECD (2000a). *Social Expenditure Database 1980–1997*, 2nd ed., OECD, Paris.

OECD (2000b). *Employment Outlook*, June, OECD, Paris.

OECD (2000c). *Labour Force Statistics 1979–1999*, October, OECD, Paris.

OECD (2000d). *Economic Outlook*, No. 68, December, OECD, Paris.

Payne, J., S. Lissenburg and M. White (1996). 'Employment training and employment action: An evaluation by the matched comparison method', Policy Studies Institute, London.

Raaum, O. and H. Torp (2002). 'Labour market training in Norway: effect on earnings', *Labour Economics*.

Regnér, H. (2002). 'A non-experimental evaluation of training programs for the unemployed in Sweden', *Labour Economics*.

Rosholm, M. (1999). 'Evaluating subsidized employment programmes in the private and public sector', *mimeo*, Center for Labour Market and Social Research, Aarhus.

Schmidt, C.M. (1999). 'Do we need social experiments? Potential and limits of non-experimental project evaluation', *mimeo*, UC Berkeley.

Schmidt, C.M. (2000a). 'Persistence and the German unemployment problem: empirical evidence on German labor market flows', *Economie et Statistique*.

Schmidt, C.M. (2000b). 'The heterogeneity and cyclical sensitivity of unemployment: an exploration of German labor market flows', *ifo Studies*.

Schmidt, C.M., K.F. Zimmermann, M. Fertig and J. Kluve (2001). *Perspektiven der Arbeitsmarktpolitik – Internationaler Vergleich und Empfehlungen für Deutschland* [Perspectives of Labour Market Policy – International Comparison and Recommendations for Germany], Springer, Berlin.

Sianesi, B. (2001). 'An evaluation of the active labour market programmes in Sweden', *mimeo*, University College London.

Smith, J.A. (2000). 'Evaluating active labor market policies: Lessons from North America', *mimeo*, University of Western Ontario.

Smith, J.A. and P.E. Todd (2002). 'Does matching overcome LaLonde's critique of nonexperimental estimators?', *Journal of Econometrics*, forthcoming.

Stanley, M., L. Katz and Alan B. Krueger (1999). 'Impacts of employment and training programs: The American experience', *mimeo*, Harvard University.

Van den, Berg, G.J. and B. van der Klaauw (2001). 'Counselling and monitoring of unemployed workers: Theory and evidence from a social experiment', IZA Discussion paper 374, IZA, Bonn.

Van Ours, J.C. (2001). 'Do active labour market policies help unemployed workers to find and keep regular jobs?', in M. Lechner and F. Pfeiffer (eds), *Econometric Evaluation of Labour Market Policies*, Physica, Heidelberg.

Vella, F. (1998). 'Estimating models with sample selection bias: A survey', *Journal of Human Resources*.

Corporate income tax
Reforms and tax competition

SUMMARY

This paper analyses the development of taxes on corporate income in EU and G7 countries over the last two decades. We establish a number of stylized facts about their development. Tax-cutting and base-broadening reforms have had the effect that, on average across EU and G7 countries, effective tax rates on marginal investment have remained fairly stable, but those on more profitable investments have fallen. We discuss two possible explanations of these stylized facts arising from alternative forms of tax competition. First, governments may be responding to a fall in the cost of income shifting, which puts downward pressure on the statutory tax rate. Second, reforms are consistent with competition for more profitable projects, in particular those earned by multinational firms.

— *Michael Devereux, Rachel Griffith and Alexander Klemm*

Economic Policy October 2002 Printed in Great Britain
© CEPR, CES, MSH, 2002.

Corporate income tax reforms and international tax competition

Michael P. Devereux, Rachel Griffith and Alexander Klemm

University of Warwick, Institute for Fiscal Studies and CEPR; Institute for Fiscal Studies and CEPR; Institute for Fiscal Studies

1. INTRODUCTION

The last two decades have seen considerable reform to corporate income taxes in major industrialized countries. Statutory rates have fallen from an average of 48% in the early 1980s to 35% by the end of the 1990s. The main wave of reforms occurred in the mid to late 1980s but the pace has continued throughout the 1990s. In 1992, the EU-appointed Ruding Committee proposed a minimum statutory corporation tax rate of 30%. At that time, only Ireland had a lower rate than this – and then only for the manufacturing industry. Less than ten years later, one third of EU member states have tax rates at or below this level. In 2001 Germany reduced its tax rate to 25%,[1] and this may well lead to further reductions elsewhere.

This work was funded by the ESRC Centre for the Microeconomic Analysis of Fiscal Policy at the IFS. Michael Devereux is also grateful for support from the CSGR at the University of Warwick, and from an ESRC grant on Multijurisdictional Economies, joint with Myrna Wooders and John Whalley. The authors would like to thank Michela Redoano for her considerable help in constructing the data used in this paper, and Tim Besley, Stephen Bond, Michael Keen, Ben Lockwood, Marco Ottaviani, Paul Seabright, Marcel Thum and participants at the April 2002 *Economic Policy* Panel meeting for helpful comments. Responsibility for errors remains the authors'.
The Managing Editor in charge of this paper was Paul Seabright.

[1] Including local corporate income taxes brings this rate up to approximately 37%.

On the face of it these reforms seem consistent with the predictions of economic theory. It has been argued that increasing capital mobility will lead to a 'race to the bottom' as countries compete with each other to attract capital. Policy-makers have been concerned that this downward pressure on corporate income taxes will lead to a loss of revenue, and thus provide a constraint on government activity. The European Commission (1997) has also expressed concern that this process is forcing governments to rely more heavily on taxes on labour, which they fear will in turn increase unemployment. The European Commission and the OECD have recently made attempts at international coordination to counter what they see as 'harmful' tax competition.

This paper presents a detailed consideration of these issues. The first part of the paper analyses the development of taxes on corporate income over the last two decades. We analyse the tax regimes in 16 countries[2] over the 1980s and 1990s. The most common reform to corporate income taxes in these countries has been to lower tax rates and to broaden tax bases. Measuring the tax base in a simple way, by the rate of allowance available for investment in plant and machinery, seven countries – including France, Germany, the UK and the USA – reduced the tax rate and expanded the tax base. A further five, mainly smaller, countries reduced their tax rates, but left the tax base unchanged.

The rate-cutting, base-broadening reform has interesting effects on firms' investment incentives. Most empirical research on the impact of taxes on investment – and most theoretical work on tax competition – has focused on the impact of taxes at the margin (Hines, 1999; Devereux and Griffith, 2002b; Wilson, 1999). Typically, corporate income taxes raise the cost of capital – the required rate of return on an investment – and therefore act as a disincentive to invest. The two aspects of these reforms have offsetting effects on this disincentive: the lower tax rate typically increases the incentive to invest, while the lower allowance decreases it. The combined effect depends on the details of each reform.

In Section 2 we describe the development of the tax rate, the tax base and the effective marginal tax rate, which measures the extent to which the tax raises the cost of capital. We develop a series of stylized facts describing the trends in tax reform. There have been marked changes in the effective marginal tax rate in some individual countries over the period considered. However, there has been no clear movement, on average, in the marginal rate across countries. On average, this rate at the end of the 1990s was similar to that in the early 1980s.

The view that corporate income tax rates have fallen in response to increased mobility of capital, as countries compete to lower the cost of capital within their jurisdictions, is therefore not generally borne out by the data. An alternative possibility is that countries may instead compete for the activities of mobile multinational

---

[2] In analysing measures based data on tax revenue, we expand this to 18 countries – the EU and G7.

firms, which have access to valuable proprietary assets, rather than simply for mobile capital. The literature on multinational firms emphasizes that such firms make discrete investment choices: for example, whether to export to a new market or to produce locally, or where within a new location to site a new production facility. Devereux and Griffith (2002a) show that the impact of taxes on such discrete decisions is not captured by the effective marginal tax rate. Instead, it depends on the proportion of total profit taken in tax, measured by the effective average tax rate. This measure also depends on both the tax rate and the tax base, so that the effect of the rate-cutting, base-broadening reforms could be either to increase or decrease this effective rate. The evidence presented in Section 2 points to a fall in the effective average tax rate averaged across countries.

In Section 3 we review possible explanations of this pattern of reforms in corporate income taxes over the last two decades. Broadly we argue that the canonical model from the theoretical tax competition literature does not explain the reforms, since it (implicitly) focuses on only one aspect of the tax schedule – the effective marginal tax rate.

The finding that there has been a decline in the effective average tax rate may indicate a process of competition to attract more profitable and mobile firms. A fall in the effective average tax rate benefits more profitable firms. If such firms are also more mobile – and if their mobility has increased over time – then governments may gain by shifting the shape of the tax schedule in order to attract them. This could be accomplished by rate-cutting and base-broadening. We explore this explanation in Section 4. We present evidence that capital has become more mobile, that more profitable firms are more mobile and that the degree of mobility of higher profitability firms has increased faster than that of lower profitability firms.

We also explore an alternative explanation for the observed reforms, based on a formal model of tax competition by Haufler and Schjelderup (2000). The idea is that, as well as competing for inward flows of capital, governments also compete for flows of taxable profit. That is, conditional on where they locate their real activities, firms may be able to shift their profit between countries in order to reduce their worldwide tax liabilities. After using up all allowances in each location, the relevant marginal tax rate for shifting profit is the statutory tax rate – which has fallen in almost all countries over the last two decades. In this model, governments use two instruments – the tax rate and allowances – to compete over two mobile resources – capital and taxable income.

One other recent policy development is also relevant to this discussion. Over the last five years there have been significant advances in international cooperation. In the late 1990s, both the EU and the OECD introduced forms of cooperation, designed to counter what was seen as 'harmful' tax competition. The exact aims of these policy initiatives are somewhat unclear. In practice, however, both initiatives appear to be concerned with combating profit shifting, which is consistent with both of the explanations of tax reforms outlined above. In Section 5 we present some brief conclusions.

2. WHAT HAS HAPPENED TO CORPORATE TAXES?

We begin with a description of the development of source-based capital income taxes over the last two decades.[3] A number of other studies have presented a description of corporate income taxes across countries in a particular year.[4] However, there has been very little description of how they have developed over time, across a wide range of countries.[5] In this paper, we therefore begin by presenting a systematic account of how such taxes have developed over time. In order to understand the measures used below, it is necessary to explain how they are derived, and what they are intended to capture. We begin this section by summarizing the measures to be used. We then apply the measures and describe a number of stylized facts about the development of corporate income taxes. We also comment on the recent moves towards international cooperation.

We use data on 18 countries – the EU and the G7. Data on tax revenue are available from 1965, and we can therefore track the development of revenue over 35 years. However, data on the rules of tax systems are more difficult to collect. We present measures of effective tax rates based on sixteen of these countries (excluding Luxembourg and Denmark) from 1982 to 2001. In the next sub-section we discuss the measures in more detail.

2.1. Some measurement issues

The main focus of this paper is on competition between national governments to attract capital. The specific form of competition we investigate is the way in which corporate income is taxed. The traditional method of measuring the impact of corporate income tax on the level of capital is through the cost of capital – defined as the pre-tax real required rate of return on an investment project.[6]

The basic idea is that a firm will invest up to the point at which the marginal product of capital is just equal to the cost of capital – so that, at the margin, the project just breaks even. As investment increases, the marginal product is assumed to decline, resulting in a unique profit-maximizing level of investment. Most theoretical papers that model the impact of corporate income tax in an open economy are based on this approach. Typically, firms are assumed to be immobile, but can raise finance for capital on the world market. A higher effective marginal tax rate pushes up the cost of capital, and therefore reduces the inflow (or increases the outflow) of capital.

---

[3] The tax data used in this paper are available at http://www.ifs.org.uk/corptax/internationaltaxdata.zip.

[4] See, for example, Jorgenson and Landau (1993), OECD (1991), European Commission (1992), Devereux and Pearson (1995), European Commission (2001b).

[5] Chennells and Griffith (1997) is a precursor of this paper, in that they present similar measures to those in this paper for a smaller number of countries and years and discuss how the broad trends relate to predictions from the tax competition literature. Mendoza *et al.* (1994) also present a time-series for taxes on 'capital'; however, for reasons explained elsewhere, we do not believe that their measure adequately captures the incentives for investment created by corporate income taxes.

[6] This approach dates back at least to Hall and Jorgensen (1967). It was further developed by King (1977) and King and Fullerton (1984), among others.

More recently, though, attention has focused on the discrete investment choices, based in part on the literature on multinational firms. One common approach to modelling the location choices of multinational firms analyses whether, and how, such firms access a foreign market.[7] One choice facing the firm is whether to produce at home and export, or whether to produce abroad. Conditional on locating abroad the firm has a choice between alternative locations of production. For example, if an American firm wants to enter the European market, it could locate production in one of a number of different European countries. Conditional on deciding where to locate the firm must also decide the scale of investment.

The first two of these decisions are discrete. Suppose that the cost structure of the firm prohibits both exporting and producing abroad, and also prohibits producing in more than one location. Suppose also that the firm has some market power so that it expects to earn a positive economic rent. Then it can be assumed that the firm chooses that option which generates the highest post-tax rent. In this model – unlike in the traditional model – taxes on economic rent can affect a firm's investment decisions. Specifically, the impact of tax can be measured by the extent to which the pre-tax economic rent is reduced by taxation. Conditional on the discrete choice – for example, having chosen a location – the decision of the scale of the investment will be determined by the point at which the expected marginal product equals the cost of capital. For this third stage, then, it is again the impact of taxes at the margin – that is, on the cost of capital – that is relevant.

The tax system affects returns to investments in a number of complex ways. Among other things, the tax paid will generally depend on the profitability of the investment, the legal status of the entity investing and the sources of finance. Data limitations, and the need to obtain interpretable measures, mean that significant simplifications are required in order to produce a description of the tax schedule facing firms. Which of these assumptions are appropriate will depend on the aims of the research. In this paper we focus primarily on measures designed to capture the impact of tax on the incentives faced by firms to locate and use capital. We briefly explain why some proposed measures do not adequately measure such incentives. We also investigate trends in tax revenue.

Broadly, measures of corporate income taxes fall into two groups. The first group is based on an analysis of the tax legislation itself. Measures in this group are based on information on the statutory tax rate, depreciation allowances and so on. We describe these measures in the next subsection. The second group comprises measures based on tax revenues. These include measures that scale observed tax revenues by GDP, total tax revenue or some approximation of the tax base. These are discussed in Section 2.3. One of the main differences between these two groups of measures is that the former is forward looking, and so captures the impact of tax on

[7] See, *inter alia*, the early literature of Dunning (1977), Caves (1974) and more recently Horstmann and Markusen (1992) and Devereux and Griffith (1998).

future expected earnings on a specific investment project, while the latter are back-ward looking, and so capture the impact of tax on the returns in any period of the whole past history of a firm's investment decisions.

2.2. Measures based on tax legislation

This group of measures includes statutory tax rates, the net present value of depre-ciation allowances and marginal and average effective tax rates. Corporate income tax liabilities are calculated by applying the statutory tax rate to the tax base, where the tax base can be defined with varying degrees of precision in tax legislation. Clearly, both the rate and base are relevant for exploring the incentives created by the tax regime. We begin by describing the development of both the tax rate and the tax base over time for the 16 countries analysed here. We then describe in more detail the measures of effective tax rates, and present estimates of these as well.

Some important simplifying assumptions are made in developing all of these measures. We consider the tax system as it applies to a mature manufacturing firm. In our main calculations we do not consider the treatment of losses or other forms of tax exhaustion, although we discuss below the impact that tax exhaustion would have on our calculations. We analyse only source-based corporate income taxes – we do not include taxes levied in the country of residence of the parent company, for example. We generally exclude industry-specific measures and we do not allow for any forms of tax avoidance.

2.2.1. The statutory tax rate.   The most basic measure of corporate income taxes is the statutory tax rate. This measure is widely used, although even defining this rate is less straightforward than might be expected. Corporate income taxes are often applied at more than one level of government. There may also be temporary or permanent supplementary taxes. Our definition includes local tax rates and any supplementary charges made.[8]

Figure 1 shows the tax rate for each country for which data are available in 1982 and 2001. Over this period, the statutory tax rate fell in most of these 16 countries. Only Italy and Spain increased their tax rate, each by around two percentage points. The Irish rate remained unchanged. Between 1982 and 2001, the unweighted mean statutory tax rate for this group of countries fell from around 48% to around 35%. Throughout the period Ireland had the minimum rate at 10% (Ireland reduced the tax rate on manufacturing activities from 45% to 10% in 1981).

---

[8] In cases where local tax rates differ across regions, we use averages weighted by production where data are available. Otherwise the rate of the region in which most production takes place is used. Where local taxes or surcharges can be set off against other taxes (e.g. against federal), this is taken into account. Where tax rates change within a year we use the rate valid at the end of the calendar year. See Chennells and Griffith (1997) and Devereux et al. (2002) for more detail on how the data were collected.

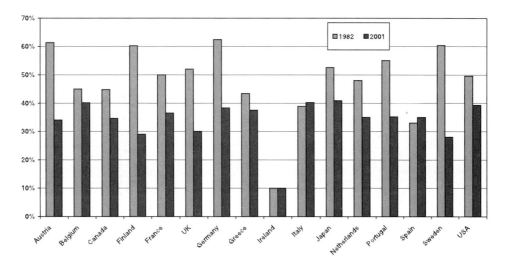

Figure 1. Statutory corporate income tax rates

Notes: For countries using different tax rates, the manufacturing rate is chosen. Local taxes (or the average across regions) are included where they exist. Any supplementary taxes are included only if they apply generally, rather than only under particular circumstances.

In Figure 2 we present the time series of the mean (weighted by GDP, measured in US dollars) and the median for these countries. The fall in tax rates was fairly continuous, though most pronounced in the late 1980s. The unweighted mean (not shown) reveals a similar pattern, though with a slightly steeper fall and lower tax rates in every single year. The median fell by more than the weighted mean.

Stylized fact 1: statutory tax rates fell over the 1980s and 1990s.

A high tax rate does not necessarily imply high tax payments, since payments depend also on the tax base. However, the tax rate may be important in its own right, since it is the marginal rate of tax applied to any additional income, given a level of allowances. It is therefore likely to be relevant in determining the incentive for firms to shift income between countries, conditional on where their real activity takes place. We return to this issue below.

2.2.2. The tax base. In all countries, the definition of the corporate tax base is extremely complex, involving a vast range of legislation covering everything from allowances for capital expenditure, to the deductibility of contributions to pension reserves, the valuation of assets, the extent to which expenses can be deducted, and so on. It is not feasible to present a measure that reflects all of these factors. We follow the empirical literature in focusing on depreciation allowances for capital expenditure.

If a firm invests £100 in capital, typically it cannot set the entire £100 cost against tax immediately. Instead, the cost can be spread over the expected life of the asset. For example, if the asset is expected to last for five years, then the allowance rate may

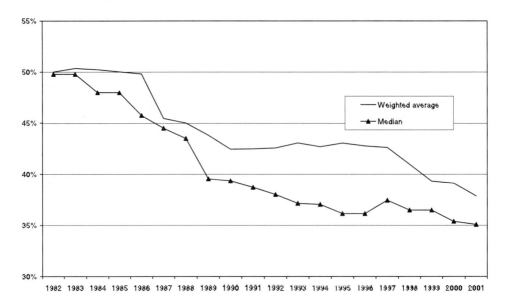

Figure 2. Average statutory corporate income tax rate

Notes: Statutory tax rate defined as in Figure 1. Average weighted by GDP in US$.

be set at 20% of the initial cost per year for each of the 5 years. The rate allowed typically depends on the type of asset, and varies considerably both across countries and over time. A natural measure of the value of such allowances is their present discounted value (PDV). In Figures 3 and 4 we present estimates of the PDV of allowances for investment in plant and machinery, expressed as a percentage of the initial cost of the asset. The PDV would be zero if there were no allowances at all and it would be 100% with a cash-flow tax that permitted the cost to be deducted immediately.

In almost all countries, allowances are based on the original cost of an asset, and are not adjusted in line with inflation. To the extent that nominal interest rates move in line with inflation, a reduction in the inflation rate (expected over the lifetime of the asset) would increase the PDV of (expected) allowances. This raises the issue of what is the appropriate way of comparing the value of allowances between countries and over time. Figure 3 shows the PDV for each country in 1982 and 2001, based on a single nominal discount rate for all countries and all years.[9] This figure therefore reflects changes in the rates of allowance set by governments, and abstracts from changes in the inflation rate and the real interest rate. However, it is possible that governments have observed or expected changes in the inflation rate (which has generally fallen over the period analysed), and adjusted their allowance rates accordingly. To allow for this, in Figure 4, we present the two versions of the weighted

[9] The nominal discount rate is 13.9%, based on inflation of 3.5% and a real discount rate of 10%.

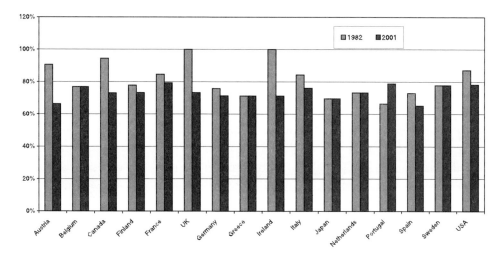

Figure 3. PDV of depreciation allowances

Notes: The PDV of allowances is calculated for an investment in plant and machinery. Special first year allowances are included if applicable. Where switching between straight-line and reducing balance methods is allowed, such switching is assumed at the optimal point. The assumed real discount rate is 10%, the assumed rate of inflation is 3.5%.

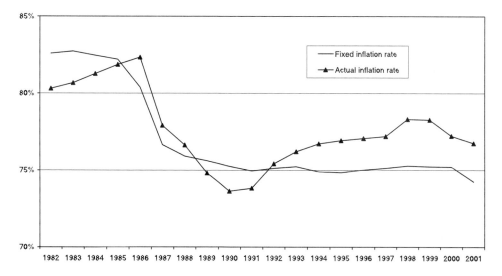

Figure 4. Average PDV of depreciation allowance

Notes: Allowances defined as in Figure 3, except for the second series which is based on actual inflation rates (implying static expectations), rather than an assumed fixed rate of 3.5%. Average weighted by GDP in US$.

average PDV of allowances. The first uses a constant nominal discount rate (as in Figure 3), while the second is based on the inflation rate actually observed in that country in period t.[10]

---

[10] Data for inflation are annual percentage changes in the consumer price index over the year. Source: IMF (2001).

Of the 16 countries analysed in Figure 3, 10 cut their allowance rates for investment in plant and machinery between 1982 and 2001 – that is, they have broadened their tax bases. Most notably, the UK and Ireland decreased their allowances substantially from 100% to 73% and 71% respectively. Five countries kept their allowances constant and only one country, Portugal, increased allowances.

Figure 4 presents the time series of the weighted mean with constant and actual inflation. Not surprisingly, given the evidence of Figure 3, when inflation is held constant, there has been a decline in the average PDV of allowances for plant and machinery; that is, the rates of allowance set by governments have become less generous. In fact, on this basis, the weighted mean fell nearly ten percentage points, from 83% to 74%. The largest part of this decline was in the late 1980s; cuts were less pronounced in the 1990s. An unweighted average (not shown) reveals the same pattern, as does the median.

Allowing for the effects of inflation on the nominal discount rate generates a slightly different pattern. The marked decline in the second half of the 1980s is even more pronounced. However, the stability of rates in the 1990s, combined with falling inflation, leads to some recovery of the average PDV. Overall, both measures indicate a decline over the period considered, but the impact of the decline in the rates has been offset by the lower discount rates implied by lower inflation.

Stylized fact 2: on average, tax bases were broadened between the early 1980s and the end of the 1990s; however, the impact of reduced rates of allowance was moderated by lower inflation.

Figures 3 and 4 show the PDV of allowances for an investment in plant and machinery. We have also calculated the PDV of allowances for investment in industrial buildings. These yield lower PDVs, corresponding to lower rates of allowance – which in turn reflects the lower economic depreciation rates of buildings. However, there was also a fall in the average PDV for buildings over the period considered.

2.2.3. Effective tax rates. We use the term 'effective tax rates', whether marginal or average, only for measures based on tax legislation. This term has also been used to refer to tax rates estimated from data on tax revenues. We differentiate by referring to those as 'implicit tax rates'.

Clearly both the tax rate and the tax base are relevant in determining incentives for investment. This is true of both types of decision described above: the discrete choice of which type of investment to undertake (or where to undertake it), and the scale of investment conditional on that choice. Given an underlying model of investment, it is possible to combine information on the tax rate and tax base in ways that summarize these incentives.

The standard approach to combining the rate and base to summarize incentives is to look at the impact of tax on a hypothetical investment project that just earns the

---

Box 1. Effective marginal and average tax rates

Consider a simple one period investment, in which a firm increases its capital stock for one period only. It does so by increasing its investment by 1 at the beginning of the period, and reducing it by $1 - \delta$ at the end of the period, where δ represents economic depreciation. The higher capital stock generates a return at the end of the period of $p + \delta$, where p is the financial return. The discount rate is r. Ignore inflation.

One unit of capital generates a tax allowance with a net present value (NPV) of A. So introducing tax reduces the cost of the asset to $1 - A$, while the saving from the subsequent reduction in investment becomes $(1 - \delta)(1 - A)$. The total return $p + \delta$ is taxed at the tax rate τ.

The NPV of the investment with tax is therefore:

$$R = \frac{(p + \delta)(1 - \tau) - (r + \delta)(1 - A)}{1 + r}.$$

The cost of capital is the value of p, denoted $\tilde{p}$, for which the investment is marginal, i.e. $R = 0$. The effective marginal tax rate (EMTR) is $(\tilde{p} - r)/\tilde{p}$.

We define the effective average tax rate (EATR) – for a given value of p – to be the NPV of tax payments expressed as a proportion of the NPV of total pre-tax capital income, $V^* = p/(1 + r)$. This is comparable to other commonly used measures of the average tax rate. For a marginal investment, EATR = EMTR. For a highly profitable investment, EATR approaches τ.

The cash flows are slightly different in the case of debt-financed investment, but the concepts of the EMTR and EATR are unchanged.

---

minimum required rate of return (a marginal investment). In general, the incentives generated by the tax system depend on the form of the investment project, including the type of asset purchased and the way it is financed. However, in practice it is not possible to account for all the features and complexities of the tax system. The form of the investment modelled is therefore typically simple. Box 1 describes our approach.[11] The basic approach is to find the impact of taxes on the cost of capital – the pre-tax required rate of return – given a post-tax required rate of return (equal to the discount rate). The proportionate difference between the pre-tax and post-tax required rates of return is known as the *effective marginal tax rate* (EMTR). The higher the EMTR, the greater the required pre-tax rate of return, and hence the lower is the incentive to invest.

---

[11] This is based on Devereux and Griffith (2002a), and is slightly different from the well-known approach of King and Fullerton (1984) (although the measures generated are very similar).

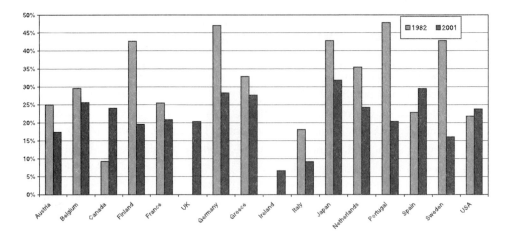

Figure 5. Effective marginal tax rates

Notes: Calculations based on a hypothetical investment for one period in plant and machinery, financed by equity or retained earnings (but not debt). Taxation at the shareholder level is not included. The project is expected to break even, i.e. there is no economic rent. Other assumptions – real discount rate: 10%, inflation rate: 3.5%, depreciation rate: 12.25%.

The impact of taxes on discrete investment choices is not captured in this frame-work. Instead, it is necessary to consider two alternative forms of investment, each of them profitable. The impact of taxation on the choice between them depends on the proportion of total profit taken in tax. We denote this the *effective average tax rate* (EATR). If one option has a higher pre-tax profit than the other, but also a higher EATR, then the tax may lead the firm to choose the option with the lower pre-tax profit. The measure of the EATR used here is also defined in Box 1. As with the EMTR, it is defined for a particular project (the same project as for the EMTR, apart from the rate of profitability), and takes into account only the broad structure of the tax system.

Our base case for the effective tax rates is an investment in plant and machinery, financed by equity. We ignore any personal taxes paid by the marginal shareholder.[12] These effective tax rates also depend on economic conditions associated with each investment, notably the real post-tax required rate of return, the economic deprecia-tion rate of the asset and the inflation rate. Throughout, we hold fixed the real post-tax required rate of return (at 10%) and the economic depreciation rate for each asset (12.25% for plant and machinery and 3.61% for industrial buildings).

Figures 5 and 6 show the development of effective marginal tax rates (EMTR) over time, using the same format as in previous figures. In Figure 5 we follow the approach

---

[12] We do not incorporate any forms of personal taxation, so there is no distinction between investment financed by new equity or retained earnings.

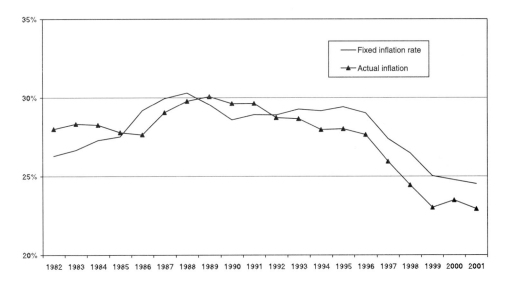

Figure 6. Average effective marginal tax rates

Notes: Effective marginal tax rate defined as in Figure 5, except for the second series which is based on actual inflation rates (implying static expectations), rather than an assumed fixed rate of 3.5%. Average weighted by GDP in US$.

of Figure 3, in holding inflation constant across all years and countries. In Figure 6 we mirror the approach of Figure 4 in presenting the weighted average across countries both with inflation fixed, and using the inflation rate actually observed in the country and period in which the investment is assumed to take place. Note that these rates correspond to the EATR evaluated for a marginal investment, that is, when the pre-tax rate of profit is equal to the cost of capital ($p = \tilde{p}$).

The development of the EMTR over time does not replicate the pattern seen in the statutory tax rates. This is because investment projects at the margin are strongly affected by the value of allowances. Considering the rates under the constant inflation assumption (Figure 5) we see that in more than half of the countries the EMTR has decreased, although in many others it has increased. Figure 6 shows that, given fixed inflation, the weighted mean EMTR remained fairly stable over the period; it rose a little during the early and mid 1980s, but has since fallen back to its initial level. On the same basis, the unweighted mean fell by nearly four percentage points over the period, and the median by six percentage points; this is consistent with a greater fall in smaller countries, as reflected in Figure 5. There is also a slight fall between 1982 and 2001 in the weighted mean EMTR based on actual inflation rates in each country and year. Again, this measure rose slightly in the 1980s; however, its subsequent decline has been greater, leaving it around three percentage points lower than in 1982. This largely reflects the evidence shown in Figure 4; with lower inflation rates, a given allowance rate is more generous, leading to a lower EMTR.

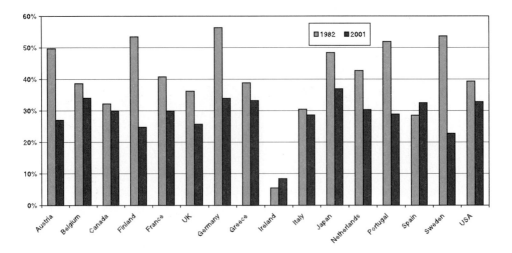

Figure 7. Effective average tax rates

Notes: Calculations based on a hypothetical investment for one period in plant and machinery, financed by equity or retained earnings (but not debt). Taxation at the shareholder level is not included. The expected rate of economic profits earned is 10% (implying a financial return, p, of 20%). Other assumptions: real discount rate: 10%, inflation rate: 3.5%, depreciation rate: 12.25%.

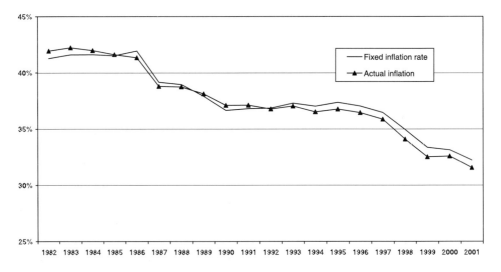

Figure 8. Average effective average tax rates

Notes: Effective average tax rate defined as in Figure 7, except for the second series which is based on actual inflation rates (implying static expectations), rather than an assumed fixed rate of 3.5%. Average weighted by GDP in US$.

Figures 7 and 8 present evidence for the EATR, following the same approach as Figures 5 and 6. In each case, the investment project is assumed to have an expected real rate of economic profit of 10% (i.e. $p - \tilde{p} = 0.10$). Figure 7 shows that, given the fixed inflation assumption, the EATR fell in all but three of the countries. The

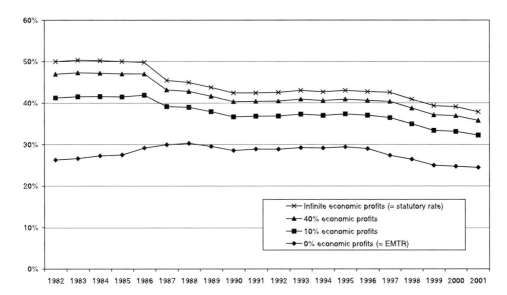

Figure 9. Average effective average tax rates at different levels of profitability

Notes: Effective average tax rates defined as in Figure 7. Average weighted by GDP in US$.

pattern of reduction reflects the pattern seen in the development of the statutory tax rate in Figures 1 and 2. The EATR for industrial buildings follows similar patterns.

Figure 8 shows that, on the basis of fixed inflation, the weighted mean EATR fell over the period from around 41% to around 34%. Based on actual inflation, the fall in the EATR was similar, from 42% to 33%. These two series are closer in the case of the EATR than in the case of the EMTR, since the EATR depends rather more on the statutory tax rate and rather less on allowances. Nevertheless, the two approaches give a similar qualitative picture of the development of effective tax rates.

Figure 9 shows the weighted mean EATR at different rates of economic profit, for the fixed inflation case. The lowest line is the weighted mean EMTR (equivalent to the EATR evaluated at zero economic profit, a marginal investment). The three higher lines represent the EATR for investments with increasing rates of profitability. The highest is simply the statutory tax rate (to which the EATR converges as profitability rises). This figure confirms the previous discussion; the reduction in the EATR is greater the higher is the profitability of the investment. At one extreme, it is equal to the statutory rate, which has fallen significantly. At the other, it has remained fairly constant.

The difference in the effective tax rate at very low and very high levels of economic profit has fallen over time. This is shown in Figure 10, again for the fixed inflation case. The top line shows the weighted average effective average tax rate in 1982 at different levels of profitability. It rises sharply as economic profits rises from 0% to

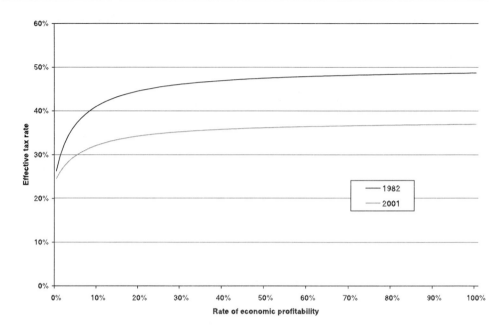

Figure 10. Effective tax rates at different levels of profitability

Notes: Effective average tax rates defined as in Figure 7, but rate of economic profits allowed to vary from 0% to 100%. Averages weighted by GDP in US$.

20% and then flattens out, converging to the statutory tax rate. The lower line shows the same relationship in 2001. At the margin, the weighted mean EATR is very similar for the two years. However, in 2001, while the effective average tax rate still rises with profitability, it does so more slowly, and never reaches the higher rates seen in 1982.

> ***Stylized fact 3: the effective marginal tax rate has remained stable over the 1980s and 1990s; effective average tax rates for projects earning positive economic profits have fallen over the 1980s and 1990s, and they have fallen more at higher levels of profitability; allowing for lower inflation implies a small reduction in the effective marginal tax rate, and a greater fall in the effective average tax rate.***

Despite the various forms of effective tax rate described already, there are other possibilities that have not yet been addressed. In particular, we discuss two issues: the impact of using debt, instead of equity, to finance the investment; and the impact of the asymmetry in most corporation taxes, which implies that taxable losses do not generate an immediate tax rebate, but must be carried forward to offset against future taxable profits (a form of tax exhaustion).

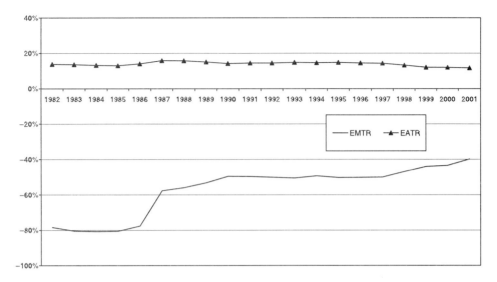

Figure 11. Effective tax rates, debt financed

Notes: Effective marginal tax defined on a tax-exclusive basis, unlike in Figure 5. Finance is by debt, all other assumptions as in Figure 5. Average weighted by GDP in US$.

The main difference in effective tax rates for investment financed by debt, rather than equity, is that interest payments to lenders are deductible from taxable profit. This plays a very important role in determining effective marginal and average tax rates.

We explore the impact of tax reforms on effective tax rates for debt-financed investment in Figure 11. Rather than use the 'tax inclusive' measure defined above ($EMTR = (\tilde{p} - r)/\tilde{p}$) we use the 'tax exclusive' measure ($EMTR* = (\tilde{p} - r)/r$), where $\tilde{p}$ is the minimum pre-tax rate of return and r is the associated post-tax rate of return. In the case of debt finance, $\tilde{p}$ can take values very close to zero, implying huge values of the EMTR. In presenting evidence of the development of such tax rates in Figure 11, we therefore scale by r instead of $\tilde{p}$. Note that this measure is therefore not directly comparable to the measure presented for the case of equity-financed investment.[13]

Figure 11 presents, for the case of fixed inflation in all years and countries, the weighted mean EATR and effective marginal tax rate for investment financed solely by debt. The EMTR for an investment financed completely by debt would be zero if allowances were set equal to our assumed economic depreciation rates. This is because interest is fully deductible. In fact, allowances are, on average, more generous than our assumed depreciation rates, so the EMTR is negative. These measures

[13] We prefer the tax inclusive measure because, for that measure, the EMTR is a special case of the EATR with economic profits set to zero.

present a somewhat different picture of the impact on incentives. The combination of the various reforms has generated a rise in the EMTR over the period, while the EATR initially rose in the mid 1980s, before falling back again to below its original level.

Differences in Figure 11 compared to the earlier evidence for equity-financed investment are due to the impact of the reduction in the statutory rates. Such reductions can increase effective marginal rates for debt-financed investment because of the reduced value of interest deductibility. However, the value of interest deductibility is lower for more profitable investments; hence this effect is less marked for effective average tax rates.

The second assumption about the measures of effective tax rates used here that we note is that we have made the assumption that when an investment takes place, the investor assumes that current tax rates will hold indefinitely. That is, we do not allow for the possibility that tax rates may change over the life of an investment.[14]

A special case of this assumption relates to the possibility that, in a given period, a firm may have, or expect to have, a negative taxable profit – a position sometimes referred to as tax exhaustion. This was common in some countries in the 1980s – particularly in the UK, where allowances were very generous. In considering an incremental investment for a firm in this position, the tax consequences of that investment may be delayed. For example, extra allowances cannot reduce tax liabilities immediately, but only when the firm returns to a tax paying position; likewise, extra revenue is not taxed immediately, but only when the firm returns to a tax-paying position.

The effect of a period of tax exhaustion on effective tax rates depends crucially on the timing of the tax exhaustion relative to the timing of the investment. Suppose the firm pays tax in periods $t-1$ and $t+1$, but not in period t. Then allowances for an investment that takes place in period t will be delayed, and hence will be less valuable; in turn, effective tax rates will be higher. However, an investment in period $t-1$ will generate allowances in period $t-1$, but the return from the investment, arising in period t will not be taxed until period $t+1$. This reduces effective tax rates. These effects can be quite large, but it is clear that they may shift effective tax rates in either direction. Allowing for such effects goes beyond the scope of the cross-country analysis in this paper.[15]

2.3. Measures based on tax revenue

We now turn to a consideration of the second group of measures. A number of studies have used data on tax revenues to measure the impact of corporate income tax on incentives for investment. Typically, a form of average tax rate is calculated,

---

[14] This is consistent with most, but not all, tax reforms. In principle, if there is an announcement of a future tax reform, then current investment should be based on the expected change.

[15] For a detailed analysis of such effects in the UK, see Devereux (1987, 1989).

expressing the tax payment as a proportion of a measure of profit or the tax base. There are a number of reasons why these measures are not appropriate for our purposes here.

The first, and most general, concerns the definition of profit used in the denominator of such a tax rate. Clearly, if the measure of profit used were defined in the same way as the tax system, then the proportion of it taken in tax would be equal to the statutory rate. Differences in such average tax rates from the statutory rate therefore reflect differences in the definition of profit used in the measure from the definition of profit used in the tax system.

Where it is the case that differences in the two measures of profit reflect the fact that legislators sometimes deliberately set the tax base to be narrower, or broader, than a conventional (or economically meaningful) measure of profit, then the measure provides meaningful information. However, in many cases the difference between the tax base and some other measure of profit may simply reflect differences in measurement, which provide no clear guide to incentives.

These differences in the true and measured tax base reflect several common features of tax systems. For example, the tax liabilities of a firm at any point in time reflects (1) the history of its investment up to that point (in determining what allowances it can claim in that period); (2) tax liabilities in possibly several jurisdictions; (3) the history of losses in the firm (that is, it may be carrying forward losses from some previous period); and (4) the history of the tax system up to that point. As such, these measures are largely backward looking and reflect the past history of investment. Each of these features may affect the tax base, but are likely to be ignored in most conventional measures of profit.

A particular example of such a tax rate, and one which has been widely used, was developed by Mendoza et al. (1994) for use with aggregate data. Their basic approach is to divide all taxes into one of three groups – labour, consumption and capital. For the last group, a tax rate is found by dividing total revenue from this group by a measure of the operating surplus of the economy.[16] Eurostat (1998, 2000) use this methodology with a few minor changes. They refer to the last group of taxes as 'taxes on other factors of production' rather than capital, but their interpretation of the measure is similar.

Such an 'implicit' tax rate has the merit of being simple to calculate across a wide range of countries, years and types of tax. But one fundamental problem with the measure in the context considered here is its very broad scope. It typically groups together a diverse range of taxes; for example, inheritance and estate taxes, property taxes, stamp duties and gift taxes. These all have different economic effects, and most

---

[16] Defined by Mendoza et al. (1994) as: 'gross output at producers' values less the sum of intermediate consumption, compensation of employees – which is wages and salaries plus employers' contributions to social security – consumption of fixed capital, and indirect taxes reduced by subsidies. Note that this definition of pre-tax capital income implicitly assumes zero net profits and an aggregate CRS technology.

are unrelated to taxes on corporate income and in particular are not necessarily applied to 'mobile' tax bases. In this measure, the denominator of the implicit tax rate depends on the treatment of different factors related to profits in national accounts, which vary widely across countries and over time.

We do not, therefore, use revenue-based measures to infer economic incentives. However, the size of revenues raised from corporate income taxes is clearly important to governments who face revenue constraints. We do, therefore, present a description of the development of revenues from corporate income taxes.

Note that these may differ in scope from the measures considered above. For example, in constructing effective tax rates, we considered only source-based corporate income taxes. However, tax revenues in any country may include both source-based taxes and residence-based taxes – typically, revenue collected from profits earned abroad and repatriated.

2.3.1. Corporate income tax revenues as a proportion of GDP or total tax revenue.
It is clearly not useful simply to compare corporate income tax revenues across countries. Two convenient ways of making such comparisons are to scale tax revenues in each country by GDP or by total tax revenues. These measures will vary for reasons other than the corporate tax system. For example, both depend on the size of the corporate sector (e.g. the degree to which business is transacted through corporate tax paying entities) and on the relative size of corporate income in GDP, which varies considerably over the economic cycle and potentially across countries.

Figure 12 presents the time series of tax revenues from corporate income as a proportion of GDP from 1965 to 1999. We use data from OECD Revenue Statistics on tax revenues from corporate income and capital gains.[17] The weighted mean of the ratio of taxes on corporate income to GDP varies over the economic cycle, but does not appear to follow any long-term trend. In most years it is within the interval from 2.5% to 3.5% of GDP. The median remains fairly constant until the early 1990s when it rises slightly.

> *Stylized fact 4: tax revenues on corporate income have remained broadly stable as a proportion of GDP since 1965.*

Despite this general observation, it should be noted that developments vary strongly across countries. The unweighted mean (not shown) increases during the period, rising from around 2.3% to 3.4%, which suggests that revenues from corporate income taxes have grown in smaller countries. Figure 13 shows corporate income tax revenue as a proportion of GDP for each country in 1965, 1982 and 1999.[18] The

---

[17] This is tax class 1200 in the OECD data.

[18] The latter two dates were chosen to correspond to the dates available for measures based on tax rules. We also show the year 1965, because tax revenue data are available over a longer period.

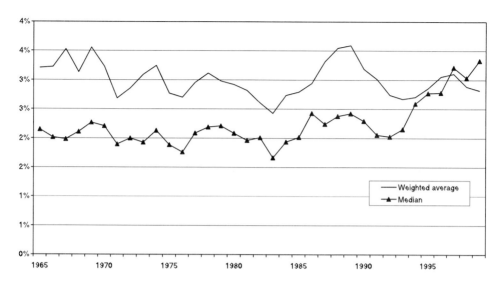

Figure 12. Corporate income tax revenue (% of GDP)

Notes: Average of the countries shown in Figure 13 weighted by GDP in US$. All taxes levied on profits and capital gains of corporations are included.

Source: OECD.

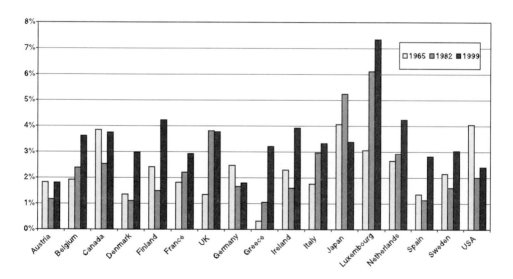

Figure 13. Corporate income tax revenue (% of GDP)

Notes: All taxes levied on profits and capital gains of corporations are included. Data for Portugal are missing.

Source: OECD.

variation across countries is considerable: several countries raised less than 2% of GDP from corporate income taxes in 1965; by contrast, Luxembourg raised over 7% in 1999. Between 1965 and 1999 most countries experienced an increase in tax revenues as a proportion of GDP. There are five exceptions, but only the USA

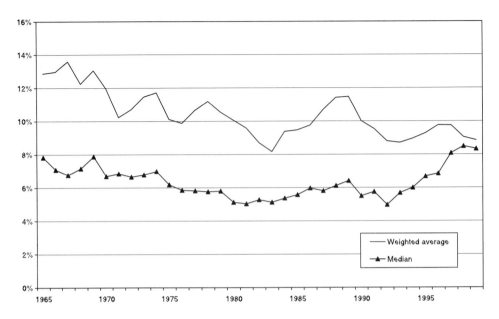

Figure 14. Corporate income tax revenue (% of total tax revenue)

Notes: Average of the countries shown in Figure 13 weighted by GDP in US$. All taxes levied on profits and capital gains of corporations are included.

Source: OECD.

experienced a drop in excess of one percentage point. Between 1982 and 1999 this ratio decreased in only two of the eighteen countries, and only one of them, Japan, experienced a large reduction – of nearly two percentage points of GDP.

This pattern of tax revenues may seem inconsistent with the stylized facts presented above, which indicate a fall in statutory tax rates and the EATR. It can be partly explained by changes in profitability. In some countries it may be partly due to the tax system itself. For example, Ireland has had a 10% tax rate on manufacturing activity since the early 1980s. One consequence has been a dramatic increase in inward investment: this in turn has boosted corporate income tax receipts as a share of GDP, despite the continuing low tax rate.[19]

Part of the explanation for the maintenance of the ratio of revenue to GDP is an increase in the size of government generally. To see this, we consider, in Figure 14, equivalent measures to Figure 12, but based on the ratio of taxes on corporate income to total tax revenue. This paints a rather different picture. Corporate income taxes have fallen on average as a share of total tax revenue. The weighted mean of the ratio of corporate income tax revenues to total tax revenues declined steadily until the mid 1980s. It then recovered in the late 1980s before falling back to the lower level. Combined with Figure 12, this suggests that taxes from sources other than

[19] It seems likely that it has also benefited from inward shifting of corporate income.

corporate income have risen rather faster than GDP, and that – relative to other taxes – governments are relying rather less on corporate income taxes.

> **Stylized fact 5: tax revenues on corporate income have declined as a proportion of total tax revenue since 1965.**

2.4. International co-operation

The discussion so far has focused on the unilateral setting of taxes on corporate income by governments in different countries. Within that framework, we have been able to identify the broad directions of reform of such taxes in EU and G7 countries. In addition, there have been three recent international attempts to introduce some form of co-ordination of corporation taxes across countries. Two of these originated with the European Commission (1997 and 2001a),[20] and one with the OECD (1998). The first European Commission initiative and the OECD initiative have much in common and they are rather different from the more recent approach of the European Commission.

2.4.1. The EU code of conduct. The 1997 initiative – agreed by the EU Council of Ministers in December 1997 – introduced a 'Code of Conduct' in business taxation, as part of a 'package to tackle harmful tax competition'.[21] The Code of Conduct was apparently designed to curb 'those business tax measures which affect, or may affect, in a significant way the location of business activity within the Community' (European Commission, 1998). Crucially, the Code specifies that only those tax measures that allow a significantly lower effective level of taxation (including paying no tax at all) than those levels that generally apply in the member state should be regarded as harmful. In other words, the Code is not aimed at the overall rate or level of corporate taxation in individual member states. It is aimed at specific, targeted measures that reduce the level of tax paid below the 'usual' level. For example, the criteria used to determine whether a particular measure is 'harmful' include whether the lower tax level applies only to non-residents, whether the tax advantages are 'ring-fenced' from the domestic market, and whether advantages are granted without any associated real economic activity taking place.

A working group examined a list of over 200 potentially harmful regimes within the EU against the agreed criteria to see if they should be classified as harmful. The group concluded that 66 of the measures were in fact harmful, although not all decisions were unanimous. Most of the measures declared harmful affect financial

---

[20] There is a long history of proposals from the European Union, dating back to the Neumark report in 1962.

[21] The other elements included measures on the taxation of savings income and cross-border interest, and the taxation of royalty payments between companies. The package was seen as necessary to achieve certain objectives, such as reducing continuing distortions in the single market, preventing excessive loss of tax revenue and encouraging tax structures to develop in a way that was thought to be more favourable for employment.

services, offshore companies and services provided within multinational groups. That is, they concentrate on those tax measures that affect the location of financial functions, but which are less likely to affect the location of real economic activity. This suggests – despite claims to the contrary – that the main concern of the working group has been to prevent revenue erosion through shifting of profits, rather than to prevent the distortion of real economic activity.[22]

Under the Code, countries commit not to introduce new harmful measures (under a 'standstill' provision) and to examine their existing laws with a view to eliminating any harmful measures (the 'rollback' provision). Member states are committed to removing any harmful measures by 1 January 2003. However, the Code is not legally binding – member states have instead made only a voluntary commitment to abide by it.

2.4.2. The OECD initiative against harmful tax competition.

At the same time as the EU Code of Conduct group was developing its recommendations, the OECD was pursuing a similar project. In 1998, the OECD published a report (OECD, 1998), which contained 19 recommendations to counter what it saw as the 'harmful' tax competition of capital income. Subsequently, it created the Forum on Harmful Tax Practices to oversee the implementation of the recommendations. The first main output of this work was published in June 2000 (OECD, 2000). The OECD distinguished two forms of 'harmful' tax practice, essentially split between OECD members and non-members.

The first form is concerned with 'harmful preferential regimes in member countries', which were defined in a broadly similar way to that used by the Code of Conduct, although lack of transparency and exchange of information were also cited as important factors.[23] The 2000 Report listed 47 preferential regimes that were 'potentially harmful'.[24] The Forum aims to verify by June 2003 whether member countries have eliminated 'harmful' regimes, although the deadline for removing them is December 2005. However, there is no legally binding agreement between countries. The 2000 report does not outline any action to be taken against countries that have not complied with eliminating such regimes, it merely states that 'other countries may wish to take defensive measures'.

---

[22] One example – out of many – of a regime which is classified as 'harmful' is that for Belgian 'Co-ordination Centres'. There are a number of criteria for eligibility for a firm to be classified as a co-ordination centre: for example, they must form part of an international group, in which at least 20% of the equity is held outside of the country in which the parent is established and which operates subsidiaries in at least four countries. Approved activities include financial co-ordination activities and preparatory or auxiliary activities for other companies in the group. Tax payments are significantly reduced because the tax rate is applied to notional income rather than real profits, where notional income is defined as a fixed percentage of expenditure (usually 8%), excluding salaries and financing expenses. Co-ordination Centres are also exempt from a number of other taxes and administrative requirements, most importantly from withholding taxes on dividends and interest. Firms that set up such a co-ordination centre face strong incentives to shift as much of their profits to such a centre as possible.

[23] The report and the recommendations were approved by the OECD Council with abstentions from Luxembourg and Switzerland.

[24] These include regimes such as the Belgian Coordination Centres, and the Irish International Financial Services Centres.

The second form of 'harmful' tax practice identified by the 1998 report concerned jurisdictions outside the OECD identified as 'tax havens'. Here the focus was on jurisdictions, rather than on specific features of their tax regimes. The criteria for identifying tax havens were again broadly similar to that for identifying harmful regimes operated by OECD members: lack of transparency and exchange of information were again important. Again, the OECD emphasized that low taxation itself was not sufficient to identify a jurisdiction as a tax haven.

The 2000 report published a list of 34 'tax havens' meeting its criteria.[25] Any jurisdiction deemed to be 'uncooperative' – essentially by not agreeing to abandon the 'harmful' aspects of their regimes by 2005 – were threatened with 'defensive measures' outlined by the OECD in its 2000 report. These measures relate partly to the enforcement of existing tax regimes.[26] However, the measures go beyond this, effectively introducing a penalty for dealing with such jurisdictions. They include proposals to impose withholding taxes on payments to their residents, deny the availability of tax credits associated with income received from them, and generally to disallow deductions, exemptions, credits or other allowances related to transactions with them. Governments are also invited to reconsider whether to direct non-essential economic assistance to 'uncooperative tax havens'. In the event, the OECD announced in April 2002 that the vast majority of 'tax havens' named in the 2000 report have committed to abandoning their 'harmful' practices, and committing to 'principles of transparency and the effective exchange of information'. The current list of 'tax havens' contains just seven states.[27]

Both the OECD initiative and the EU Code of Conduct appear not to be directed at affecting the broad nature of tax competition for capital, as they focus on the existence of specific regimes. Both initiatives claim specifically that tax regimes with low general rates of capital income tax – but without special regimes – are outside their scope. Instead, they seem directed towards preventing tax avoidance by shifting taxable profits between jurisdictions. Special low tax-rate regimes may be vehicles into which companies can shift their profits on other activities; reducing the scope for firms to do this is likely to reduce – although not eliminate – such tax avoidance.

2.4.3. The European Commission proposals.

A more recent initiative from the European Commission (2001a) is quite different from previous policy initiatives. It is more broadly aimed at eliminating tax obstacles within the internal market. Under

---

[25] Just prior to the publication of the report, six further jurisdictions made a public political commitment to eliminate their 'harmful' tax practices and to comply with the principles of the 1998 report. As a result, they were not named in the 2000 report.

[26] For example, they include the enhancement of auditing and enforcement activities, a requirement for comprehensive information reporting rules, and a recommendation to adopt controlled foreign corporation (CFC) rules, all with respect to uncooperative tax havens.

[27] Andorra, Liechtenstein, Liberia, Monaco, Marshall Islands, Nauru and Vanuatu.

a two-track strategy, it encompasses smaller measures to address the most urgent problems, e.g. by extending the existing Merger and the Parent-Subsidiary Directives to cover a wider range of companies and transactions. It also covers the promotion of a more comprehensive approach to tax reform, by suggesting the introduction of an EU-wide consolidated tax base, and the use of formula apportionment. The current requirement to identify the profit earned in each separate country would be abandoned. Under the proposed system companies would need to compute profits only once for the whole of the EU, using just one set of rules. The obtained taxable profit would then be apportioned to member states, according to a pre-agreed formula, which could be based on factors such as capital, payroll or sales or a combination thereof.[28]

The tax rate at which these apportioned profits would be taxed, would remain under the sovereignty of each member state and would not be harmonized. Apart from addressing the compliance costs of computing taxable profits in every European jurisdiction, this proposal would also eliminate the possibilities firms have to manipulate transfer prices to shift profits within the EU. The initiative, however, does not deal with profit shifting in and out of the EU. Nor would it eliminate tax competition: tax rates would not be harmonized, and firms may be able to relocate factors used in the allocation formula.

3. CAN THEORY EXPLAIN THE STYLIZED FACTS?

The previous section established a number of stylized facts about the development of corporation taxes over the last two decades. Over roughly the same period of time, there has been a great deal of theoretical work on tax competition. In this section, we ask whether this explosion of theory can explain the stylized facts.

The central results of the tax competition literature were established by Wilson (1986) and Zodrow and Mieszkowski (1986). In the context of perfectly mobile capital between many jurisdictions, the post-tax rate of return earned on capital must be equated between jurisdictions. As a result, any tax on capital levied within a jurisdiction will raise the required pre-tax rate of return and, in doing so, drive part of the capital stock elsewhere. This spillover effect between jurisdictions creates an additional cost to levying a source-based tax on capital. As a result, the optimal tax rate is lower than it otherwise would be, and if this is the only source of revenue, this leads to an under-provision of public goods. This canonical model is at the heart of concerns about capital tax competition within the EU.

In a closely related paper, Gordon (1986) also considers other tax-raising opportunities. He compares source-based and residence-based capital income taxes in a

---

[28] For a discussion of the economic issues of formula apportionment, see, *inter alia*, Gammie *et al.* (2001), European Commission (2001b), Gordon and Wilson (1986), Goolsbee and Maydew (2000).

two period model of a small open economy. The source-based tax has the same effects as in the canonical model, driving up the pre-tax required rate of return and driving away capital. However, the residence-based tax does not have these effects. Hence in this model, the source-based tax should not be used; instead revenue should be raised from a residence-based tax. This type of analysis[29] has led to fears of a 'race to the bottom', in which source-based capital income taxes disappear altogether.[30]

Of course, there are considerable practical problems in levying a residence-based tax on capital income, especially if the tax is to apply to income earned but not repatriated. As a result, as the survey by Wilson (1999) suggests, the theoretical literature has generally investigated models where residence-based taxes are either limited or not available.

At first glance it seems that these models are a good starting place for understanding at least part of the stylized facts described in the previous section. Beginning with some degree of imperfect capital mobility, and allowing an exogenous increase in mobility over time, would result in the optimal tax rate on capital falling over time (as seen in the stylized facts).

However, the models in these papers – as with most others in the literature – do not specifically allow for the two broad instruments which governments have available for taxing capital income: the tax rate and the tax base. Instead the tax base is generally assumed to be equal to capital income net of true economic depreciation, but before any costs of financing investment. An advantage of this formulation is that it is tractable, since it becomes possible to write the required post-tax rate of return (r) as a simple function of the tax rate (t) and the pre-tax marginal product of capital (F_K): $F_K(1 - t) = r$. But, clearly from this expression, t is an effective marginal tax rate (EMTR): it reflects the difference between the required return on capital in the presence and absence of tax. Yet t is typically assumed to be the statutory rate. In general, then, these models do not permit governments to choose separately the tax rate and tax base. But there are many combinations of the rate and base that can generate a given EMTR. A tax base equal to net capital income is a special case.

In fact, it is straightforward to show that the key results of the canonical model do not survive if governments can choose the two instruments separately. As long as the revenue requirement is not too high, governments can use a cash flow tax, in which all capital expenditure is deductible in the period in which it is incurred. It is well known that such a tax generates an EMTR of zero. Revenue is generated from the infra-marginal returns, assumed in the canonical model to accrue to immobile domestic residents. In this case, an optimal tax rate can be set which generates the appropriate level of public good provision, without distorting capital flows. This is shown by Haufler and Schjelderup (2000).

---

[29] See also Razin and Sadka (1991).

[30] Gordon and Mackie-Mason (1995) consider two tax instruments: corporation tax and personal income tax. They contrast the corporate income shifting between countries with income shifting between the personal and corporate sectors.

However, this extension of the canonical model is clearly not sufficient to explain the pattern of existing corporate income taxes, since in fact, as shown above, the EMTR is typically not zero. One possible explanation of this is that the revenue requirement – determined by the preference for public goods – exceeds the immobile infra-marginal returns (which is certainly plausible if generally capital earns only a normal return). In this case, it may be necessary to raise revenue from a tax on capital as well – i.e. to have an EMTR greater than zero.

But whether this is the case depends also on the other tax instruments available to governments. One issue here is whether a labour income tax is more or less distorting than a tax on capital flows. In the canonical model, labour is typically assumed to be immobile. In this case, any taxes on capital are effectively borne by labour, so it is generally better to tax labour directly, than to distort the availability of capital by taxing capital. But the European Commission (1997) has argued that switching tax bases from capital to labour – as a result of increasing tax competition – has had serious implications for unemployment in Europe. Daveri and Tabellini (2000) present evidence that taxes on labour have impacted on unemployment rates. However, there have been no studies that investigate the impact of corporate income tax on unemployment, using detailed measures of taxes on corporate income that reflect both the rate and the base.

Another extension of the canonical model would consider the possibility that infra-marginal returns are mobile. In this case, imposing a tax on economic rent would also distort the location of capital; this is at the heart of the model discussed above, in which multinational firms make discrete location choices. In this case, the EMTR is not the only measure of taxation that affects location decisions; the EATR also matters.

This raises the question of the extent to which governments can rely on taxes on economic rent to raise revenue. There may be location-specific rents in a particular country – that is, economic rent over and above that which could be earned else-where. In principle, such location-specific rents could be taxed without distorting the location of firms and capital.[31] But it is likely that such location-specific rents vary – across industries, firms and time. It is simply not possible to capture location-specific rents with a general tax system which applies to all investment projects, while avoiding tax on rents which are not location-specific.

But if all economic rents cannot be fully taxed, it will generally be optimal to tax different kinds of internationally mobile capital differently. All else equal, source-based tax rates should be lower, in terms of the pursuit of national welfare, on more mobile forms of capital. At one extreme, location-specific rents can still be taxed at

---

[31] For example, in the 1980s the UK government raised substantial amounts of revenue from a tax on North Sea oil production in the form of the Petroleum Revenue Tax.

100%. At the other extreme, if the same rent is available in another country, then such rents cannot be taxed at a higher rate than in the other country without causing the capital to locate there. If some location-specific rents, which accrue to foreigners, cannot be fully taxed, then it is generally optimal for a small open economy to levy a distorting source-based capital income tax as a rent-shifting device. That is, setting a tax system to capture at least some of the location-specific rent will involve having a positive EMTR. We discuss these issues further below.

The theoretical literature has explored cases in which optimal tax rates may vary according to economic circumstances. For example, Bucovetsky (1991) and Wilson (1991) present models in which large countries maintain higher tax rates than small countries. The tax rate levied in large countries will have a greater effect on the equilibrium post-tax rate of return, and hence a smaller impact on the pre-tax required rate of return. Hence larger countries can maintain a higher source-based capital income tax rate. This could be interpreted in terms of a location-specific rent associated with large countries.

Baldwin and Krugman (2000) present a model in which an agglomeration in one country creates a location-specific economic rent. Given the presence of an agglomeration, small changes in the source-based capital income tax rate may have little effect. However, larger changes may end up collapsing the agglomeration, which could have large welfare effects.

Our discussion in this paper so far has implicitly assumed a benevolent welfare-maximizing government. That is, we have been attempting to understand observed patterns of tax setting behaviour by identifying whether they are consistent with the optimization of social welfare. But what if governments are not benevolent?[32] Suppose, for example, that a Leviathan government puts greater weight on public goods than private goods, since the government itself gains some private benefit from the public provision. In a static model, that might lead the Leviathan government to set taxes on capital higher than a benevolent government; consequently there would be lower capital in the economy; and the lower welfare associated with the lower private consumption would exceed the greater welfare arising from higher public goods provision.

Suppose we start from such a situation and observe an increase in capital mobility. This changes the relative cost of public good provision – it becomes more expensive to provide public goods in terms of the amount of private consumption that must be given up. As long as the Leviathan government attaches some positive value to private goods for its citizens, then the higher 'price' of public goods would lead to lower tax rates and public goods, just as with the benevolent government.

---

[32] Two papers which explore alternatives in this vein are Edwards and Keen (1996) and Wilson and Gordon (2001).

The relevant question here is not whether different types of government would set different tax rates, but how their chosen tax rates would respond to increases in mobility. We are not aware of any model which predicts that tax rates would increase as a result of increased mobility because the government is not welfare-maximizing.[33]

4. POSSIBLE EXPLANATIONS OF THE STYLIZED FACTS

The discussion above suggests that the canonical tax competition literature is not able to explain the observed behaviour of governments over the last two decades of cutting tax rates on corporate income as well as broadening the associated tax bases. In this section we discuss two possible explanations based on the notion of tax competition. Of course, there could be reasons, unconnected to tax competition, why governments have followed rate-cutting, base-broadening tax reforms. For example, they could simply be learning from each other about the construction of (more) optimal tax structures. The first major rate-cutting, base-broadening corporation tax reform was in the UK in 1984. The rationale for the reform given at the time was to reduce distortions to the investment and financial policy for UK firms, by reducing the dispersion in effective marginal tax rates across different forms of investment and sources of finance. A similar rationale was at least partly behind the corporation tax reforms included in the US Tax Reform Act of 1986.[34] It is possible that other countries could have simply followed suit in an attempt to reduce distortions in the domestic economy. Indeed, anecdotally, there is some evidence of this occurring in the 1980s' wave of reform. However, this seems less persuasive as an explanation of the continuing rate-cutting, base-broadening reforms, up to the German tax reform of 2001.

An alternative, but related explanation, has been offered by Sinn (1988, 1989). This explanation begins by noting that, given three conditions, the cost of capital is equal to the real interest rate. These conditions are: (1) that the personal tax rate of the marginal shareholder is equal to the corporate tax rate; (2) that the marginal shareholder does not pay capital gains tax; and (3) that capital allowances are set equal to the true economic depreciation rate. Compared to this, Sinn argues that, in the past, corporation taxes subsidized investment by being more generous in setting allowances. A tax cutting reform that cut personal and corporate tax rates equally would have only a small impact on the cost of capital. However, combining this with a reduction in allowances would reduce the subsidy to investment. A similar

---

[33] There is at least one model in which greater mobility leads to higher tax rates, but in a setting of a benevolent government. Janeba (1998) begins from a trade model in which two firms, resident in different countries, compete in an imperfectly competitive market in a third country. In this model, if the firms are immobile, each government has an incentive to subsidize its own firm in order to give it a competitive advantage. However, introducing capital mobility restricts this inefficient activity, since a high subsidy would attract the foreign firm, and would be captured by its non-resident owners. In this case, tax competition for mobile capital enhances efficiency, and reduces subsidies.

[34] An extensive literature has analysed this reform. See, for example, Slemrod (1990), and Auerbach and Slemrod (1997).

argument holds if the two tax rates are not exactly equal, but are both simultaneously cut.

However, this explanation relies on the tax reform reducing both the corporate tax rate and the personal tax rate. While many countries did indeed institute such reforms, these taxes have rather different properties. The corporate tax is generally levied on a source basis – where activity takes place. The personal tax is generally levied on a residence basis – where the recipient of the income resides. If, in the context of an international capital market, the marginal shareholder of the firm resides in a different country, then the source country has no control over that shareholder's personal tax rate. For the corporate and personal tax rate to be simultaneously cut requires either the marginal shareholder to be a domestic resident (which seems unlikely in the case of a capital-exporting country), or the two countries to co-ordinate on the rate cut.

We consider two possible explanations of the stylized facts presented in Section 2. Both are based on forms of tax competition and both focus on the impact of taxes on economic profits on firms' investment behaviour. They differ, however, in that each considers some form of mobility other than capital. The first considers taxable profit to be mobile, independently of the location of capital. The second considers the mobility of firms (multinationals) with access to valuable proprietary assets (be these technological knowledge, management skills or brand name).

4.1. Income shifting

One possibility is that income shifting between jurisdictions is driving these reforms. Such income shifting can take simple forms: the manipulation of transfer prices on intermediate goods traded between members of the same group, for example, or lending from low tax countries to subsidiaries in high tax rate countries. Or it can take rather more complex forms, which may or may not use 'special regimes' available in some countries, allowing taxpayers to reduce their overall tax liabilities. There is empirical evidence of income shifting behaviour by firms (see Hines, 1999 for a survey), and as we have seen the EU and OECD measures have to a large extent been targeted at regimes that exploit such activity by firms.

One response governments can make to income shifting is to attempt to impose greater constraints on such activities. For example, one approach is to tighten and more rigorously enforce taxes on controlled foreign companies (CFCs). This may drive firms to use more sophisticated, and more costly, techniques of income shifting, which in turn reduce the net benefit. This would imply less income shifting, although this strategy may also be costly to governments in the form of administrative and compliance costs.

Income shifting itself might be seen as giving rise to competition between jurisdictions. Shifting income between jurisdictions creates spillovers just as shifting capital does; in the case of movement of income, it is the tax base – and hence tax revenues – which move, as opposed to capital. But there is nothing to rule out countries also competing over such tax revenue. One theoretical paper, Haufler and Schjelderup (2000), has addressed the optimal choice of source-based capital income tax parameters in a model with profit shifting. This paper starts from what is essentially the canonical model described above, although in a two-country setting. The paper begins by demonstrating the result referred to above: that if the government has two instruments at its disposal – the tax base and the tax rate – then it will define the tax base to be cash flow, ensuring an EMTR of zero.

Haufler and Schjelderup go on to consider the case in which firms can shift their profits between jurisdictions with some convex costs. They can do so by over-pricing an input purchased from the other country. The higher the price given to this input, the lower the tax base in the home country and the higher the tax base in the foreign country. The amount of income shifted out of a jurisdiction depends on its tax rate relative to that in some lower taxed jurisdiction. Conditional on the foreign tax rate, the higher the home country tax rate, the greater the benefit of shifting income out of the home country. The firm will therefore increase the price of the input, in the process raising the marginal cost of doing so, until the marginal cost is equal to the difference in the tax rates.

This additional factor constrains the tax-setting of the home country government. The tax rate cannot be raised without a cost in terms of a smaller tax base due to greater income shifting. With a fixed revenue requirement, the government is forced to reduce allowances in order to recoup the tax revenue lost from being obliged to have a lower tax rate. In effect, the optimal policy is then to accept some distortion to capital flows in the form of lower allowances in order to reduce the incentives to shift capital out of the country.

Note that in this simple formulation, the amount of income shifted does not depend on the generosity of tax allowances; lower allowances have no direct effect on the degree of income shifting. The optimal tax rate depends on the degree of convexity of the cost of overpricing the input. It also depends, in conjunction with the rate of allowances, on the sensitivity of the capital stock to the EMTR.

Suppose now, in the context of this model, that there is an exogenous reduction in the cost of profit shifting. In particular, suppose that, for any given difference between the two tax rates, there is greater profit shifting. Other things being equal, this would change the trade-off in the welfare costs of income shifting compared to the distortion to capital. Since income shifting has become cheaper, we would expect the tax rate to fall and allowances to fall as well.

This is a possible explanation of the rate-cutting, base-broadening reforms in the 1980s and 1990s. As Haufler (2001) points out, in the absence of income shifting, the optimal policy is to have a cash flow tax. Introducing profit shifting implies lower allowances and hence raises the EMTR from zero to some positive number.

Beginning with no income shifting this model therefore predicts a rise in the EMTR. However, this is not necessarily the case for all combinations of the tax rate and tax base. Beginning from some positive value of the EMTR, a revenue-neutral fall in allowances and fall in the tax rate may raise or lower the EMTR.

This is therefore a possible explanation for the rate-cutting, base-broadening reforms of the 1980s and 1990s. The explanation also fits well with the interpretation of the EU Code of Conduct and OECD measures as being designed to make income shifting more difficult. If governments can increase the cost of income shifting, then they at least partially relax the constraints on their tax-setting behaviour. The fact that the Code cannot eliminate income shifting is irrelevant to this argument. Any increase in the cost of income shifting would ease constraints faced by governments.

4.2. Multinational firms

Another possible explanation for these reforms is that governments are particularly interested in attracting certain types of investment project – those carried out by multinational firms. The theory of the multinational firm suggests that they have access to proprietary assets, and that their projects will, on average, be more profitable. These assets may, for example, be technological knowledge, management skills or brand name. These investment projects may be thought to be more desirable if they bring greater social benefits through positive externalities. As shown in Section 2, the effect of rate-cutting, base-broadening reforms has generally been to reduce the tax rate on profitable investments by more than on less profitable investments.

In particular, while a revenue-neutral rate-cutting and base-broadening reform may leave the EATR on the *average* project unchanged, it will tend to lower the EATR on projects of above-average profitability and raise the EATR of those of below average profitability. Figure 10 illustrates the impact that reforms over the past two decades have had on projects of varying levels of profitability. It indicates that there has been a greater fall in the EATR at higher rates of profitability.

Given this non-linear pattern of the EATR, there are two plausible related reasons for the observed tax reforms. One possibility is simply that more profitable activities are thought to have greater benefits to the domestic economy. Hence, even if all activities were equally mobile, governments would want to attract more profitable activity. The second is that, irrespective of any such benefits, more profitable firms may also be more mobile.

It has been argued that multinational firms may increase productivity and generate positive externalities through technological spillovers or increases in competition. The introduction of new technologies benefits consumers (to the extent that the goods were not previously traded), workers (to the extent that they benefit from training, or capture some of the economic rent) and possibly also domestic firms (to the extent that they are able to copy the technically superior multinational to improve their own efficiency).[35] Thus, to the extent to which multinational firms do generate positive externalities, it may be optimal to tax them at a lower rate. An alternative explanation would be that large multinationals might have more resources to lobby for lower taxes than less profitable local firms.

These factors may help explain the stylized facts of Section 2, if the cost of shifting profitable investment projects between countries has decreased over time. That is, if governments have undertaken tax reforms in order to attract higher profit firms, then the fact that they have done so suggests that the degree of competition has increased, which in turn is consistent with greater mobility. An alternative explanation is that the mobility of such firms has increased more sharply than that for lower profit firms. In this case, governments may have responded by reducing effective tax rates more quickly for such firms, even if all firms generated the same benefit to the domestic economy. What evidence is there to support these assertions?

There have been a number of policy reforms which can be expected to have led to an increase in the mobility of capital. These include the relaxation of capital controls and trade liberalization across a broad range of countries. It is very difficult to document the increase in capital mobility or the mobility of certain types of firm or investment project over time. We cite several types of evidence here to give an indicative picture of the increase in cross-border corporate activity over the past few decades.

One indicator is the upward trend in foreign direct investment (FDI) across OECD countries. Figure 15 shows that in 1981 FDI was around 0.5% of GDP (weighted average across OECD countries) and that this increased to around 3% by 1999. FDI statistics capture flows of financial capital across borders.

Another indicator looks at the real activity of firms. Griffith and Simpson (2001) show that the proportion of investment in physical assets in the UK production sector that was accounted for by foreign-owned firms rose from 20.9% in 1980 to 39.3% in 1996. Lipsey (2001) shows that the value of foreign non-official assets in the USA has risen from $188 billion in 1976 (current value) to $6102 billion in 1999.

To provide further information, we use firm level data from Thomson Financial Datastream between 1975 and 1999 on 811 firms listed on the London Stock Exchange. We investigate the share of employees of these firms that were located abroad.[36] This is clearly not a direct measure of mobility. Rather a measure of mobility would be more properly based on the elasticity of activity abroad with respect to, say, post-tax profitability. However, it seems plausible to suppose that more mobile firms would have a greater share of their employees located abroad, and that

---

[35] Empirical research is unclear on the sign, size or importance of these externalities. The early literature suggested that there were large positive spillovers or externalities from multinationals to other firms see, *inter alia*, Blomstrom (1989), Borensztein *et al.* (1998), Caves (1974) and Globerman (1979). The more recent literature finds a much smaller impact, see Aitken and Harrison (1999), Griffith *et al.* (2001) and Criscuolo and Martin (2002).

[36] This is measured as 1-ds216/ds219, where ds216 is the number of domestic employees and ds219 is the total number of employees (and where the number refers to Datastream account items).

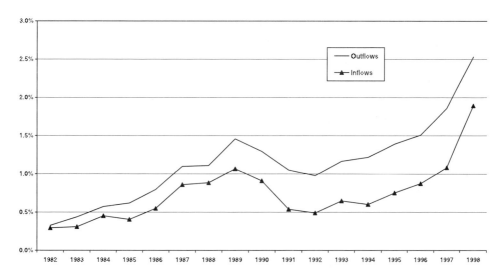

Figure 15. Foreign direct investment (% of GDP)

Notes: Average weighted by GDP in US$. The average is across all EU and G7 countries except the following, which have missing data in some years: Austria, Belgium, Greece, Ireland, Luxembourg, Sweden.
Source: OECD.

increased mobility is likely to be associated with a higher share of employees being located abroad.

In fact, the average share of employees located abroad rose from around 6% in the mid 1970s to around 15% by the late 1990s. In a regression of the share of workers located abroad on a time trend, allowing for individual firm constants, the time trend is positive and significant. The same data reveal a positive correlation between profitability[37] and the share of employees located abroad. Splitting firms into those above and those below median profitability, less profitable firms have an average share of workers abroad of around 9%, while among more profitable firms it is around 13%. In a regression of the share on a time trend and profitability, allowing for individual effects, the coefficient on profitability is positive and significant.[38] These facts suggest that activity abroad has increased and that there is a correlation between higher profitability and activity abroad.

The increase in mobility has been faster for more profitable firms. In the late 1970s lower profitability firms had on average around 6% of employees located abroad while higher profitability firms had on average around 6.5%. By the late 1990s the average for lower profitability firms had increased to 10% while for higher profitability firms it had increased to 17%. Separate regressions of the share of employees located abroad on a time trend for low and high profitability firms (split by the

[37] We measure profitability by earned for ordinary – full tax (ds182) over total sales (ds104).
[38] The coefficient is 0.045 with a standard error of 0.025.

median) reveal a positive and significant coefficient in both cases, but it is significantly larger for more profitable firms.[39]

Using different data Bloom and Griffith (2001) show that UK firms are increasingly conducting R&D abroad and that the share of R&D conducted by foreign-owned firms in the UK has increased over time.

While these figures reflect the experience only for the UK, they are consistent with the proposition that the mobility of projects of above-average profitability has risen relative to other projects. This is also consistent with the literature on the activities – and indeed existence – of multinational firms, which suggests that they are more profitable than purely domestic firms. Theory suggests that multinationals should have some superiority over domestic firms, based on the presumption that, because there are costs to setting up production in a foreign country, a multinational must have some other advantages[40] to compete with local firms (which do not face such costs). Such advantages may take a number of forms. They may reflect lower production costs or a higher quality product, made possible, for example, by research and development undertaken in the multinational's home country or elsewhere. They may reflect a better organized and managed structure. However, the advantage may also reflect market power, due perhaps to advertising and branding.

There is one important caveat to the notion that multinational firms are more mobile. That is, that the capital owned by immobile firms may nevertheless be mobile. In the canonical model described above, firms are immobile, but raise finance on the world market. A higher domestic tax rate will reduce the demand for finance for capital by domestic firms; the available capital will instead be used elsewhere. Such immobile firms may be relatively unprofitable; indeed they may make only a normal return. If so, then the relevant measure of taxation for the movement of capital is the EMTR.

Nevertheless, one interpretation of recent corporation tax reforms may be that governments have aimed to attract investment by multinationals, by shifting the distribution of effective tax rates across levels of profitability, because they believe it brings access to valuable proprietary assets. The evidence in Section 2 indicates that effective tax rates have fallen furthest at higher rates of profitability.

This might appear to be inconsistent with international cooperation in the form of the Code of Conduct. The Commission has effectively argued that, beginning from a position of relatively high taxes on capital, the creation in some jurisdictions of 'special' low-tax regimes for some types of capital induces not only a reduction in revenue, but also greater distortions to the location of capital. Setting up such regimes would certainly be consistent with governments attempting to attract specific forms of activity. In this context, 'special' regimes could be seen as a further attempt to reduce taxes on specific, targeted, forms of mobile capital, as has been suggested by Keen (2002).

---

[39] The coefficient (standard error) is 0.049 (0.004) for lower profitability firms and 0.117 (0.005) for more profitable firms.

[40] This is known as the OLI approach of Dunning (1977).

But as Keen points out, if special regimes are eliminated, then the opportunity which governments have had to differentiate between different forms of capital investment (e.g. foreign-owned versus domestic-owned) through special regimes will be lost. To continue to compete for such activities will put additional downwards pressure on general levels of corporation tax (although more profitable activities can still be targeted by an appropriate movement in the distribution of the EATR). But, if this is the effect of the Code of Conduct, then the Code itself is inconsistent with this interpretation of two decades of corporation tax reform.

However, an alternative reading of the Code of Conduct, as was given above, is that it is primarily aimed at profit shifting activities. Certainly, the measures which the Code of Conduct Group has identified as being 'harmful' include very few which are likely to affect the location of real activity. If the Code of Conduct is not targeted towards removing regimes specifically set up to attract real capital, then it does not contradict the second explanation of tax reforms put forward here.

5. SUMMARY AND CONCLUDING REMARKS

In this paper we have analysed the development of taxes on corporate income in EU and G7 countries over the 1980s and 1990s. We have developed a number of stylized facts about the development of such taxes over this period:

- statutory tax rates fell over the 1980s and 1990s;
- tax bases were broadened between the early 1980s and the end of the 1990s;
- the effective marginal tax rate has remained stable over the 1980s and 1990s;
- effective average tax rates for projects earning positive economic profits have fallen over the 1980s and 1990s, and they have fallen more at higher levels of profitability;
- tax revenues on corporate income have remained broadly stable as a proportion of GDP since 1965; and
- tax revenues on corporate income have declined as a proportion of total tax revenue since 1965.

We have argued that the standard or canonical theoretical economic models of tax competition are not sufficient to explain these developments. The main reason is that such models typically do not model the tax rate and the tax base separately. Instead, they make assumptions about the tax base which imply that the tax rate is equal to the effective marginal tax rate. We have seen that such an assumption does not generally hold. And in any case, it is not possible to model the observed developments in corporate income tax if the tax base is assumed not to change. We have discussed two possible explanations of the past two decades of reform.

The first draws on a paper by Haufler and Schjelderup (2001), which considers the impact of income shifting by firms, and focuses on competition for capital and tax revenue. The two broad instruments available to governments – the rate and base –

can be combined in an optimal combination to pursue both forms of competition. As income shifting becomes less costly, a likely response by governments is to reduce the rate and expand the base.

The second possible explanation begins by noting that the observed tax reforms have had different effects on projects of different profitability. Specifically, they have tended to reduce the effective average tax rate by more for more profitable projects. Governments may compete more intensely over such projects, either because they generate more social benefits, or because they are more mobile. We provided evidence that capital and firms have become more mobile and that more profitable firms have become more mobile relative to less profitable firms.

While the share of GDP attributed to corporate tax revenues has remained fairly stable, the proportion of total tax revenues raised from corporate income taxes has fallen over time. Combined with theoretical predictions of a 'race to the bottom' from some theoretical models, this has led policy-makers to be concerned about the revenue stream likely to be available from corporate income taxes in the longer run. In turn, this has helped to generate new forms of international co-ordination in taxes on corporate income. These new forms of co-ordination are targeted primarily towards combating tax avoidance and evasion in the form of shifting income between countries, irrespective of the location of real activities.

Discussion

Marcel Thum
Dresden University of Technology, ifo Dresden and CESifo

In the last twenty years, we have experienced a general trend in corporate tax reforms around the world. Tax rates have been cut and, at the same time, tax bases have been broadened. A significant public finance literature has evolved analysing the economic effects of such reforms. However, surprisingly little effort has been made to understand why governments undertake tax-cut-*cum*-base broadening reforms at all. Of course, the literature on tax competition offers arguments as to why tax rates are cut, but usually there is no discussion of what happens to the tax base. The paper by Devereux, Griffith and Klemm bridges this gap and offers interesting insights into the effects of tax-cut-*cum*-base broadening policies.

The authors argue that firms have become more mobile during the previous two decades. However, the increase in mobility has not been the same for all firms; more profitable firms, which are of the most interest to tax authorities, have experienced a greater increase in mobility. In a word, due to tax competition for profitable firms, governments have had to offer more favourable conditions to these mobile firms. At the same time, the governments do not want to offer lower taxes to all firms, as this would erode their tax revenue. This is where tax-cut-*cum*-base-broadening comes in. This type of tax reform works similarly to price discriminations as it allows the average tax rate for highly profitable firms to be reduced. Those firms clearly benefit from a reduced tax rate as a larger share of pure profits accrues to the investor. In contrast, the deterioration of tax allowances due to a broader tax base is relatively unimportant because capital costs only comprise a small share of total revenues.

The approach taken by Devereux, Griffith and Klemm is certainly a very useful and innovative attempt to explain tax-cut-*cum*-base-broadening. Nevertheless, I am not yet fully convinced that their explanation is the right one, and I believe that future research has to complement various aspects of the current study. First, the argument critically hinges on the fact that firms have become more mobile and, in addition, that this increase in mobility has been stronger for more profitable firms. Mobility is measured by a firm's share of overseas employees. As this share has increased by more for more profitable firms, the authors argue that the more profitable firms have become more mobile, which requires targeted reforms in tax competition. Is the share of overseas employees really an appropriate measure for mobility? From a theoretical point of view, no relocation of firms has to occur in equilibrium with a decrease in mobility costs. And from an empirical point of view, there are many reasons why we should observe this pattern quite naturally (other than due to lower mobility costs). For instance, more profitable firms expand more quickly. Hence, it is also more likely that their share of employees abroad should also increase compared to less profitable companies which hire no new employees.

Secondly, the paper analyses the tax-cut-*cum*-base-broadening strategy along the profitability dimension of firms and mostly neglects another important dimension, namely the types of investor. The impact of a tax-cut-*cum*-base broadening reform depends significantly on an investor's investment alternatives. This can be clearly seen from the recent reform of the corporate income tax in Germany (Sinn and Scholten, 1999). The typical domestic investor faces the alternative of a taxed financial investment. For this investor, the tax cut has increased the net return on financial investments and, due to base broadening, made real investments less attractive. Therefore, the tax reform has led to significant increases in the cost of capital for the typical domestic investor. However, things are somewhat different for investors whose alternative investments are either untaxed or consist of real investments abroad (foreign direct investors). Here, the tax reform has led to reductions or only slight increases in the cost of capital.[41] As the typical domestic investor is – almost by definition – less mobile than the foreign direct investor, one could argue that the tax-cut-*cum*-base-broadening reform allows governments to discriminate between different types of investors. In contrast to the profitability dimension employed in the paper, the

---

[41] The precise magnitude and direction depends on the investment category. For instance, the cost of capital has remained roughly constant for investments in industrial construction.

argument of different investors does not require the tricky measurement of mobility costs across firms; it simply requires that the costs of foreign direct investments have fallen over time.

Finally, the authors provide an explanation for the widespread phenomenon of tax-cut-*cum*-base broadening reform but the analysis still lacks clear-cut policy con-clusions. Are the effective corporate tax rates too high or too low from a welfare point of view? Is the discrimination in effective tax rates desirable? A first approach would suggest that this is not the case, as the effective tax burden on pure profits is reduced requiring *ceteris paribus* higher distorting taxes on other factors. Furthermore, inter-nationally agreed limits on direct subsidies (e.g., at the EU level) might trigger further tax-cut-*cum*-base-broadening reforms. When national governments no longer have the choice of attracting profitable footloose firms through subsidies, they might be tempted to rely more heavily on their use of tax-cut-*cum*-base-broadening policies. On the one hand, limiting direct subsidies curbs detrimental tax competition, but on the other hand it might increase the distortions in the tax systems. So it is not obvious whether such limits increase welfare given that there is tax competition and that governments circumvent such rules through tax reforms.

Marco Ottaviani
London Business School and CEPR

This paper establishes some stylized facts on the evolution of corporate taxation in the EU and G7 countries over the last two decades. After establishing these facts, the authors go on to argue that the trends can be explained by an increase in inter-national tax competition. In this discussion, I give my critical summary of the facts and explanation proposed by the authors. I then present some difficulties in developing the theory of tax competition highlighted in this paper. Finally, I cast some doubts on whether tax competition is the only explanation for the facts.

Here are the facts. First, there has been a pronounced reduction in statutory tax rates. Second, some countries have reduced the depreciation allowances for capital expenditure, resulting in increased tax bases.[42] Third, the effective marginal tax rates have overall remained stable, while the tax rates on infra-marginal investments have gone down. Fourth and fifth, government tax revenues from corporate income have remained broadly unchanged as a fraction of GDP, but have declined as a proportion of total tax revenues. These facts seem consistent with the perception I have gleaned from the literature on the topic. It is nevertheless useful to summarize these facts, as their understanding will guide the academic and policy debate.

The authors explain these facts as the outcome of tax competition among countries attempting to attract mobile capital investments by firms. Firms have heterogeneous levels of profitability and are thus affected in different ways by changes in tax rate

---

[42] This second trend is not as strong as the first. I wonder whether it could be reinforced by showing that the measured tax base tended to over-estimate the actual tax base more in the past when investment tax credits were more pervasive.

and base. The effective average tax rate for more profitable ventures has decreased as a result of rate cutting and base broadening. More profitable ventures are shown to have become more mobile over the last two decades, inducing a reduction in tax rates and increase in bases in all countries.

This story sounds very reasonable and I liked it so much that I tried to derive its implications in a simple model. Unfortunately, this was not as straightforward an exercise as I anticipated. More work is needed to untangle this insight with a fully specified model.[43] One could then derive additional implications in order to test the theory. For example, heterogeneity among countries could be exploited. The incentive to reduce the tax rate seems greater the lower the fraction of highly profitable firms already present in a country. Similarly, when it comes to taxes, smaller countries could be tougher competitors.

The income-shifting theory proposed by Haufler and Schjelderup (2000) is not very different from the investment-location theory proposed here. In Haufler and Schjelderup's model profits are shifted directly by manipulating transfer prices. According to Devereux, Griffith, and Klemm's story, profits are shifted indirectly through foreign direct investment that later results in profits. The common aspect of both explanations is that companies end up shifting profits to countries with lower effective taxation. Overall, there are more conceptual similarities than differences between the two theories.

In support of their investment-location explanation, the authors show that foreign direct investment by multinational firms has increased in the last decades. It would be interesting to verify whether these investments are made in countries with more favourable corporate tax treatments. If instead investment locations do not depend on differences in corporate taxation, this increased mobility could be just due to globalization trends. How much of the increased mobility is actually toward countries outside the OECD with lower cost of labour?

While the incentive to reduce tax rates as firms become more mobile or are able to better shift income is quite clear, it seems more difficult to obtain base broadening as an equilibrium phenomenon. For example, Haufler and Schjelderup essentially assume base broadening by restricting governments to run a balanced budget, so that a reduction in tax rate necessarily results in an increase in the tax base. I wonder whether rate broadening could instead result from a Leviathan government without the revenue constraint.

Both variants of the tax competition explanation sound very natural and appealing. Yet, I am uncomfortable with the fact that the main (first two) stylized facts do not seem to be unique to corporate income taxation. In the last twenty years we have witnessed similar trends in personal income taxation. Tax legislation passed by the US Congress in the early 1980s and culminating in the 1986 tax reform involved

---

[43] There are some interesting parallels between the theory of tax competition and the theory of competition between firms with differentiated products.

either rate reduction or base broadening, or a combination of both.[44] But it would be hard to argue that this trend in personal income taxation is also due to tax competition. Could it be that the same forces that have been determining personal income taxation reform at the national level also drive corporate taxation trends?

This observation also suggests an alternative interpretation of base broadening. The tax reforms of the 1980s were a reaction to the many tax provisions previously enacted to boost particular sectors of the economy. At the time of their implementation, these reforms were seen as a response to the perception of unfairness generated by excessive tax benefits and in particular to the tax benefit transfer systems.[45] The investment tax credit regime tended to result in low effective tax rates, further lowered by combining liberal capital cost recovery provisions with interest deductions associated with debt financing. The elimination of the investment tax credit was mostly aimed at reducing these 'horizontal' iniquities. If so, base broadening was introduced to increase horizontal equity. The authors argue that these policies ended up creating more 'vertical' iniquities.

In conclusion, I do not think that we can unambiguously rule in favour of a tax competition explanation for the stylized facts. More economic analysis of the issue is needed to inform the policy debate. Given the importance of the topic in the current debate, this work is bound to have an impact.

Panel discussion

Michael Devereux replied to Marcel Thum that the authors had deliberately played down the discussion of welfare in their analysis because it would be extremely complicated. Rachel Griffith added that an adequate treatment of welfare issues would require taking account of many kinds of externality for which it was difficult to obtain credible empirical measures.

Thomas Piketty asked the authors to provide more evidence on the politics of base broadening. Whereas he considered the evidence on the motives for reductions in statutory corporate income tax rates to be convincing, he had doubts about the explanation for base broadening. He pointed out that depreciation allowances had decreased substantially only in the UK, Ireland, Canada and Austria. He thought more information would need to be provided before the presented evidence could be called a stylized fact.

---

[44] The actual timing of the reforms might reveal some information. In the US, tax rate cuts tended to precede base broadening measures. Was this a more general trend? It might be worthwhile to complement future analyses with careful case studies.

[45] A stressed by Weiss (1996): 'It is hard to overemphasize the degree to which horizontal equity was the driving force behind the Tax Reform Act of 1986. Publicity in the early 1980s about high-income individuals and large corporations that paid little or no tax was perhaps the most important force that kept the Act alive on its perilous legislative journey. Members of the Congress were sensitized to perception of unfairness that can arise when items of income are omitted from the tax base.'

Jean-Marie Viaene thought that it was not clear that lower tax rates attract international firms given the existence of treaties on the avoidance of double taxation. Once a firm is located in one country it is indifferent to tax rates abroad. Karen-Helene Midelfart-Knarvik thought, however, that because of large differences in tax treaties across countries and multinational firms, it was unlikely that such treaties achieved neutrality.

Richard Lyons suggested an explanation in terms of threshold effects. Given that firms obtain tax credit in the US for repatriated earnings, it makes sense for countries to lower the statutory rate to 35% (the US corporate tax rate) and then broaden the base to increase tax revenue.

Philip Lane pointed out that income shifting might have become easier over time as firms have become more specialized vertically. He emphasized that attracting capital was different from attracting firms and that the latter was important. He added that corporate revenues had remained high in Ireland because the tax base had increased substantially so that corporate tax revenues are now as important as income tax revenues.

REFERENCES

Aitken, B. and A. Harrison (1999). 'Do domestic firms benefit from direct foreign investment? Evidence from Venezuela', *American Economic Review*, 89, 605–18.

Auerbach, A.J. and J. Slemrod (1997). 'The economic effects of the Tax Reform Act of 1986', *Journal of Economic Literature*, XXXV, 589–632.

Baldwin, R. and P. Krugman (2000). 'Agglomeration, integration and tax harmonization', CEPR Discussion Paper, 2630.

Blomstrom, M. (1989). *Foreign Investment and Spillovers: A Study of Technology Transfer to Mexico*, Routledge, London.

Bloom, N. and R. Griffith (2001). 'The internationalisation of UK R&D', *Fiscal Studies*, 22(3), 337–55.

Borensztein, E., D. Gregario and J.-W. Lee (1998). 'How does foreign direct investment affect economic growth?', *Journal of International Economics*, 45, 115–35.

Bucovetsky, S. (1991). 'Asymmetric tax competition', *Journal of Urban Economics*, 30, 167–81.

Caves, R. (1974). 'Multinational firms, competition and productivity in host-country markets', *Economica*, 41, 176–93.

Chennells, L. and R. Griffith (1997). *Taxing Profits in a Changing World*, Institute for Fiscal Studies, London.

Criscuolo, C. and R. Martin (2002). 'Multinationals, foreign ownership and productivity in UK businesses', mimeo presented at Workshop on Recent Developments in Productivity Analysis using the British Annual Respondents Database, University of Nottingham, January.

Daveri, F. and G. Tabellini (2000). 'Unemployment, growth and taxation in industrial countries', *Economic Policy*, 30, 47–88.

Devereux, M.P. (1987). 'Taxation and the cost of capital: the UK experience', *Oxford Review of Economic Policy*, 3.4, xvii–xxxii.

Devereux, M.P. (1989). 'Tax asymmetries, the cost of capital and investment', *Economic Journal*, 99, 103–12.

Devereux, M.P. and R. Griffith (1998). 'Taxes and the location of production: evidence from a panel of US multinationals', *Journal of Public Economics*, 68(3), 335–67.

Devereux, M.P. and R. Griffith (2002a). 'Evaluating tax policy for location decisions', *International Tax and Public Finance*, forthcoming.

Devereux, M.P. and R. Griffith (2002b). 'The impact of corporate taxation on the location of capital: a review', *Swedish Economic Policy Review*, forthcoming.

Devereux, M., Lockwood, B. and Redoano, M. (2002). 'Do countries compete over corporation tax rates?', CEPR Discussion Paper 3400.

Devereux, M.P. and M. Pearson (1995). 'European tax harmonisation and production efficiency', *European Economic Review*, 39, 1657–81.

Dunning, J. (1977). 'Trade, location of economic activity and MNE: a search for an eclectic approach', in B. Ohlin, P.O. Hesselborn and P.M. Wijkman (eds), *The International Allocation of Economic Activity*, Macmillan, London.

Edwards, J.S.S. and M. Keen (1996). 'Tax competition and Leviathan', *European Economic Review*, 40, 113–34.

European Commission (1992). 'Report of the Committee of Independent Experts on Company Taxation', Office for Official Publications of the European Communities, Luxembourg.

European Commission (1997). 'Towards tax co-ordination in the European Union: a package to tackle harmful tax competition', Communication from the European Commission COM(97) 495 final.

European Commission (1998). 'Conclusions of the ECOFIN Council meeting on 1 December 1997 concerning taxation policy', *Official Journal of the European Communities*, C2, 6/1/98, 1–6.

European Commission (2001a). 'Towards an International Market without Tax Obstacles', Communication from the European Commission COM(2001) 582 final.

European Commission (2001b). 'Company Taxation in the Internal Market', Commission Staff Working Paper SEC(2001) 1681 final.

Eurostat (1998, 2000). 'Structures of the Taxation Systems in the European Union', Office for Official Publications of the European Communities, Luxembourg.

Gammie, M., A. Klemm and C. Radaelli (2001). 'EU corporate tax reform', Report of a CEPS Task Force, Centre for European Policy Studies, Brussels.

Globerman, S. (1979). 'Foreign direct investment and spillover efficiency benefits in Canadian manufacturing industries', *Canadian Journal of Economics*, 12, 42–56.

Goolsbee, A. and E. Maydew (2000). 'Coveting thy neighbor's manufacturing: The dilemma of state income apportionment', *Journal of Public Economics*, 75(1), 125–43.

Gordon, R.H. (1986). 'Taxation of investment and savings in the world economy', *American Economic Review*, 76, 1086–102.

Gordon, R.H. and J.D. Wilson (1986). 'An examination of multijurisdictionl corporate income taxation under formula apportionment', *Econometrica*, 54(6), 1357–73.

Gordon, R.H. and J.K. Mackie-Mason (1995). 'Why is there corporation taxation in a small open economy? The role of transfer pricing and income shifting', in M. Feldstein and J. Hines (eds), *Issues in International Taxation*, University of Chicago Press, Chicago.

Griffith, R. and H. Simpson (2001). 'Characteristics of foreign-owned firms in British manufacturing', IFS Working Paper W01/10.

Griffith, R., H. Simpson and S. Redding (2001). 'Catch-up at the plant level', IFS mimeo.

Hall, R.E. and D. Jorgenson (1967). 'Tax policy and investment behavior', *American Economic Review*, 57.

Haufler, A. (2001). *Taxation in a Global Economy*, Cambridge University Press, Cambridge.

Haufler, A. and G. Schjelderup (2000). 'Corporate tax systems and cross country profit shifting', *Oxford Economic Papers*, 52, 306–25.

Hines, J.R. (1999). 'Lessons from behavioural responses to international taxation', *National Tax Journal*, 52, 305–22.

Horstmann, I. and J. Markusen (1992). 'Endogenous Market Structures in International Trade (natura facit saltum)', *Journal of International Economics*, 32, 109–29.

IMF (2001). *World Economic Outlook Database*, May 2001, International Monetary Fund.

Janeba, E. (1998). 'Tax competition in imperfectly competitive markets', *Journal of International Economics*, 44, 135–53.

Jorgenson, D.W. and R. Landau (1993). *Tax Reform and the Cost of Capital: An International Comparison*, Brookings, Washington DC.

Keen, M. (2002). 'Preferential regimes can make tax competition less harmful', *National Tax Journal*, 54, 757–62.

King, M.A. (1977). 'Taxation, investment and the cost of capital', *Review of Economic Studies*, 41, 21–35.

King, M.A. and D. Fullerton (1984). *The Taxation of Income from Capital*, University of Chicago Press, Chicago.

Lipsey, R.E. (2001). 'Foreign Direct Investment and the Operations of Multinational Firms: Concepts, History, and Data', NBER Working Paper No. w8665.

Mendoza, E.G., A. Razin and L.L. Tesar (1994). 'Effective tax rates in macroeconomics: Cross country estimates of tax rates on factor incomes and consumption', *Journal of Monetary Economics*, 34, 297–323.

OECD (1991). *Taxing Profits in a Global Economy: Domestic and International Issues*, OECD, Paris.

OECD (1998). *Harmful Tax Competition: An Emerging Global Issue*, OECD, Paris.

OECD (2000). *Towards Global Tax Co-operation: Progress in Identifying and Eliminating Harmful Tax Practices*, OECD, Paris.

Razin, A. and E. Sadka (1991). 'Efficient investment incentives in the presence of capital flight', *Journal of International Economics*, 31, 171–81.

Sinn, H.W. (1988). 'The 1986 US tax reform and the world capital market', *European Economic Review*, 32, 325–333.

Sinn, H.W. (1989). 'The policy of tax-cut-cum-base-broadening: implications for international capital movements', in M. Neumann and K.W. Roskamp (eds), *Public Finance and Performance of Enterprises*, Wayne State University Press, Detroit.

Sinn, H.W. and U. Scholten (1999). 'Steuerreform, Kapitalkosten und Sozialprodukt', (Tax reform, cost of capital, and domestic product), IFO Research Report 28, 14–18.

Slemrod, J. (ed.) (1990). *Do Taxes Matter? The Impact of the Tax Reform Act of 1986*, MIT Press, Cambridge, MA.

Weiss, R.D. (1996). 'The Tax Reform Act of 1986: Did Congress love it or leave it?', *National Tax Journal*, 49(3), 447–59.

Wilson, J. (1986). 'A theory of interregional tax competition', *Journal of Urban Economics*, 19, 296–315.

Wilson, J. (1991). 'Optimal public good provision with limited lump-sum taxation', *American Economic Review*, 81, 153–66.

Wilson, J. (1999). 'Theories of tax competition', *National Tax Journal*, 52, 269–304.

Wilson, J. and R.H. Gordon (2001). 'Expenditure competition', NBER Working Paper No. 8189.

Zodrow, G.R. and P. Mieszkowski (1986). 'Pigou, Tiebout, property taxation, and the underprovision of public goods', *Journal of Urban Economics*, 19, 356–70.

Financial services VAT in Europe?

EU financial services are exempted of VAT for technical reasons. This paper argues that the changed nature of bank–client relationships and advances in information technology have opened the door to a practical way of redressing this exemption. The proposed solution is to charge the regular VAT on services supplied to households, but no VAT on those supplied to businesses, while allowing financial institutions the normal VAT credit for all of their purchased inputs. Financial services would, as a result, be priced differently for households and businesses so banks would have to verify their customers' VAT status. While this may be burdensome, the OECD-wide fight against tax evasion and the international struggle against terrorism have forced financial institutions to know much more about their clients. Verifying clients' VAT status should thus be fairly simple. The paper also evaluates the economic impact of reform and finds that reform would significantly increase VAT revenues, while having little impact on overall welfare. Households would see an increase in the price of financial services but given the relatively high incomes of mortgage takers, the burden of the tax would be approximately proportional across income classes.

— *Harry Huizinga*

A European VAT on financial services?

Harry Huizinga

Tilburg University, European Commission and CEPR

1. INTRODUCTION

Value Added Tax (VAT) is supposed to be a broad tax applied to virtually all final consumption. For technical reasons, however, most financial services in the EU are exempt from VAT. Since the financial services sector is quite large – accounting for something like 3.5% of EU output – and VAT rates are fairly high – 15% to 25% – this exemption creates some important distortions. For instance, the exemption means that EU banks are not, in principle, given rebates for the VAT that they pay on most of their purchased inputs. This puts them at a disadvantage with respect to banks located in nations (like the US) that have no VAT. The complexity of the exemption also entails an important administrative burden for EU banks. Most, but not all financial services are exempted, so banks are required to keep detailed records that allow tax authorities to calculate how much value-added is created by the taxable services (e.g., safekeeping boxes and investment advisory services) as opposed to the untaxed services (e.g., loans, deposit taking, foreign exchange transactions and insurance). As we shall see, the complexity also faces EU tax authorities with a temptation to engage in race-to-the-bottom fiscal competition via lax application of the rules.

The findings and conclusions expressed in this paper are those of the author and they do not necessarily represent the views of the European Commission. I thank the referees, Quentin Bradshaw, Arthur Kerrigan and Søren Bo Nielsen for many useful comments and suggestions.
The Managing Editor in charge of this paper was Richard Baldwin.

Finally, as we explain below, the exemptions lead to an over-pricing of financial services provided to business users and an under-taxation of financial services provided to households.

While the exemption may seem odd, the EU's example is widely followed in the OECD. The reason is that exemption has hereto been judged as the only practicable way of dealing with the peculiar problems of measuring value added in the financial sector. These problems are easy to describe. The value added created by a business is the value of its sales minus the value of its purchased capital and intermediate inputs. For most businesses, calculating total sales and purchases is straightforward. The problem with financial services, however, is that a major input is financial capital, and pricing such capital is difficult.

Banks, for example, do not 'buy' capital, so it is difficult for them to document how much they paid for this particular input. Rather, banks raise capital by taking in deposits or by accessing the capital markets. This difference implies many problems for value-added calculations. First, determining the price that banks pay for capital is difficult. The interest rate banks pay to depositors, for example, understates the cost since a whole array of services are tied to bank deposits and these are typically 'paid' for by offering depositors a lower interest rate. But even if it were possible to determine the price banks paid for the capital they use in providing financial services, this would not be enough. The loan interest rate charged to any particular business accounts for some default risk. And while banks surely evaluate such risks, their evaluations are not verifiable. Consequently, the amount of value added created by any given loan is very hard to calculate. The crux of the problems is that it is virtually impossible for tax authorities to determine whether a high rate of interest on a loan represents big profits, which constitutes value added and thus should be taxed, or a big risk premium, which constitutes a cost and thus should not be taxed. Analogous difficulties arise for a wide range of financial services, including foreign exchange transactions and insurance.

In attempts to remedy these distortions, Denmark and France have introduced compensatory wage taxes on exempt sectors such as banking. These measures are rather imperfect, however, and indeed they actually worsen some of the distortions. (e.g., the over-taxation of the business use of financial services). In 1998 the European Council adopted the Financial Services Action Plan (FSAP) as a blueprint for an integrated EU financial system (see European Commission, 2001a, for a recent evaluation). The FSAP does not address the VAT of financial services, but European Commission (2001b, p. 12) refers to financial services as an area where 'further work is being undertaken'.

Be that as it may, a more fundamental approach to dealing with currently exempt financial services is *a priori* appealing, but can only be considered seriously, if two conditions are met. First, a way has to be found to solve or circumvent the technical difficulties of subjecting financial services to VAT. Second, reform has to be preceded by economic analysis of its implications for the public and private sectors alike. Analysis, in particular, is necessary to address fears that reform might have negative implications for overall VAT revenues or for the distribution of income.

1.1. Purpose of this paper

The purpose of this paper·is two-fold. First, it discusses the rationale for eliminating the current VAT exemption of financial services and the options available for doing so. The main options are shown to be economically equivalent, but they differ in whether VAT is assessed for each financial transaction separately, as with the standard VAT, or instead is calculated on a more aggregate basis. Studies and pilot testing undertaken by the European Commission have attempted to establish whether calculating VAT for each financial transaction is practicable. The experience gained from this helps to clarify current options. A fresh look at an old problem is also warranted, as information technology opens up new possibilities.

A second aim of the paper is to evaluate some of the economic implications of reform. Reform increases the VAT on household-use of financial services, while reducing the VAT on business-used services. This introduces the possibility that reform lowers overall VAT revenues, dampening the enthusiasm for reform among tax administrators. This paper's analysis, however, suggests that VAT revenues from banking would increase by around €12 billion in the EU. Thus, the increased VAT revenue from higher taxes on household use of financial services considerably exceeds the VAT revenue reduction from lower-taxed, business-used services. This somewhat surprising result materializes, as currently tax authorities allow banks VAT credits for almost all of their inputs, and not just for their inputs used to produce currently taxed services. Authorities allow generous input tax credits – through a combination of explicit regulation and lax tax enforcement – to safeguard the competitive position of their banking systems. The generosity of tax authorities in this regard, to the extent that it differs across member states, leads to competitive distortions. Financial VAT reform would eliminate the apparent tax competition in this area, and thereby contribute to the creation of a single, level European financial market.

Financial VAT reform primarily leads to higher indirect financial taxes on households. Higher taxes are manifested in higher mortgage interest rates and lower deposit rates. This raises the concern that financial VAT reform has undesirable redistributive consequences. The redistributive effects, clearly, depend on the propensity of households in different income brackets to use banking services such as bank deposits and mortgages. As is shown in detail below, household data for the Netherlands suggest that financial VAT reform affects low-income and high-income households proportionately. This result reflects that bank deposits – as a share of wealth – decline with income, that the use of mortgages rises with income, and that income taxes are progressive. The fear that financial VAT reform would unduly harm the poor appears to be misplaced.

1.2. Organization of the paper

The paper starts with a more thorough exposition of the difficulties of applying VAT to financial services and the distortions that exemptions implies. The following section considers reform options, focusing mainly on the zero-rating and cash-flow approaches. While quite different in their administrative implementation, these approaches turn out to be economically equivalent, and the subsequent section, Section 4, studies the economic implications of reform. The analysis concentrates on three elements: the implications for tax revenue, the implications for social welfare, and the redistributive consequences. Also, the main reform options are evaluated as to their administrative ease and potential compliance and enforcement problems. The last section, Section 5, sums up the findings and provides some comments on the politics of financial services sector taxation.

2. THE PROBLEM

We open the analysis by first taking a closer look at the problem. The first step is to get a handle on the magnitude of the problem and how it varies across EU nations.

2.1. The magnitude of the problem

In the EU, VAT revenues are a crucial source of government revenue and the importance of VAT has been increasing. The total VAT 'take' in the EU, for instance, has increased from 3.8% of GDP in 1965 to 7.1% in 1990, and to 7.3% in 1998 (see Genser, 2001). The increased reliance on VAT makes the special treatment of the banking sector all the more noticeable.

The banking sector produces 3.5% of total EU value added in 1997 (see Table 1), but this average hides a wide dispersion. Banking accounts for only 2% of GDP in nations such as Finland and Sweden. In nations such as Portugal and Denmark, however, the figure is in excess of 5%.

Moreover, as Table 2 shows, the standard VAT rate also varies widely. While in most EU members the rate clusters around the 20% mark, Luxembourg's is as low as 15% and Denmark's is as high as 25%.

2.2. Why is it so hard to apply VAT to financial services?

This question, it turns out, is much easier to answer once one understands how VAT works in standard industries, so we illustrate the basic functioning of VAT with a simple example before turning to the specific problems of the financial sector.

2.2.1. How VAT works normally.   The basic idea of VAT is really rather simple and is best understood by thinking of it as a sales tax with a built-in enforcement

Table 1. Credit institutions in the EU, 1997

	Value added in billion euro	Value added/ total value added as %	Persons employed in thousands	Persons employed/ total employment as %
Austria	8.2	4.5	73.8***	2.0***
Belgium	5.0	2.3	77.4	2.0
Denmark	9.7	6.5	47.5	1.8
Finland	2.2	2.0	26.3	1.2
France	46.3	3.7	366.4	1.6
Germany	61.6*	3.3*	751.5	2.1
Greece	3.2	3.0	54.8	1.4
Ireland			32.3**	2.4**
Italy	36.2	3.5	345.7	1.7
Luxembourg			19.8	11.7
Netherlands	12.1	3.6	121.0***	1.7
Portugal	5.0	5.6	61.0	1.3
Spain	20.4	4.1	247.7	1.9
Sweden	4.1	2.0	47.2	1.2
UK	39.3	3.4	463.9	1.7
EU-15	253.3	3.5	2704.0	1.8

Notes: Employment data are for 1998. * 1996, ** 1997, *** estimated.

Source: Banking in Europe (1999, Tables 12 and 14, both of Section 2, and Table 1 of national sections, and 2000, Tables 13 and 15 of Section 2) and own calculations.

Table 2. VAT rates, 1999

	Standard VAT rate		Standard VAT rate
Austria	20	Ireland	21
Belgium	21	Italy	20
Denmark	25	Luxembourg	15
Finland	22	Netherlands	17.5
France	20.6	Portugal	17
Germany	16	Spain	16
Greece	18	Sweden	25
		UK	17.5

Source: PricewaterhouseCoopers, *World Tax Summaries*, 1999/2000 Edition.

device. Consider the example of the simplified value-added chain behind a photo-copying shop that makes copies for consumers. To keep things simple, we suppose that this is a highly competitive business so that the consumer price of copies exactly equals the cost of making copies plus VAT. Again to be simple, suppose the cost of copies consists only of the cost of labour, say €2 per thousand copies, and the cost of the paper, say €1 per thousand copies (no other inputs are used in this simplified example). The consumer price would therefore be €3 per thousand copies in a world without VAT. If we were considering a sales tax of, say, 20%, the consumer price would be €3 plus €0.6 in sales tax, and tax authorities would collect the full €0.6 from the copy shop. The VAT ends up having an identical impact on the final consumer price, but the tax authorities collect the €0.6 in a more roundabout manner.

The way VAT is administered, the paper producer who sells paper to the copy shop is obliged to pay VAT on the full value of his sales. The VAT-inclusive price of paper to the shop will be €1.2 per thousand, assuming a VAT rate of 20% (i.e., €1 plus €0.2 in tax). Thus the tax authorities collect €0.2 in tax from the supplier of intermediate goods to the photocopying store. The copy shop is also obliged to pay VAT on all its sales to consumers, but if it can prove that it purchased intermediate goods as inputs into its service, the authorities will grant the copy shop a credit for all the VAT paid on its purchased inputs. That is to say, the copy shop should pay €0.6 in tax to the authorities, but it can claim a €0.2 credit for the VAT contained in the price of its purchased inputs. In the end, the tax authorities collect €0.6 on the sale of €3 worth of photocopying, but part of this is collected at each stage in the value-added chain.

Note that the ultimate consumer price is the same when the tax is collected at various points along the value-added chain as when it is collected only at the final point of sale. With the VAT rebated on its purchased inputs, the true cost of paper to the copy shop is €1 per thousand (i.e., it pays a VAT-inclusive price of €1.2 but gets a VAT credit of €0.2). Thus the pre-VAT price charged to consumers will be €1 for the paper plus €2 for the labour; the VAT-inclusive consumer price will be €3.6 (i.e., €3 plus €0.6 in VAT).

The big difference between VAT and a simple sales tax is that VAT is self-enforcing. The self-enforcing mechanism lies in the fact that the copy shop must report its purchase of paper in order to get a VAT credit. Thus, even if the paper producer would like to under-report his actual sales in order to avoid some VAT, the copy shop, and all the paper producer's other customers, will demand documentation (an invoice) so that they can get a VAT credit. These invoices leave a paper trail that tax authorities can use to detect tax evasion on business-to-business sales.

2.2.2. Problems specific to the financial sector.   As the simple example makes clear, determining the price of purchased input prices is essential. Due to the nature of financial services, however, it is very difficult to determine the price of one essential input, namely capital. Banks need capital to make loans just like the copy shop needed paper, but unlike the copy shop, banks do not 'buy' capital. What, then, should be the price of the capital used in calculating the bank's VAT credit on its inputs be?

To illustrate the difficulty, consider the example of a bank loan extended to a small business owner. The cost of the loan consists of the labour of the bankers who make and administer the loan as well as the cost of some purchased inputs like computers and paper. On top of this, however, the bank needs to 'purchase' the loan capital, by, for example, taking in deposits and paying savers an interest rate. One idea would be to use the deposit rate to find the cost of the capital input. This, however, would understate the true cost to the bank because banks provide all sorts of services to their depositors and they typically 'charge' for these services by paying a lower interest rate.

Moreover, even if one knew what the true cost of capital to the bank was on average, the cost of capital for any particular loan will depend upon the riskiness of each loan. Banks charge higher interest rates on risky loans in order to compensate themselves for potential problems (defaults, non-performance, etc.). In essence, the cost of capital on any particular loan is the average cost plus a loan-specific risk premium. In a perfect world, the bank should only pay VAT on the loan interest minus the cost of all purchased inputs including the risk-adjusted cost of capital. The crux of the problem is that tax authorities cannot know what part of the variance in lending rates reflects profits (which should be subject to VAT) and what part reflects the risk premium (which should not be subject to VAT since it is part of the cost of inputs). In pricing their loans, banks surely have to assess a risk premium, but this assessment is not verifiable by the tax authorities and thus cannot be a basis for taxation. Similar difficulties stand in the way of determining the value created through bank deposits and many other financial products and services.

2.3. Real world practices and the EU's exemption

Countries have created a broad array of schemes to address this difficulty, but by far the most common solution is to avoid the problem altogether. The EU and almost all other OECD nations 'exempt' most financial services from VAT. That is to say, banks and other financial institutions are not obliged to pay VAT on most of the services they provide, but neither are they allowed to take VAT credits for the purchased inputs they use providing those services. In the EU, this exemption was instituted by the EC Sixth VAT Directive of 1977. The exemption, in particular, applies to deposit taking, lending, securities and foreign exchange transactions as well as insurance (see Box 1). Exemption thus essentially discards with financial sector output taxation, and replaces this with financial sector input taxation.

2.4. Market distortions caused by VAT exemption

Not surprisingly, the oddity of the VAT exemption of financial services creates a host of economic distortions relative to regular VAT (this is the gist of studies of the optimal taxation of financial services, as reflected in Box 2).

2.4.1. Consumer versus business price distortion. A key principle of market efficiency is that the price of a single good should be the same for all users. The exemption violates this since financial services are used both by businesses and by consumers. Because banks do not get VAT rebates for the VAT they pay on their purchased inputs (office space, computers, printed forms, etc.), banks pass this on to the buyers of financial services. When the buyer is a consumer – say an apartment

---

Box 1. Financial services exempt from VAT in the EU

The key financial activities exempted by the EC's Sixth VAT Directive are: *Insurance* described as 'Insurance and reinsurance transactions, including related services performed by insurance brokers and insurance agents'; *Dealings in bank notes and coins* defined as 'Transactions, including negotiation, concerning currency, bank notes and coins used as legal tender, with the exception of collectors' items'; *Payment activities* or 'Transactions, including negotiation, concerning deposit and current accounts, payments, transfers, debts, cheques and other negotiable instruments, excluding debt collection and factoring'; *Credit activities* consisting of 'The granting and negotiation of credit and management of credit by the person granting it and also the negotiation of or any dealings in credit guarantees or any other security for money and the management of credit guarantees by the person who is granting the credit'; *Dealings in securities* specified as 'Transactions, including negotiation, excluding management and safekeeping, in shares, interests in companies or associations, debentures and other securities'. Thus, most banking activities are in fact exempt, including the main activities of deposit taking and loan making.

The Sixth VAT Directive gives member states the choice to provide taxpayers with the option to treat all banking activities mentioned above as normally taxable under VAT rather than exempt. Thus, member states have to decide which activities are always exempt, and which activities are exempt or taxed at the discretion of the taxpayer. Germany, France and Belgium have provided their taxpayers with options in this regard. In Germany, the option to tax is broadly available, while in France it is restricted to specified financial services and institutions (see Cnossen, 1999).

---

owner taking out a mortgage – this is not a problem. Indeed, if financial services were subject to VAT, the mortgage-taker would have had to pay VAT on the value added by the bank as well. In other words, exempting financial services from VAT means that final users of financial services see a price that is lower than it otherwise would be.

For business buyers of financial services, the result is just the opposite. Financial services are productive inputs as far as business borrowers are concerned, so the normal logic of VAT would allow businesses to get VAT credits for the VAT contained in the price of financial services. Since financial services are exempted, however, businesses do not get these VAT credits. This means that businesses pay more for financial services than they would without the exemption. The central point here is that banks pass on to the price of financial services all the VAT they paid on purchased inputs. Thus even though banks do not charge VAT on financial services

---

Box 2. Should financial services be subject to VAT?

A broad-based VAT at a standard rate corresponds to a flat-rate tax on all final consumption. The VAT is often advocated on efficiency grounds, as it equally relates to present and future consumption but excludes present savings. The VAT thus leaves the saving choice undistorted.

Financial services yield no direct utility to the consumer and frequently they facilitate saving rather than spending on current consumption. Several authors have argued that these properties make financial services special and justify excluding these services from VAT. Auerbach and Gordon (2001), however, maintain that an efficient VAT should be broad-based and also apply to financial services. The VAT is equivalent to a proportional labour income tax plus a tax on existing assets, as labour and accumulated capital together ultimately give rise to final output. A constant labour income tax (and tax on existing assets) ensures an efficient allocation of labour in all production (including financial-sector production) without distorting individual saving. The same holds for a comprehensive VAT that includes financial services. Thus, such a VAT ensures production efficiency. A standard VAT also implies consumption efficiency (regarding the choice between financial services and other output and regarding saving).

Income taxes differ from VAT in that they are also tax saving and tend to be progressive to facilitate income redistribution. Over time, the weight of the VAT in the EU tax mix has been increasing, suggesting that concerns over proper savings incentives and reduced preferences for redistribution hold sway. Similar forces have lead to the introduction of dual income taxes – with relatively low capital income taxes – in several EU member states. The retrenchment of statutory capital income taxes in the EU, however, is accompanied by increased efforts to combat the evasion of income tax on international interest flows – witness the EU proposal to introduce generalized exchange of information on interest flows by 2009. This suggests that both income taxes and the VAT are in the EU to stay, in part because the coexistence of multiple tax handles reduces the scope for tax evasion. With the VAT in place, the proper design of the VAT on financial services remains a key issue.

directly, the price of financial services does contain some VAT. Under exemption this is never rebated to business users, but under normal VAT treatment it would be. As a consequence, the exemption means that businesses pay more for financial services than they would if financial services were subject to VAT (see Box 3 for a more structured exposition of this point).

Box 3. VAT and the prices of financial services

The price of, say, a loan is the loan interest margin that the bank charges above its cost of funds (in addition, there may be a risk premium to account for credit risk). This loan margin reflects the real resource costs incurred by the bank. To illustrate, let the loan margin reflect the cost of computer inputs, of labour and the VAT itself. As an example, we can assume that a single loan is 'produced' with c computers and i units of labour input, while the VAT rate equals τ. This means that the loan margin free of any VAT, denoted p^f, would be $c + i$ (with the pre-VAT price of computers and the wage set to one). The bank, however, has to buy computers at their VAT-inclusive price of $1 + \tau$. Under the exemption system, the bank does not receive any input credits for this VAT on computers. Hence, the loan margin under exemption will be $c(1 + \tau) + i$. This will be the market price of the loan. For households, this also is the effective loan price under exemption, denoted p^e_h, as households do not pay VAT themselves.

Businesses, however, have to pay VAT on their own output, and this will change the effective price of the loan. To illustrate, we will assume that a business uses the loan as the only input to produce one unit of a non-financial output. This output is subject to VAT so that its tax-inclusive price will be $c(1 + \tau)^2 + i(1 + \tau)$ given that the firm receives no VAT input credit for use of the loan. Thus, the effective rate of VAT on computer inputs now equals $\tau(2 + \tau)$, or more than double the regular VAT rate. The effective, tax-inclusive price of the loan for businesses, denoted p^e_b, equals the VAT-inclusive output price or $c(1 + \tau)^2 + i(1 + \tau)$.

Under standard VAT, the VAT-inclusive price of the loan, denoted p^t, will be $(c + i)(1 + \tau)$ for households and businesses alike. Reform thus lowers the effective loan price to businesses by $c\tau(1 + \tau)$, while households see a price increase of $i\tau$. Equivalently, the effective loan price to businesses declines by a share $\gamma\tau(1 + \tau)$ of the pre-VAT loan price p^f, where $\gamma = c/(c + i)$ is the share of computer inputs in total inputs (more generally, γ is the share of bank inputs with unrecoverable VAT under the exemption system). Reform, instead, increases the VAT-inclusive loan price to households by a share $(1 - \gamma)\tau$ of p^f. In a numerical example, let the pre-VAT loan margin p^f be 3%, while $\tau = 0.15$ and $\gamma = 0.2$. Reform then reduces the effective loan margin for businesses by 0.1035% with $0.1035 = 0.2*0.15*(1 + 0.15)*3$, while the margin for households increases by 0.36% with $0.36 = (1 - 0.2)*0.15*3$.

2.4.2. Administrative burden and competitive distortions of tracking input usage.

The next distortion stems from the fact that not all services provided by financial institutions are exempt. Some services, like safety box rentals and investment advisory services, do not involve capital and so do not engage the problems of valuing capital inputs. The EU therefore insists that they be subject to normal VAT in the EU. Input VAT related to the production of regularly taxed financial services remains normally creditable, while inputs used to produce exempt services are not creditable. This saddles banks with the administrative burden of determining which inputs are used to produce taxable services. In practice, banks are required to track the actual use of inputs in their production process, or they can apply simple input allocation rules based on, say, the receipts of payments for various types of transactions. Rules like these are notoriously difficult to enforce. (OECD, 1998 provides a survey of these rules.)

Moreover, a sort of race-to-the-bottom logic may encourage national tax authorities to allow banks to get VAT credit on most purchased inputs, regardless of what they are used for. If one nation provides very generous credits while another does not, financial service providers based in lenient nations will have a cost advantage when competing for business against providers based in stringent nations. Thus we see that countries have limited incentives to enforce these accounting rules. Below, this paper provides evidence that banks in the EU do in fact receive rather generous input credits, and this in turn suggests that the exemption causes EU member states to engage in financial VAT competition, with the potential for intra-EU competitive distortions.

The current exemption also leads to distortions in financial services trade with non-EU countries. Again the point turns on un-refunded VAT that EU banks pay on their purchased inputs. Since financial services are exempt from VAT, financial services that are 'imported' from non-EU nations are also exempted. For example, consider an EU business that needs a loan. Whether it borrows from an EU bank or a US bank, no VAT will be paid directly, however, the US bank pays no VAT on its purchased inputs while the EU bank does. This puts the EU bank at a competitive disadvantage. This is true whether the imports come from a country without domestic VAT, such as the US, or from countries that zero-rate their exports of financial services. (The OECD has instituted an informal working group in January 2000 to examine the significance of this type of distortion.)

2.5. Attempts to redress the distortions

The realization that the current exemption is distortive naturally leads to searches for ways to mitigate the drawbacks of exemption or, more fundamentally, to repeal it altogether. In efforts to improve the current situation, Denmark and France have imposed compensatory wage taxes on the financial sector as a substitute for regular VAT. Such taxes potentially correct the under-use of labour in the production of financial services under the current exemption. They are no proper substitute for the VAT, however, as they exacerbate the current over-taxation of the business use of financial services (as the additional labour taxes are not creditable to firms using financial services).

Along similar lines, Israel combines the VAT exemption of financial services with a compensatory tax on banking sector labour inputs and profits. A somewhat different approach has been taken by Quebec that combines the so-called zero-rating of financial services (i.e., banks pay no VAT but they still get VAT credits on their traditionally purchased inputs) with a tax on financial institutions' labour and capital inputs.

None of these approaches solves the underlying problem of properly valuing financial services for VAT purposes, and hence these approaches remain unsatisfactory. At present, only a few countries attempt to impose regular VAT on a few specific financial services. Mexico, for instance, levies VAT on bank accounts and on credit card interest, while New Zealand charges VAT on general and fire insurance through its Goods and Services Tax. Viable options to impose proper VAT on the range of financial services, however, are available, as discussed next.

3. THE REFORM OPTIONS

This section discusses the two main avenues for imposing standard VAT on financial services dubbed the 'cash-flow method' and 'zero-rating business-use of financial services'. These two alternative arrangements are economically largely equivalent, but they differ substantially in their implementation.

3.1. The cash-flow method

Regular VAT assessment, as discussed, requires information about the value of the taxed goods or services. The basic difficulty with a financial services VAT is that the exact taxable margin of, say, a loan is not known, as data on the bank's cost of funds and the risk premium are not available on a transaction-by-transaction basis. Lenders, however, will make correct risk assessments 'on average', and thus the *ex post* default rate on a loan portfolio can serve as an estimate of the *ex ante* risk premium.

This observation underlies the cash-flow method of assessing VAT on financial services. The cash-flow method requires financial institutions (and businesses) to treat any cash receipt (of either interest or principle) from, say, a loan as a 'sale' subject to VAT, while any cash payment (again of interest or principal) is treated as an input 'purchase' (with creditable VAT). Households remain entirely outside the scheme, while banks are allowed full VAT input credits. The scheme allows a bank facing a loan default to reduce its VAT payment, as the diminished cash flow from the loan is seen as reduced 'sales'.

The cash-flow method implies that financial flows between banks and their business customers generate no net VAT, as the taxes to be paid on the cash flows of banks and their customers are exactly opposite. Put differently, VAT paid by banks on financial services to businesses is exactly matched by VAT input credits to these businesses. The cash-flow system thus eliminates the current over taxation of business use of financial services, as businesses pay regular output VAT while banks obtain full input credits. The cash-flow method also ensures that the value of household use of financial services, measured by the positive cash flow of financial institutions vis-à-vis households, is properly subject to VAT. The basic cash-flow method is straightforward and produces a neutral VAT on financial services (see Poddar and English, 1997).

The cash-flow approach, however, is not without problems. An undesirable feature is that a firm taking out a loan, generating positive cash flow, immediately has to pay VAT on this 'sale'. This could force the firm to borrow additional money simply to cover this upfront VAT liability. At the time of loan repayment, the firm registers a cash out-flow, or a 'purchase', yielding a VAT rebate to pay off any loan taken out to finance the upfront VAT payment.

3.1.1. The TCA methodology. To avoid cumbersome VAT assessments on capital transfers like these, borrowers can in principle be allowed to defer VAT on loan disbursements. A modified cash-flow method, allowing for such deferrals, has been studied in detail by the European Commission (see European Commission, 2000c). In this scheme, so-called Tax Calculation Accounts (TCAs) are created to register deferred tax on initial credit disbursements. At the time of principal repayment, the deferred tax is expunged from the TCA. The TCA methodology solves the problem of large VAT payments associated with capital transfers, but at the cost of introducing a dynamic accounting framework for each and every financial transaction. In the years 1996–98, the European Commission conducted case studies of the cash-flow method with TCAs involving ten EU financial institutions (six banks, three insurance institutions and one stock broker) to see whether it could work in practice. The experience gained from this suggests that such a system would indeed be cumbersome to implement (see the discussion of administrative issues in Section 4).

3.2. Zero-rating business-use of financial services

The cash-flow system of financial VAT, with or without TCAs, delivers VAT assessments for each and every transaction in symmetry with standard VAT. This level of detail, however, is not necessary to levy a neutral VAT on financial services. Neutrality with respect to business use of financial services can also be achieved by zero-rating these services. This arrangement enables banks to deliver financial services to businesses free of any VAT (as banks would obtain rebates for all their input VAT). Neutrality would then be guaranteed, if businesses subsequently keep financial services out of the calculation of their own output VAT.

Under zero-rating, financial services to households should be subject to the normal VAT. One way to do this is to apply the cash-flow method, as outlined above, to each and every financial transaction involving households. This would yield an estimate of the value added for each and every financial transaction. In the case of households, however, this information is not needed, as households do not pay VAT themselves and thus cannot claim VAT input credits for their use of financial services. This suggests that a sufficient and much simpler way to tax household-used services is to apply cash-flow taxation to banks' aggregate transactions with households.

Zero-rating business use of services implies that banks need to charge higher tax-inclusive prices to households than to businesses. This requires that financial institutions are able to check whether or not a customer is a VAT-paying business. Such a requirement, while substantial, is not entirely new to VAT administration, as exporters (including banks) currently have to verify the international status of their business customers before supplying them with zero-rated goods or services. Zero-rating financial services to domestic businesses, however, expands the need to check the VAT status of bank customers to the entire domestic economy. The feasibility of this approach is discussed in Section 4.

3.3. Reform needs to be comprehensive

Reform means replacing the current exemption of the financial services listed in Box 1 with a new regime of financial VAT applied to these services. VAT on financial services under this regime will only be payable by financial institutions. Hence, a first concern is to define financial institutions broadly enough to capture all firms that are significant providers of financial services. Second, the financial VAT regime has to be sufficiently comprehensive to prevent VAT-motivated arbitrage across financial products or across financial service providers.

Arbitrage across different financial products would be possible if the VAT treatment of largely equivalent financial instruments were different. A portfolio of shares can be equivalent to a combination of bonds and share derivatives. The VAT treatment of activities of financial intermediaries regarding these various financial instruments, hence, has to be equivalent as well. Similarly, the VAT should be neutral to banks' portfolio choices, for instance, regarding the securitization of mortgages. This requires that the financial service of administering securitized mortgages is also subject to VAT. All financial institution income should equally enter into VAT calculations so that simple reclassifications of interest income as capital gains or rental income do not affect VAT liabilities.

All financial institutions, including banks, insurers and pension funds, should be subject to financial VAT. Credit card companies and other financial service providers, that are not traditionally defined as banks, need to be included as well.[1] A difficult problem is to eliminate arbitrage through financial institutions located abroad. As already discussed, the present exemption puts EU banks at a competitive disadvantage, as financial imports from third countries are generally free of all VAT (output VAT and input VAT). Reform eliminates the import-bias for domestically located businesses, as it eliminates the over-taxation of domestically provided financial services to

---

[1] European Commission (2000c) works out in detail how various financial instruments and institutions can be taxed under the modified cash-flow system with TCAs. Zero-rating business use of financial services would imply simplification in some instances compared to this standard.

domestic businesses. Reform, however, potentially exacerbates the import-bias for domestic households, as it serves to increase the taxation of domestically provided financial services to them.

To counter this, one can think of schemes that require non-EU banks to pay VAT to an EU treasury commensurate with their business with EU private residents. Permission to deal with these residents, or perhaps access to EU legal systems could be made contingent on the contribution of VAT. All the same, some financial services imported by households will always continue to escape VAT. The best way to reduce the scope of this problem is the adoption of financial-sector VAT by a relatively large set of countries, perhaps going beyond the EU. In any case, reform needs to be comprehensive and to provide clarity on a number of important issues. Reform at EU-level in practice thus has go beyond the enunciation of main principles.

4. EVALUATION

This section provides an evaluation of the economic consequences of VAT reform in the EU. First, it looks at prospective changes in financial services demand, VAT revenues and overall welfare within a public finance approach. Second, it considers the implications of reform for the distribution of income using data for the Netherlands. Finally, the section evaluates some administrative issues regarding the reform options discussed in Section 3.

4.1. Financial services demand and VAT revenue

Financial VAT reform increases the prices of financial services to households, while it lowers effective prices for businesses. These price changes alter the sectoral demand for financial services, VAT revenues and ultimately overall welfare. This section presents some illustrative calculations of how revenues and overall welfare could be affected in the EU. Calculations of this kind require information on the demand for financial services by various using sectors, and on the current and prospective VAT burdens on financial services. Therefore, this section begins with evidence on the sectoral demand for the chief financial services of bank depositing and bank lending in the EU. Then we provide some information on the VAT burden of financial services implicit in the current exemption, followed by some evidence on how taxation affects the volume and location of financial intermediation. Finally, this section turns to calculations of the VAT revenue and welfare effects of reform.

4.1.1. Demand for financial services. Ambiguities regarding the value generated by a single financial transaction also imply that it is difficult to measure the sectoral demand for financial services. This has frustrated efforts by statisticians to determine GDP, as only financial services to end users (households and the government) should be counted towards GDP. To remedy this problem, the EU is currently experimenting

Table 3. Demand by domestic residents for FISIM from domestic banks, 1998

	FISIM in billion euro	FISIM/bank production as %	Loan share in FISIM as %
Austria	4.8	42.2	39.5
Belgium	5.2	42.0	41.0
Denmark	3.1	52.4*	67.2
Finland	2.3	76.3	52.4
France	30.0	42.5	48.8
Germany	63.3	69.4	73.8
Greece	5.0		22.6
Italy	25.9	66.9	52.9
Netherlands	9.2		62.6
Portugal	3.9		61.8
Spain	16.3		56.1
Sweden	5.6	81.8	48.5
UK	31.7		63.0

Note: * 1997. See Web Appendix Part III for data sources and details on calculations. No data available for Ireland and Luxembourg.

with ways to assign financial-sector output to various sectors after all (see European Commission, 1998). In these exercises, financial-sector output – from deposit and lending activities – is called Financial Intermediation Services Indirectly Measured (FISIM). Essentially, FISIM is the banking sector's net interest income derived from its deposit and loan activities. The main problem is to split the bank's overall interest margin – or the difference between its lending and deposit interest rates – into separate loan and deposit margins vis-à-vis some central reference rate. At this experimental phase, six possible definitions of the reference rate are being considered.[2] The choice of reference rate clearly affects the division of overall FISIM between deposit and lending activities – with a lower reference rate leading to a larger share of total FISIM from lending activities.

Table 3 provides FISIM estimates for EU member states in 1998. FISIM just represents banking-sector output from deposit and loan activities, and thus it is interesting to see how important FISIM is in total bank output. Total bank production includes FISIM, the production of exempt services other than FISIM, and of services normally subject to VAT. FISIM on average represents 59.2% of total bank output for eight EU member states. The last column of the table indicates that the loan share in national FISIM varies considerably across member states.[3]

Next, Table 4 presents information on the sectoral composition of the demand for total FISIM (from loans as well as deposits) for several main business, household and government sectors. Specifically, the table aggregates all FISIM users into five distinct

---

[2] After review of these experimental data, the Commission will adopt a final method for the sectoral allocation of FISIM by 31 December 2002, if the results obtained during the trial period are deemed positive.

[3] The relatively high loan share in FISIM in Denmark and Germany could reflect that in these countries banks have relatively more market power in their lending markets than in their deposit markets.

Table 4. Composition of domestic demand for FISIM from domestic banks, 1998

	Businesses as %	Other financial firms as %	Households as %	Government as %	Non-profits as %	Households, government, non-profit as %
Austria	50.8	3.4	36.0	9.7	–	45.7
Belgium	37.4	2.1	54.7	5.6	0.1	60.5
Denmark	34.2	0.9	63.1	1.4	0.5	64.9
Finland	27.8	0.4	68.9	1.7	1.3	31.8
France	53.9	3.6	33.3	8.0	1.2	42.5
Germany	48.4	−13.9	55.7	7.8	1.9	65.4
Greece	48.2	1.6	39.2	5.4	5.7	50.3
Italy	50.8	0.6	44.7	3.9		48.6
Netherlands	31.3	−4.0	69.9	3.0		72.9
Portugal	23.2	17.6	43.3	15.5	0.4	59.2
Spain	42.2	4.0	49.0	3.7	1.0	53.7
Sweden	45.4	1.9	47.9	2.8	1.9	52.7
UK	23.9	0.5	74.5	−0.4	1.5	75.6

Note: See Web Appendix Part III for data sources and details on calculations. No data available for Ireland and Luxembourg.

categories: (1) *businesses* defined as non-financial corporations and households as owners of unincorporated businesses, (2) *other financial firms* (other than the banks for which FISIM is calculated) such as financial auxiliary firms, insurance companies and mutual funds, (3) *households* in their roles of consumers and of dwellers (mortgage holders), (4) *government* defined as the overall government sector, and (5) *non-profits* being non-profit institutions serving households. In the table, we see that households are the largest purchasers of FISIM in most countries, typically followed by the business and government sectors.[4]

For VAT purposes, the main distinction is whether a sector has to account for VAT. Hence, we need to know which of the five sectors in Table 4 are VAT paying. First, businesses are certainly VAT registered. Second, other financial firms are also taken to be VAT paying, as most activities of these firms, such as insurance, are likely to be included in a reformed financial VAT (even if they are currently exempt). Finally, households, the government sector, and non-profits are taken to be non-VAT paying. In Table 4, the last column adds up the FISIM demand shares for these three non-VAT paying sectors. We see that non-VAT payers purchase a relatively large share of FISIM in Finland, the Netherlands and the UK.[5]

[4] Note that FISIM associated with Other Financial Firms oddly is estimated to be negative in the Netherlands and Germany. To understand how this can arise, note that in the Netherlands there are various large financial holding companies that own both banks and insurance companies. These holding companies can shift profits from their banks to their insurance companies by letting the banks give cheap loans to the insurance companies. Such intra-holding company profit shifting can possibly explain negative FISIM associated with Other Financial Firms, and it presents an argument for also including insurance in a revised financial VAT.

[5] Differences in the share of non-VAT payers in the demand for FISIM may reflect international differences in the degrees of competition in banking markets serving households and businesses. Relatively little competition in the retail market serving households, for instance, would give rise to large interest margins in this market translating into a relatively high share of non-VAT payers in total FISIM demand.

4.1.2. Magnitude of currently unrecoverable VAT on banking inputs. As seen in Box 3, reform increases the effective price of financial services to households less (and reduces the price of financial services to businesses more), the higher is the share of bank inputs with currently unrecoverable VAT, denoted γ. One way to estimate γ is to take the ratio of banking-sector intermediate and capital inputs to total banking-sector production (on the assumption that exempt and taxable financial services require all inputs in equal proportion).[6] This yields an average estimated share of inputs with unrecoverable VAT of 41.7% for eight EU member states (for individual country calculations see Web Appendix Part I on http://www.economic-policy.org). This figure suggests that VAT reform would provide banks with ample opportunities to claim additional VAT input credits.

Far lower estimates of the share of bank inputs with currently unrecoverable VAT are obtained from data on a group of European financial institutions gathered in EC case studies. For a set of six banks and three insurance firms in the EU, estimates of γ range from 8.0% to 35.9% with an average of 16.5%.[7] The estimate of the share for the Dutch banking sector is 18.8% as based on the EC case study, against 59.1% as estimated from actual input use. One reason for this discrepancy may be that some bank inputs are VAT exempt or zero-rated so that no input credits will be available anyway, but the main reason must be that tax administrations currently provide banks with almost full VAT input credits – against the letter of the exemption system. It is impossible to disentangle to what extent the discrepancy is due to tax evasion or simply to lenient regulation and enforcement.

The generous provision of VAT input credits to the banking system implies that the current exemption system almost operates like a system where all banking services, supplied to businesses and households, are zero-rated. Making financial services to businesses officially zero-rated at EU level therefore only 'legalizes' actual national practice, while doing away with some of the VAT compliance burdens on banks. The current practice of (almost) zero-rating all financial services also implies that reform will lead to substantially higher indirect taxes on household use of financial services. The implications of reform for VAT revenues and for the distribution of income thus derive primarily from a higher VAT on household use of financial services.

4.1.3. The demand for financial services and taxation. Financial services are varied and supplied to varied customers, and hence the impact of tax reform on financial pricing and demand is likely to be diverse as well. In competitive segments of financial markets, the pass-through of taxation into pricing is likely to be complete,

---

[6] Countries in general do not appear to have direct information on this. Note, however, that the estimate of Genser and Winker (1997) of a VAT revenue increase from financial VAT reform in Germany of around DM 10 billion in 1994 is based on a direct estimate of the unrecoverable VAT on bank inputs.

[7] This average reflects six banks in the Netherlands, Ireland, Germany, Italy, the UK and France and three insurance companies in France, the UK and Germany.

at least in the long run. Financial institutions that have some market power may opt for a less-than-complete pass-through of higher financial-sector taxes, instead reducing profits.

There is some sketchy evidence of how financial taxation can be expected to affect the volume and location of financial services demand. As discussed by Feige (2000), elasticity estimates of how transaction costs reduce trading volumes on stock exchanges range from 0.26 in US equity markets (Epps, 1976), to 0.70 on the London security exchange (Jackson and O'Donnell, 1985), and 1.0 for the Stockholm stock exchange (Lindgren and Westlund, 1990). Consistent with this, Umlauf (1993) presents evidence that the increase of the Swedish security transaction tax to 2% in 1986 led to the migration of a large proportion of trading activity to London. More recent evidence by Coelho *et al.* (2001) indicates that bank debit taxes introduced in six Latin American countries in recent years have led to considerable declines in banking transactions. Huizinga and Nicodème (2001) in turn find that international deposit flows among BIS member countries are in part motivated by domestic interest income taxes and by the reporting of interest payments by banks to the tax authorities.[8]

Traditional banking transactions, as represented by FISIM, still constitute the bulk of value added in the banking sector. The evidence on how financial taxes affect bank deposit activity thus is more pertinent than the evidence on how transaction taxes affect stock market turnover. All the same, the available evidence reflects mostly small open economies, and hence may tend to overstate the impact of financial VAT reform in a major economic area such as the EU. Much certainly also depends on the effective exclusion of tax-favoured substitutes available to households. In the assessment of financial VAT reform below, we will take several values for the underlying elasticity of demand for financial services given that precise estimates are unavailable.

4.1.4. Impact of reform on revenues and welfare. VAT reform would substantially increase the indirect taxation of household use of financial services, while slightly reducing the taxation of business use of financial services. With the aid of a simple partial equilibrium model, we now calculate the possible implications for overall VAT revenues and economic welfare (see Web Appendix Part II for details). Following the logic from Box 3, we assume that banks use VAT paid inputs and a basic factor of production in a fixed proportion to produce financial services. Financial services prices simply reflect the various inputs and the VAT.

The impact of VAT reform on business use of financial services is illustrated by Figure 1. Reform causes a price drop from p_b^e to p^t, prompting an increase in demand from D_b^e to D_b^t. In textbook fashion, business-sector surplus increases by the sum of areas 1 and 2, while VAT tax revenues increase by area 4 but decline by area 1. Similarly, Figure 2 illustrates the impact of VAT reform on the household use of

---

[8] The adoption of domestic bank interest reporting is estimated to increase external bank deposits by 28%.

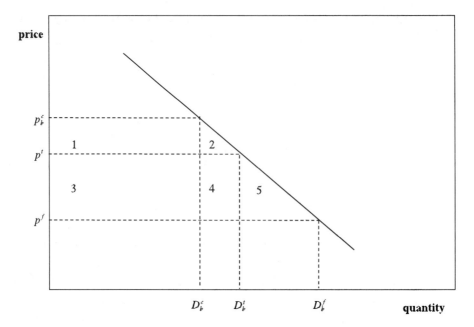

Figure 1. Business demand for financial services

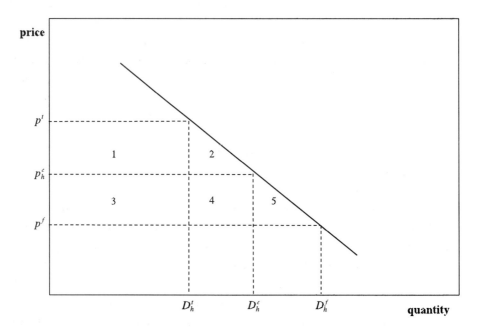

Figure 2. Household demand for banking services

financial services. Reform increases the VAT inclusive price facing households from p_h^e to p^t so that household use of financial service drops from D_h^e to D_h^t. Household surplus falls by the sum of areas 1 and 2, while VAT revenues increase by area 1 and decline by area 4.

Table 5. Revenue and welfare effects of VAT reform in the EU in billions of euros for 1998

Elasticity	Private sector surplus	VAT revenues	National welfare, $\rho = 1$	National welfare, $\rho = 1.5$	National welfare, $\rho = 2$
0	−15.0	15.0	0	7.5	15.0
1	−13.6	12.2	−1.3	4.8	10.9
2	−12.2	9.5	−2.7	2.1	6.8

Notes: Figures are for entire EU minus Ireland and Luxembourg. ρ is the marginal cost of public funds. For further details on the calculations, see Web Appendix Part II. For a description of data sources, see Web Appendix Part III.

To proceed, we can first make the simplifying assumption that the demand for financial services is totally inelastic (unlike in the pictures). In this instance, VAT reform potentially increases VAT revenues at the cost of an equal reduction in private-sector surpluses. For the entire EU (minus Luxembourg and Ireland), we estimate that total VAT revenues increase by €15.0 billion, if we assume the share of bank inputs with currently unrecoverable VAT is 16.5%, as indicated by the EC case studies. This reflects a reduction of taxes on businesses of €2.9 billion, and higher taxes on households of €17.9 billion.

Next, we realistically assume that the demand for financial services is elastic. This introduces the possibility that VAT reform affects the dead weight loss from VAT, and hence has a significant impact on welfare. To estimate the impact on welfare, we take national welfare to be the sum of private-sector surpluses and total VAT revenues. The weight on VAT revenues in this sum can be equal to or more than one, reflecting that raising tax revenues with alternative tax instruments may involve dead weight losses as well. Table 5 gives estimates of the aggregate impact of reform on welfare in the EU (minus Luxembourg and Ireland) for several values of a common demand elasticity η. The other key parameter is the relative value of tax revenues in national welfare, denoted as ρ in the table. This allows us to suppose that a euro of tax revenue raised is worth more to society than a euro of output loss caused by the tax-induced distortions. Specially, the elasticity η takes on the values 0, 1, and 2, while ρ ranges from 1 to 1.5 and 2. A realistic value of η would be between 0 and 1, given that the demand for banking services is probably less elastic than that for stock market transactions (with estimated elasticities in the 0–1 range). Also, the VAT reform considered here would cover the entire EU thereby curtailing the potential for conducting activities abroad to escape domestic financial VAT.

Increasing the elasticity η from zero to one causes the aggregate VAT revenue gain to decline to €12.2 billion. The estimated welfare gain from reform is positive, in the order of €4.8 billion a year, if the relative value of tax revenues ρ is taken to be 1.5. Sensitivity analysis reveals that an unrealistically high elasticity of 2.77 is necessary to reduce the welfare gains to zero for a ρ of 1.5 (while the elasticity has to rise to 3.67 to erase all welfare gains, if instead ρ is set to 2). At an even higher elasticity of 5.50 VAT reform would become revenue neutral.

These numbers, clearly, are only indicative. A more thorough analysis would also take into account that reform eliminates current production inefficiencies in the banking sector, and potentially alters incentives to import financial services. Further, comprehensive VAT reform is likely to also apply to brokerage services, exchange transactions, and insurance with probable additional revenue and welfare gains. The overall conclusion, however, remains that VAT reform is likely to increase VAT revenues and overall economic welfare.

4.2. Redistributive implications of VAT reform

VAT reform makes financial services more expensive for households, translating into lower deposit rates and higher lending rates. Reform affects all major bank interest rates, including those paid on savings accounts and payable on mortgages. Households in different income classes are likely to be affected unevenly by these various interest rate adjustments, and hence it is not *a priori* clear what will be the impact of VAT reform on the distribution of income.

This section provides some indication of the likely distributional effects of reform on the basis of household data for the Netherlands in 1999. The data are from the Social Economic Panel, which surveys the incomes and the wealth composition of about 5000 households. For each household, we have information on four types of bank exposure: the value of current accounts, of savings accounts and similar instruments, of mortgages, and of personal loans and revolving credit.

On the basis of disposable income, households are divided into quintiles, while we also distinguish the top 5% of the income distribution. Table 6 reports the percentages of households in different income classes reporting particular kinds of bank exposure. Higher-income households are seen to be more frequent users of all bank financial instruments. Higher-income households are especially more likely to hold savings accounts and to have mortgages. The table also provides information on the various bank instruments as percentages of net worth. As net worth increases, all bank financial instruments – apart from mortgages – appear to become less important. The weight of mortgages is so great, however, that the sum of all bank financial instruments as a percentage of net worth is relatively even across income classes.

Let us assume that the pre-VAT interest margins on current accounts, savings balances, mortgages and personal loans, margins equal 1.5, 1.5, 2.5 and 3%, respectively. As discussed in Box 3, VAT reform increases all these margins by a proportion of $(1 - \gamma)\tau$ (with γ being the share of bank inputs with unrecoverable VAT, and τ the VAT tax rate). Taking γ to be 18.8% for the Netherlands and with $\tau = 0.175$, we see that reform increases all bank interest margins by 14.2% of the pre-VAT margins. The mortgage interest margin, for instance, would rise from 2.5 to 2.86%. Table 7 presents the income reductions on account of the various interest rates changes – relative to disposable income. To complete the picture, we have to take into account

Table 6. The use of banking services across income classes in the Netherlands, 1999

	Income class						
	0–20%	20–40%	40–60%	60–80%	80–100%	Top 5%	All
Average disposable income*	8	15	20	27	40	53	22
Average wealth*	20	38	72	98	163	220	77
Percent of households with							
Checking accounts	95	96	99	99	99	100	98
Savings accounts**	58	69	80	88	90	89	77
Mortgages	11	20	48	71	78	75	45
Personal loans/revolving							
credit	11	15	19	20	19	21	17
Category as percentage of							
net wealth							
Current accounts	5	4	3	2	3	2	3
Savings accounts*	21	16	14	11	12	14	13
Mortgages	33	30	40	51	42	36	42
Personal loans/revolving	2	2	2	2	1	1	1
Sum	60	51	59	66	57	53	59

Notes: * thousands of euros, ** including savings deposits and certificates. See Web Appendix Part III for data sources and details on calculations.

Table 7. Simulated effect of VAT reform on incomes in the Netherlands, 1999

	Income class						
	0–20%	20–40%	40–60%	60–80%	80–100%	Top 5%	All
Reduction in income from*							
Current accounts	2	2	2	2	2	2	2
Savings accounts**	11	9	10	8	10	12	10
Mortgages	29	27	50	65	61	53	53
Personal loans/							
revolving credit	2	2	2	2	2	2	2
Sum	44	40	65	77	75	69	66
Sum, net of tax	28	20	33	31	30	28	

Notes: * gross, hundredths of percent of disposable income, ** including savings deposits and certificates, *** net-of-tax, hundredths of percent of disposable income. Note that the marginal tax rates for the income quintiles are 37.05, 50, 50, 60, and 60%. See Web Appendix Part III for data sources and details on calculations.

the progressivity of the tax system.[9] From the bottom of the table, we see that all income groups, apart from perhaps the second quintile, are affected proportionately by VAT reform. Fears that reform would disproportionately affect the poor thus appear to be unjustified.

---

[9] We continue to ignore that interest income up to €454 per individual is exempt from income tax (€908 for a married couple), while non-mortgage interest payments are tax deductible only up to €2361 per individual (€4721 for a married couple). This means that a lower deposit interest rate hurts low-income households (with relatively little interest income) relatively much, while a higher personal loan interest rate hurts high-income households (who may have personal loan interest payments exceeding the deductible amount) relatively much. Hence, these omissions may not affect the conclusion that low and high-income households are about proportionately affected by VAT reform.

4.3. Administrative issues

The current exemption and the two main reform options of the cash-flow method and zero-rating business use differ in the compliance burdens they create for banks and businesses, and also in the tax evasion risks they introduce. This section reviews some of the main compliance and enforcement difficulties for each of the three methods. On the basis of this review, the option of zero-rating business use of financial services appears to offer the best prospects for reform.

4.3.1. Compliance with exemption. Intra-EU financial services currently are exempt or taxable on the basis of national regulations implementing the EU Sixth VAT Directive, while all financial services supplied to non-EU customers are zero-rated. Banks have to classify their output accordingly with the potential of misrepresentation if, for instance, a EU customer claims to be a non-EU customer. Banks only receive VAT rebates for intermediate and capital inputs used in the production of taxable and zero-rated financial services. Again, banks have to follow national regulation to determine exactly which input VAT is creditable. This process is cumbersome and yields the result that input VAT of banks is largely rebated in several EU member states. The current VAT yield from the banking system thus is low, probably with the explicit or implicit approval of tax administrations.

4.3.2. Compliance with the cash-flow method. The cash-flow method eliminates the need to distinguish between exempt and taxable financial services. Supplies to non-EU residents would presumably remain zero-rated with some potential for misrepresentation. Intra-EU transactions, in turn, create the least difficulties if they are made taxable in the country of bank location.[10] The cash-flow system also does away with the need to distinguish between recoverable and unrecoverable input VAT.

These gains come at the cost of requiring banks and businesses to account for the VAT on each financial transaction. Specifically, banks would be required to present their business customers with VAT invoices for each financial instrument each VAT reporting period so they can reclaim input VAT. To gain insight into the practicality of operating a cash-flow VAT with TCA accounts, the European Commission sponsored case studies encompassing six banks (along with four non-bank financial institutions) during the years 1996–98. This study did not yield precise estimates of anticipated compliance costs of a cash-flow system, but all the same it provided the Commission with valuable feedback from participating institutions and from consulted national tax administrators. Participating institutions indicated that the

---

[10] Alternatively, intra-EU financial services can be made zero-rated if supplied to businesses, and be taxable in the country of customer location if supplied to households. This treatment would be analogous to the current treatment of intra-EU trade in non-financial goods and services, but it creates the need for banks to distinguish between domestic and other-EU household customers.

accounting and information systems necessary to deal with VAT on individual transactions would entail significant costs. These costs derive from the high volume of transactions to be tracked by financial institutions, their business customers and ultimately tax administrators. There would also be considerable costs in learning about such a system. Banks, for instance, may find themselves explaining to their business customers that the taxable margin of a loan does not represent an expendable profit margin, but rather the real resource costs of originating and servicing the loan.

4.3.3. Compliance with zero-rating of business use.

Under this option, services supplied to intra-EU households are taxable, while services to all businesses and to non-EU households are zero-rated. Banks would be allowed to calculate VAT applicable to intra-EU households on an aggregate basis with low compliance costs. In this scheme, businesses do not have to deal with financial VAT at all. The zero-rating option also obviates the need for banks to track the use of intermediate inputs in the production of varying financial services.

Businesses would receive financial services free of VAT under zero-rating, providing households with an incentive to masquerade as businesses. Thus, banks need to be able to verify the business status of their customers.[11] This requires banks to be able to check in real time whether businesses present valid VAT numbers, which should pose no technical difficulties at this stage. Also, banks need to corroborate whether customers claiming to represent bona fide businesses are telling the truth. Valid businesses should be willing to aid banks in this verification process, as this is the only way for them to obtain VAT-free financial services. Effective enforcement requires that banks that wrongly supply VAT-free services to households are penalized.

Recently, bank–customer relationships have changed greatly on account of policy initiatives to combat tax evasion, money laundering, and the financing of terrorism. Banks increasingly are subject to 'know your customer rules' that require them to know the identity of their customers and the nature of their activities. As part of this, banks in OECD countries now typically require adequate proof of customer identity before opening a bank account.[12] EU countries have also stated their intention to rely on the exchange of information to improve the taxation of cross-border investment income. This initiative also requires adequate identification of bank customers. These

---

[11] Keen and Smith (1996) have advocated a system of 'Viable Integrated VAT' or VIVAT as an alternative to the present system of VAT on intra-EU transactions. VIVAT consists of an EU-wide common VAT rate for transactions among businesses, while countries are free to levy a VAT applied to final customers at different rates. For this scheme to work, suppliers must be able to distinguish between business and non-business customers. Hence, VIVAT involves similar needs of customer identification as zero-rating business use of financial services.

[12] OECD (2000) indicates that most countries require banks to verify the name and address of a client by some type of official documentation. Most countries that use tax identification numbers (TINs) require the domestic TIN to be provided to open a bank account, but only ten OECD countries (including EU member states Denmark, Finland, Portugal, Spain and Sweden) require the customer to provide documentary evidence of the TIN.

developments imply that the requirement that banks know the VAT status of customers can hardly be considered a great additional burden. At the same time, planned international cooperation to improve the taxation of international interest income can easily be combined with efforts to verify the VAT status of international banking customers.

Zero-rating currently applies to intra-EU exports of non-financial goods and services. In practice, this arrangement appears to lead to extensive fraud where zero-rated goods are never exported or, if exported, subsequently are not declared as imports.[13] This has given zero-rating a bad name, but it does not follow that similar problems will occur with zero-rating business use of financial services. A main difference is that businesses have no incentive to misrepresent their use of zero-rating financial services, as these services do not register in their VAT calculations at all. Thus, the delivery of financial services to businesses free of VAT is not as problematic as it is in the case of standard, tradable goods.

As indicated, the zero-rating option requires banks to offer financial services at different prices to businesses and households. This should pose no great problems, as banks already treat their business and household customers very separately. Business and personal loans, for instance, tend to be priced differently by most banks. Some fear that lower-priced services to business may prompt households to set up businesses simply to get cheaper financial services. This problem is not specific to financial services, as households similarly may attempt to set up a business to claim VAT input credits for, say, a car purchase. VAT auditors currently deal with this problem by re-imposing VAT on inputs, if a firm fails to produce any sales subject to VAT. This kind of enforcement should also be effective in the financial services area.

5. CONCLUSION

Financial services make up an important share of Europe's economy yet they are exempted from VAT. This exemption naturally creates a host of economic distortions. VAT exemption of financial services is a major obstacle on the road to a more harmonized VAT base. It raises the price of financial services faced by EU businesses while lowering the price faced by households. It puts EU banks at a competitive disadvantage vis-à-vis banks based in nations that have no VAT. And, since the operation of the exemption is complex, it fosters indirect fiscal competition among EU tax authorities in the financial sector.

Practicality has been the only justification of the exemption. This paper argues that the changed nature of bank–client relationships and advances in information

---

[13] See European Commission (2000a, 2000b) for an assessment of these difficulties and proposed policy responses, including more effective exchange of information.

technology have opened the door to a practical way of redressing the inefficiencies that arise from the financial services exemption. The solution proposed here is to 'zero-rate' financial services supplied to businesses while applying regular VAT to services supplied to households. Financial services would, as a result, be priced differently for households and businesses, so financial institutions would have to verify the VAT status of their customers. While this may be burdensome, the OECD-wide fight against tax evasion and the international struggle against terrorism have forced financial institutions to know much more about their clients. Verifying a client's VAT status should thus be fairly simple.

An alternative reform, the so-called cash-flow method, is also evaluated. The cash-flow method calculates VAT separately for each financial transaction parallel to standard VAT practice. The option of zero-rating business use of financial services instead uses data on aggregated transactions at the level of the bank to assess financial VAT. The cash-flow method is economically equivalent to zero-rating, so the choice between these two options in large part has to be based on their relative ease of compliance and enforcement. As argued above (Section 4) the cash-flow approach is administratively much more difficult because it requires transaction-by-transaction accounting for VAT by banks and businesses.

This paper estimates that financial sector VAT reform using either method would *increase* VAT revenues from the main banking activities of deposit taking and lending by around €12 billion in the EU. This estimate reflects the fact that the zero-rating or cash-flow options would significantly increase taxes on financial services purchased by households while slightly reducing the indirect taxation of services purchased by EU businesses. Reform would eliminate the distortions to household and business demand of financial services relative to standard VAT treatment and hence should increase overall economic welfare.

Policy-makers have been hesitant to consider zero-rating business use of financial services, in part as it breaks with standard VAT practice. Also, there may be fears that other sectors will demand the same treatment, even if tax administrations should have no difficulty to 'hold the line'. A further perceived problem with zero-rating is that it potentially leads to net VAT payments to some financial institutions, if their VAT input credits exceed the VAT due on financial services to households. The sight of net VAT payments to certain financial institutions is admittedly not pretty, but our calculations suggest that in the aggregate VAT revenues will increase. Objections of this kind should not stand in the way of reform.

The currently low taxation of financial services to businesses also raises the question whether international competitive pressures, and perhaps the political influence of banks and their business customers, will stand in the way of VAT reform in the EU. Reform will only reduce the VAT on business use of financial services, and thus businesses are not likely to oppose reform. Reform, however, will increase the overall VAT on financial services and thus may negatively affect financial sector profits, at least in the short run. Banks therefore may have an interest in opposing reform. Any pressures

of this kind, and also national incentives to reduce financial sector VAT for competitive reasons, are best overcome by collective action at the EU level. National barriers
to taxing the financial sector thus do not imply an impossibility of reform in the EU.

Reform would require the adoption of a new EU directive that amends the
current exemption of financial services as laid down in the Sixth VAT Directive of
1977. Reform proposals have to be comprehensive and implemented evenly throughout the EU to prevent VAT avoidance. The directive would also have to specify
national options as to the VAT rate to be applied to financial services. Countries
would presumably wish to tax financial services at the standard rate. A narrow
range of financial VAT rates in the EU would be advisable to minimize tax-motivated
cross-border banking by households. The European Commission, however, has so far
not indicated plans to come forward with a proposal for a new financial services VAT.

Discussion

Stijn Claessens
World Bank

The major financial services are exempt from VAT in almost all countries and most
attempts to introduce them have been short-lived. Apart from some special cases,[14]
few countries have adopted VAT for financial services in full force, with technical
reasons of administrating VAT typically stated as the main barrier.

The application of VAT to financial services is nevertheless an important and
interesting topic for a number of reasons. First, exempting (many) financial services
from VAT can lead to distortions in economic transactions. Second, VAT on financial
services can be a significant source of government revenues, also as financial services
become increasingly important in economies' overall value-added. Third, the taxation of financial services through VAT may be desirable because of its distributional
consequences. Fourth, while the practical challenges of applying VAT to financial
services have been large, if overcome, there may be valuable lessons for applying VAT
to other type of services that currently are exempt (such as e-commerce which shares
some features with financial services).

While important and interesting, the 'doability' of taxing financial services can be
questioned. Much political support will be necessary, but it is not clear how urgent a
topic this is within the EU. Building on earlier work, the European Commission has
been exploring the practicality of a VAT for financial services within the EU, and the
current paper relates to this ongoing effort. However, the single market for financial

---

[14] Some transition economies where the IMF has recommended to (and obtained agreement from) that they should apply VAT
in this area.

services has been slower to come about than many observers argued for, in part as the impetus from Brussels in the last decade seems to have been less, suggesting that reforms affecting financial services have had little political support at the European level.

In recent years, the recognition that many barriers in financial services still need to be removed and that effective competition in financial services industries is some way off seems to have increased, and a new financial services action plan has been adopted. The delay and need to catch up with reforms, however, also in light of large global changes in financial services industries, make for a substantial reform agenda in itself. Whether policy-makers and the industry itself are ready to deal with a reform of the taxation of financial services is unclear, but the paper makes a serious attempt to convince the reader that adopting the VAT for financial services is not only a relevant, but also doable topic.

Let me comment first on the analytical framework used first, then discuss the practical options available to implement a VAT and finally discuss the empirical application. I will end with some thoughts on the realism of the approach.

The analytical framework used

This is not an easy analytical, or empirical area, as indicated by the limited work to date. The analytical framework used here is a basic one and the paper presents the standard arguments in favour of extending VAT to financial services. The section raises the problem that one needs to tax the financial intermediation margin, not the interest rate or the risk premium, and to separate investment from consumption. The paper could have usefully expanded further on the list of economic arguments in favour of fully adopting a VAT to financial services. Besides the issue of under-taxation and loss of revenues, there are the issues of tax cascading, the bias toward self-supply and intra-group supply, the foreign supply bias, and distorted competition due to lack of uniformity. Another general issue which may deserve some attention is that changes in the taxation of financial intermediaries can alter the scale on which they operate, the risk-profile of their portfolios, the scale of their transactions' services and their market-power (pricing of loans and deposits, profit per unit-scale).

The framework also raises a few questions. The author uses, for example, the argument that the application of the VAT to financial services is a key issue as both income taxes and VAT are to stay in the EU. This of course is not starting from first principles. Nevertheless, the conclusion that there are no good economic rationales for exempting financial services from VAT, except for the practical problems, is a very reasonable one and seems shared by most others.

The practical options available

The paper discusses the various options available to apply VAT to financial services. I have little to add here, except that there seems to be some variations of the models that can be used beside the three discussed here (exemption, cash-flow method and zero-rating). Poddar (2002), for example, mentions not only full taxation, which covers the cash flow and TCA method, but also several more types of modified exemption and compensatory systems. The paper also discusses the implementation issues with or without VAT and the relative benefits of the various proposals. This list includes issues like: the specification of which financial services to exempt from VAT can get very detailed; how to treat non-bank financial institutions; the fact that banks bundle services, some of which are fees based and some of which are 'financial intermediation' based; the issues of the incidental services; the need for systems in banks to track financial transactions; and the fact that a lack of uniformity across countries leads to legal uncertainty and administrative costs.

The one major comment I want to make on this section relates to the issue of financial products versus institutions. The paper follows most other papers on this issue by looking at the issue of taxation largely from an institutional perspective. But, the rapidly changing nature of the financial sector with financial products overlapping and becoming closer substitutes, different types of financial institutions integrating into single financial conglomerates, and more trading of financial assets through markets will make the traditional, institutional way of taxation much more difficult. For example, what is the definition of a bank if one can obtain bank services in many other ways, e.g., from financial markets or non-bank financial institutions? Looking ahead, whether financial sector taxation is best approached from an institutional perspective or from a financial instrument perspective is a big question in my mind. The implications for the analytical and empirical framework are considerable, as are the policy recommendations.

The empirical application

The paper's empirical assessment uses a basic public finance framework. The paper does a reasonable job of working with the available data, but inevitably many assumptions need to be made to analyse the tax incidence of a VAT on financial services (or any other tax for that matter), and the responses of households and firms. Many of the assumptions made are not unreasonable, and the paper is open on each of the assumptions, but one wonders whether they collectively add to a realistic framework. It is hard to reconstruct the analysis oneself, and the empirical application may not be meant to be more than a very rough, back of the envelope exercise, but I do have a few points.

One, the assumed response of financial intermediaries/institutions and their customers to various forms of explicit and implicit taxation is clearly key. Other analyses with taxes on financial service, mentioned in the paper, suggest very high elasticities. This includes the securities taxes used in Sweden that drove much trading from Stockholm to London. Also the referenced work by Kirilenko and Summers at the IMF on the experiences with financial sector taxation in some Latin American countries suggests high elasticities and finds significant deadweight losses from financial taxation. Although these experiences are not in the form of a VAT, the response of market participants to (increases in) taxation thus seems to be high. The paper still uses a relatively low elasticity, with the argument that household deposits are not as mobile. That is debatable, however. Many alternative financial instruments will become more easily available, even to households.

Second, the competitive environment and the tax-treatment of substitutes for banks' major products will matter for the ability to impose a VAT. In the paper, there is little analysis of the effects of competition between different types of financial intermediaries or other forms of cross-subsectoral competition. On the empirical side, the data used to establish the overall tax revenues and possible welfare costs are very aggregate. Household surveys would be useful to review as to the actual use of different financial services, their respective elasticity with respect to price, and the incidence of a possible VAT. There is some of this in the redistributive section on the Netherlands, but perhaps more use could be made of this tool, also using other countries. In addition, the empirical treatment of non-bank financial services at the household level is quite limited, with scant attention to pension and insurance services and even less to securities markets activities.

Finally, the analysis does not explicitly consider other forms of financial sector taxation. This should be part of any public finance analysis, as each form of taxation has some economic cost. Such an extension would help answer questions like: Is a VAT more attractive than taxation at source (e.g., a withholding tax)? Are 'deemed' taxes at the personal income level more attractive? Given the problems in taxing financial services at the intermediary level, can one argue for a financial wealth tax at the consumer level instead of a VAT on household use of financial services? How do these taxes compare to the current wage-tax applied to financial intermediaries in Denmark and France? Although I realize that a general equilibrium model is too much to ask for, a more fully specified model would be useful to be able to asses the merits of a VAT relative to other taxes and their implementation problems.

Avoidance issues and realism of approach

The paper acknowledges the implementation issues and devotes much attention to it, but I think there are more problems with the idea of a VAT (or any other tax for that matter at the intermediary level) for financial services than indicated here. For businesses, there has always been the possibility of avoiding VAT by having banks book business outside the EU, and the paper acknowledges this, although it does not incorporate this formally in the analysis. The standard exemption for foreign trade remains and there are many zero-VAT tax countries that can serve as places to book financial services.

Individuals may be able to avoid the tax more easily than suggested, particularly as European financial markets become more integrated with the common currency and increasingly easy Internet access to cross-border financial services. While efforts aimed at reducing money-laundering have increased, and technology will aid the tracking of deposits, the full exchange of information that would be necessary to apply VAT (or any other taxes) in a consistent manner will surely take considerable time. And even with full information exchange, the problem of tax-shopping and the different VAT rates within the EU will remain. Also, the increased integration of international financial markets itself raises issues in the harmonization of rules on tax collection, which are not uniform yet and can create some legal uncertainty and administrative costs.

The focus of the paper is on banks and traditional financial services, but there are many other forms of financial intermediation. How does one tax the use of options by households, for example? More generally, as noted, financial services are becoming less institutional and more functional-based, which calls for a different approach. Don't these developments require a different approach to financial sector taxation than an institutional-based one and do they still allow the methods suggested here?

This brings me to the final point – the feasibility and political economy of implementing VAT. The practice of levying VAT on financial services seems to have had little support so far. As the paper notes, few tax authorities with the EU seem to impose the statuary VAT on non-exempt services, but rather allow banks to subtract all VAT paid. This suggests either that competition among countries does not allow VAT to be charged, or, and this could be a complementary explanation, that the political economy does not make tax authorities want to levy taxes on financial institutions/services. The author makes the point that corporations will benefit from the introduction of VAT, but a coalition of households and financial institutions may have been stronger in the past and may continue to be so.

These concerns seem to be supported by the fact that the EC has so far not come out with any proposal for a (new) financial services VAT. This makes one wonder whether there is actually sufficient political support for this approach or whether the administrative and political economy hurdles are simply perceived to be too large. The future will tell, but some assessment would have been useful.

Fiona Scott Morton
Yale University

First, I think the author's main motivation, which is to remove distortions from taxation, is a good reason to look at the financial service sector's exemptions from VAT. The paper makes two important points that somewhat undercut the motivation for reform. One is that, in contrast to the official policy, banks are, in fact, rebated most of the VAT on their inputs through various subsidy programmes and lax tax enforcement. The author suggests (reasonably) that these subsidies might be motivated by a desire to support the national bank or banking sector. This seems like an important distortion in itself. These subsidies will impede exit of inefficient banks and give governments a lever over bank decisions (such as loans to large employers in the country). Thus reform of subsidies seems desirable, regardless of policy towards VAT on financial services.

The second point is that a numerical example shows that the impact of bank exemption on business users of financial services is negligible. Because there are two steps in the chain of production between the extra tax and the final consumer price, the effect is much diluted. (The bank charges a higher price to its business customers who then charge a higher price to their final customers.) I would like more discussion of why the estimates of unrecoverable VAT for banks are so different between author and EU study (16.5% versus 41.7%). These two features of the situation suggest that the distortion from not being able to deduct the VAT is negligible, and this should be made clear earlier in the paper. However, the implicit subsidy to consumer financial services remains.

The paper presents zero-rating as the best option for reform, and this seems clearly to be the case. In fact, operationalizing zero-rating seems like a very mild reform. All that would occur is that (a) we officially recognize that banks get VAT rebate on inputs; (b) we allow businesses to subtract financial services costs from revenue before assessing VAT; and (c) we allow banks to charge higher interest rates unless the customer demonstrates they are a VAT-paying business. In addition, current abilities of information technology are likely to make compliance costs reasonable.

The direction in which tax revenue will move is obvious – up – once the fact that banks are getting VAT rebated already is known. The paper presents this as a question of concern to EU governments, which it may not be. Consumption of financial services by consumers would presumably fall. Notice that one does not want to interpret this reduction in consumption of financial services as creating deadweight loss. The original motivation of the paper was that the current system implicitly subsidizes financial services for consumers. Thus any reduction in consumption would simply represent a better allocation of society's resources.

The question of whether a VAT on financial services to consumers is a good policy idea hinges on the elasticity of demand for those services. What is odd about this case is that we are not interested in the 'true' elasticity of demand, i.e. whether consumers need to borrow money to purchase a house, but rather the elasticity of demand for particular financial products. For example, if mortgage interests were taxed, perhaps consumers would finance their house purchases using 'rent-to-own' transactions that involve no interest payments. To the extent that the effect of a financial transaction can be achieved another way, using other instruments or agents, the elasticity of demand for some narrowly defined financial services may be very high. If so, VAT on financial services will create an industry of financial engineers who strive to stay one step ahead of the EU tax authorities.

It would be interesting to know what the incidence of this tax would be across member states of the EU. Presumably as national tendencies to save in savings accounts or buy houses with mortgages vary, incidence would vary also.

Finally, if consumer elasticity is relatively high, then reform will cause lower consumption of financial services. In addition, wealthy customers may be induced to purchase financial products outside the EU where they can avoid VAT. We would expect this reduction in market size to cause bank exit or consolidation in the medium-run. If this proposed reform shrinks the market for financial services, increases IT costs, and requires a bank to employ financial engineers, then financial intermediaries may resist reform.

Panel discussion

Many panellists stressed a point made by both discussants, namely the importance of the potential for tax avoidance. Kenneth Rogoff found the proposal for a VAT tax reform sensible from a theoretical point of view but had doubts on its feasibility in practice. If implemented in a slightly wrong way, the tax would become a tax on financial transactions. The evidence from developing countries indicates that such taxes imply massive distortions. Charles Goodhart pointed out that unless the VAT would be imposed on all interest flows, one should expect big distortions on financial organization and location because of the ease with which interest payments can be shifted. Harry Huizinga agreed that all institutions would have to be taxed to avoid distortions. Moreover, distortions could arise resulting from self-production. Marcel Thum mentioned that much on the elasticity of consumption of financial services could be learned from past tax reforms. For example, intra-family lending might make the use of final services quite elastic. Pursuing a related theme, Philipp Hartmann wondered whether there would be a stronger case for tax harmonization within the EU than before. Harry Huizinga replied that tax harmonization indeed would be necessary to prevent tax competition. Moreover, non-EU institutions should be forced to pay taxes on loans to businesses within the EU by implementing a financial service import VAT. To bring this about, pressure could be exerted by not providing access to the legal system for non-EU banks that do not comply.

Hans-Werner Sinn questioned the basic premise that VAT should be applied to financial services. He thought that a VAT on financial services would be an implicit tax on transactions of households transferring current resources to the future. He thought that it would not be optimal to tax such transactions. Harry Huizinga replied that in the tax reform transactions would not be taxed (see Box 2 in the paper for a discussion of this issue).

Rachel Griffith pointed out that the figures reported in Table 6 indicate that households have substantial other net worth such as stocks and shares. Hence, both Rachel Griffith and Carol Propper suspected the effect of the reform on the business sector that is passed through to shareholders had been neglected. Moreover, Rachel Griffith thought that the results of the distributional impact of the tax reform for the Netherlands could not be taken as representative for the EU because of big cross-country differences.

Rafael Repullo wondered how the tax would be assessed on different transactions. For example, he asked what would happen if the deposit rate is zero or if interest rates are above the benchmark rate implying a negative value added. Harry Huizinga answered that deposits as such will not be taxed and that within the zero-rating approach only aggregate cash flows are taxed. These will be necessarily positive for the firm to remain in business. Rafael Repullo also pointed out that the risk premium is not constant across borrowers so that small businesses are taxed disproportionately.

WEB APPENDIX

This can be downloaded for free from http://www.economic-policy.org.

REFERENCES

Auerbach, A. and R. Gordon (2001). 'Taxation of financial services under a VAT', mimeo, University of California, Berkeley.

Banking in Europe, various issues, Eurostat, Luxembourg.

Cnossen, S. (1999). 'VAT treatment of financial services', in Lindencrona, Lodin and Wiman (eds), *International Studies in Taxation: Law and Economics*, Kluwer Law International.

Coelho, I., L. Ebrill and V. Summers (2001). 'Bank debit taxes in Latin America: An analysis of recent trends', IMF Working Paper WP/01/67, Washington, DC.

Epps, T.W. (1976). 'The demand for broker's services: The relations between security trading volume and transaction cost', *The Bell Journal of Economics*.

European Commission (1996). 'Council Regulation on the European System of National and Regional Accounts in the Community', No. 2223/96.

European Commission (1998). 'Council Regulation with Respect to the Allocation of Financial Intermediation Services Indirectly Measured Within the European System of National and Regional Accounts', No. 448/98.

European Commission (2000a). 'Report on Administrative Cooperation in the Field of Indirect Taxation (VAT) and on VAT Collection and Control Procedures', COM(2000) 28 final.

European Commission (2000b). 'A Strategy to Improve the Operation of the VAT System within the Context of the Internal Market', COM(2000) 348 final.

European Commission (2000c). 'TCM/TCA System of VAT for Financial Services'.

European Commission (2001a). 'Financial Market Integration in the EU', in *The EU Economy: 2001 Review*.

European Commission (2001b). 'Tax Policy in the European Union – Priorities for the Years Ahead', COM(2001) 260 final.

Feige, E. (2000). 'Taxation for the 21st century: the automated payment transaction (APT) tax', *Economic Policy*, 31, 475–511.

Genser, B. (2001). 'Coordinating VATs between member states', mimeo, University of Konstanz.

Genser, B. and P. Winker (1997). 'Measuring the fiscal revenue loss of VAT exemption in commercial banking', *FinanzArchiv*, 54, 563–85.

Gottfried, P. and W. Wiegard (1991). 'Exemption versus zero rating, a hidden problem of VAT', *Journal of Public Economics*, 46, 307–28.

Huizinga, H. and G. Nicodème (2001). 'Are international deposits tax-driven?', *Economic Paper* 156, European Commission.

Jackson, P.D. and A.T. O'Donnell (1985). 'The effects of stamp duties on equity transactions and prices in the UK Stock Exchange', Discussion Paper No. 25, The Bank of England.

Keen, M. and S. Smith (1996). 'VIVAT, an alternative VAT for the EU', *Economic Policy*, 23, 373–420.

Lindgren, R. and A. Westlund (1990). 'Transactions costs, trading volume, and price volatility on the Stockholm Stock Exchange', Stockholm School of Economics Working Paper.

OECD (1998). *Indirect Tax Treatment of Financial Services and Instruments*, OECD, Paris.

OECD (2000). *Improving Access to Bank Information for Tax Purposes*, OECD, Paris.

Poddar, S. (2002). 'Indirect Taxes II: Consumption Taxes', mimeo, Ernst & Young, Toronto.

Poddar, S.N. and M. English (1997). 'Taxation of financial services under a value-added tax: Applying the cash-flow approach', *National Tax Journal*, 50, 87–111.

Umlauf, S. (1993). 'Transaction taxes and the behavior of the Swedish Stock Market', *Journal of Financial Economics*, 33, 227–240.

Forex markets and the euro

Dollar spreads: mark versus euro

SUMMARY

We compute bid-ask spreads for the dollar/euro exchange rate market and find them to be substantially larger than their deutschemark counterparts before introduction of the euro. We show that larger percentage spreads are not explained by volatility, trade intensity, and other standard explanatory variables in our data sets. But we also show that spreads have not increased in terms of the unit ('pip') used in exchange rate quotations to the fourth decimal point. Since the euro is worth about two marks, and was initially worth more than a dollar, this finding suggests that larger percentage spreads reflect the more pronounced 'granularity' of quoting conventions in euro-dollar rather than dollar-mark trading. We discuss whether mandating quotations to the fifth decimal point might be advisable, and conclude that such a policy might, but need not, increase the foreign exchange market's liquidity.

— *Charles Goodhart, Ryan Love, Richard Payne and Dagfinn Rime*

Economic Policy October 2002 Printed in Great Britain
© CEPR, CES, MSH, 2002.

Analysis of spreads in the dollar/euro and deutschemark/ dollar foreign exchange markets

Charles Goodhart, Ryan Love, Richard Payne and Dagfinn Rime

Financial Markets Group, London School of Economics (LSE); Financial Markets Group, LSE; Financial Markets Group, LSE; Stockholm Institute for Financial Research and Norges Bank

1. INTRODOUCTION

The dollar is used in most global foreign exchange (FX) transactions.[1] When the euro was created, it was suggested that the new European currency might challenge the dollar's position as *the* dominant vehicle currency. In fact, market participants gener-ally choose the transactions medium with the lowest costs and, as the fixed order processing costs of market makers is spread across large volumes, costs fall further by economies of scale. This virtuous cycle implies the existence of multiple equilibria: any one of many currencies may play a hegemonic role in financial markets, and inertia plays an important role in determining the identity of *the* international vehicle currency. The world's financial markets can however shift from one equilibrium to

The paper has benefited hugely from comments by Philipp Hartmann, Richard Portes, Rich Lyons, Ken Rogoff, Paul Seabright, an anonymous referee, the Managing Editors and the participants of the *Economic Policy* Panel Meeting in Madrid on 12–13 April 2002. Goodhart, Love and Payne acknowledge financial assistance from the Economic and Social Research Council. All errors are the joint responsibility of the authors. The comments and opinions expressed here do not represent those of Norges Bank.

Giuseppe Bertola was the Managing Editor for this paper.

[1] In April 2001 the US dollar was on one side of 90.4% of all currency trades (BIS press release, 9 October 2001). This is a slight increase from the corresponding figure for April 1998, which was 87.3%.

another if a large enough shock occurs, and the arrival of the euro could potentially end the dollar's hegemonic status (see Portes and Rey, 1998; for a more extensive discussion of these issues see Hartmann, 1998a).

But how has the euro performed since its birth in its role as a possible international transaction medium? One approach to answering this is to consider the costs that FX market participants face when trading euro. If the costs of trading in the euro markets have fallen compared to those seen for the euro's 'predecessor', the deutschemark, then one can argue that the euro is more liquid and stands a better chance of breaking the hegemony of the dollar.

From this perspective, costs of trading euro in the foreign exchange markets are important.[2] Hau, Killeen and Moore (2002a), from here on referred to as HKM, examine spreads for a number of currencies from January 1998 to August 1999, i.e. twelve months prior to the euro's introduction and eight months post euro introduction. As we do in this paper, they consider the spread, the difference between the price at which one buys and sells euro (EUR) or deutschemarks (DEM) against US dollars (USD). They find that the DEM/USD to USD/EUR spreads increased from 3.76 basis points to 5.26 basis points, an increase of 40%. They also consider spreads against the Japanese yen (JPY) and the British pound (GBP), finding that JPY/DEM-EUR and GBP/DEM-EUR spreads increased over the same period. Their 'market transparency hypothesis' suggests that, after currency unification, imbalances and desired trading positions of market makers became more easily identifiable by other market participants to imply, on the basis of microstructure approach arguments, that larger spreads are quoted by FX dealers to compensate for this increased risk.

Our analysis makes use of a unique dataset that allows us to analyse real time firm, tradable spreads. The data, taken from the Reuters D2000-2 broking system, shows the quoted prices and spreads at which trades actually occur, rather than indicative spreads which have often been used in previous analysis, including Hartmann (1998b, 1999) and HKM. 'Indicative' quotes need not give an accurate indication of actual market spreads, which tend to be smaller. Tradable spreads show more precisely the cost of transactions for the agents participating in the market and the cost of providing liquidity for the specialist dealers. Our data also make it possible to study how other relevant statistics (number of trades, volatility, etc.) have changed since the introduction of the euro, and to give a much more accurate impression of how the cost of trading has changed.

We find that spreads, when defined as a percentage of mid-quote, have increased significantly from the DEM/USD to the USD/EUR eras. This evidence is consistent with HKM. However, we also offer a different and simpler explanation for this increase. In both the DEM/USD and USD/EUR periods, spreads are set by market makers as a number of pips, the absolute difference between the bid and ask prices,

---

[2] Of course, a more complete assessment of the euro's role should consider other financial markets, such as debt instruments and other securities; see Detken and Hartmann (this volume).

and *not* as a percentage of mid-quote. For example a market maker may buy euro at a bid price of 0.8900 dollars per euro and sell euro at an ask price of 0.8902 dollars per euro, with a mid-quote rate of 0.8901. This implies a spread of 2 pips. We find that pip spreads have not changed significantly between the two exchange rate periods, and we suggest that the redefinition of the exchange rate may have caused the spread (as a percentage of mid-quote) to increase for the USD/EUR.

The idea that the change in denomination could lead to a jump in percentage spreads was already proposed by Patrick Honohan in his discussion of the HKM paper (*Economic Policy* 34, p. 180). The pip defines the minimum bid-ask spread, and 1 pip as a percentage of 0.8901 (USD/EUR mid-quote) is obviously greater than 1 pip as a percentage of 1.7530 (DEM/USD mid-quote). If dealer competition led to a fair number of observations of spreads at their minimum level, one would quite naturally expect observed percentage spreads in the subsequent USD/EUR market to be higher. Dealers would be prevented from competing spreads down to their prior magnitudes (in percentage terms) simply due to the granularity of the pricing system.

The practical relevance of this phenomenon can be assessed in light of an existing literature that studies changes in effective pip or 'tick' sizes, focusing mainly on regulatory changes of minimum price variation in North American equity markets. In June 1997, both the NYSE and the NASDAQ stock markets lowered the minimum nominal price variation from one eighth to one sixteenth of a dollar. By the end of January 2001, the minimum price variation had been further lowered in the NYSE, to one cent. Empirically, these reductions in tick size as a proportion of prices led to a decline of quoted (and effective) spreads, as well as of the 'depth' (allowed trade size) of these quotes.[3] Thus the US evidence suggests that larger tick sizes imply larger transaction costs, at least for some market participants. In the situation under study in the current paper, tick sizes have increased in percentage terms upon transition from DEM/USD to USD/EUR quotes, and evidence from the US equity markets raises the possibility of a resultant increase in percentage spreads/costs of trade. This has adverse implications not only for transactions costs but also for something which is not as easy to observe: liquidity.[4] The higher spreads *may* be an equilibrium response to increased difficulties in inventory control due to lower liquidity, making risk management more difficult. However, it could well be the case that spreads are relatively tighter in the USD/EUR market than in the DEM/USD market for larger

[3] See, for example, Goldstein and Kavajecz (2000) and Jones and Lipson (2001) for evidence on the 1997 reforms and Bacidore *et al.* (2001) for evidence on the effects of the NYSE decimalization. Harris (1999) provides a survey of the debate surrounding the implementation of decimalization.

[4] As reported in the BIS 71st annual report, evidence on how liquidity has changed, when proxied by volumes, spreads and volatility, is inconclusive. Bid-ask spreads and short-term volatilities in the USD/EUR market in 2000 were broadly similar to those present in 1998. However the BIS also report that foreign exchange market activity declined substantially between 1998 and 2001. Daily average spot transactions for April fell from US$568 billion in 1998 to US$387 billion in 2001. This is also consistent with Goldman Sachs, which shows that monthly spot foreign exchange turnover through EBS (Electronic Broking Services) between the dollar and the dominant European currency was lower in 1999 than 1998, i.e. lower for the USD/EUR than the DEM/USD. BIS suggests that the decrease in volume is due to the loss of trading in former EMS currencies and the widespread adoption of electronic brokers.

trade sizes. These large volumes have tended to move from direct inter-dealer to electronically brokered trading, such as Reuters D2000-2 and EBS, since it is possible to hide your true position and trade size on these systems.[5]

The remainder of the paper is organized as follows. Section 2 discusses the data and presents summary statistics for the two periods. Section 3 explains our spread determination exercise, presents our regression results and includes a more detailed comparison of the spreads after taking into consideration the different market conditions in the two samples. Only the main findings are reported, but interested readers can consult the Appendix for further results and information. Section 4 discusses our findings and their policy implications, and Section 5 concludes.

2. DATA AND ANALYSIS

We have data for the dollar/euro (USD per EUR) exchange rate from 28 September 1999 to 8 March 2000, obtained from Reuters D2000-2 via the Bank of England, and for the deutschemark/dollar (DEM per USD) exchange rate between 6 and 10 October 1997, obtained directly from Reuters. Two datasets are available to us for each of the DEM/USD and USD/EUR periods.

The first contains the date, time (hour and minute) together with the best *bid* and *ask* prices. From these data we computed mid-quote rates as the simple average of the bid and ask prices, $mq = (bid + ask)/2$. Then we computed percentage spreads, $s = 100(ask - bid)/mq$, and spreads in terms of pips, $pip = 10000*(ask - bid)$, for every observation over the entire period. We removed all observations with zero bid or ask, since this suggests erroneous data, or non-positive spreads, which primarily represent the matching of market orders on the Reuters D2000-2 system. (See the Appendix for a more detailed explanation of this data removal/cleaning process.)

Since spreads tend to be large late at night and early in the morning, when trading activity is thin, we decided to use only data from periods of significant trading. For the USD/EUR, 97.5% of all trades took place in the ten hours between 0700 and 1700 London time; for the DEM/USD, 95.3% of all trades took place between 0600 and 1600 GMT. The apparent one hour delay for the USD/EUR data comes from the fact that these data were already adjusted for daylight saving time pre 31 October 1999, while the DEM/USD data were not. We decided to consider only these ten-hour periods of each day.

When averaging percentage and pip spreads over each hour and each day, we computed both the simple arithmetic mean of all observations and a time-weighted mean, where each spread is weighted according to how long it lasted in the market. For each hour (day), we also computed the standard deviation of spreads and a measure of return volatility: each hour (day) was split into five-minute intervals and

[5] From the BIS 71st annual report, between 85% and 95% of inter-bank trading took place using electronic broking in 2000 compared to only 50% in 1998.

the percentage change between the first calculated mid-quotes in each interval was defined as the return from one interval to the next. Hourly return volatility was computed as the sum of the 12 relevant squared return observations, and daily return volatility as the sum of the 120 relevant squared return observations.[6]

The second data set contained data on trade flows: the date, time (hour and minute), the direction of the trade (buyer initiated or seller initiated), and the price at which the transaction occurred. We computed total trades, defined as the number of times a transaction (buy or sell) occurred in the hour (day). Unfortunately we were not given information on the size of the trades or market depth, but only the number of trades. We also computed absolute imbalance, defined as the absolute difference between the number of market buys (buyer initiated trades) and the number of market sells (seller initiated trades) in each time period.

2.1. Summary statistics

Table 1 reports the summary statistics for average spread (AS), time weighted average spread (TWAS) average pip spread (ASPIP), time weighted average pip spread (TWASPIP), trades (TRAD), absolute imbalance (ABIM), volatility (VOLAT), standard deviation of spreads (STDSP) and standard deviation of pip spread (STDSPPIP), for our USD/EUR and DEM/USD samples, together with the indicative spread results of HKM.

2.2. Spread results

We see in Table 1 that the average hourly spread, as a percentage of mid-quote, for the USD/EUR market was 2.77 basis points, an increase of 71% from the 1.62 basis point average spread seen for the DEM/USD. This is consistent with the results of HKM, who found an increase of 40%, although our findings are more extreme. Unsurprisingly, the time weighted average spread also increased, this time by 84% from 1.45 to 2.67 basis points.[7] Only rarely did the daily USD/EUR spreads fall below 2 basis points whereas the DEM/USD spread was consistently below this level.

However, in terms of pips the spread only increased by 7% for the time weighted average, and actually fell by 1% for the average spread. We see in Figure 1 that the USD/EUR spread fluctuated roughly between 2 and 3.5 pips, and in Figure 2 that the same was true of the DEM/USD spread. The average daily spread for the USD/EUR over the sample period was fairly stable until mid December. The Christmas period has been excluded because very thin trading may distort the evidence, but

---

[6] For this definition of volatility see Andersen *et al.* (2001).

[7] For both hourly and daily statistics the time weighted average spread is lower than the average spread in both the DEM/USD and USD/EUR periods. This is not surprising, since spreads persists longer in the market when the market is rather quiet (less uncertainty, fewer large speculative trades) and these conditions are likely to be characterized by smaller spreads.

Table 1. Summary statistics[a]

	Hourly[b]			Daily[c]		
	DEM/USD[d]	USD/EUR[e]	% change	DEM/USD[d]	USD/EUR[e]	% change
AS (basis points)	1.62 (0.4783)	2.77 (1.2823)	71	1.63 (0.2917)	2.77 (0.6592)	70
TWAS (basis points)	1.45 (0.5310)	2.67 (1.4189)	84	1.44 (0.2474)	2.69 (0.6654)	87
ASPIP	2.84 (0.8339)	2.82 (1.2843)	−1	2.85 (0.4997)	2.82 (0.6264)	−1
TWASPIP	2.53 (0.9274)	2.71 (1.4305)	7	2.53 (0.4246)	2.74 (0.6379)	8
TRAD	602.74 (313.279)	289.55 (146.127)	−52	6027.4 (914.319)	2864.13 (735.043)	−52
ABIM	51.3 (47.473)	30.22 (26.566)	−41	86.6 (129.009)	104.16 (88.400)	20
VOLAT	0.0318 (0.05996)	0.0387 (0.05800)	22	0.3178 (0.2181)	0.3888 (0.2930)	22
STDSP	1.11 (0.5660)	2.00 (1.7955)	80	1.25 (0.4110)	2.58 (1.2311)	106
STDSPPIP	1.93 (0.9888)	2.03 (1.8531)	5	2.19 (0.7133)	2.63 (1.2682)	20
HKM Spread	3.76	5.26	40			

Notes:
[a] Standard deviations in parentheses.
[b] For hourly data, statistics were only calculated if there were full data over the hour. Hours during which the Reuters computer feed crashed have been omitted.
[c] Daily statistics were only computed if there were ten complete hours of data and this explains the slight variations between the daily and hourly results.
[d] DEM/USD data used 0600 to 1600 observations from 6 to 10 October 1997.
[e] USD/EUR data were calculated using 0700 to 1700 observations from 28 September 1999 to 8 March 2000. All statistics were calculated excluding the Christmas period from 24 December 1999 to 3 January 2000.

Sources: Authors' calculations using Reuters D2000-2 data as previously described. HKM data from Hau *et al.* (2002a).

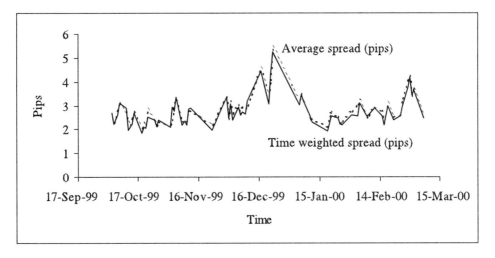

Figure 1. Time weighted and average pip spreads (daily USD/EUR)

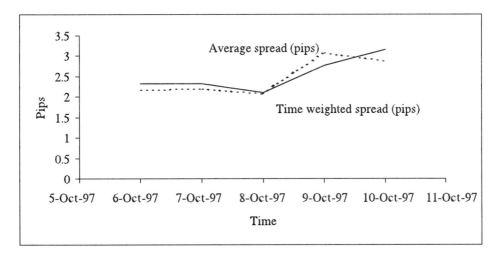

Figure 2. Time weighted and average pip spreads (daily DEM/USD)

spreads increased to over 5 pips leading up to Christmas, and only returned below 3 pips on 10 January 2000.

As for the DEM/USD data, we see in Figure 2 that the spread did appear to increase on 9 and 10 October 1997 for both the average and time weighted definitions. This is almost certainly due to the change in interest rates in Germany, announced at 1130 GMT on 9 October, the fourth day of our series. As reported in the *Financial Times* (10/10/1997), the Bundesbank, to the surprise of many analysts, increased its securities repurchase (repo) rate from 3% to 3.3%. This caused volatility in the DEM/USD rate to rise dramatically. Whereas hourly volatility never increased

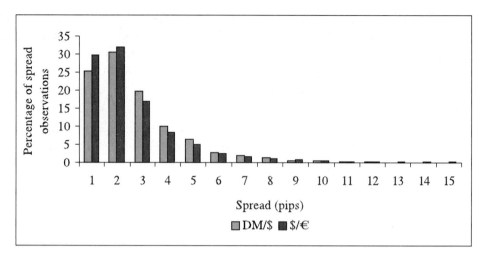

Figure 3. Breakdown of spreads for the DEM/USD and USD/EUR markets

above 0.05 in previous observations, volatility was 0.45 in the hour containing the announcement. In Table 1, the average hourly return volatility for the USD/EUR and DEM/USD is 0.0387 and 0.0318 respectively. However, if we exclude the observation for 1100 on 9 October for the DEM/USD, the DEM/USD return volatility measure falls to 0.0237, which is substantially below the figure for the USD/EUR.

The dataset for the DEM/USD is much smaller than that for the USD/EUR, and it may have been the case that the week observed for the former was in some way out of the ordinary. However, the data offer considerable evidence that spreads against the dollar (when defined as a percentage of mid-quote) have risen post-introduction of the euro.[8] This is consistent with the results of HKM. However, there is also considerable evidence to suggest that the spread, when given in pips, has not changed. When testing the null hypothesis of equal population pip spreads, the test statistic for the time weighted average is 1.29 and that for the average spread is only 0.16. The null hypothesis of equal spreads can therefore not be rejected at any reasonable level. If we examine the breakdown of the pip spreads for both DEM/USD and USD/EUR datasets (Figure 3), we can see that the distribution of spreads is broadly similar.

From this analysis, we therefore claim that, first, the spreads in the DEM/USD and USD/EUR markets are set as a number of pips, and secondly, that these pip spreads have not significantly changed post-introduction of the euro. Of course, FX dealers decide their spread as a number of pips, since what they actually set are the

---

[8] Testing the null hypothesis that the two population basis point spreads (hourly data) are equal results in test statistics of 14.37 for average spreads and 13.74 for time weighted average spreads. The 1% critical value for the standard normal distribution is 2.57 for a two-tailed test. Therefore the null of equal spreads can be rejected at any reasonable level.

bid and ask prices. From this the percentage of mid-quote spread can be calculated but is not directly chosen by the dealers. If our hypothesis is true then it can help explain the findings of HKM, in that the same number of pips as a percentage of a lower mid-quote will naturally lead to a higher spread when given as a percentage of this mid-quote. The 'granularity' hypothesis is also consistent with some of the other findings of HKM, namely the increased spreads in the GBP/DEM-EUR foreign exchange markets where again the mid-quote has changed, and the much smaller changes in the JPY/USD and USD/GBP markets where no re-factoring of the mid-quote has occurred.[9]

2.3. Trade results

Moving on to the trades data, it is quite clear that the number of trades in our USD/EUR data is considerably smaller in comparison to DEM/USD data. The average number of trades for the euro was 2864 per day (one trade every 12.5 seconds). As is the case for spreads, there is a Christmas effect where trading volume fell off leading towards Christmas. For the deutschemark, the average daily trades was 6027 (one trade every 6 seconds), more than double the euro figure. In fact the highest number of daily trades in the USD/EUR market was 4417, on 17 February 2000, and this is still below the minimum number of trades seen in the DEM/USD market (5375, on 10 October 1997). When considering the same week in October for the USD/EUR market, 4–8 October, so avoiding criticism of ignoring calendar effects, the daily average number of trades was 3045.8, 50.5% of the DEM/USD figure.

3. DETERMINANTS OF SPREADS

We now turn to the factors that determine the pip spreads for the two currency pairs. Standard microstructure theories suggest that the greater the number of trades, the lower should be the spread, since fixed order processing costs may be spread across more trades. More precisely, expected trades should have a negative effect on spreads while unexpected trades should have a positive effect.[10] Also, greater volatility and more pronounced absolute imbalances should increase spreads, since a more volatile market or one-way trading pressure indicate arrival of new information and make inventory control more difficult. Building on work by Hartmann (1998b, 1999), we regressed average and time weighted pip spreads on return volatility, number of trades, absolute imbalance; we also included the standard deviation of spreads as a

---

[9] See Detken and Hartmann (this volume) for further evidence corroborating the hypothesis we test here. HKM find in their data that spreads have increased in the JPY/EUR market, which is inconsistent with our granularity hypothesis. However, this is not confirmed in longer-run data, and that counter-example uses a very small and illiquid market: on the basis of the spreads reported by HKM, it would be considerably cheaper to convert between deutschemarks/euro and yen using the dollar as a vehicle.

[10] Following Hartmann (1999), attempts were made to break down trades into expected and unexpected components by fitting trades to an ARMA process and taking the residual from this regression as unexpected trades. However, this proved unsuccessful.

Table 2. Deseasonalized spread regressions[a]

	DEM/USD[b]		USD/EUR	
	TWASPIP	ASPIP	TWASPIP	ASPIP
C	0.5307 (12.08)	0.6143 (11.59)	0.7823 (17.57)	0.8082 (13.39)
VOLAT		0.0487 (2.04)	0.0311 (3.93)	0.0421 (3.70)
STDSPPIP	0.4352 (9.28)	0.3887 (11.37)	0.2643 (6.41)	0.2422 (3.91)
TRAD		−0.0700 (−1.73)	−0.0773 (−3.70)	−0.0920 (−4.58)
AR(1)	0.3211 (2.22)		0.2952 (5.60)	0.4068 (7.61)
AR(2)			0.1578 (3.46)	0.1105 (2.14)
AR(3)			0.1938 (4.91)	0.1794 (3.78)
Dummy	0.1045 (2.70)	0.0642 (3.27)		
R^2	0.86	0.91	0.73	0.78

Notes:
[a] Test statistics in parentheses. Newey–West consistent standard errors were used throughout. All variables are deseasonalised as described in the text. However, for the DEM/USD data, due to the distortionary effects the 1100 GMT 4th day data may have, it was excluded in the deseasonalization procedure, i.e. the intra-day pattern for 1100 GMT was found by averaging only the 1st, 2nd, 3rd and 5th days' data.
[b] The dummy variable D takes the value '1' for observations from 1200 GMT on 9 October 1997 onwards and zero otherwise. The observation for 1100 GMT has been removed. Pre and post interest rate announcement, it was found that the responsiveness of the spread to changes in the explanatory variables remained unchanged.

Sources: Authors' calculations using Reuters D2000-2 data as previously described.

regressor, in order to account for the changing market position of Reuters D2000-2.[11] Due to the presence of obvious seasonal patterns in the data ('U' shaped spreads and 'M' shaped trades within the day for example) all data were deseasonalized.[12]

Before any regressions were performed, each series was tested for stationarity. We would expect every series to be stationary and for the USD/EUR data standard Augmented Dickey–Fuller (ADF) tests confirmed these hypotheses. However for the DEM/USD data average spread, time weighted spread, and the standard deviation of spreads were all found to be non-stationary. This appears implausible. The interest rate change made by the German Bundesbank at 1130 GMT on 9 October 1997 suggests a possible structural break around the time of the announcement.[13] Indeed, when eyeballing the deseasonalized spread series for the DEM/USD, after removing the observation for 1100 on 9 October, it is quite clear that average spreads are higher post interest rate announcement than pre-announcement.

The deseasonalized spread was therefore modelled with a structural break around the time of the interest rate announcement. Box 1 outlines the regression procedure, and Table 2 reports the results for the DEM/USD data along with those for the USD/EUR spread.

[11] If the spread increased from 1 pip to 6 pips this will naturally cause average spread and spread standard deviation to increase. However this is likely to be due to D2000-2 becoming uncompetitive with trading activity moving to the competing EBS system. Regressions were also performed omitting the standard deviation of spreads, and the results are given in the Appendix.

[12] Hourly deseasonalized data are calculated as proportional deviations from the average (across days) of each hour's data in the sample.

[13] It has been shown that ADF tests tend to accept the null hypothesis of unit root processes far too often when the series is in fact stationary but with a structural break. See, for example, Perron (1990).

Box 1. Spread regressions: technical details

Microstructure theory suggests that volatility and trades will affect the spread. In turn, the spread influences the number of trades: a system of simultaneous equations would be needed to account for the fact that transaction costs deter market participants from trading. However, we use simple single equation regression techniques, and we also disregard econometric issues arising from the fact that pip spreads are integers. We are looking at averages over each hour, and also deseasonalizing the data, hence discreteness of the original data does not introduce the same econometric problems as in tick-by-tick data – where one might, following Huang and Stoll (1997), let the error term capture the discreteness and use Generalized Method of Moments estimators, which put few distributional constraints on the error.

The following dummied regression was therefore performed for deseasonalized USD/EUR pip spreads (average and time weighted) and the results are shown in Table 2.

$$TWASPIP_t^{DS} = X_t^{DS}\gamma_1 + X_t^{DS}D\gamma_2 + \varepsilon_t \tag{1}$$

Where $X_t^{DS} = [1, VOLAT_t^{DS}, STDSPPIP_t^{DS}, TRAD_t^{DS}, ABIM_t^{DS}]$ and γ_1 and γ_2 are 5*1 vectors of coefficients, i.e. we regress the pip spreads on trades, volatility, etc. but allow for a structural change at the time of the interest rate announcement by introducing the dummy variable D. D takes the value of '1' for observations from 1200 GMT on 9 October onwards and zero otherwise. If there were a jump change in the spread, then the first element of γ_2, corresponding to the constant in the regression, would be statistically significant. However, if the responsiveness of the spread to the explanatory variables changed following the Bundesbank announcement, then the other γ_2 coefficients would be shown to be significant. Insignificant explanatory variables were sequentially removed in a general to specific approach and upon further investigation, an AR(1) process was suggested for time-weighted spreads. However for average spreads, no evidence was found to suggest using lagged dependant variables.

For the EUR/USD data, the following model was fitted:

$$TWASPIP_t^{DS} = X_t^{DS}\gamma + \varepsilon_t \tag{2}$$

where X_t^{DS} is as above and γ is a 5*1 vector of coefficients to be estimated. On more detailed inspection of the residuals, an AR(3) process was suggested. The model presented in Table 2 was therefore estimated and found to work well, further AR terms failed to significantly improve the fit of the model. For average spreads the same procedure resulted in the same model specification, and the results given in the same table.

We see in the results of Table 2 for pip spreads that those for the USD/EUR are affected by return volatility and the number of trades, as well as by the spread standard deviation and by lagged spreads. Determination of the DEM/USD spread proved more awkward, largely due to the shorter dataset and to the unexpected interest rate increase by the Bundesbank on the fourth day of the data series. For the purpose of the spread determination exercise, a structural break was tested and indeed found around the time of the interest rate change and this has been incorporated into our spread model. There appeared to be a jump in the spread following the interest rate change (which was sure to die out in subsequent days) and it was found that the responsiveness of the spread to changes in the exogenous variables remained the same post-interest rate announcement. However, despite the higher R^2 for the DEM/USD spread model, fewer variables were found to affect the spread. Trades were only significant at barely the 10% level for average spread and, along with return volatility, were found to be insignificant when looking at the time weighted average.

3.1. The role of different market conditions

We have shown that, in terms of pips, the USD/EUR spreads are approximately the same as those seen in the DEM/USD period. To see whether the spreads set by the market makers are structurally different, however, we need to control for factors that may affect these spreads differently in the two samples, such as higher volatility and smaller number of trades. We compared the actual spreads observed in the DEM/USD sample to those predicted by the USD/EUR model of Table 2 on the basis of the trades and volatility observed in the DEM/USD period. Of course, the comparison is meaningful only if the linear model fitted for the USD/EUR can be extrapolated to the DEM/USD data. This appears optimistic since the number of trades for the DEM/USD were more than double that for the USD/EUR. There were also two other major structural changes between the DEM and the euro data periods, namely the rapid expansion of electronic broking discussed above, and greater concentration in the banking industry (in 2001 there were 2772 banks in 48 countries reporting to the BIS, as opposed to 3087 in 43 countries in 1998). Since concentration can reduce competition, both phenomena are likely to result in reduced numbers of trades and may affect liquidity, but we cannot control for these developments with our data. Another possible problem is that available data for the DEM/USD period cover only five days (including a major interest rate change), and may not be representative of the foreign exchange market at the time. However, corroborating evidence comes from Lyons (1995) who found a median bid-ask spread of 3 pips when using five days of data from August 1992 and Bjonnes and Rime (2001) who examined data from one dealer operating on Reuters D2000-1 in March 1998, finding an

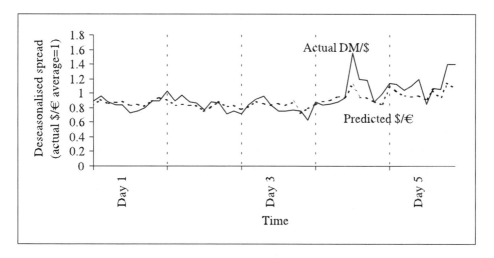

Figure 4. Actual DEM/USD and predicted USD/EUR time weighted pip spreads

average spread of 1.985 pips.[14] At this stage it should also be noted that anecdotal evidence suggests that D2000-2's share of the foreign exchange market has declined between our two data periods, at least for the USD/DEM-EUR. This itself could cause spreads (as a percentage of mid-quote) to rise.

Keeping in mind these important caveats, we plot in Figure 4 the actual DEM/USD spreads and those predicted by the USD/EUR model. The two series track each other reasonably well. Towards the end of the sample, the USD/EUR model under-predicts the DEM/USD spreads and this is largely due to the structural break at the time of the interest rate announcement, after which DEM/USD spreads experienced a jump shift. In the figure, a value of 1 refers to the USD/EUR average, 2.71 pips for the time weighted average spread. Since trades were higher for the DEM/USD and both volatility measures lower, one would naturally expect the predicted USD/EUR spreads to be lower than those seen in the actual USD/EUR market. This is indeed the case since the predicted pip spreads are nearly always below unity. Since the actual DEM/USD and predicted USD/EUR spreads follow each other quite well, then we conclude that after taking into consideration the differing levels of volatility and trades, the USD/EUR spreads in pip terms are no different to those seen in the DEM/USD period. In fact, the coefficients of the spread model are statistically significant but very small, and predicted spreads are not substantially affected by the number of trades in the DEM/USD period (more than twice that for the USD/EUR) and much lower return volatility.

---

[14] Although Evans (1998) found a larger average DEM/USD spread of 6 pips when using data from May to August 1996. However, his data were from the bilateral D2000-1 system, which included all large trades where spreads are naturally higher.

4. DISCUSSION AND POLICY IMPLICATIONS

In summary, the USD/EUR market on D2000-2 has been shown to be characterized by a smaller number of trades and higher volatility compared with the previous D2000-2 DEM/USD market. We have found that the USD/EUR spreads, when defined as a percentage of mid-quote, are considerably higher than those observed in the preceding DEM/USD market, consistent with the findings of HKM. However, we argue that this is due to the re-factoring of the European currency, approximately 1.75 DEM per USD and 1 USD per EUR in the periods under review. The data suggest that an unchanged pip spread implied larger proportional transaction costs. In light of the institutional set-up of the market, this is not surprising. The DEM/USD spreads during peak hours were no more than 1 or 2 pips. In order to bring the percentage of mid-quote spreads down to DEM/USD levels in the current USD/EUR era, pip spreads should have fallen, but no market maker will provide liquidity services at a zero spread! As seen in Figure 1, there is in fact a slightly greater concentration of spreads at one and two pips for the USD/EUR market than for the DEM/USD: 61.5% of USD/EUR spreads were at either 1 or 2 pips, compared with 55.8% for the DEM/USD. If after redefinition of the exchange rate the market makers wanted to reduce the percentage spread down to the level seen in the DEM/USD period, however, there would be a *much* greater concentration of spreads at 1 or 2 pips. Thus, we suggest that the market makers are earning extra rents, at least on small trades in the USD/EUR market compared to the preceding DEM/USD market.

In our view, larger spreads are due to the 'granularity' of the market (prices being given only to four decimal places) rather than to the risk sharing mechanism proposed by HKM. If the DEM/USD exchange rate had been defined the other way round, i.e. 0.57 USD per DEM rather than 1.75 DEM per USD, and pip spreads remained the same when moving to the USD/EUR period, then the percentage of mid-quote spreads would have fallen dramatically. The current discussion would then have been focused on the cause of the 'increased liquidity' of the euro, and the possible demise of the dollar as an international currency.

It may in fact be the case that quoting the euro in dollars, rather than in per dollar terms as was the case for the deutschemark, reflected an expectation of dollar 'demise' in early January 1999. The euro was the most expensive currency in January 1999, hence one pip was less as a percentage of a USD/EUR mid-quote than a EUR/USD mid-quote. And since both the ECU and mark had been appreciating against the dollar, and some expected the euro to continue on this path as it became a reserve currency, USD/EUR pips would have been even less as a percentage of the mid-quote during the spring. History proved this expectation wrong, but in late 1998 and early 1999 one could not know.

The persistence of absolute spreads is reminiscent of the phenomenon studied by Christie and Schultz (1994), who found that market makers in NASDAQ avoided odd eighth quotes through collusion, earning excess rents. If foreign exchange market makers are earning extra rents via pip persistence, could this be viewed as a case of market maker collusion? In our opinion, the answer is no! Whereas dealers in NASDAQ were colluding to offer the same even eighth spread, each FX dealer offers spreads of multiple pips, and it is competition that brings spreads down to one or two pips. In fact, it is usually the case that the best bid and ask prices, which form the spread that we observe, are quoted by different dealers/banks.

One may, however, ask why a fifth decimal was not introduced in practice. Conversations with dealers indicate that the network suppliers, EBS and Reuters, had no incentive to do this as long as the dealers did not demand it. And why should the dealers not demand it? First they may believe that five decimals would be confusing and increase the risk of keying in mistakes. Second, as providers of liquidity they enjoyed making the extra money from the higher percentage spread. Also, the dealers claim that the spreads to customers have decreased over the last couple of years so customers are not hurt by the four-decimal constraint.

Of course, even though dealers may not be colluding to prevent spreads from falling, the current system does imply a lower bound on the minimum spread, that being one unit of the fourth decimal, 0.0001. Would a policy-induced move to using five decimals when quoting prices have helped? From the data in Table 1, one can calculate that a 1.65 pip spread in the USD/EUR market was needed to support the same percentage spread as in the DEM/USD market. Clearly, five decimal quotes would facilitate achieving a 16 'pips' spread (as a pip would be one movement of the fifth decimal, not the fourth). The introduction of fifth decimal quoting would see the lower bound on spreads fall to 0.00001 and *should* see rents made by dealers on small trades fall to those seen pre-introduction of the euro.

The issue, however, is not as simple as it appears. In the North America equity markets, the move from eighths to sixteenths and then to cent spreads was indeed motivated by concerns about the market's liquidity. However, depths decreased along with spreads (see Jones and Lipson, 2001, and Goldstein and Kavajecz, 2000). If you wanted to trade at the smaller spreads, you could only trade smaller volumes. It may well be the case, although this is purely a conjecture, that a move to five decimals might have the same effects in the USD/EUR market, improving the tightness of the market (the spread at the smallest trade size) but reducing the depths of available quotes. In the new situation, the costs of trading may or may not be lower, depending on trade sizes. Indeed, anecdotal evidence from traders suggests that despite the increase in spreads that we report, trades are moving to larger sizes, where spreads are relatively lower compared to those for comparative sizes in the DEM/USD market. So the total costs of trade may *not* have increased when moving to the USD/EUR period but, again, this is a conjecture and cannot be verified using our data.

5. CONCLUSION

From the above analysis we can conclude that the USD/EUR spreads did increase significantly from those seen in the DEM/USD period but only when defining spreads as a percentage of mid-quote. This, we argue, is due to the re-factoring of the mid-quote along with the fact that pip spreads have remained unchanged. We successfully model the spread as a function of trades and return volatility, and when we allow for the higher volumes and lower volatility in the DEM/USD era, the spreads predicted by the USD/EUR model are essentially the same as those actually observed. This suggests that the market makers are setting the same pip spreads in the USD/EUR market as in the preceding DEM/USD market, *ceteris paribus*. When comparing the spreads in the DEM/USD and USD/EUR markets, it is tempting to claim that liquidity has fallen in the euro markets, as suggested by HKM. Such claims are, however, difficult to substantiate once one considers the significant structural changes that have taken place in recent years, namely banking sector consolidation and an increased use of electronic broking, together with anecdotal evidence that trades have moved to larger sizes where spreads are relatively tighter in the USD/EUR period.

Despite the increased percentage spreads, we do not believe that the USD/EUR market is characterized by collusion, as was the case for NASDAQ. The introduction of a fifth decimal in quoting USD/EUR prices will indeed reduce the lower bound on spreads and will probably reduce the costs of trading the smallest quantities. However if the depths associated with the tightest spreads also fall, then when one conditions on trade size, trading costs may not necessarily be reduced. The introduction of a fifth decimal may then not increase the market's overall liquidity.

APPENDIX

See http://www.economic-policy.org.

DISCUSSION AND REFERENCES

The Discussion and References for the three 'Forex markets and the euro' papers appear on pages 592–7.

Forex markets and the euro

Comprehensive early evidence

SUMMARY

Three years after the euro's introduction, we discuss its role in foreign exchange and international debt securities markets on the basis of a comprehensive set of data sources. In spot foreign exchange markets the euro's role resembles that of the deutschemark, with a dominant position in the Nordic and several Central European countries. Transaction costs in the important dollar-euro market are larger than they used to be for dollar-mark, but the same does not hold for any other major spot market. We discuss how this phenomenon may be explained by persistence of bid-ask quoting conventions in this market in the face of changed nominal parities. We show a notable reduction in euro swap trading and explain it, inter alia, with the elimination of dollar swaps meant to hedge exchange rate risk between currencies now subsumed in the euro. We observe strong growth of euro-denominated debt securities, while international euro bond investments are stable at the level of the 'synthetic euro' aggregate of legacy currencies.

— *Carsten Detken and Philipp Hartmann*

Economic Policy October 2002 Printed in Great Britain
© CEPR, CES, MSH, 2002.

Features of the euro's role in international financial markets

Carsten Detken and Philipp Hartmann

European Central Bank, DG Research; European Central Bank, DG Research, and CEPR

1. INTRODUCTION

Economic and monetary union (EMU) prompted some speculation as to the future international role of the new European currency. Some thought the euro might soon challenge the dollar's post-World War II dominance, while others even doubted it would come into existence. Three years after the introduction of the euro and only a few months after the circulation of notes and coins, it is still much too early to pass judgement on the euro's international fate. However, it is interesting to try and ascertain whether and why introduction of the euro has yet caused significant changes in the international financial system.

In this paper we refrain from long-range speculation. Following up on similar previous work,[1] we compare indicators of the euro's early international role to similar

Any views expressed are only the authors' own and do not necessarily reflect the views of the ECB or of the Eurosystem. We thank two anonymous referees for their comments and Vincent Brousseau, Gabriele Galati, Paola Gallardo, Jerome Haegeli, Andreas Hasenbalg, Antonio Manzini, Brian Martin, Francesco Mazzaferro, Philippe Mongars, Eoin O'Donovan, Jim O'Hagan, Graham Parkinson, Thorsten Polleit, Jouni Timonen, Arwed Max von Poser, Dirk Wegener, and participants at the April 2002 *Economic Policy* Panel Meeting in Madrid and at an ECB internal seminar for discussions. We are particularly grateful to Electronic Broking Services (EBS) and Capital Access International for generous data provision. Research assistance by Sandrine Corvoisier and Andres Manzanares as well as editorial help by Sabine Wiedemann are very much appreciated. The Managing Editor in charge of this paper was Giuseppe Bertola.

[1] See Hartmann (1998) for methodology, and Detken and Hartmann (2000) for a discussion of the euro's international role about one year after its introduction, including cautious observation of some increase of spot foreign exchange bid-ask spreads in relatively noisy daily quoted data.

indicators for the aggregate of its predecessors, i.e. the 11 'legacy' currencies replaced by the euro on 1 January 1999 (Portuguese escudo, Belgian and Luxembourg franc, French franc, Dutch gilder, Italian lira, Finnish mark, German mark, Spanish peseta, Irish pound and Austrian shilling; the Greek drachma also joined on 1 January 2001). To compare the international role of the euro and of legacy currencies, one needs to recognize that the 'international' character of currency use was redefined by the euro's introduction. For example, German mark holdings and transactions in France were international before 1999, but euro usage anywhere within the euro area is domestic rather than international. To obtain a 'synthetic euro' series from historical data, one needs to deduct from aggregate currency statistics the portion that reflected trading among legacy currencies, or usage that used to be external for a legacy currency but is now internal for the euro. This is the so-called 'simple arithmetics of EMU'. The resulting series can be meaningfully compared to the actual observation of euro usage after the euro's introduction.[2]

We focus on foreign exchange trading and international debt security denomination, two important aspects of currencies' international role (see e.g. Hartmann, 1998a, or Portes and Rey, 1998) that have attracted significant attention recently. Since excessive attention to partial indicators can easily be misleading, we strive to offer a comprehensive picture, tapping new data and comparing all available euro indicators to historical 'synthetic' data. Section 2 highlights salient features of recent experience in the foreign exchange market, from both aggregate and microstructure perspectives. We cover global and regional spot markets (trading volumes and transaction costs) as well as global swap markets (volumes). Section 3 briefly reports on whether the evolution of international bond markets conforms predictions and earlier analyses. The final section concludes, and an Appendix offers more detailed empirical evidence.

2. FOREIGN EXCHANGE MARKETS

Foreign exchange market developments have recently attracted considerable attention. In two papers Hau, Killeen and Moore (2002a and 2002b) show that intra-day data – 21 months of indicative bid-ask spreads from the Reuters FXFX page and 2 months (August 1998 and August 1999) of traded spreads from Electronic Broking Services (EBS) – indicate that transaction costs were systematically higher during 1999 for bilateral euro markets than they were during 1998 for bilateral

---

[2] Estimates of the 'synthetic' euro on this basis for a variety of international currency dimensions have been made before the start of stage 3 of EMU by Hartmann (1996), Henning (1997), McCauley (1997) and Hartmann (1998). For several important dimensions, such as e.g. foreign exchange trading, it turned out that – as a percentage share of total currency uses – the 'synthetic' euro was actually quite close to the mark, partly related to the fact that Germany possessed the only currency in Europe with a relatively large international role at the time. One implication of this finding was that the initial 'shock' on the international monetary system through the introduction of the euro could be expected to be relatively moderate.

mark markets.[3] Their data also indicate that euro trading volumes in EBS during 1999 were lower than mark volumes during 1998, and the authors argue that elimination of euro legacy currency markets increased transparency in spot trading and thereby inventory risk, so that dealers had to increase spreads (the transparency hypothesis). Goodhart *et al.* (this volume) offer a very different explanation. They find that EUR / USD relative transaction spreads in Reuters Dealing 2000-2 between October 1999 and February 2000 were higher than mark-dollar spreads during five days in 1997. They show that standard explanatory variables, such as volatility or trading activity, cannot account for the increase in transaction costs, and suggest that 'granularity' of price quotes may be responsible for it instead (the 'pip' hypothesis).

We proceed to re-assess these empirical findings in light of better and more comprehensive data, offering time series evidence, wider coverage of FX market segments, and more systematic integration of evidence from particular trading systems and from global survey data.

2.1. Is the current global trading volume of the euro surprising?

We update the 'simple arithmetics of EMU' procedure of Hartmann (1996, Tables 9 and 10) for spot markets, and apply it also to swap and total turnover.[4]

2.1.1. No surprises in spot markets. Table 1 shows global dollar (USD), yen (JPY), 'synthetic' euro (EUR) and mark (DEM) spot turnovers (interbank and customer) as well as their shares of total global spot turnover for the central bank survey years of 1992, 1995 and 1998 (Bank for International Settlements, 1993, 1996, 1999a). It also shows the aggregate spot turnover between euro area currencies that were eliminated through EMU. The bottom row reports USD, yen and euro spot turnover, as reported in the latest survey (BIS, 2002).

In 2001, the euro share of spot turnover is exactly the same as the 1998 DEM share: at 43%, the euro is the second largest currency in the spot foreign exchange market, clearly behind the USD (84%) and also clearly in advance of the yen (26%). The 1998 share of the 'synthetic euro' (aggregating all legacy currencies) was only slightly larger at 47%. So, the euro's relative role is not very surprising from a 'simple arithmetics of EMU' perspective.

Table 1 also shows that the 34% reduction in absolute euro spot volume (from USD252 billion to USD166 billion) closely corresponds to a 33% volume reduction

---

[3] EBS is one of the two main broking systems now reckoned to turn over together more than half of inter-dealer spot trading in global foreign exchange markets. The other system is Reuters Dealing 2000-2. FXFX is an information page on Reuters terminals displaying indicative bid and ask prices, mainly considered in relation to wholesale dealer customer transactions. Spreads derived from these indicative bid and ask prices tend to be 2–3 (or sometimes more) times larger than the ones' implied by prices that are traded high frequency in the wholesale inter-dealer market, e.g. through EBS or Reuters Dealing.

[4] For the smaller market segment of outright forwards this is reported in the Appendix, Table A1. See also McCauley (1997) for total turnover computations on the 1995 BIS survey (BIS, 1996).

Table 1. Level and currency composition of *spot* foreign exchange trading volume before EMU and in 2001

	USD		JPY		EUR[b]		Total[b]		Elim. EUR legacy currency volume		Memorandum: DEM	
	USD bn	%[a]	USD bn	%[a]	USD bn	%[a]	USD bn	%	USD bn	%[c]	USD bn	%[c]
1992	283.8	79.2	79.2	22.1	201.7	56.3	358.3	100	35.5	9.0	209.3	53.2
1995	351.4	82.2	109.0	25.5	236.4	55.3	427.6	100	66.6	13.5	268.3	54.3
1998	455.2	84.3	142.9	26.5	252.3	46.7	539.7	100	38.1	6.6	246.8	42.7
2001	326.7	84.4	100.6	26.0	166.4	43.0	387.0	100	–	–	–	–

Notes: This is an amended and extended version of tables 9 and 10 in Hartmann (1996). Daily averages over the months of April. The horizontal sum of USD, EUR and JPY volumes is larger than 100 percent of global spot turnover, because direct exchanges between currencies listed are counted twice. If all currencies were listed the total would amount to 200 percent.

[a] Percentage of volume in column 'total'.

[b] Excluding trading volume between euro legacy currencies for 1992, 1995 and 1998.

[c] Percentage of the sum of volume in column 'total' and 'eliminated euro legacy currency volume'.

Sources: Bank for International Settlements (1993, 1996, 1999, 2001), own calculations.

in total spot trading (from USD540 billion to USD387 billion) during the same three years. The USD38 billion of spot trading among euro legacy currencies in 1998 accounts for a quarter of the spot volume that disappeared. The rest of the decline in total spot trading has been explained with bank consolidation, international corporate sector concentration and the advance of electronic broking (see Galati, 2001). Trading in (synthetic or actual) euro remained constant as a proportion of a shrinking spot market.[5]

2.1.2. News from swap markets. We next consider swaps, the largest segment of the foreign exchange market.[6] Here, the picture is different (see Table 2). The main currencies' shares did not change very much between 1992 and 1998 (with the exception of the yen in 1998), but the euro experienced a sharp 35% reduction in turnover from USD337 billion to USD221 billion. This decline was much larger than that of overall swap turnover, which declined by only 11%, of which only 1.5 percentage points can be explained by the elimination of the euro legacy currency turnover. One may note, however, that in contrast to spot markets the absolute euro volume is still much larger than the DEM volume was before, and that the euro share of 34% is also 14 percentage points larger than the previous DEM share of 20%.

The results for spot, swap and forward markets add up to the totals reported in Table 3. They show that the 9 percentage points reduction in the euro's relative share in total global foreign exchange markets compared to the aggregate of its legacy currencies was mainly a swap market phenomenon.

We believe, also on the basis of interviews with foreign exchange market participants, that three interrelated phenomena may explain why euro swap volume is so much lower than that of its synthetic legacy counterpart.

First, it is apparent in Table 2 that almost all foreign exchange swap trading has the dollar on one side of the transaction, and that hardly any swaps were written directly between two legacy currencies. To hedge the risk of legacy currency positions at the end of the trading day, dealers would usually swap the USD against the relevant legacy currencies.[7] To the extent that all swap transactions went through the USD, even when intended to hedge exchange rate risk between legacy currencies, the mechanical elimination of legacy currency turnover would affect both USD and euro volume. However, since the USD share is almost 100%, only the euro share would decrease through this effect.

---

[5] Similarly, volume fluctuations in specific trading systems should not be confused with volume changes at the aggregate level. For example, they could simply reflect shifts between different trading systems (such as EBS or Reuters) or between the electronic broking segment and the bilateral inter-dealer market. In the Appendix, Figure A1, we show that the decrease of euro volumes relative to the dollar in the EBS system between 1998 and 1999 did not persist in our newly available December 1999 to January 2002 data obtained from EBS.

[6] A swap transaction entails exchange of currencies both immediately ('spot') and at a specified future time ('forward'), in opposite directions.

[7] A particularly popular version of this technique was 'tom-next funding' (for 'tomorrow/next day') at a short-term maturity of 1 day.

Table 2. Level and currency composition of *swap* foreign exchange trading volume before EMU and in 2001

	USD		JPY		EUR		Total		Elim. EUR legacy currency volume		Memorandum: DEM	
	USD bn	%	USD bn	%	USD bn	%	USD bn	%	USD bn	%	USD bn	%
1992	309.0	96.5	83.4	26.0	119.6	37.4	320.0	100	4.3	1.3	72.6	22.4
1995	518.3	97.1	136.7	25.6	231.6	43.4	533.7	100	12.2	2.2	112.1	20.5
1998	699.2	96.6	122.6	16.9	336.7	46.5	723.5	100	10.7	1.5	146.8	20.0
2001	623.0	95.0	132.2	20.2	220.8	33.7	655.5	100	–	–	–	–

Notes and sources: see Table 1.

Table 3. Level and currency composition of *total* foreign exchange trading volume before EMU and in 2001

	USD		JPY		EUR		Total		Elim. EUR legacy currency volume		Memorandum: DEM	
	USD bn	%	USD bn	%	USD bn	%	USD bn	%	USD bn	%	USD bn	%
1992	637.0	86.7	178.0	24.2	347.8	47.3	734.6	100	41.9	5.4	303.2	39.0
1995	946.7	90.0	274.1	26.0	510.3	48.5	1052.4	100	84.5	7.4	410.7	36.1
1998	1260.0	90.8	300.1	21.6	643.0	46.4	1386.9	100	54.6	3.8	430.0	29.8
2001	1060.4	90.4	266.1	22.7	441.6	37.6	1173.1	100	–	–	–	–

Notes and sources: see Table 1.

Second, trading of USD-euro legacy currency swaps may have been unusually high at the time of the BIS survey (April 1998). In the run-up to EMU, swaps were widely used in 'convergence plays', that is, bets on the speed of the interest rate convergence across countries. In fact, countries with the largest initial interest rate differentials experienced the strongest growth in swap turnover among EU countries (excluding Greece). Between 1995 and 1998 swap turnover of both the Irish pound and the Portuguese escudo grew by 154% and of the Italian lira by 94%, while the whole swap market grew only by 34% (BIS, 1996, 1999). In April, a few days before the final announcement of the conversion rates, these and other currencies still featured significant 3 months interest rate differentials with Germany, while other currencies had already fully converged.[8] If late 'convergence plays' for specific countries blew up swap trading at the time of the central bank turnover survey, the 1998–2001 drop may be overstated from a longer-run perspective.

Finally, financial innovation may also be relevant. A traditional foreign exchange swap is subject to supervisory capital requirements and, to relax those requirements, Continental European banks have recently preferred off-balance sheet instruments that save on regulatory capital. For example, the same positions that can be taken with forex swaps can be replicated with interest rate swaps in two countries (such as EONIA swaps newly created in the euro area).[9] Consistently with this explanation, euro- and USD-denominated interest rate derivates turnover in 2001 was almost twice as large as the aggregate of legacy currency turnovers (BIS, 1999, 2002).

2.2. Are there any 'anomalies' in euro bid-ask spreads?

Bid-ask spreads are a widely used measure of foreign exchange market liquidity, and a transaction cost factor that can play an important role in the use of currencies in the FX market.[10] In this sub-section we first check with longer high-frequency data series whether the observation of increased euro spreads is really a robust and sustained feature. For the bilateral markets where this is the case we then look for an explanation for this phenomenon.

We can compute FX spreads in EBS across main euro and USD spot exchange rates and over time. The data span the period February 1997 to February 2002, i.e. almost two years before the introduction of the euro and more than three years afterwards. For each year ultra-high frequency (second-to-second) quoted and traded bid and ask prices are available for the months of February and August, except for February 2001. For the most recent months, August 2001 to February 2002, continuous data is available.

---

[8] For example, three-month forward discounts against the German mark were 2.4% for Ireland, 1.6% for Italy, 0.9% for Portugal, 0.8% for Spain. We illustrate the convergence process of the 'late' countries in the Appendix, Figure A2.

[9] EONIA stands for European overnight index average, a standardized measure of the daily overnight deposit rate in the euro area.

[10] See e.g. the various microstructure analyses in Hartmann (1998) and references therein.

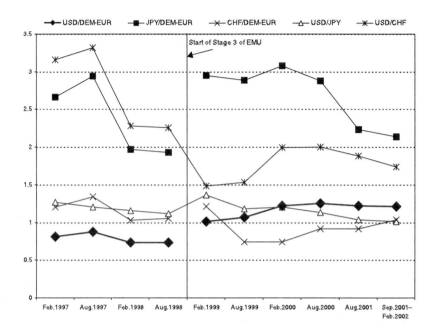

Figure 1. Traded/tradable spot foreign exchange bid-ask spreads in basis points

Source: Electronic Broking Services, ECB staff calculations.

Figure 1 displays the traded relative spread in terms of what we regard as the most reliable measure of transaction costs. We calculated the absolute spread for each second when a transaction occurred as the difference between the transacted ask and bid prices. When there was a trade only on one side of the market in this second, the spread is completed by adding the latest quoted or transacted price (whichever is closer in time) on the 'empty' side. Then the absolute spread is divided by the mid-point of the resulting spread measure, and multiplied by 10 000 to express it in basis points. Finally, the unweighted average of these spreads is taken over the respective reporting period.[11]

Spot bid-ask spreads appear to be quite variable over time. This is not surprising, since spreads can be theoretically and empirically explained in the short run by variables like exchange rate volatility, trading volume or information arrival. From a medium-term perspective, the data give no indication of permanent structural shifts

[11] We also calculate two other spread measures from the EBS data. One is the hourly measure from transaction prices used by Hau *et al.* (2002) and the other is measuring quoted spreads again at the secondly frequency. Our preferred transaction spread measure yields the narrowest spreads, the hourly transaction spreads are slightly larger and the quoted spreads are significantly larger than the other two. There are some differences in the results across spread measures. In particular, observed changes can be larger or smaller and sometimes even change sign depending on the measure used. However, our main conclusions are perfectly robust for all three measures. The full results for all spread measures and data periods are summarized in Tables A2, A3 and A4 in the Appendix.

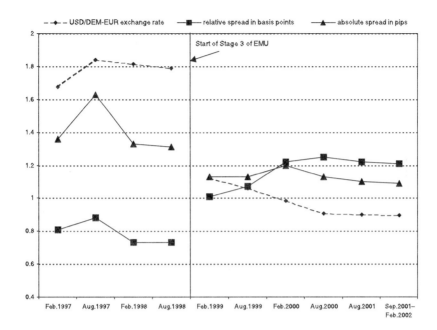

Figure 2. USD/DEM-EUR exchange rate and bid-ask spreads

Sources: Electronic Broking Services, ECB staff calculations.

in the spread between the deutschemark or euro and the yen or the Swiss franc. However, in the first two years of EMU spreads in euro-USD trading in EBS have consistently been 20–50% higher than previously observed spreads in mark-USD trading, and appear to have stabilized after a marked increase upon EMU inception.

Hence, the data do not support the idea that euro spreads are systematically higher than DEM spreads before EMU, an indicator of systematically worse liquidity of the euro, which has the potential to reduce its international use. The only market where there is so far a sustained increase in transaction costs is the EUR/USD market. This is of course a very important market, the largest foreign exchange market in the world, as was the DEM/USD market before EMU. An increase of transaction costs in this market (from 0.7–0.9 basis points to about 1.2 basis points) damages both the euro's and the dollar's liquidity, and it is obviously important to discuss what may have caused this development.

We consider the 'pip' or 'granularity' hypothesis advanced by Goodhart *et al.* (this volume) using Reuters data, approaching it in a slightly simpler way with our more comprehensive EBS data. Figure 2 shows the EUR/USD exchange rate and absolute EUR/USD spreads (in pips; i.e. in hundreds of a dollar cent per euro, the fourth digit behind the decimal point) as well as relative EUR/USD spreads (in basis points) over the whole sample period. Observe first that with the euro changeover, the average absolute spread size is now very close to 1 pip, the lowest possible spread at FX dealers' current quoting conventions and given the corresponding design of trading software. This is similar to Goodhart *et al.*'s evidence from Reuters data, and indicates that most EUR/USD spreads are now quoted at 1 pip. Second, note that since the euro changeover the relative EUR/USD spread moves inversely to the exchange rate. Third, the quoting convention was changed from DEM per USD to USD per EUR, to imply a smaller denominator for proportional bid-ask spreads. And on top of that, the euro depreciated in the first two years. The conclusion from these three observations is very similar to the one by Goodhart and others. A pip became a larger percentage of nominal exchange rates, as the typical quoted rate first jumped down, and then depreciated.

We can also check the other four spot markets for similar associations between exchange rate and spread size, but in none could we find anything comparable to the USD/EUR phenomenon. The USD/EUR market stands out in this respect, and the reason seems to lie with the peculiarly changed relationship between the market convention of a minimum spread of 1 pip and exchange rate levels.[12]

2.3. Are there signs of a vehicle currency role of the euro?

The emergence of one currency as a medium of exchange in currency trading is an important dimension of a currency's role in international financial markets, and is intimately related to a currency's trading volume and trading costs.[13] In this section we seek signs of a vehicle currency role for the euro, considering the USD and euro shares in global spot trading as well as evidence from a new data set on regional spot foreign exchange trading volumes.

From the global data it turns out that, in 2001, 98% of total inter-dealer spot volume had the USD or the euro on one side of the transactions. Hence, only these two currencies can possibly play some role as vehicle currency, and most of it must be with the USD on the global level (85% of trading). This situation closely mirrors the one with USD and DEM before EMU.

Table 4 breaks the spot interbank turnover in each trading centre in 1998 and 2001 down into the euro's (mark's) and the USD's share. The euro dominates spot interbank trading in the Nordic countries and several Central and Eastern European countries, as the DEM did before EMU. In Denmark and Norway the euro share increased to 83% and 93% compared to 1998 and in Sweden it almost remained constant at around 80%. Large euro shares between 80% and 98% also exist in the Czech Republic, Hungary, the Slovak Republic and Slovenia, with a fundamental change in Hungary from a USD-dominated market in 1998 to a euro-dominated market in 2001. These shares are so high that one can be reasonably confident that

---

[12] In the Appendix we show with a simple numerical example that no similar phenomenon is relevant in the EUR/CHF market, and we report figures similar to those displayed here for other currencies (Figures A3, A4, A5 and A6).

[13] See Swoboda (1969), Krugman (1980), Hartmann (1998), Portes and Rey (1998).

Table 4. Regional roles of dollar and euro/mark in the interbank spot foreign exchange market (in per cent of total interbank spot turnover in the respective country)

Region Country	2001				1998			
	USD Total volume[a]	EUR Total volume[a]	USD/EUR Direct volume	Residual volume[b]	USD Total volume[a]	DEM Total volume[a]	USD/DEM Direct volume	Residual volume[b]
Europe (excl. euro area)								
Western Europe								
Denmark	43.2	83.2	28.4	1.9	56.2	66.6	25.8	3.0
Norway	71.4	93.4	66.2	1.4	62.3	88.9	52.3	1.1
Sweden	46.5	78.9	29.8	4.4	42.4	80.6	31.9	9.0
Switzerland	70.2	49.0	25.9	6.6	67.3	59.9	30.1	2.8
United Kingdom	83.9	48.8	33.5	0.8	75.2	54.0	30.6	1.4
Central and Eastern Europe								
Czech Republic	39.6	91.3	31.0	0.1	24.8	87.1	13.3	1.4
Hungary	64.2	86.3	51.9	1.4	77.4	55.6	39.8	6.7
Russia	99.7	3.8	3.5	0.0	96.3	25.8	22.5	0.4
Slovak Republic	82.0	80.6	63.0	0.3	n.a.	n.a.	n.a.	n.a.
Slovenia	2.4	97.6	0.0	0.0	n.a.	n.a.	n.a.	n.a.
Turkey	91.7	70.7	62.5	0.0	n.a.	n.a.	n.a.	n.a.
Africa								
South Africa	88.1	25.0	14.3	1.1	94.1	24.2	21.6	3.3
Latin America								
Brazil	95.6	5.8	1.7	0.3	100.0	0.0	0.0	0.0
Chile	99.8	2.1	1.9	0.1	99.7	3.4	3.3	0.2
Middle East								
Bahrain	86.5	35.2	22.3	0.5	95.3	23.9	19.4	0.2
Saudi Arabia	91.7	39.1	33.6	2.8	97.2	30.3	27.8	0.3
Asia								
Hong Kong	90.9	34.0	27.8	2.9	86.1	39.9	31.1	5.1
Japan	89.3	22.9	14.0	1.8	88.6	20.0	10.0	1.3
Singapore	91.7	32.6	26.4	2.1	86.3	35.4	23.0	1.4
Thailand	98.2	5.5	4.6	0.9	94.0	5.5	3.7	4.2
India	97.8	15.5	13.8	0.5	95.3	19.0	14.7	0.4
Oceania								
Australia	94.2	18.9	14.9	1.9	91.5	24.1	18.1	2.5

Notes: This table is an updated and extended version of Table 4.2 in Hartmann (1998a, p. 83).

[a] Includes USD/EUR turnover (USD/DEM prior to 1999). A large part of this turnover has usually the respective local currency on the other side.

[b] Residual calculated as 100 − (column 2 + column 3 − column 4). Includes remaining cross-currency turnovers and gaps in reporting. Residual might show minor inconsistencies due to rounding. n.a. means not available.

Sources: Bank for International Settlements, national central banks, ECB staff calculations.

the euro plays a role as a vehicle currency between the respective home currencies and some outside currencies, in particular other European currencies.[14]

For all other countries around the globe that we can cover, the USD clearly dominates trading. This is particularly the case for Asia, the Middle East, North and Latin America; in the European periphery, there are also a few countries that are USD dominated, in particular Russia and perhaps to a lesser extent Turkey (see Table 4). Again, the picture closely corresponds to the situation prevailing before the introduction of the euro. In the Appendix we show that these observations are robust for a larger number of countries per region and for a longer period before EMU, including 1992 and 1995 (see Table A5). In trading with non-EMU currencies, the euro's role closely resembles the earlier one of the deutschemark.

3. INTERNATIONAL BOND AND MONEY MARKETS

In this section we briefly broaden the picture beyond the foreign exchange market. Earlier studies found evidence of increasing use of the euro as an international debt financing currency combined with a relatively constant role in international bond investment (Detken and Hartmann, 2000; Hartmann and Issing, 2002). Here, we ascertain the robustness of these findings on the basis of updated empirical information and in light of a new data set.[15]

Figure 3 displays the main currencies' shares in the stock of bonds and money market instruments outstanding that has been issued by non-residents (international financing currency use). The data cover corporate and sovereign issuance from five years before the introduction of the euro to more than three years afterwards, and a 'synthetic euro' share can be computed for the period before January 1999. The euro share displays an increasing trend, starting in 1998, and grows by almost 10 percentage points reaching 29% of the world total by early 2002. Most of this stock change came at the expense of the Japanese yen, which declines visibly (to 13%), and only little at the expense of the USD so far (now 43%). Flow data are very volatile (for bonds), however it bears mentioning that the flow of euro-denominated external issuance jumped up quite significantly in early 1999.[16]

The economic explanation for the increased international issuance of euro denominated bonds, notes and money market instruments can probably be found in the unification of the bond demand side through the introduction of the single currency in the euro area. Apparently liability managers found greater liquidity in the euro bond market than was the case for the previous national bond markets, which were separated

---

[14] As an anonymous referee rightly pointed out to us, a forex vehicle role cannot be ascertained from aggregated data. However, we see in Table 4 that there are several cases (Czech Republic, Denmark, Slovenia, Sweden) in which euro trading, even excluding all direct EUR/USD volume, exceeds dollar trading substantially. This is an indicator of some vehicle role for the euro, although it is of course quite impossible to say anything about the exact quantitative dimension of it. Qualitatively, the point also applies to the dollar, but the quantities around the globe are probably less ambiguous.

[15] A strong increase in euro denominated bond issuance at the beginning of stage 3 of EMU (not corrected for home currency financing) was first reported in BIS (1996b) and Bishop (1999), and confirmed conjectures by McCauley (1997, p. 42).

[16] For a detailed picture of the corresponding flows see the Appendix, Figures A7 (bonds) and A8 (money market instruments).

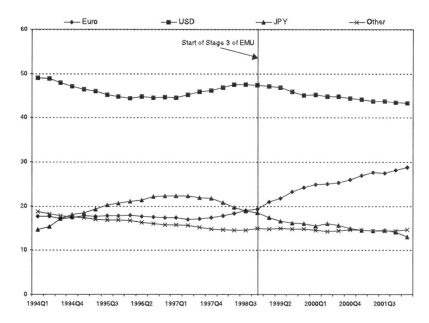

Figure 3. Currency shares in international debt securities, excluding home currency issuance (amounts outstanding at constant end of 1994Q1 exchange rates, in per cent of total, 1994Q1 to 2002Q1)

Note: Time series derived following Detken and Hartmann (2000).

Sources: Bank for International Settlements, own calculations.

through different currencies. In fact, as Santos and Tsatsaronis (2002) argue, non-resident entry by corporate bond underwriters brought down underwriting fees in euro/legacy currencies from very high levels to levels closely in line with those in the dollar-denominated segment. So, it seems that the external underwriters anticipated the increased attractiveness of a unified domestic demand side and through their entry made the euro-denominated market much more competitive than previously the case. Although this evidence suggests a structural change in the primary euro bond market, which may well have permanent effects, only the future can tell whether the euro's international financing use will remain at the current levels.

Let us now turn to the investment side. We first report in Figure 4 the bond holdings by 8–9 major international fund managers, as provided quarterly by *The Economist* magazine. After a brief 'in-and-out' behaviour in the first quarter of 1999 the euro's share in bond investments stabilized around one quarter to one third of the total, compared to a 50% share of the USD and roughly a 15% share for the yen. Since in these data the 'euro' only included the DEM and French franc before the fourth quarter of 1998, it turns out that since the introduction of the euro its share is close to the previous aggregate of legacy currencies.

Since Figure 4 is limited to only a few large fund managers, we also tapped a new database by Capital Access International (2002). From this source a currency breakdown of international bond investments could be calculated for the last quarter

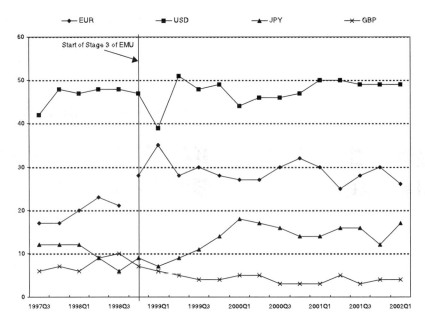

Figure 4. Currency shares in bond holdings by a small sample of large fund managers (in per cent of total, 1997Q3–2002Q1)

Note: Euro before 1998Q4 equals the sum of DEM and FRF only (structural break). Note that these data are uncorrected for holdings in domestic currency, because of the global character of the 8–9 institutions polled. Thus no correction for EMU effects prior to 1999 is undertaken.

Sources: *The Economist*, own calculations.

Table 5. Currency shares in international bond investments (end 2001)

	Amount (USD)	Share
EUR	59.488.853	24.51
USD	115.581.505	47.62
JPY	48.187.881	19.85
GBP	17.718.817	7.30
CHF	1.751.405	0.72
Total	242.728.461	100.00

Notes: Bond holdings of non-residents of the country issuing the respective currency. Data exclude foreign currency bond holdings of Japanese firms, i.e. currency shares represent an upper bound for JPY and lower bounds for all other currencies.

Source: Capital Access International (2002).

of 2001 (Table 5). It should be kept in mind that while the database has generally broad coverage (including a broad mix of financial firms in Europe and North America), it does not include much information on foreign currency bond holdings by Asian, in particular Japanese firms. As a consequence the currency shares reported constitute upper bounds for the yen and lower bounds for USD and euro. So, at least one quarter of international bond investment is in euro and at least 48% in USD. Less than 20% are in yen. In other words, the new Capital Access data seem to confirm the picture provided by *The Economist* portfolio poll.

The static character of international bond investments does not call for a detailed economic interpretation. Our earlier analysis of 1998 and 1999 return correlations did not imply any dramatic adjustments in global portfolio investments, while Kool (2000) found with a mean-variance framework (using data from the first half of 1999) that some net euro disinvestment could occur. Our bond investment data do not bear out the latter effect. The data in Figures 3 and 4 as well as Table 5 show that the euro's bond financing share merely caught up with the investment share, and future research could fruitfully explore why international euro financing developed so much faster than international euro investment.

4. CONCLUSIONS

Our broad approach to all available data strives to offer a comprehensive picture, even for market microstructure issues, and to avoid possible pitfalls from consideration of specific market segments or trading systems.

We find that in global spot foreign exchange markets the euro's relative role closely resembles that of the deutschemark before EMU, and features a dominant position in spot trading (with a likely role as a vehicle currency) in the Nordic and several Central European countries. As to trading spreads, only USD-euro transaction costs appear to have increased permanently. Building on the contribution by Goodhart *et al.* in this volume, our data confirm that this phenomenon may be explained by a combination of the persistence of 'granular' quoting conventions, establishing a lower bound for absolute spreads, with the inversion of the USD-euro exchange rate and the appreciation of the dollar. We also find that the share of euro foreign exchange swap trading is substantially smaller than that of its predecessor 'legacy' currencies. We argue that this may be explained by another arithmetic effect related to the elimination of USD swap trades meant to hedge exchange rate risk between legacy currencies, a final wave of convergence trading in the run-up to EMU and by financial innovation.

International euro bond investments remain static at about the level of the pre-stage 3 aggregate. Unification of the domestic demand side appears to be the most relevant explanation for the so far sustained increase in international euro financing activity. Overall, the euro remains on a gradualist path towards developing its role in international financial markets.

APPENDIX

See http://www.economic-policy.org.

DISCUSSION AND REFERENCES

The Discussion and References for the three 'Forex markets and the euro' papers appear on pages 592–7.

Forex markets and the euro

Theoretical perspective

SUMMARY

I provide theoretical perspective on recent findings of increased transaction costs in the new dollar-euro market relative to the prior dollar-mark market, and assess the welfare significance of this drop in liquidity. In theory, transaction costs arise from information disadvantage costs, inventory management costs, and other market-making costs (e.g., order-processing costs). A review of theoretical reasons for the underlying costs to be rising can allow one to discriminate among hypotheses for the liquidity drop. New data on public trades support a customer liquidity hypothesis, based on the idea that the ultimate providers of liquidity in this market are customers rather than market-makers. However, the hypothesis is not consistent with the totality of the evidence, and I discuss how a combination of various mechanisms can influence transaction costs and the FX market's information efficiency.

— *Richard K. Lyons*

Economic Policy October 2002 Printed in Great Britain
© CEPR, CES, MSH, 2002.

Theoretical perspective on euro liquidity

Richard K. Lyons

U.C. Berkeley

1. INTRODUCTION

I used to view bid-ask spreads in foreign exchange as a nuisance parameter, bad manners next to an otherwise elegant approach. Anyone sharing this view will find it curious, then, that recent empirical work on FX spreads should cause such a stir. Two papers published in this journal find that there has been an increase in transaction costs in the new dollar-euro market relative to the prior dollar-mark market: Hau, Killeen and Moore (2002a), hereafter HKM, and Goodhart *et al.* (this issue). My objective in this paper is to frame the theoretical and welfare significance of such changes in liquidity.[1] How does theory help us to identify the underlying causes of changing transaction costs? And, whatever the cause, why should anyone care, since transaction costs in these markets are and remain very small?

To answer these two questions, one needs to examine the supply side of the market for liquidity. Transaction costs (i.e., the size of bid-ask spreads as a function of trade

For helpful comments I thank Rich Adams, Carsten Detken, Philipp Hartmann, Michael Moore, Ken Rogoff, two anonymous referees, the Managing Editors, and participants in the April 2002 *Economic Policy* Panel Meeting. I also thank the US National Science Foundation for financial assistance.

Giuseppe Bertola was the Managing Editor for this paper.

[1] Versus addressing the empirical finding's robustness. Accordingly, I focus instead on interpreting the finding and its welfare implications. Though robustness of the initial HKM finding was hotly contested (see the discussion in Hau *et al.*, 2002 by Honohan and Franks, and especially Portes's comments), recent confirming evidence by Detken and Hartmann (this issue) that dollar-euro spreads did increase, has shifted attention toward identifying underlying causes and implications.

size) are composed of three underlying costs of liquidity provision, the economics of which are quite different. These component costs arise due to market-maker information disadvantage, market-maker inventory management, and other market-making costs.

To understand how information disadvantage bears on bid-ask spreads, consider a simple example. As a market-maker, you are asked to provide a bid-ask quote for a $100 million trade. If your counterparty chooses to sell, you are now long $100 million. But if at the same time that counterparty was also selling $100 million to nine other market-makers, then the market price would likely to move downwards to induce steady-state absorption of the $1 billion position.[2] Being long dollars as the market price is falling is clearly costly. To protect yourself, you need to widen your initial spread: this way, when your counterparty's sale is only $100 million in total (and the exchange rate move will be negligible) you make enough money to cover losses when your counterparty's total sale is much more than $100 million.

To understand the role of market-maker inventory management, suppose you know the counterparty's trade was only $100 million in total, so the subsequent market price is just about as likely to move in your favour as it is to move against you. But because you are risk averse, you would still like to restore your inventory to a neutral 'flat' position. One way to do so is to lower your subsequent bid-ask quotes, to increase the likelihood that the next person requesting a quote will buy and thereby take the position off your hands. This shading of your price, of course, is also costly, and needs to be factored into the width of your initial quote.

Finally, the 'Other' market-making cost component is a catch-all that captures traditional price factors from the theory of industrial organization.[3] These factors include costs of back-office trade processing, such as clearing and settlement, which have both fixed and variable components; market-maker salaries; and – if the market is less than perfectly competitive – market-maker profits.

Having defined the three cost components, one can turn to theory for guidance on identifying which component or combination of components is driving the spread increase.[4] This is important not only for discriminating among the theories, but also from a welfare perspective. If, for example, the increase in spreads is due to an increase in market-maker information disadvantage, this may indicate lower market resiliency: as information asymmetries become more acute, models show that market

---

[2] Absorption by the quoting market-makers is transitory – most FX market-makers hold positions only intraday – hence my addition of the term 'steady state'. Note too that the counterparty need not trade the full $1 billion simultaneously: until the quoting market-maker rids himself of the $100 million long position, subsequent sales by the quote-hitting counterparty will continue to produce losses.

[3] The first cost component is non-traditional in that it involves asymmetric information, whereas the second is non-traditional in that it involves producer risk aversion.

[4] HKM offer a model – the increased transparency hypothesis – that predicts that the spread increase is due to additional costs of inventory management. One can test whether this prediction is borne out, i.e., whether the spread component that increased was indeed the inventory management component. I return to this below.

breakdowns, or other liquidity collapses, become more likely.[5] Note too that identifying the cause of increasing spreads will help determine whether an increase is likely to persist – obviously relevant for determining welfare significance.

In the context of my theoretical overview I also offer a model of increasing spreads that is qualitatively different from those considered in previous work. This 'customer liquidity hypothesis' views increasing spreads as an increase in market-maker *costs*, rather than an increase in market-maker *profits*, as would typically be implied by the price granularity hypothesis offered by Goodhart *et al.* I test implications of the customer liquidity hypothesis using new data on public trades from January 1998 to December 2000 and find them borne out.

A second issue for which transaction costs are relevant involves the FX market's information efficiency. In traditional models of exchange rate determination, transactions *per se* play no role in price determination. Rather, because all information relevant to exchange rates is publicly observed, shifts in that information induce demand and price shifts without actual transactions causing the movement in price. In that information environment – which rules out the type of market-maker information disadvantage described above – transactions convey no incremental information, making them irrelevant to fundamentals and price. But assuming all price-relevant information to be shared by all market participants is rather simplistic. For perspective, consider the following question: Does the foreign exchange market aggregate information? Of course it does; that's what all securities markets do. There are thousands of bits of dispersed information that are relevant for market clearing prices (such as banks' changing risk preferences, firms' changing hedging demands, and individuals' changing interpretations of macro news). This dispersed information is transmitted to prices via the trading process. If increased transaction costs alter the trades process (e.g., by altering trades' signal-to-noise ratios), then this will affect prices, even over long horizons.[6] Then, spreads are not simply a nuisance parameter, but can affect the determination of price *levels* (a point also made by Romer 1993, who shows how small transaction costs impede large, warranted adjustments in asset prices). Given there is no exchange rate other than the one that these market-makers quote, their models for processing market information deserve attention.

The remainder of this paper is in four sections. Section 2 summarizes the theory of spread determination, including the extent to which that theory is relevant to the spot FX market (as opposed to equity markets, for example, many of which are organized differently than FX). Section 3 applies the theoretical guidance from Section 2 to the

---

[5] One needs only to remember the dramatic reduction of liquidity that occurred in the dollar/yen market in the wake of the LTCM collapse to recognize that major FX markets are not immune to such events. On a single day in early October 1998, the yen price of a dollar fell from over 130 to under 120 and persisted at that new level, with spreads in that market at the time being about 50 times their usual size (roughly 1 yen versus a typical spread for $10 million transactions around 0.02 yen). For an analysis, see Cai *et al.* (2001).

[6] For empirical evidence that the trades process affects exchange rates over longer horizons, see Evans and Lyons (2002a), Payne (1999), Rime (2000), Killeen *et al.* (2001), and Froot and Ramadorai (2001).

empirical result that dollar (USD)/euro (EUR) spreads have increased from those in USD/deutschemark (DEM). Specifically, what prescriptions does theory offer for disentangling different spread components, and in so doing, disentangling the competing theoretical explanations? Section 4 turns to the 'Why-should-we-care?' question. Perspective developed in Sections 2 and 3 are essential for addressing this question. Broken into parts, the substantive welfare considerations can be separated from those of lesser significance. Section 5 concludes with some thoughts on the open questions and how interested researchers might address those open questions.

2. THEORY OF SPREAD COMPONENTS

As noted, microstructure theory breaks bid-ask spreads into three components: information disadvantage, inventory management, and other market-making costs (such as order-processing costs and rents). Understanding what these components are and how to identify them will help us discriminate among theoretical explanations for the increasing spreads result.[7] The remainder of this section is a brief review of that underlying spread theory, including its relevance for FX markets (as opposed to equity markets, for which much of it was developed).

To be precise, theory that addresses these three components is split into three rather distinct approaches. Each approach demonstrates how non-zero spreads can arise even when the only factor driving spreads is the factor focused on by that approach. For example, the literature treating asymmetric information begins by assuming that market-makers are risk neutral and bear no other costs of carrying inventory, so that inventory management is a non-issue. This literature also assumes that market-makers bear no other costs of market-making (like salary or back-office costs), and are forced by competition to price their market-making services with zero profit. In this setting, the only factor driving non-zero spreads is the market-maker's need to protect himself from information disadvantage (i.e., trading with someone better informed about future prices). Though these theoretical approaches generate their respective spread components in isolation, empiricists have devised methods of disentangling them in the data. The first part of this section follows the theory in motivating each of the three components in a 'pure' setting. The later part clarifies how empiricists disentangle them in the data.

2.1. Spotlight on each component

To understand the component of spreads arising from market-maker information disadvantage, consider the trading losses a market-maker might face.[8] For example,

---

[7] The three-component structure of spreads theory is never explicitly recognized in the HKM paper or the published comments on HKM, hence my choice to use it as an organizing framework in this paper. Of course, that structure is well known, see Huang and Stoll (1997) for a review. In the FX setting, see the analysis by Hartmann (1998a, pp. 134–35; 1999) of how transaction volume can affect each of the three spread components.

[8] Theoretical literature uses the term 'effective spreads' to denote the spread that is operative at all trade sizes, i.e., it is the market-maker's quoted price schedule as a function of order sizes from $-\infty$ to ∞ (negative sign denotes an incoming sell order).

in the canonical market-maker model of Glosten and Milgrom (1985), the market-maker faces a pool of potential counterparties, some of whom have superior information relevant to future prices. Because the market-maker cannot distinguish those who are better informed from those who are not, the market-maker quotes a spread wide enough so that losses to informed traders are balanced against spread revenues from traders with no special information. In that model the spread arises wholly because of this information asymmetry (the market-maker is assumed risk neutral, and faces no other costs, such as settlement costs, back-office costs, cost of this time).

The inventory cost component of the spread is best understood using models from the inventory-control branch of microstructure theory. (See, for example, the multiple-market-maker inventory model of Ho and Stoll, 1983.) In these models, market-makers are risk averse (in contrast to the risk neutrality assumed in the Glosten–Milgrom model) and therefore have to be compensated for temporarily absorbing risky positions (mismatches in non-market-maker supply and demand). The spread that arises in these models is wholly due to this compensation for taking risk; there are no information asymmetries (by assumption), and no other costs of market-making. For technical convenience, some models replace risk-averse market-makers with risk-neutral market-makers who face some unspecified inventory 'hold-ing' cost; qualitatively, the results are quite similar.

The third 'other' component is more of a catch-all category than a specific type of cost. The earliest models of market-makers focus on costs in the traditional sense of production costs: labour costs, input costs such as back-office services, etc. (e.g., Demsetz, 1968). Spreads arise in these models to produce the revenues that cover these costs. This cost category is a catch-all in that a market-maker's production function can involve many types of input cost (some fixed, some variable). Moreover, if market-making is not perfectly competitive, then spreads (revenues) will also include some monopoly profit. This, too, is lumped into the order-processing cost category (a point I return to when evaluating Goodhart *et al.*'s price granularity hypothesis).

Empiricists do not have the luxury of considering spread components in isolation: their methods have to accommodate all the components and distinguish between them. A popular method for doing so goes by the name of the 'trade indicator' approach (Glosten and Harris, 1988; Huang and Stoll, 1997). Perhaps the best way to communicate how the trade indicator approach accomplishes this is to do so graphically. Suppose the only cost component that enters the spread is that arising from information disadvantage. The top panel of Figure 1 provides an illustration. The figure shows the path of bid and ask prices over time, as well as the bid-ask midpoint. In this context, a customer sell order (denoted with the solid dot at the market-maker's bid price) pushes the market-maker's beliefs about future market prices down, inducing him to lower his subsequent bid and ask quotes. This adjust-ment in quoted prices persists as long as the shift in the market-maker's beliefs

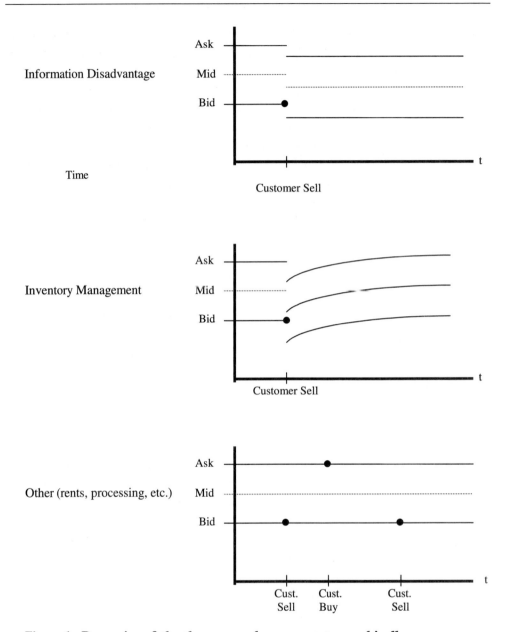

Figure 1. Dynamics of the three spread components graphically

persists.[9] (The underlying information can be any information that has persistent price effects; more on specific FX examples below.)

Now consider the case in which the spread arises because of costs from inventory management only. In this case too, the market-maker's bid and offer prices fall (see

---

[9] Price can of course be moving over time for other reasons. I hold these other reasons constant in the figure to highlight this specific source of transaction-price variation.

the middle panel of Figure 1). This is the inventory effect that is standard in the microstructure literature: after the customer's sell order, the market-maker is long (or at least longer than he was), so to restore his previous position the market-maker lowers his quotes. This induces subsequent customer purchases at those lower prices (subsequent transaction dots not shown), which returns the market-maker's position gradually to its original level.[10] Once restored, the original prices are restored, illustrating the transitory and position-dependent nature of inventory effects.

Finally, suppose the only cost component that enters the spread is the set of 'Other' costs such as those arising from order processing or market-maker profits. The bottom of Figure 1 provides an illustration of how the sequence of transaction prices would look if this were the only component. Because order flow conveys no information in this case, nor is there any inventory cost, the only connection between transaction prices and order flow is the bouncing of transaction prices from bid to ask (so-called bid-ask bounce). Transactions induce no changes in subsequent bid-ask quotes or quote midpoints.

It is important to note that innovations to public information (e.g., news about macroeconomic variables) are not reflected in any of the three panels of Figure 1. Prices can and certainly do change in response to public macro news. But in a rational expectations world, information of this type should move price *for reasons orthogonal to transaction flow* (i.e., price adjustments are not dependent on the flow of executed trades). This type of price movement is treated as an unexplained residual in microstructure models. How important is this direct channel between macro news and exchange rates empirically? The largely disappointing event-study literature on macro-news effects on exchange rates suggests that this channel is not as important as theory would suggest. More directly, Evans and Lyons (2002b) estimate that order flow accounts for about 65% of daily variation in the (log) daily DEM/USD rate, whereas the direct effect of macro announcements on the DEM/USD rate accounts for only about 10%. The evidence suggests that direct price effects from public information shocks do not swamp order-flow effects, as one might presume, and instead appear to be swamped by them.

To my knowledge, the trade-indicator approach has not yet been applied to FX markets. The difficulty is data availability. In particular, one needs data for constructing the indicator variable that captures the direction of trade (i.e., identifies which side is quoting and which side is the initiator who acts on the quote). In addition, one needs data on the quoted spreads that produced the transaction price data. I do not know of any data set currently in use that fulfills these two criteria over a sample period spanning the euro's launch. But such a data set certainly could be constructed (e.g., from EBS transaction data).

---

[10] In this case, too, prices can be moving over time for other reasons. Also, the figure assumes that the width of the spread does not change. This is the simplest case and can be shown to hold in some inventory models. It is not a general property of inventory models however. See O'Hara (1995) for more detail along these lines.

	Risk-neutral Fundamentals	**Risk-related Fundamentals**
Concentrated Information		
Dispersed Information		

Figure 2. Partitioning the class of private information

2.2. Non-public information in FX: dispersed versus concentrated

This is all well and good, you say, but why is asymmetric information relevant to the FX market? After all, asymmetric-information models of equity trading were devised to understand things like insider trading in individual stocks. Insider trading of that kind simply doesn't exist in FX markets.

This is a good question. Answering it requires a bit more perspective on the information environment of the FX market. For most financial economists, information comes in two forms, public and private. I would like to provide a bit more detail within the private information category.

Private information can be split into the 2 × 2 classification shown in Figure 2. When people claim that private information in FX does not exist, they have in mind the upper left-hand cell of this diagram. By risk-neutral fundamentals, I mean any variable that would drive price determination in a risk-neutral world. In the case of a stock, this is essentially the expectation of future dividends. In FX, the equivalent is any variable that would drive prices in, for example, a monetary model with no risk premium, i.e., future interest differentials, money supplies and real outputs. For a stock, it is natural that concentrated inside information about a firm's earnings and dividends may be conveyed by the trades of those people who have that information (see, e.g., the celebrated model of insider trading by Kyle, 1985). However, it is hard to imagine that such phenomena play a major role in the major FX markets, where concentrated inside information would have to concern (for example) future interest-rate movements.

The lower right-hand cell is where the action is likely to be in FX markets: dispersed information about risk-related fundamentals (or, in the terms of modern asset pricing, information about 'stochastic discount factors'). This includes dispersed information about any variables that determine risk premia. Examples include information about participants' risk aversions, hedging demands, money demands, or even transaction demands (all of which would *persistently* affect the equilibrium exchange rate in traditional portfolio-balance models of risk premia).[11] Note, however, that although this information is initially dispersed, it is not aggregated and impounded in price in a single step. Rather, dispersed information about these variables is first impounded in the customer orders received by FX market-makers, which constitutes roughly one-third of total trading volume in the major markets. Importantly, the rest of the market does not observe these initial customer orders (there are no disclosure or other transparency regulations in the major FX markets). The engendered trades between market-makers, which account for the remaining two-thirds of total volume, now involve increasingly concentrated information, giving rise to the types of information asymmetries that motivate information-based trading models.

Aggregating dispersed information is one of asset markets' central functions.[12] Yet models of exchange rate determination abstract completely from this aggregation. These models (e.g., monetary models, portfolio balance models, new open-economy macro models) posit an information environment in which all relevant information is publicly known. This approach is sensible if the abstraction misses little, i.e., if dispersed information is rapidly summarized in the public macro variables we rely on to estimate our models. Only recently has this common assumption been subjected to scrutiny, and empirical work on exchange rates using what I call the 'dispersed information approach' has enjoyed some success. This work relies on micro models of how, specifically, asset markets accomplish information aggregation. When coupled with the poor performance of public information models, these positive results imply that the above assumption – that dispersed information is rapidly summarized in public information – is dubious.

3. POSITIONING INCREASING SPREADS WITHIN THE BROADER THEORY

Let me begin this section by reviewing the theory that HKM (2002a) offer to account for the increase in transaction costs in the new USD-EUR market.[13] Their market transparency model accounts for increasing spreads through an increase in inventory management costs, i.e., the second of the three components in the framework presented above. The model is not based on increasing transparency of the USD-EUR market *per se* relative to the USD-DEM market. Rather, it is based on a reduction in market-makers' ability to trade in multiple markets. Pre-euro, market-makers had the ability to trade in both USD/DEM and in markets where the USD was exchanged for

[11] For a survey of the portfolio balance approach to exchange rates, see Branson and Henderson (1985).

[12] Nobel laureate Friedrich Hayek (1945) provides an early and powerful articulation of this point: 'the problem of rational economic order is determined precisely by the fact that knowledge of the circumstances of which we must make use never exists in concentrated or integrated form, but solely as dispersed bits of incomplete and frequently contradictory knowledge which all the separate individuals possess. The economic problem of society is thus a problem of the utilization of knowledge not given to anyone in its totality.'

[13] The authors of HKM (2002a) offer a broader menu of theoretical rationales for their result in HKM (2002b). A possibility related to the transparency hypothesis in HKM (2002a) focuses on market-makers in USD/otherEMS markets rather than those in USD/DEM. Specifically, market-makers in USD/otherEMS markets were surely using the USD/DEM for hedging, thereby injecting liquidity into the USD/DEM market.

European Monetary System (EMS) currencies other than the DEM. With the launch of the euro, all of the USD/otherEMS markets disappeared, making the management of inventory by USD/EUR market-makers more difficult (or 'costly', from the perspective of the previous section).[14] This increase in cost was passed on in their spreads.

Note that if their model is correct, then the increase in spreads should not only increase the total spread, it should increase a particular component of the spread, namely that due to inventory management costs. This is inherently testable. One could make use of the Huang and Stoll (1997) extension of the trade indicator approach, which allows a disentangling of the asymmetric information and inventory management spread components.

Consider the alternative hypotheses that were proposed by discussants and others at the Panel meeting that addressed the HKM paper and how these hypotheses fit into the three-component framework. In his comment on HKM, Honohan proposes another inventory-based rationalization when he alludes to an increase in 'uncertainty about how smoothly the operating procedures of the European Central Bank would work'. This idea could be formalized with an increase in *ex ante* conditional variance, increasing the cost of inventory management, and increasing the inventory-management component of the spread to cover those costs.[15] However, Honohan adopts a hybrid perspective when he suggests 'heightened uncertainty is also compatible with the finding that information embodied in order flow could have become more significant.' For this additional channel to be operative, the key role is not that of increased policy uncertainty, but rather that of higher information content about policy (dollar for dollar) in market trades. In this case, part of the spread increase is coming from the increase in costs from information disadvantage, a conceptually distinct type of cost.

This information channel can be activated not only by the increase in macro uncertainty put forward by Honohan, but also by uncertainty about what I will term micro portfolio balance effects. In a world where different-currency assets are imperfect substitutes, shocks to asset demands shift equilibrium exchange rates. Importantly, those shocks to asset demands need not be public information, and in the case of euro-denominated assets, those shocks were most assuredly not public information. Rather, as thousands of portfolios were being adjusted in response to the euro launch, signals of these adjustments were reaching the FX market in the form of order flow.

---

[14] 'Transparency' enters in their model because (by assumption) USD/DEM market-makers are able to dispose of unwanted inventory discreetly through the USD/otherEMS markets, with less price impact than if they had used the USD/DEM market directly. These other markets could provide a proxy hedge because the EMS currencies were pegged to one another. As they note, part of the reduction in price impact from this indirect trading can come from reducing other market-makers' ability to forecast one's trades. When trades are forecastable, other market-makers will have incentives to trade in advance of them (i.e., front run), thereby causing prices to move against the inventory-managing market-maker before he gets rid of the full position. See Hirschleifer (1971) on the fascinating question of how greater revelation of information may be welfare reducing in that it can impede risk sharing.

[15] Using realized volatilities, HKM do provide some evidence (Table 4) that volatility did not have the spread effect in USD/euro that the Honohan model would predict.

Think, for example, of global bond fund managers shifting their allocations in response to near-perfect correlation of Euroland term structures. These potentially permanent portfolio shifts engender long-lived exchange rate effects, making the price impact of order-flow dollars larger. Under this model, too, the information cost of market-making would increase, inducing market-makers to quote larger total spreads.[16]

Another model proposed at the earlier Panel meeting involves an increase in the 'Other' component of the spread. Recall that this component is a catch-all, and one element it catches is market-maker rents. De Ménil suggested that increasing bank concentration could be the root cause of the increase in spreads. If this were true, then one would expect an increase in the Other component, an inherently testable prediction (see Weston, 2000). Honohan also suggested that rents might have increased when he pointed out the possibility that discreteness may be behind the increase in the spread (one 1/100th of a US cent is worth more than 1/100th of a German pfennig), which is the 'price granularity hypothesis' echoed and tested by Goodhart *et al*. This, too, should manifest as an increase in the Other component of spreads, and I discuss the point further below.

Thus, when surveyed, the models in the HKM paper and those offered by Panel participants span all three of the theoretical approaches to spread determination. Another possible explanation tends more in the direction of spread *measurement* and deserves mention for completeness. Even if spreads did increase for brokered trading between market-makers (the source of the HKM and Goodhart *et al*. data), they may not have increased for other trading, for example, direct bilateral trading between market-makers. It may be that in response to the euro's launch market-makers substituted away from the multilateral broker systems and toward bilateral trading. It is common for market-makers to do this in times of heightened uncertainty, because placing limit orders on an electronic broking system like EBS is like writing a free option available to other market-makers, an option that becomes more valuable to those other market-makers as volatility rises. If so, then one would expect spreads to increase on broker systems as liquidity is drained away from them. One would also expect greater price impact per dollar traded on EBS (another of the HKM findings) because the EBS limit-order book provides less quantity available at any given price, causing arriving orders to eat further into the book (more price impact).

3.1. The price granularity hypothesis

If increased spreads were indeed a more or less mechanical implication of discrete quoting convention, one might be tempted to think that the microstructure theory outlined above is beside the point. Not true. Indeed, as suggested by the discussion

---

[16] Note that individual contributions to this aggregate portfolio shift are dispersed across many market participants, it is not necessary (or likely) that trading by any particular customers would be strategic.

of HKM by Honohan and the more focused treatment in Goodhart *et al.* (this issue), it is natural to associate price granularity of this type with market-maker rents. Market-maker rents, in turn, play a clear and identifiable role within the three-component theoretical framework outlined above. In fact, a prediction quite similar to that of the granularity hypothesis was recently tested in the Nasdaq equity market by Weston (2000). He asks whether competition-increasing reforms on the Nasdaq reduced effective spreads by, in particular, reducing the Other component of the spread (which is what one would expect if pre-reform competition among market-makers was less than perfect). He finds that not only did spreads fall, but the reduction was in fact due to the Other component, consistent with pre-reform spreads having a significant rent component. The bottom line is that theoretical spread decomposition provides a concrete way to address the granularity hypothesis empirically.

Let me turn to the two arguments offered by HKM against the granularity hypothesis. The first is that the euro launch also increased spreads in the Japanese yen (JPY)/EUR market (relative to JPY/DEM), despite these markets not having undergone a shift in the pip numeraire (both were, and still are, quoted in JPY pips). If the percentage spread increase were due purely to granularity in the change of numeraire, as the analysis of Goodhart *et al.* suggests, then we should not have observed this increase in JPY/EUR spreads, while the increase in JPY/EUR spreads is consistent with the HKM increased transparency hypothesis. Though an appealing argument, I do not find it as compelling as I did at first blush. For example, suppose the increase in USD/EUR spreads were in fact due to price granularity, as the Goodhart *et al.* results suggest, then wouldn't we *expect* to find an increase in JPY/EUR spreads for exactly the kind of increased-cost-of-risk-management reasons that underlie the increased transparency hypothesis? If a market-maker in JPY/DEM (now JPY/EUR) finds it more expensive to hedge positions through the USD/EUR market than it was in USD/DEM, he would pass this increased cost on in his JPY/EUR spreads. Thus, spread increases in JPY/EUR (if any) need not undermine the granularity hypothesis.

The second argument offered by HKM against the granularity hypothesis is that spreads of 2–3 pips are not so plausible as minimum boundaries for pip-spreads. Even a 1 pip spread (to 4 decimal places) is not a minimum, they argue, because market-makers are free to quote to the fifth decimal place (for both direct trading between market-makers and for brokered trading between market-makers). This is an essential issue in the debate. I would add only two (small) points that make this argument, too, less than fully compelling, at least in my judgment. First, in models of less-than-perfect competition (a modelling approach suggested by the granularity hypothesis, as noted above), the condition under which spreads (to four decimal places) would not be reduced another pip should be determined by a non-negative profit constraint. For example, under normal market conditions profits could be negative at 1 or 2 pips but not at 3 pips, leaving 3 pips as a plausible equilibrium. Second, market-makers may not move to 5 decimals because this imposes additional costs: communication costs, negotiation costs, and costs of foregone flexibility. (For models of market-maker costs of these types see Harris, 1991 and Grossman *et al.*, 1997.) Trading spot FX is, after all, a ferociously intense endeavour. Once these incremental costs are considered, sticking to 4-decimal spreads might be privately optimal – but not necessarily socially optimal, with important policy implications: for related issues in equity markets that have engendered some of the strongest policy responses in decades, see Christie and Schultz (1994), Christie *et al.* (1994), and Barclay *et al.* (1999).

What should one make of the granularity hypothesis? I offer three distinct thoughts. First, while apparently elegant, the granularity hypothesis is only elegant at its surface. Theoretically minded readers cannot help but be puzzled by how a substantial increase in rents could be sustained in such a competitive environment (my comments above about moving to 5 digits notwithstanding). Until more theoretical progress is made on that front, it seems hard to subscribe to the granularity hypothesis in any substantial way, given the Detken–Hartmann results regarding persistence of the spread increase. Second, one has to ask about the *power* of the granularity hypothesis test. That is, suppose the true driver of the spread increase is an increase in inventory management cost (e.g., some combination of the transparency hypothesis of HKM and another hypothesis I outline in the next paragraph). If the percentage increase in inventory costs were within a wide band around the percentage spread change implied by constant pip-spreads, then one would (mistakenly) accept the simple granularity explanation. There is a real power issue here, given the nature of the data Goodhart *et al.* bring to bear.

Third, I would add that my views about the granularity hypothesis are heavily conditioned by conversations I have had with FX market practitioners (both spot market-makers and proprietary desk traders). A common view from the trenches is that percentage spreads in spot USD/EUR were indeed higher in the first months of 1999, but that those spreads have likely settled down. One specific comment by the manager of a proprietary trading desk caught my attention, and is something to which hard numbers can be brought to bear. Specifically, this trader told me that the book of limit orders submitted to his bank by customers in USD/DEM, normally very full, was virtually empty at the changeover of 1 January 1999. It seems that customers did not want to provide these limit orders – which amount to the provision of liquidity to the market-making community – at a time of such radical transition.[17] Participants were less certain about how the new currency would actually trade, including uncertainty about (1) limit order execution, (2) the meaning of 'best efforts' by market-makers, and (3) the flow supply of liquidity to the market by other participants. He also said that it took several months for their customer limit book in USD/EUR to look as full as was normal in USD/DEM.

---

[17] While macro institutions like the European Central Bank were in place well before 1 January 1999, the trading environment changed abruptly on that date.

3.2. The customer liquidity hypothesis

This observation leads me to consider a complementary explanation, namely the possibility that percentage spreads increased following the euro's launch because of an increase in market-maker *costs*, in particular, an increase in the costs of providing liquidity at the marketwide level. Customer unwillingness to provide this market with lower-frequency liquidity by submitting limit orders could well have made it more difficult for market-makers to share position risk with the broader market. Then, more costly management of inventory risk was reflected in EBS and Reuters 2000-2 broker spreads, reflecting larger costs rather than larger rents. The increase in inventory management costs that underlies this hypothesis comes from a different source than in the transparency hypothesis of HKM.

I will refer to this mechanism as the customer liquidity hypothesis, or CLH. It has the following empirical implication:

Implication 1: Under the CLH customers should significantly reduce their trading in USD/EUR in the period following 1 January 1999.

This is not terribly strong, since a similar development would be implied by any increase in transaction costs, regardless of origin. The following is stronger:

Implication 2: Under the CLH the customer segment that exhibits the greatest reduction in trading should be the *providers* of liquidity to the market-making community, known both in theory and empirically to be *hedge funds*.

To test these implications I have gathered all of the customer trading records from Citibank, one of the top three market-making banks in FX, over a three-year period extending from one year before euro launch to two years after euro launch (from 1 January 1998 to 31 December 2000). These data reflect all of the customer orders received worldwide by Citibank in all of the predecessor currencies against the dollar (1 January to 31 December 1998) and in the euro against the dollar (1 January 1999 to 31 December 2000). For the pre-euro portion of the sample, daily customer order flows in USD/EUR are constructed from the underlying predecessor currencies using the conversion weights. I am also able to separate the trading of hedge funds (a customer segment that Citibank refers to as leveraged investors) from the trading of the other two main customer segments: non-financial corporations and unleveraged investors (the latter includes mutual funds, pension funds, and insurance companies). Each segment accounts for about one third of total FX trading by customers at Citibank.

Table 1 assesses whether hedge funds traded less aggressively after the euro's launch. The first row shows that the variance of hedge fund order flows was not significantly different when comparing the first and last six months of 1998 (both periods are pre-launch). But a significant reduction did occur in the six months following the launch, and hedge fund trading remained significantly less aggressive for at least two years (see the third row of the table). Note too that the variance of *total* customer flow in the USD/EUR fell in the first six months following the launch,

Table 1. Does the variance of customer order flow change with euro launch?[a]

	Observations	Std Dev. (daily, EUR millions)[b]	p-value: no change in order flow variance
Hedge Funds USD/EUR			
First half 1998	128	155	0.43
Last half 1998	131	157	
Hedge Funds USD/EUR			
Last half 1998	131	157	0.001
First half 1999	129	118	
Hedge Funds USD/EUR			
Last half 1998	131	157	0.001
Last half 1999 + all 2000	391	127	
All Customers USD/EUR			
Last half 1998	131	238	0.01
First half 1999	129	193	
All Customers USD/JPY			
Last half 1998	131	276	0.33
First half 1999	129	265	

[a] Daily data from Citibank. 'Hedge Funds' corresponds to a customer segment that Citibank calls 'leveraged investors', which includes hedge funds and proprietary trading desks. (This is one of three main customer segments, each of which is about one-third of Citibank's worldwide flow of customer orders in FX. The other two segments are unleveraged investors – mutual funds, pension funds, life insurance companies, and so forth – and non-financial corporations.) 'All Customers' is the sum of the order flows from each of the three categories. *p*-value denotes the marginal significance of the *F*-test that there was no change in the variance of the daily order flow across the two samples.
[b] The last row of this column, which corresponds to the USD/JPY market, is in USD millions.

driven by the hedge fund component. (The variance of order flow from unleveraged investors fell, but the drop is not significant – *p*-value 17% – whereas that from non-financial corporations actually rose – *p*-value 3%.) These results are consistent with the two implications above of the CLH, and are hard to reconcile with the idea that transactions costs faced by customers increased across the board (unless the response of demand to transactions costs has different signs for different customer groups). The last row shows that less aggressive trading in USD/EUR did not extend to the USD/JPY market: the event was a euro event rather than a USD (or JPY) event.[18] There is another fact with which the CLH is not consistent, however, namely that the increase in USD/EUR spreads was persistent, as shown by Detken and Hartmann (this volume). My motivation of the CLH stressed that increased uncertainty about the trading environment is what caused hedge funds to retrench. This type of uncertainty is unlikely to have persisted beyond a few months.

[18] One concern is that the fateful day in USD/JPY in October 1998 is artificially inflating activity in the last half of 1998 (see note 5). It is comforting that the reduction in trading applies to USD/EUR but not to USD/JPY and that the two halves of 1998 did not differ. At the same time, the distress suffered by macro hedge funds in the fall of 1998 might very well account for the persistent drop in the intensity of their trading over the following two years.

4. WELFARE SIGNIFICANCE

There are two fundamental functions of financial markets: risk sharing and information aggregation. As we have seen, HKM's transparency model focuses on how changes in the FX market (the elimination of legacy currencies) affects risk sharing, in particular, market-makers' ability to share risk before price fully adjusts. In this section, I provide theoretical perspective on the second of these fundamental functions, information aggregation, and specifically on how the elimination of legacy currencies might have altered the process of impounding information in exchange rates.

How did the information environment of the USD/DEM market change with the euro launch? This question is important from the perspective of exchange rate determination. Honohan suggests (indirectly) that euro launch increased the amount of dispersed information about macro policy fundamentals (or what I have called risk-neutral fundamentals). I suggested a related model in which launch of the euro increased dispersed information about risk-related fundamentals (portfolio balance information). These theoretical partitions of the information environment provide additional resolution for considering the relevant information economics.

Given that trades *per se* – specifically order flow – account for most exchange rate variation at daily and lower frequencies (Evans and Lyons, 2002a; Payne, 1999), it is important to consider how increasing spreads might affect the order flow process.[19] In microstructure theory, asset demands have two components: an information component and a hedging component. When extending these models to FX, one needs to add a transactions component (e.g., exports/imports) because there is a *bona fide* transactions demand for currencies that does not exist in most securities markets. Thus, we can write the aggregate order flow A (for the denominator currency in terms of the numerator currency) as the sum of the information-based component, the hedging (risk sharing) component, and transactions demand. If one observes only a subset of the aggregate order flow, say the component A_i generated by institution or individual i, then inferences about the components of A will be based on signal extraction. To the extent that euro launch changes the relative variances of the three individual components, the market's ability to discriminate between them will change. Suppose, for example, that the regime shift induces significant variance in the hedging component, while the information-based component is the variable of interest (the 'signal'). In this case, the signal to noise ratio will be reduced, thereby reducing the degree to which price can impound information embedded in the information component.

For this last idea it is important to distinguish between concentrated and dispersed information (recall the two rows of Figure 2). If non-public information is concentrated

---

[19] Order flow and transaction volume are not the same: order flow is a measure of signed volume, where the sign depends on the direction of the initiating party. My focus here on order flow is distinct from the emphasis on volume that characterizes previous work on international currencies (e.g., Hartmann, 1998a, 1999; Portes and Rey, 1998).

in the hands of a few, there is no way that a small change in transaction costs is going to alter the trading of those few 'insiders'. But if information is dispersed widely among a large number of market participants, the incentive for any single participant to trade on the basis of his or her knowledge may be small. In this setting, small changes in transaction costs can matter a lot because large fractions of these minutely informed agents may choose not to trade: macroeconomist David Romer (1993) offers a lovely exposition of this insight.

Disaggregated data similar to that used above to test implications of the CLH can be used to test whether different FX order flow types have different price impact, as the above signal extraction model suggests. For example, Lyons (2001, ch. 9) shows that at the monthly frequency, the price impact per dollar of order flow from financial institutions is significantly higher than that for non-financial corporations. This suggests that the orders of financial institutions are especially potent in an informational sense. (Or, put differently, order flow is not just undifferentiated demand; for price determination at monthly and lower frequencies, where it comes from matters.) This result does not prove that the 'information-processing' view of transactions flows is the right view. But in conjunction with the myriad papers that document significant and persistent effects of flows on prices, these results provide a solid frame within which the information efficiency of the FX market can be addressed in a disciplined way.

Note that the focus of the above welfare discussion has less to do with spreads than with order flow. The welfare significance of a change in the order flow process is clear from microstructure theory (through the channel of price determination over longer horizons). Indeed, I think it is the effects of spread changes on this order flow process that has the first-order welfare implications, not the effects of spread changes *per se*.[20]

4.1. Transaction-cost frictions

In discussing HKM, Honohan wondered what would be the right base from which to calculate the total dollar value (cost) of spread increases (p. 180). Does the fact that the trading examined by HKM and Goodhart *et al.* is purely between market-makers imply that gains and losses are zero sum? No, it does not, because the costs of trading between market-makers get passed on to customer trading costs. If we assume a one-to-one passing on of these costs, one can use customer to market-maker volumes to calculate the total cost to the non-market-maker public. To what extent is this a pure efficiency loss, as opposed to (at least partially) a transfer of wealth? That depends on

---

[20] There are basically three views on the question of whether an increase in spreads can change information efficiency. The first view is the Tobin Tax view: higher spreads can increase information efficiency. The second view is the Traditional view: higher spreads have no effect on information efficiency because the effects of transactions on prices are too short lived to matter. The third view is the view I outline above, the Informative Flow view: higher spreads can reduce information efficiency by censoring the flow of informative trades.

which of the spread components has increased. If the increase is rents, then significant wealth (welfare) transfer is occurring. If it is inventory management costs, then the effect is more purely welfare destroying. And if it is asymmetric information, the added costs are paying (at least in part) for price discovery in a changed information environment.

5. CONCLUDING REMARKS

My main objective in this paper is to frame the theoretical and welfare significance of reductions in liquidity like that which occurred in the USD/EUR market. The framework of spread decomposition provides a disciplined way to discriminate among competing explanations. I then introduce a hypothesis that is qualitatively different from those considered elsewhere in that it recognizes that providers of liquidity in FX are ultimately customers, not FX market-makers, who generally go home with no position each day. Using new data on public trades from January 1998 to December 2000, I find the model's basic implications borne out. Nevertheless, the model predicts that the drop in liquidity should be temporary, due to temporary uncertainty about the trading environment *per se*. This is not consistent with the persistent drop in liquidity in the data.

Using spread decomposition as an organizing framework concentrates attention on the following question: Which market-maker cost components account for the spread increase empirically? I outlined the trade indicator approach that has been applied fruitfully in other contexts as a means for pinning this down. Qualitatively, we now have the kind of data for FX markets that allow us to estimate models of this type. The problem is that extant samples of requisite richness do not cover the period spanning the euro's launch. I suspect the necessary data will become available soon.

When determining which cost components underlie the change in liquidity, several factors need to be taken into account, as suggested in the text. First, in FX, the issue is not just the number of currencies being traded (e.g., parallel markets emphasized by HKM), but also a mix of competing trading mechanisms in FX (e.g., bilateral versus brokered trading). In this competing-mechanism environment, we need to be careful not to over-interpret spread-variation results derived from any one of those mechanisms. In the future, as data sets come on line that integrate trading across multiple mechanisms, we will have a stronger basis for addressing 'the' market's liquidity, as opposed to liquidity in a particular segment of trade types. Finally, as pointed out to me by Michael Moore, spread decomposition is a stickier wicket empirically than it is theoretically. As an empirical matter, even if the catalyst for spread change is from inventory or information costs, volumes will be affected, which can in turn influence costs in the Other category (e.g., the per unit share of fixed order-processing costs; see Hartmann, 1999). This interaction across the cost categories complicates inference.

More broadly, I have addressed the question of why anyone should care about increasing transaction costs (irrespective of the causes), given that they are so small. I show how increasing transaction costs affect the FX market's information efficiency, which, from a welfare perspective, can be first order (relating, as it does, to the dynamics of exchange rates over longer horizons). An open research question along these lines is whether order flow conveys information about both risk-neutral fundamentals and its complementary information partition, risk-related fundamentals. A related question, more specific to the issue at hand, is whether the euro's launch increased the dispersion of information about risk-neutral fundamentals (macro policy), as Honohan indirectly suggests in his discussion of HKM. These questions parallel a question that is central to modern asset pricing more generally, namely, whether asset price variations are due to changing payoff expectations or stochastic discount factors. Much empirical progress is being made in that broader literature along these lines and I anticipate significant advances within exchange rate economics along the same lines over the coming few years.

Are spreads really just a nuisance parameter? Or, more precisely: Should we care about the economics underlying spreads? To this I would answer yes, unequivocally. Spreads tell us about how effective markets are in sharing risk and aggregating information. These are the fundamental functions of financial markets and spreads give us insights into how well a market is fulfilling these functions. These issues are important for policy as well. Over the last ten years, work in equity markets along the lines of that addressed in this symposium has engendered profound policy shifts (such as changes in minimum tick sizes, changes in transparency, changes in allowable fragmentation, and changes in order handling rules). The same issues have only recently hit the policy radar screen in FX.

Finally, did spreads increase and, if so, why? In my judgment the evidence provided by HKM and by others subsequently does indeed make a convincing case that transaction spreads increased (for brokered trading between market-makers) and that the increase persisted for a year or more. Is it possible that these increased spreads between market-makers were not passed on as higher spreads to non-market-maker customers (perhaps because spreads for bilateral trading between market-makers did not rise)? I doubt it: these broker spreads are too important a part of the market for their effects to be isolated (they accounted at the time for a third to a half of total spot trading in USD/EUR). As to what might have caused the increase in spreads, in the end the proposed hypotheses offer considerable complementarity. In my judgment the granularity hypothesis interpreted as rents is not sufficient to account for the increase: if the pass-through of higher broker spreads to customers were more than a small percentage, the rents involved would be enormous and too difficult to sustain. Adding costs to the granularity hypothesis helps, in particular the additional costs in terms of communication, negotiation and foregone flexibility that would be entailed by moving to five-digit quotes. But even this is unlikely to allow so large and sustained an increase in spreads. Rather, I believe the resulting spreads are due to a combination of the granularity and inventory hypotheses, the latter including the set of stories that rely on an increase in inventory management costs:

- the HKM transparency hypothesis that USD/EUR market-makers could no longer pass positions off into other EMS markets;
- the related but distinct hypothesis that USD/otherEMS market-makers were no longer providing liquidity to USD/EUR market-makers via their hedging trades; and
- the customer liquidity hypothesis that liquidity-providing customers backed away from this market.

With these three factors contributing to higher market-maker costs, the increase in rents otherwise resulting from the maintenance of pip spreads was much reduced, perhaps to the point where the added costs of moving to five-digit pricing was not attractive for individual market-makers.

Forex markets and the euro: Discussion

Kenneth Rogoff
International Monetary Fund

This is an interesting set of papers on the micro-market structure of the nascent euro foreign exchange market. The starting point for the debate is the provocative paper by Hau, Killeen and Moore (2002a) – henceforth HKM – that appeared in the last issue of *Economic Policy*. All three papers make independent contributions of their own, but it is nevertheless useful to first view them through the lens of the HKM paper.

HKM demonstrated the startling result that bid-ask spreads for the euro were actually higher than bid-ask spreads for the largest legacy currency, the deutschemark (DEM). Their result provoked sharp debate at the last Economic Policy Panel meeting since it runs so contrary to what one would expect. The market for euro is hardly thin; according to the March 2002 BIS Triennial Central Bank Survey, the euro was involved in 38% of all foreign exchange rate transactions (versus 90% for the dollar and 23% for the yen). Thirty per cent of all global turnover in currencies in 2001 consisted of euro/dollar trades, or roughly $360 billion per day out of a total of $1200 billion per day. HKM offer an intriguing, if extravagant, explanation of the apparent fall in liquidity, having to do with less effective aggregation of information in a thinner market. Total trade including DEM was higher than total trade in euro, presumably because the advent of the euro killed all trade across the various legacy currencies of the euro system (e.g., the franc, the escudo, the lira, etc.).

To make a long story short, none of the three authors in this symposium are able to reverse HKM's surprising findings. Panelists at the April *Economic Policy* Panel meeting had suggested the HKM result was an illusion, partly because the market they study is unrepresentative and partly because the years they look at are unrepresentative. In fact, surprisingly, HKM's facts seem to hold up, at least with the data available to date.

Goodhart *et al.* offer a disarmingly simple explanation of the HKM result, having to do with indivisibilities in the foreign exchange market. The bid-ask spreads we observe in foreign exchange markets are generally set in absolute currency units (e.g., fraction of a euro) rather than in percentages, and quotes only go to 4 decimal places. Furthermore, many quotes are in the range of 1–2 'pips', e.g., 0.0002 euro might be the spread on euro/dollar trades. The lowest possible spread is 0.0001, because market participants resist 5 decimal point bids, on the grounds that they are harder to key in at high speeds or communicate verbally. Since, in terms of dollars, the old DEM was generally worth less than a euro (say 0.6 instead of 0.9) the 0.0001 DEM minimum bid-ask spread in old DEM/dollar market was lower (in *dollar* terms) than a 0.0001 euro spread is today (at the euro's present value). This 'granularity' in the euro market raises transactions costs if the minimum spread is 1 pip. Correspondingly, volume is lower than it otherwise might be, and there are potentially large efficiency losses. Goodhart *et al.*'s granularity hypothesis seems implausible (HKM say that such behaviour would amount to simple money illusion) until one realizes that similar problems have arisen in other markets. For example, NASDAQ quotes used to be in minimum units of 1/16 until the exchange converted to a decimal system. Dealers resisted the charge since they feared a changeover to decimal quotes would lower profits, as apparently did happen when the change took place. How can a fifth decimal place rounding error make the slightest difference? When a market is clearing 3–4 hundred billion dollars per day, a difference at 5 decimal places can loom quite large, potentially in the tens of billions of dollars per year. Would traders be aware of this fine point? Of course they understand the issue, but clearly they have no incentive to change. So have we got to the bottom of the problem? I'm still not sure, but Occam's razor favours the granularity hypothesis.

Detken and Hartman provide what will no doubt be, for a while, the definitive empirical paper on the early evolution of liquidity in markets for euro foreign exchange swaps and bonds. Empirical evidence on the actual performance of the euro is important, because much was written before the fact. There were optimists, but the real pessimists in 1995 were euroskeptics, particularly in the United States, who thought the euro would never come to pass. I must admit to having been one of them at one time (Rogoff, 1985; Froot and Rogoff, 1991). I was wrong; through an admirable and determined effort, the euro was created and thus far, has been a signal success – even if the HKM empirical evidence is confirmed in a longer data series of euro/dollar spreads. Hip-hip-hooray for the euro!

Richard Lyons's paper contributes additional evidence on order flows and an especially useful overview of theoretical issues underlying the market microstructure literature. As creative and interesting as the analysis is, I still do not find compelling the notion that market absorption of asymmetric information (in the hands of individual traders) can have more than a very transitory impact on the market for major currency cross rates. Indeed, it seems meaningless to me to analyse information about exchange rates in isolation from the thousands of other pieces of macro data available for major economies. As Stock and Watson (2001) have shown, one can explain a very large part of the movements of most available macroeconomic data with a relatively small-dimension latent variable model. Of course, I have to admit that it is still an open question whether the exchange rate, which should depend on a broad range of aggregate data, is reliably correlated with any macroeconomic variables. Certainly, if it is, no one has ever been able to prove it: see, e.g., Meese and Rogoff (1983), and Rogoff (2001). If so then, in principle, the welfare effects of larger spreads may be important along the lines Lyons suggests, but more evidence is needed.

Looking to the broader question underlying this debate, what will it take for the euro to become a vehicle currency on par with dollar? Certainly, if there are small imperfections in the trading systems, these will be ironed out in time. A far more serious issue, at present, is the balkanization of cross-border payments systems across Europe. The combination of lack of competition and lack of transparency still adds significant transactions to cross-border business dealings. Depending on which routing and payments system is used in any particular transaction, these costs can easily be half a per cent or more to any cross-border transaction. This problem, too, should be sorted out in time, even if some national banking systems kick and scream before allowing themselves to be fully exposed to pan-European competition.

At the macro level, the first step towards becoming an international currency is to become solidly established as the national currency across Europe. Predictably low inflation, transparent monetary policy, and conservative anti-inflation central bankers are essential ingredients. To become an international currency, one should add to the list deep, liquid, bond markets, and the general absence of financial transactions taxes and capital controls.

Of course, even if one does everything right, there is no guarantee the euro will match or pass the dollar in importance any time soon. Virtually even high-theory model of currency competition (e.g., Matsuyama et al., 1993) finds that there are multiple equilibria; see also, Portes and Rey (1998). The theoretical models tell us that whether the euro or dollar dominates, or whether they cohabit roughly equally, depends on fragile initial conditions. Of course, the euro can be a great success even without surpassing the dollar. Finally, there is the question of whether the euro might fail even as the national currency for Europe. This seems most unlikely at present, but there is no question that the long-term sustainability of the system is much more likely if Europe succeeds in deepening the process of political and economic integration, and ensuring more flexible markets. Admitting these caveats, it is still hard indeed to be a euroskeptic these days in the face of the tremendous success the euro project has enjoyed to date.

Panel discussion

Stijn Claessens pointed out that a minimum pip-size might not necessarily be a bad thing if it prevents dealers from obtaining information about the demand schedule in a world of imperfect competition and market power. Richard Portes pointed out that spot markets are much more important for the euro as a vehicle currency than swap markets. His work on the subject, with Helene Rey, envisioned a possible vehicle currency role for the euro only in 5–10 years. Liquidity is crucial for the euro bond market, whose volume has increased by 50% in recent years, and liquidity depends on turnover volume as well as on transaction costs. Charles Goodhart agreed that the euro-dollar market appears very liquid, if only on the basis of casual impression rather than hard data. He also pointed out that the EBS data on spreads are not reliable for the yen. Richard Lyons agreed that turnover could be included in a broader measure of liquidity, but stressed that larger spreads are a clear feature of recent evidence. There are no hard data on other liquidity-relevant aspects, such as depth. Harry Huizinga thought banks' accounts could provide more information as to the structure of trading costs.

FOREX MARKETS AND THE EURO: REFERENCES

Andersen, T., T. Bollerslev, F. Diebold and P. Labys (2001). 'The distribution of realized exchange rate volatility', *Journal of the American Statistical Association*.

Bacidore, J., R. Battalio, R. Jennings and S. Farkas (2001). 'Changes in order characteristics, displayed liquidity, and execution quality on the New York Stock Exchange around the switch to decimal pricing', NYSE working paper 2001–02.

Bank for International Settlements (1993). Central bank survey of foreign exchange market activity in April 1992.

Bank for International Settlements (1996). Triennial central bank survey of foreign exchange market activity in April 1995.

Bank for International Settlements (1999a). Triennial central bank survey of foreign exchange and derivatives market activity in April 1998.

Bank for International Settlements (1999b). International banking and financial market developments, *BIS Quarterly Review*.

Bank for International Settlements (2002). Triennial central bank survey of foreign exchange and derivatives market activity in April 2001.

Barclay, M., W. Christie, J. Harris, E. Kandel and P. Schultz (1999). 'The effect of market reform on the trading costs and depths of Nasdaq stocks', *Journal of Finance*, 54, 1–34.

Bishop, G. (1999). 'The euro's first quarter: a progress report on bonds', Salomon Smith Barney.

Bjonnes, G. and D. Rime (2001). 'FX trading . . . LIVE! Dealer behavior and trading systems in the foreign exchange market', available at www.sifr.org/dagfinn.html.

Branson, W. and D. Henderson (1985). 'The specification and influence of asset markets', in R. Jones and P. Kenen (eds), *Handbook of International Economics*, Volume 2, North-Holland, Amsterdam.

Cai, J., Y. Cheung, R. Lee and M. Melvin (2001). 'Once in a generation yen volatility in 1998: Fundamentals, intervention, or order flow?', *Journal of International Money and Finance*, 20, 327–47.

Capital Access International (2002). http://eMAXX.capital-access.com.

Christie, W. and P. Schultz (1994). 'Why do Nasdaq market-makers avoid odd-eighth quotes?', *Journal of Finance*, 49, 1813–40.

Christie, W., J. Harris and P. Schultz (1994). 'Why did Nasdaq market-makers stop avoiding odd-eighth quotes?', *Journal of Finance*, 49, 1841–60.

Detken, C. and P. Hartmann (2000). 'The euro and international capital markets', *International Finance* (statistical annexes in ECB working paper, no. 19, http://www.ecb.int/pub/wp/ecbwp019.pdf).

Demsetz, H. (1968). 'The cost of transacting', *Quarterly Journal of Economics*, 82, 33–53.

European Monetary Institute (1998). Convergence report.

European Central Bank (2001). Review of the international role of the euro.

Evans M. (1998). 'The microstructure of foreign exchange dynamics', working paper, Department of Economics, Georgetown University.

Evans, M. and R. Lyons (2002a). 'Order flow and exchange rate dynamics', *Journal of Political Economy*, 110, 170–80 (long version at www.haas.berkeley.edu/~lyons).

Evans, M. and R. Lyons (2002b). 'How is macro news transmitted to exchange rates?', typescript, U.C. Berkeley, June (at www.haas.berkeley.edu/~lyons).

Froot, K. and T. Ramadorai (2001). 'Currency returns, institutional investor flows, and exchange-rate fundamentals', typescript, Harvard Business School, November.

Froot, K. and K. Rogoff (1991). 'The EMS, the EMU, and the transition to a common currency', *NBER Macroeconomics Annual*, 6, 269–317.

Galati, G. (2001). 'Why has global FX turnover declined? Explaining the 2001 triennial survey', *BIS Quarterly Review*.

Galati, G. and K. Tsatsaronis (2001). 'The impact of the euro on Europe's financial markets', BIS Working Paper, no. 100.

Glosten, L. and L. Harris (1988). 'Estimating the components of the bid-ask spread', *Journal of Financial Economics*, 21, 123–42.

Glosten, L. and P. Milgrom (1985). 'Bid, ask, and transaction prices in a specialist market with heterogeneously informed agents', *Journal of Financial Economics*, 14, 71–100.

Goldman Sachs release, September 2000. 'New realities of the international monetary system'.

Goldstein, M. and K. Kavajecz (2000). 'Eighths, sixteenths and market depth: Changes in tick size and liquidity provision on the NYSE', *Journal of Financial Economics*.

Grossman, S., K. Cone, M. Miller, D. Fischel and D. Ross (1997). 'Clustering and competition in asset markets', *Journal of Law and Economics*, 40, 23–60.

Harris, L. (1991). 'Stock price clustering and discreteness', *Review of Financial Studies*, 4, 389–415.

Harris, L. (1999). 'Trading in pennies: A survey of the issues', USC working paper.

Hartmann, P. (1996). 'The future of the euro as an international currency: a transactions perspective', *LSE Financial Markets Group Special Paper*, no. 91.

Hartmann, P. (1998a). *Currency Competition and Foreign Exchange Markets: The Dollar, the Yen and the Euro*, Cambridge University Press, Cambridge.

Hartmann, P. (1998b). 'Do Reuters spreads reflect currencies' differences in global trading activity', *Journal of International Money and Finance*.

Hartmann, P. (1999). 'Trading volumes and transaction costs in the foreign exchange market: evidence from daily dollar-yen spot data', *Journal of Banking and Finance*.

Hartmann, P. and O. Issing (2002). 'The international role of the euro', *Journal of Policy Modeling*.

Hau, H., W. Killeen and M. Moore (2000). 'The euro as an international currency: explaining puzzling first evidence', CEPR discussion paper 2510.

Hau, H., W. Killeen and M. Moore (2002a). 'How has the euro changed the foreign exchange market?', *Economic Policy*.

Hau, H., W. Killeen and M. Moore (2002b). 'The international role of the euro: Explaining puzzling first evidence from foreign exchange markets', *Journal of International Money and Finance*, June.

Hayek, F. (1945). 'The use of knowledge in society', *American Economic Review*, September.

Henning, R. (1997). 'Cooperating with Europe's monetary union', Policy Analysis in *International Economics*, no. 49.

Hirschleifer, J. (1971). 'The private and social value of information and the reward to inventive activity', *American Economic Review*, 61, 561–74.

Ho, T. and H. Stoll (1983). 'The dynamics of dealer markets under competition', *Journal of Finance*, 38, 1053–74.

Huang, R. and H. Stoll (1997). 'The components of the bid-ask spread: A general approach', *Review of Financial Studies*, 10, 995–1034.

Issing, O. (1998). 'Von der D-Mark zum Euro', *Beiträge zur Ordnungstheorie und Ordnungspolitik*, no. 155.

Jones, C. and M. Lipson (2001). 'Sixteenths: Direct evidence on institutional trading costs', *Journal of Financial Economics*.

Killeen, W., R. Lyons and M. Moore (2001). 'Fixed versus flexible: Lessons from EMS order flow', NBER Working Paper 8491, September.

Kool, C.J.M. (2000). 'International bond markets and the introduction of the euro', *Federal Reserve Bank of St. Louis Review*.

Krugman, P. (1980). 'Vehicle currencies and the structure of international exchange', *Journal of Money, Credit, and Banking*.

Kyle, A. (1985). 'Continuous auctions and insider trading', *Econometrica*, 53, 1315–35.

Lyons, R. (1995). 'Tests of microstructural hypotheses in the foreign exchange market', *Journal of Financial Economics*.

Lyons, R. (2001). *The Microstructure Approach to Exchange Rates*, MIT Press, Cambridge MA.

Madhavan, A. (2000). 'Market microstructure: A survey', *Journal of Financial Markets*.

Matsuyama, K., N. Kiyotaki and A. Matsui (1993). 'Toward a theory of international currency.' *Review of Economic Studies*, 60 (April), 283–307.

McCauley, R. (1997). 'The euro and the dollar', *Essays in International Finance*, no. 205.

Meese, and K. Rogoff (1983). 'Empirical exchange rate models of the seventies: Do they fit out of sample,' *Journal of International Economics*, 14 (February), 3–24.

O'Hara, M. (1995). *Market Microstructure Theory*, Blackwell Business, Cambridge, MA.

Payne, R. (1999). 'Informed trade in spot foreign exchange markets: An empirical investigation', typescript, London School of Economics, January.

Perron, P. (1990). 'Testing for a unit root in a time series with a changing mean', *Journal of Business and Economic Statistics*.

Portes, R. and H. Rey (1998). 'The emergence of the euro as an international currency', *Economic Policy*.

Rime, D. (2000). 'Private or public information in foreign exchange markets? An empirical analysis', typescript, Norwegian School of Management, April (available at www.uio.no/~dagfinri).

Rogoff, K. (1985). 'Can exchange rate predictability be achieved without monetary convergence?: Evidence from the EMS,' *European Economic Review*, 28 (June–July), 93–115.

Rogoff, K. (2001). 'The failure of empirical exchange rate models: No longer new but still true,' *Economic Policy Web Essay*, (October), Issue 1, Vol. 1.

Romer, D. (1993). 'Rational asset price movements without news', *American Economic Review*, 83, 1112–30.

Santos, J. and K. Tsatsaronis (2002). 'The cost of barriers to entry: evidence from the market for corporate euro bond underwriting', paper presented at the April 2002 launching workshop of the ECB-CFS research network on 'Capital Markets and Financial Integration in Europe' at the European Central Bank.

Stock, J.H. and M.W. Watson (2001). 'Macroeconomic forecasting using diffusion indexes,' *Journal of Business and Economic Statistics*, forthcoming.

Swoboda, A. (1969). 'Vehicle currencies and the foreign exchange market: the case of the dollar', in R. Aliber (ed.), *The International Market for Foreign Exchange*, Praeger, New York.

Weston, J. (2000). 'Competition on the Nasdaq and the impact of recent market reforms', *Journal of Finance*, 55, 2565–98.

Wyplosz, C. (1999). 'An international role for the euro?', in J. Dermine and P. Hillion (eds), *European Capital Markets with a Single Currency*, Oxford University Press, Oxford.

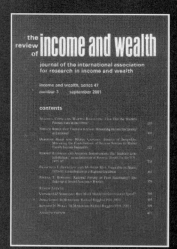

REVIEW OF INCOME AND WEALTH

Published on behalf of
The International Association for Research in Income and Wealth

Edited by
EDWARD N. WOLFF

The major objectives of *The Review of Income and Wealth* are the furthering of research on national and economic and social accounting, including the development of concepts and definitions for the measurement and analysis of income and wealth; the development and further integration of systems of economic and social statistics; and related problems of statistical methodology. In particular, the *Review* is concerned with the international aspects of these questions, such as: international comparisons of income and wealth; the use of economic and social accounting for budgeting and policy analysis in different countries; and the experiences of different countries in the development of economic and social accounting systems.

ISSN: 0034-6586. VOLUME 48 (2002) CONTAINS 4 ISSUES.
WWW.BLACKWELLPUBLISHERS.CO.UK/JOURNALS/ROIW

108 Cowley Road, Oxford OX4 1JF, UK   350 Main Street, Malden, MA 02148, USA
j n l i n f o @ b l a c k w e l l p u b l i s h e r s . c o . u k

visit our website for contents listings, abstracts, samples, and to subscribe
b l a c k w e l l p u b l i s h i n g . c o m